THREE PLAYS
OF
EUGENE O'NEILL

THREE PLAYS

of Eugene O'Neill

DESIRE UNDER THE ELMS

STRANGE INTERLUDE

MOURNING BECOMES ELECTRA

VINTAGE BOOKS
A DIVISION OF RANDOM HOUSE
New York

VINTAGE BOOKS

are published by ALFRED A. KNOPF, INC.

and RANDOM HOUSE, INC.

Manufactured in the United States of America

CONTENTS

DESIRE UNDER THE ELMS 3

STRANGE INTERLUDE 61

MOURNING BECOMES ELECTRA

HOMECOMING 227

THE HUNTED 281

THE HAUNTED 333

Desire Under the Elms

CHARACTERS

EPHRAIM CABOT

SIMEON, PETER, EBEN — *His sons*

ABBIE PUTNAM

Young Girl, Two Farmers, The Fiddler, A Sheriff, and other folk from the neighboring farms.

The action of the entire play takes place in, and immediately outside of, the Cabot farmhouse in New England, in the year 1850. The south end of the house faces front to a stone wall with a wooden gate at center opening on a country road. The house is in good condition but in need of paint. Its walls are a sickly grayish, the green of the shutters faded. Two enormous elms are on each side of the house. They bend their trailing branches down over the roof. They appear to protect and at the same time subdue. There is a sinister maternity in their aspect, a crushing, jealous absorption. They have developed from their intimate contact with the life of man in the house an appalling humaneness. They brood oppressively over the house. They are like exhausted women resting their sagging breasts and hands and hair on its roof, and when it rains their tears trickle down monotonously and rot on the shingles.

There is a path running from the gate around the right corner of the house to the front door. A narrow porch is on this side. The end wall facing us has two windows in its upper story, two larger ones on the floor below. The two upper are those of the father's bedroom and that of the brothers. On the left, ground floor, is the kitchen—on the right, the parlor, the shades of which are always drawn down.

Desire Under the Elms

PART ONE · SCENE ONE

Exterior of the farmhouse. It is sunset of a day at the beginning of summer in the year 1850. There is no wind and everything is still. The sky above the roof is suffused with deep colors, the green of the elms glows, but the house is in shadow, seeming pale and washed out by contrast.

A door opens and EBEN CABOT *comes to the end of the porch and stands looking down the road to the right. He has a large bell in his hand and this he swings mechanically, awakening a deafening clangor. Then he puts his hands on his hips and stares up at the sky. He sighs with a puzzled awe and blurts out with halting appreciation.*

EBEN God! Purty! (*His eyes fall and he stares about him frowningly. He is twenty-five, tall and sinewy. His face is well-formed, good-looking, but its expression is resentful and defensive. His defiant, dark eyes remind one of a wild animal's in captivity. Each day is a cage in which he finds himself trapped but inwardly unsubdued. There is a fierce repressed vitality about him. He has black hair, mustache, a thin curly trace of beard. He is dressed in rough farm clothes.*

He spits on the ground with intense disgust, turns and goes back into the house.

SIMEON *and* PETER *come in from their work in the fields. They are tall men, much older than their half-brother* [SIMEON *is thirty-nine and* PETER *thirty-seven*], *built on a squarer, simpler model, fleshier in body, more bovine and homelier in face, shrewder and more practical. Their shoulders stoop a bit from years of farm work. They clump heavily along in their clumsy thick-soled boots caked with earth. Their clothes, their faces, hands, bare arms and throats are earth-stained. They smell of earth. They stand together for a moment in front of the house and, as if with the one impulse, stare dumbly up at the sky, leaning on their hoes. Their faces have a compressed, unresigned expression. As they look upward, this softens).*

SIMEON (*grudgingly*) Purty.

PETER Ay-eh.

SIMEON (*suddenly*) Eighteen years ago.

PETER What?

SIMEON Jenn. My woman. She died.

PETER I'd fergot.

SIMEON I rec'lect—now an' agin. Makes it lonesome. She'd hair long's a hoss' tail—an' yaller like gold!

PETER Waal—she's gone. (*This with indifferent finality—then after a pause*) They's gold in the West, Sim.

SIMEON (*still under the influence of sunset—vaguely*) In the sky!

PETER Waal—in a manner o' speakin'—thar's the promise. (*Growing excited*) Gold in the sky—in the West—Golden Gate—Californi-a!—Goldest West!—fields o' gold!

SIMEON (*excited in his turn*) Fortunes layin' just atop o' the ground waitin' t' be picked! Solomon's mines, they says! (*For a moment they continue looking up at the sky—then their eyes drop*).

PETER (*with sardonic bitterness*) Here—it's stones atop o' the ground—stones atop o' stones—makin' stone walls—year atop o' year—him 'n' yew 'n' me 'n' then Eben—makin' stone walls fur him to fence us in!

SIMEON We've wuked. Give our strength. Give our years. Plowed 'em under in the ground,—(*he stamps rebelliously*)—rottin'—makin' soil for his crops! (*A pause*) Waal—the farm pays good for hereabouts.

PETER If we plowed in Californi-a, they'd be lumps o' gold in the furrow!

SIMEON Californi-a's t'other side o' earth, a'most. We got t' calc'late—

PETER (*after a pause*) 'Twould be hard fur me, too, to give up what we've 'arned here by our sweat. (*A pause.* EBEN *sticks his head out of the dining-room window, listening*).

SIMEON Ay-eh. (*A pause*) Mebbe—he'll die soon.

PETER (*doubtfully*) Mebbe.

SIMEON Mebbe—fur all we knows—he's dead now.

PETER Ye'd need proof.

SIMEON He's been gone two months—with no word.

PETER Left us in the fields an evenin' like this. Hitched up an' druv off into the West. That's plum onnateral. He hain't never been off this farm 'ceptin' t' the village in thirty year or more, not since he married Eben's maw. (*A pause. Shrewdly*) I calc'late we might git him declared crazy by the court.

SIMEON He skinned 'em too slick. He got the best o' all on 'em. They'd never b'lieve him crazy. (*A pause*) We got t' wait—till he's under ground.

EBEN (*with a sardonic chuckle*) Honor thy father! (*They turn, startled, and stare at him. He grins, then scowls*) I pray he's died. (*They stare at him. He continues matter-of-factly*) Supper's ready.

SIMEON *and* PETER (*together*) Ay-eh.

EBEN (*gazing up at the sky*) Sun's downin' purty.

SIMEON *and* PETER (*together*) Ay-eh. They's gold in the West.

EBEN Ay-eh. (*Pointing*) Yonder atop o' the hill pasture, ye mean?

SIMEON *and* PETER (*together*) In Californi-a!

EBEN Hunh? (*Stares at them indifferently for a second, then drawls*) Waal—supper's gittin' cold. (*He turns back into kitchen*).

SIMEON (*startled—smacks his lips*) I air hungry!

PETER (*sniffing*) I smells bacon!

SIMEON (*with hungry appreciation*) Bacon's good!

PETER (*in same tone*) Bacon's bacon! (*They turn, shouldering each other, their bodies bumping and rubbing together as they hurry clumsily to their food, like two friendly oxen toward their evening meal. They disappear around the right corner of house and can be heard entering the door*).

CURTAIN

SCENE TWO

The color fades from the sky. Twilight begins. The interior of the kitchen is now visible. A pine table is at center, a cookstove in the right rear corner, four rough wooden chairs, a tallow candle on the table. In the middle of the rear wall is fastened a big advertizing poster with a ship in full sail and the word "California" in big letters. Kitchen utensils hang from nails. Everything is neat and in order but the atmosphere is of a men's camp kitchen rather than that of a home.

Places for three are laid. EBEN *takes boiled potatoes and bacon from the stove and puts them on the table, also a loaf of bread and a crock of water.* SIMEON *and* PETER *shoulder in, slump down in their chairs without a word.* EBEN *joins them. The three eat in silence for a moment, the two elder as naturally unrestrained as beasts of the field,* EBEN *picking at his food without appetite, glancing at them with a tolerant dislike.*

SIMEON (*suddenly turns to* EBEN) Looky here! Ye'd oughtn't t' said that, Eben.

PETER 'Twa'n't righteous.

EBEN What?

SIMEON Ye prayed he'd died.

EBEN Waal—don't yew pray it? (*A pause*).

PETER He's our Paw.

EBEN (*violently*) Not mine!

SIMEON (*dryly*) Ye'd not let no one else say that about yer Maw! Ha! (*He gives one abrupt sardonic guffaw.* PETER *grins*).

EBEN (*very pale*) I meant—I hain't his'n—I hain't like him—he hain't me!

PETER (*dryly*) Wait till ye've growed his age!

EBEN (*intensely*) I'm Maw—every drop o' blood! (*A pause. They stare at him with indifferent curiosity*).

PETER (*reminiscently*) She was good t' Sim 'n' me. A good step-maw's scurse.

SIMEON She was good t' everyone.

EBEN (*greatly moved, gets to his feet and makes an awkward bow to each of them—stammering*) I be thankful t' ye. I'm her—her heir. (*He sits down in confusion*).

PETER (*after a pause—judicially*) She was good even t' him.

EBEN (*fiercely*) An' fur thanks he killed her!

SIMEON (*after a pause*) No one never kills nobody. It's allus some thin'. That's the murderer.

EBEN Didn't he slave Maw t' death?

PETER He's slaved himself t' death. He's slaved Sim 'n' me 'n' yew t' death—on'y none o' us hain't died—yit.

SIMEON It's somethin'—drivin' him—t' drive us!

EBEN (*vengefully*) Waal—I hold him t' jedgment! (*Then scornfully*) Somethin'! What's somethin'?

SIMEON Dunno.

EBEN (*sardonically*) What's drivin' yew to Californi-a, mebbe? (*They look at him in surprise*) Oh, I've heerd ye! (*Then, after a pause*) But ye'll never go t' the gold fields!

PETER (*assertively*) Mebbe!

EBEN Whar'll ye git the money?

PETER We kin walk. It's an a'mighty ways—Californi-a—but if yew was t' put all the steps we've walked on this farm end t' end we'd be in the moon!

EBEN The Injuns'll skulp ye on the plains.

SIMEON (*with grim humor*) We'll mebbe make 'em pay a hair fur a hair!

EBEN (*decisively*) But t'aint that. Ye won't never go because ye'll wait here fur yer share o' the farm, thinkin' allus he'll die soon.

SIMEON (*after a pause*) We've a right.

PETER Two-thirds belong t' us.

EBEN (*jumping to his feet*) Ye've no right! She wa'n't yewr Maw! It was her farm! Didn't he steal it from her? She's dead. It's my farm.

SIMEON (*sardonically*) Tell that t' Paw—when he comes! I'll bet ye a dollar he'll laugh—fur once in his life. Ha! (*He laughs himself in one single mirthless bark*).

PETER (*amused in turn, echoes his brother*) Ha!

SIMEON (*after a pause*) What've ye got held agin us, Eben? Year arter year it's skulked in yer eye—somethin'.

PETER Ay-eh.

EBEN Ay-eh. They's somethin'. (*Suddenly exploding*) Why didn't ye never stand between him 'n' my Maw when he was slavin' her to her grave—t' pay her back fur the kindness she done t' yew? (*There is a long pause. They stare at him in surprise*).

SIMEON Waal—the stock's got t' be watered.

PETER 'R they was woodin' t' do.

SIMEON 'R plowin'.

PETER 'R hayin'.

SIMEON 'R spreadin' manure.

PETER 'R weedin'.

SIMEON 'R prunin'.

PETER 'R milkin'.

EBEN (*breaking in harshly*) An' makin' walls—stone atop o' stone—makin' walls till yer heart's a stone ye heft up out o' the way o' growth onto a stone wall t' wall in yer heart!

SIMEON (*matter-of-factly*) We never had no time t' meddle.

PETER (*to* EBEN) Yew was fifteen afore yer Maw died—an' big fur yer age. Why didn't ye never do nothin'?

EBEN (*harshly*) They was chores t' do, wa'n't they? (*A pause—then slowly*) It was on'y arter she died I come to think o' it. Me cookin'—doin' her work—that made me know her, suffer her sufferin'—she'd come back t' help—come back t' bile potatoes—come back t' fry bacon—come back t' bake biscuits—come back all cramped up t' shake the fire, an' carry ashes, her eyes weepin' an' bloody with smoke an' cinders same's they used t' be. She still comes back—stands by the stove thar in the evenin'—she can't find it nateral sleepin' an' restin' in peace. She can't git used t' bein' free—even in her grave.

SIMEON She never complained none.

EBEN She'd got too tired. She'd got too used t' bein' too tired. That was what he done. (*With vengeful passion*) An' sooner'r later, I'll meddle. I'll say the thin's I didn't say then t' him! I'll yell 'em at the top o' my lungs. I'll see t' it my Maw gits some rest an' sleep in her grave! (*He sits down again, relapsing into a brooding silence. They look at him with a queer indifferent curiosity*).

PETER (*after a pause*) Whar in tarnation d'ye s'pose he went, Sim?

SIMEON Dunno. He druv off in the buggy, all spick an' span, with the mare all breshed an' shiny, druv off clackin' his tongue an' wavin' his whip. I remember it right well. I was finishin' plowin', it was spring an' May an' sunset, an' gold in the West, an' he druv off into it. I yells "Whar ye goin', Paw?" an' he hauls up by the stone wall a jiffy. His old snake's eyes was glitterin' in the sun like he'd been drinkin' a jugful an' he says with a mule's grin: "Don't ye run away till I come back!"

PETER Wonder if he knowed we was wantin' fur Californi-a?

SIMEON Mebbe. I didn't say nothin' and he says, lookin' kinder queer an' sick: "I been hearin' the hens cluckin' an' the roosters crowin' all the durn day. I been listenin' t' the cows lowin' an' everythin' else kickin' up till I can't stand it no more. It's spring an' I'm feelin' damned," he says. "Damned like an old bare hickory tree fit on'y fur burnin'," he says. An' then I calc'late I must've looked a mite hopeful, fur he adds real spry and vicious: "But don't git no fool idee I'm dead. I've sworn t' live a hundred an' I'll do it, if on'y t' spite yer sinful greed! An' now I'm ridin' out t' learn God's message t' me in the spring, like the prophets done. An' yew git back t' yer plowin'," he says. An' he druv off singin' a hymn. I thought he was drunk—'r I'd stopped him goin'.

EBEN (*scornfully*) No, ye wouldn't! Ye're scared o' him. He's stronger—inside—than both o' ye put together!

PETER (*sardonically*) An' yew—be yew Samson?

EBEN I'm gittin' stronger. I kin feel it growin' in me—growin' an' growin'—till it'll bust out—! (*He gets up and puts on his coat and a hat. They watch him, gradually breaking into grins.* EBEN *avoids their eyes sheepishly*) I'm goin' out fur a spell—up the road.

PETER T' the village?

SIMEON T' the village?

SIMEON T' see Minnie?

EBEN (*defiantly*) Ay-eh?

PETER (*jeeringly*) The Scarlet Woman!

SIMEON Lust—that's what's growin' in ye!

EBEN Waal—she's purty!

PETER She's been purty fur twenty year!

SIMEON A new coat o' paint'll make a heifer out of forty.

EBEN She hain't forty!

PETER If she hain't, she's teeterin' on the edge.

EBEN (*desperately*) What d'yew know—

PETER All they is . . . Sim knew her—an' then me arter—

SIMEON An' Paw kin tell yew somethin' too! He was fust!

EBEN D'ye mean t' say he . . . ?

SIMEON (*with a grin*) Ay-eh! We air his heirs in everythin'!

EBEN (*intensely*) That's more to it! That grows on it! It'll bust soon! (*Then violently*) I'll go smash my fist in her face! (*He pulls open the door in rear violently*).

SIMEON (*with a wink at* PETER—*drawlingly*) Mebbe—but the night's wa'm—purty—by the time ye git thar mebbe ye'll kiss her instead!

PETER Sart'n he will! (*They both roar with coarse laughter.* EBEN *rushes out and slams the door—then the outside front door—comes around the corner of the house and stands still by the gate, staring up at the sky*).

SIMEON (*looking after him*) Like his Paw.

PETER Dead spit an' image!

SIMEON Dog'll eat dog!

PETER Ay-eh. (*Pause. With yearning*) Mebbe a year from now we'll be in Californi-a.

SIMEON Ay-eh. (*A pause. Both yawn*) Let's git t' bed. (*He blows out the candle.They go out door in rear.* EBEN *stretches his arms up to the sky—rebelliously*).

EBEN Waal—thar's a star, an' somewhar's they's him, an' here's me, an' thar's Min up the road—in the same night. What if I does kiss her? She's like t'night, she's soft 'n' wa'm, her eyes kin wink like a star, her mouth's wa'm, her arms're wa'm, she smells like a wa'm plowed field, she's purty . . . Ay-eh! By God A'mighty she's purty, an' I don't give a damn how many sins she's sinned afore mine or who she's sinned 'em with, my sin's as purty as any one of 'em! (*He strides off down the road to the left*).

CURTAIN

SCENE THREE

It is the pitch darkness just before dawn. EBEN *comes in from the left and goes around to the porch, feeling his way, chuckling bitterly and cursing half-aloud to himself.*

EBEN The cussed old miser! (*He can be heard going in the front door. There is a pause as he goes upstairs, then a loud knock on the bedroom door of the brothers*) Wake up!

SIMEON (*startedly*) Who's thar?

EBEN (*pushing open the door and coming in, a lighted candle in his hand. The bedroom of the brothers is revealed. Its ceiling is the sloping roof. They can stand upright only close to the center dividing wall of the upstairs.* SIMEON *and* PETER *are in a double bed, front.* EBEN'S *cot is to the rear.* EBEN *has a mixture of silly grin and vicious scowl on his face*) I be!

PETER (*angrily*) What in hell's-fire . . . ?

EBEN I got news fur ye! Ha! (*He gives one abrupt sardonic guffaw*).

SIMEON (*angrily*) Couldn't ye hold it 'til we'd got our sleep?

EBEN It's nigh sunup. (*Then explosively*) He's gone an' married agen!

SIMEON *and* PETER (*explosively*) Paw?

EBEN Got himself hitched to a female 'bout thirty-five— an' purty, they says . . .

SIMEON (*aghast*) It's a durn lie!

PETER Who says?

SIMEON They been stringin' ye!

EBEN Think I'm a dunce, do ye? The hull village says. The preacher from New Dover, he brung the news—told it t' our preacher—New Dover, that's whar the old loon got himself hitched—that's whar the woman lived—

PETER (*no longer doubting—stunned*) Waal . . . !

SIMEON (*the same*) Waal . . . !

EBEN (*sitting down on a bed—with vicious hatred*) Ain't he a devil out o' hell? It's jest t' spite us—the damned old mule!

PETER (*after a pause*) Everythin'll go t' her now.

SIMEON Ay-eh. (*A pause—dully*) Waal—if it's done—

PETER It's done us. (*Pause—then persuasively*) They's gold in the fields o' Californi-a, Sim. No good a-stayin' here now.

SIMEON Jest what I was a-thinkin'. (*Then with decision*) S'well fust's last! Let's light out and git this mornin'.

PETER Suits me.

EBEN Ye must like walkin'.

SIMEON (*sardonically*) If ye'd grow wings on us we'd fly thar!

EBEN Ye'd like ridin' better—on a boat, wouldn't ye? (*Fumbles in his pocket and takes out a crumpled sheet of foolscap*) Waal, if ye sign this ye kin ride on a boat. I've had it writ out an' ready in case ye'd ever go. It says fur three hundred dollars t' each ye agree yewr shares o' the farm is sold t' me (*They look suspiciously at the paper. A pause*).

SIMEON (*wonderingly*) But if he's hitched agen—

PETER An' whar'd yew git that sum o' money, anyways?

EBEN (*cunningly*) I know whar it's hid. I been waitin'— Maw told me. She knew whar it lay fur years, but she was waitin' . . . It's her'n—the money he hoarded from her farm an' hid from Maw. It's my money by rights now.

PETER Whar's it hid?

EBEN (*cunningly*) Whar yew won't never find it without me. Maw spied on him—'r she'd never knowed. (*A pause. They look at him suspiciously, and he at them*) Waal, is it fa'r trade?

SIMEON Dunno.

PETER Dunno.

SIMEON (*looking at window*) Sky's grayin'.

PETER Ye better start the fire, Eben.

SIMEON An' fix some vittles.

EBEN Ay-eh. (*Then with a forced jocular heartiness*) I'll git ye a good one. If ye're startin' t' hoof it t' Californi-a ye'll need somethin' that'll stick t' yer ribs. (*He turns to the door, adding meaningly*) But ye kin ride on a boat if ye'll swap. (*He stops at the door and pauses. They stare at him*).

SIMEON (*suspiciously*) Whar was ye all night?

EBEN (*defiantly*) Up t' Min's. (*Then slowly*) Walkin' thar, fust I felt 's if I'd kiss her; then I got a-thinkin' o' what ye'd said o' him an' her an' I says, I'll bust her nose fur that! Then I got t' the village an' heerd the news an' I got madder'n hell an' run all the way t' Min's not knowin' what I'd do— (*He pauses —then sheepishly but more defiantly*) Waal—when I seen her, I didn't hit her—nor I didn't kiss her nuther—I begun t' beller like a calf an' cuss at the same time, I was so durn mad—an' she got scared—an' I jest grabbed holt an' tuk her! (*Proudly*) Yes, sirree! I tuk her. She may've been his'n—an' your'n, too— but she's mine now!

SIMEON (*dryly*) In love, air yew?

EBEN (*with lofty scorn*) Love! I don't take no stock in sech slop!

PETER (*winking at* SIMEON) Mebbe Eben's aimin' t' marry, too.

SIMEON Min'd make a true faithful he'pmeet! (*They snicker*).

EBEN What do I care fur her—'ceptin' she's round an' wa'm? The p'int is she was his'n—an' now she b'longs t' me! (*He goes to the door—then turns—rebelliously*) An' Min hain't sech a bad un. They's worse'n Min in the world, I'll bet ye! Wait'll we see this cow the Old Man's hitched t'! She'll beat Min, I got a notion! (*He starts to go out*).

SIMEON (*suddenly*) Mebbe ye'll try t' make her your'n, too?

PETER Ha! (*He gives a sardonic laugh of relish at this idea*).

EBEN (*spitting with disgust*) Her—here—sleepin' with him—stealin' my Maw's farm! I'd as soon pet a skunk 'r kiss a snake! (*He goes out. The two stare after him suspiciously. A pause. They listen to his steps receding*).

PETER He's startin' the fire.

SIMEON I'd like t' ride t' Californi-a—but—

PETER Min might o' put some scheme in his head.

SIMEON Mebbe it's all a lie 'bout Paw marryin'. We'd best wait an' see the bride.

PETER An' don't sign nothin' till we does!

SIMEON Nor till we've tested it's good money! (*Then with a grin*) But if Paw's hitched we'd be sellin' Eben somethin' we'd never git nohow!

PETER We'll wait an' see. (*Then with sudden vindictive anger*) An' till he comes, let's yew 'n' me not wuk a lick, let Eben tend to thin's if he's a mind t', let's us jest sleep an' eat an' drink likker an' let the hull damned farm go t' blazes!

SIMEON (*excitedly*) By God, we've 'arned a rest! We'll play rich fur a change. I hain't a-going to stir outa bed till breakfast's ready.

PETER An' on the table!

SIMEON (*after a pause—thoughtfully*) What d'ye calc'late she'll be like—our new Maw? Like Eben thinks?

PETER More'n' likely.

SIMEON (*vindictively*) Waal—I hope she's a she-devil that'll make him wish he was dead an' livin' in the pit o' hell fur comfort!

PETER (*fervently*) Amen!

SIMEON (*imitating his father's voice*) "I'm ridin' out t' learn God's message t' me in the spring like the prophets done," he says. I'll bet right then an' thar he knew plumb well he was goin' whorin', the stinkin' old hypocrite!

CURTAIN

SCENE FOUR

Same as Scene Two—shows the interior of the kitchen with a lighted candle on table. It is gray dawn outside. SIMEON *and* PETER *are just finishing their breakfast.* EBEN *sits before his plate of untouched food, brooding frowningly.*

PETER (*glancing at him rather irritably*) Lookin' glum don't help none.

SIMEON (*sarcastically*) Sorrowin' over his lust o' the flesh!

PETER (*with a grin*) Was she yer fust?

EBEN (*angrily*) None o' yer business. (*A pause*) I was

thinkin' o' him. I got a notion he's gittin' near—I kin feel him comin' on like yew kin feel malaria chill afore it takes ye.

PETER It's too early yet.

SIMEON Dunno. He'd like t' catch us nappin'—jest t' have somethin' t' hoss us 'round over.

PETER (*mechanically gets to his feet.* SIMEON *does the same*) Waal—let's git t' wuk. (*They both plod mechanically toward the door before they realize. Then they stop short*).

SIMEON (*grinning*) Ye're a cussed fool, Pete—and I be wuss! Let him see we hain't wukin'! We don't give a durn!

PETER (*as they go back to the table*) Not a damned durn! It'll serve t' show him we're done with him. (*They sit down again.* EBEN *stares from one to the other with surprise*).

SIMEON (*grins at him*) We're aimin' t' start bein' lilies o' the field.

PETER Nary a toil 'r spin 'r lick o' wuk do we put in!

SIMEON Ye're sole owner—till he comes—that's what ye wanted. Waal, ye got t' be sole hand, too.

PETER The cows air bellerin'. Ye better hustle at the milkin'.

EBEN (*with excited joy*) Ye mean ye'll sign the paper?

SIMEON (*dryly*) Mebbe.

PETER Mebbe.

SIMEON We're considerin'. (*Peremptorily*) Ye better git t' wuk.

EBEN (*with queer excitement*) It's Maw's farm agen! It's my farm! Them's my cows! I'll milk my durn fingers off fur cows o' mine! (*He goes out door in rear, they stare after him indifferently*).

SIMEON Like his Paw.

PETER Dead spit 'n' image!

SIMEON Waal—let dog eat dog! (EBEN *comes out of front door and around the corner of the house. The sky is beginning to grow flushed with sunrise.* EBEN *stops by the gate and stares around him with glowing, possessive eyes. He takes in the whole farm with his embracing glance of desire*).

EBEN It's purty! It's damned purty! It's mine! (*He suddenly throws his head back boldly and glares with hard, defiant eyes at the sky*) Mine, d'ye hear? Mine! (*He turns and walks quickly off left, rear, toward the barn. The two brothers light their pipes*).

SIMEON (*putting his muddy boots up on the table, tilting back his chair, and puffing defiantly*) Waal—this air solid comfort—fur once.

PETER Ay-eh. (*He follows suit. A pause. Unconsciously they both sigh*).

SIMEON (*suddenly*) He never was much o' a hand at milkin', Eben wa'n't.

PETER (*with a snort*) His hands air like hoofs! (*A pause*).

SIMEON Reach down the jug thar! Let's take a swaller. I'm feelin' kind o' low.

PETER Good idee! (*He does so—gets two glasses—they pour out drinks of whisky*) Here's t' the gold in Californi-a!

SIMEON An' luck t' find it! (*They drink—puff resolutely—sigh—take their feet down from the table*).

PETER Likker don't 'pear t' sot right.

SIMEON We hain't used t' it this early. (*A pause. They become very restless*).

PETER Gittin' close in this kitchen.

SIMEON (*with immense relief*) Let's git a breath o' air. (*They arise briskly and go out rear—appear around house and stop by the gate. They stare up at the sky with a numbed appreciation*).

PETER Purty!

SIMEON Ay-eh. Gold's t' the East now.

PETER Sun's startin' with us fur the Golden West.

SIMEON (*staring around the farm, his compressed face tightened, unable to conceal his emotion*) Waal—it's our last mornin'—mebbe.

PETER (*the same*) Ay-eh.

SIMEON (*stamps his foot on the earth and addresses it desperately*) Waal—ye've thirty year o' me buried in ye—spread out over ye—blood an' bone an' sweat—rotted away—fertilizin' ye—richin' yer soul—prime manure, by God, that's what I been t' ye!

PETER Ay-eh! An' me!

SIMEON An' yew, Peter. (*He sighs—then spits*) Waal—no use'n cryin' over spilt milk.

PETER They's gold in the West—an' freedom, mebbe. We been slaves t' stone walls here.

SIMEON (*defiantly*) We hain't nobody's slaves from this out—nor no thin's slaves nuther. (*A pause—restlessly*) Speakin' o' milk, wonder how Eben's managin'?

PETER I s'pose he's managin'.

SIMEON Mebbe we'd ought t' help—this once.

PETER Mebbe. The cows knows us.

SIMEON An' likes us. They don't know him much.

PETER An' the hosses, an' pigs, an' chickens. They don't know him much.

SIMEON They knows us like brothers—an' likes us! (*Proudly*). Hain't we raised 'em t' be fust-rate, number one prize stock?

PETER We hain't—not no more.

SIMEON (*dully*) I was fergittin'. (*Then resignedly*) Waal, let's go help Eben a spell an' git waked up.

PETER Suits me. (*They are starting off down left, rear, for the barn when* EBEN *appears from there hurrying toward them, his face excited*).

EBEN (*breathlessly*) Waal—thar they be! The old mule an' the bride! I seen 'em from the barn down below at the turnin'.

PETER How could ye tell that far?

EBEN Hain't I as far-sight as he's near-sight? Don't I know the mare 'n' buggy, an' two people settin' in it? Who else . . . ? An' I tell ye I kin feel 'em a-comin', too! (*He squirms as if he had the itch*).

PETER (*beginning to be angry*) Waal—let him do his own unhitchin'!

SIMEON (*angry in his turn*) Let's hustle in an' git our bundles an' be a-goin' as he's a-comin'. I don't want never t' step inside the door agen arter he's back. (*They both start back around the corner of the house.* EBEN *follows them*).

EBEN (*anxiously*) Will ye sign it afore ye go?

PETER Let's see the color o' the old skinflint's money an' we'll sign. (*They disappear left. The two brothers clump upstairs to get their bundles.* EBEN *appears in the kitchen, runs to window, peers out, comes back and pulls up a strip of flooring in under stove, takes out a canvas bag and puts it on table, then sets the floorboard back in place. The two brothers appear a moment after. They carry old carpetbags*).

EBEN (*puts his hand on bag guardingly*) Have ye signed?

SIMEON (*shows paper in his hand*) Ay-eh. (*Greedily*) Be that the money?

EBEN (*opens bag and pours out pile of twenty-dollar gold pieces*) Twenty-dollar pieces—thirty of 'em. Count 'em. (*Peter does so, arranging them in stacks of five, biting one or two to test them*).

PETER Six hundred. (*He puts them in bag and puts it inside his shirt carefully*).

SIMEON (*handing paper to* EBEN) Har ye be.

EBEN (*after a glance, folds it carefully and hides it under his shirt—gratefully*) Thank yew.

PETER Thank yew fur the ride.

SIMEON We'll send ye a lump o' gold fur Christmas. (*A pause.* EBEN *stares at them and they at him*).

PETER (*awkwardly*) Waal—we're a-goin'.

SIMEON Comin' out t' the yard?

EBEN No. I'm waitin' in here a spell. (*Another silence. The brothers edge awkwardly to door in rear—then turn and stand*).

SIMEON Waal—good-by.

PETER Good-by.

EBEN Good-by. (*They go out. He sits down at the table, faces the stove and pulls out the paper. He looks from it to the stove. His face, lighted up by the shaft of sunlight from the window, has an expression of trance. His lips move. The two brothers come out to the gate*).

PETER (*looking off toward barn*) Thar he be—unhitchin'.

SIMEON (*with a chuckle*) I'll bet ye he's riled!

PETER An' thar she be.

SIMEON Let's wait 'n' see what our new Maw looks like.

PETER (*with a grin*) An' give him our partin' cuss!

SIMEON (*grinning*) I feel like raisin' fun. I feel light in my head an' feet.

PETER Me, too. I feel like laffin' till I'd split up the middle.

SIMEON Reckon it's the likker?

PETER No. My feet feel itchin' t' walk an' walk—an' jump high over thin's—an'. . . .

SIMEON Dance? (*A pause*).

PETER (*puzzled*) It's plumb onnateral.

SIMEON (*a light coming over his face*) I calc'late it's 'cause school's out. It's holiday. Fur once we're free!

PETER (*dazedly*) Free?

SIMEON The halter's broke—the harness is busted—the fence bars is down—the stone walls air crumblin' an' tumblin'! We'll be kickin' up an' tearin' away down the road!

PETER (*drawing a deep breath—oratorically*) Anybody that wants this stinkin' old rock-pile of a farm kin hev it. T'ain't our'n, no sirree!

SIMEON (*takes the gate off its hinges and puts it under his arm*) We harby 'bolishes shet gates, an' open gates, an' all gates, by thunder!

PETER We'll take it with us fur luck an' let 'er sail free down some river.

SIMEON (*as a sound of voices comes from left, rear*) Har they comes! (*The two brothers congeal into two stiff, grim-visaged statues.* EPHRAIM CABOT *and* ABBIE PUTNAM *come in.* CABOT *is seventy-five, tall and gaunt, with great, wiry, concentrated power, but stoop-shouldered from toil. His face is as hard as if it were hewn out of a boulder, yet there is a weakness in it, a petty pride in its own narrow strength. His eyes are small, close together, and extremely near-sighted, blinking continually in the effort to focus on objects, their stare having a straining, ingrowing quality. He is dressed in his dismal black Sunday suit.* ABBIE *is thirty-five, buxom, full of vitality. Her round face is pretty but marred by its rather gross sensuality. There is strength and obstinacy in her jaw, a hard determination in her eyes, and about her whole personality the same unsettled, untamed, desperate quality which is so apparent in* EBEN).

CABOT (*as they enter—a queer strangled emotion in his dry cracking voice*) Har we be t' hum, Abbie.

ABBIE (*with lust for the word*) Hum! (*Her eyes gloating on the house without seeming to see the two stiff figures at the gate*) It's purty—purty! I can't b'lieve it's r'ally mine.

CABOT (*sharply*) Yewr'n? Mine! (*He stares at her penetratingly, she stares back. He adds relentingly*) Our'n—mebbe! It was lonesome too long. I was growin' old in the spring. A hum's got t' hev a woman.

ABBIE (*her voice taking possession*) A woman's got t' hev a hum!

CABOT (*nodding uncertainly*) Ay-eh. (*Then irritably*) Whar be they? Ain't thar nobody about—'r wukin'—'r nothin'?

ABBIE (*sees the brothers. She returns their stare of cold appraising contempt with interest—slowly*) Thar's two men loafin' at the gate an' starin' at me like a couple o' strayed hogs.

CABOT (*straining his eyes*) I kin see 'em—but I can't make out. . . .

SIMEON It's Simeon.

PETER It's Peter.

CABOT (*exploding*) Why hain't ye wukin'?

SIMEON (*dryly*) We're waitin' t' welcome ye hum—yew an' the bride!

CABOT (*confusedly*) Huh? Waal—this be yer new Maw, boys. (*She stares at them and they at her*).

SIMEON (*turns away and spits contemptuously*) I see her!

PETER (*spits also*) An' I see her!

ABBIE (*with the conqueror's conscious superiority*) I'll go in an' look at *my* house. (*She goes slowly around to porch*).

SIMEON (*with a snort*) *Her* house!

PETER (*calls after her*) Ye'll find Eben inside. Ye better not tell him it's *yewr* house.

ABBIE (*mouthing the name*) Eben. (*Then quietly*) I'll tell Eben.

CABOT (*with a contemptuous sneer*) Ye needn't heed Eben. Eben's a dumb fool—like his Maw—soft an' simple!

SIMEON (*with his sardonic burst of laughter*) Ha! Eben's a chip o' yew—spit 'n' image—hard 'n' bitter's a hickory tree! Dog'll eat dog. He'll eat ye yet, old man!

CABOT (*commandingly*) Ye git t' wuk!

SIMEON (*as* ABBIE *disappears in house—winks at* PETER *and says tauntingly*) So that thar's our new Maw, be it? Whar in hell did ye dig her up? (*He and* PETER *laugh*).

PETER Ha! Ye'd better turn her in the pen with the other sows. (*They laugh uproariously, slapping their thighs*).

CABOT (*so amazed at their effrontery that he stutters in confusion*) Simeon! Peter! What's come over ye? Air ye drunk?

SIMEON We're free, old man—free o' yew an' the hull damned farm! (*They grow more and more hilarious and excited*).

PETER An' we're startin' out fur the gold fields o' Californi-a!

SIMEON Ye kin take this place an' burn it!

PETER An' bury it—fur all we cares!

SIMEON We're free, old man! (*He cuts a caper*).

PETER Free! (*He gives a kick in the air*).

SIMEON (*in a frenzy*) Whoop!

PETER Whoop! (*They do an absurd Indian war dance about the old man who is petrified between rage and the fear that they are insane*).

SIMEON We're free as Injuns! Lucky we don't skulp ye!

PETER An' burn yer barn an' kill the stock!

SIMEON An' rape yer new woman! Whoop! (*He and* PETER *stop their dance, holding their sides, rocking with wild laughter*).

CABOT (*edging away*) Lust fur gold—fur the sinful, easy gold o' Californi-a! It's made ye mad!

SIMEON (*tauntingly*) Wouldn't ye like us to send ye back some sinful gold, ye old sinner?

PETER They's gold besides what's in Californi-a! (*He retreats back beyond the vision of the old man and takes the bag of money and flaunts it in the air above his head, laughing*).

SIMEON And sinfuller, too!

PETER We'll be voyagin' on the sea! Whoop! (*He leaps up and down*).

SIMEON Livin' free! Whoop! (*He leaps in turn*).

CABOT (*suddenly roaring with rage*) My cuss on ye!

SIMEON Take our'n in trade fur it! Whoop!

CABOT I'll hev ye both chained up in the asylum!

PETER Ye old skinflint! Good-by!

SIMEON Ye old blood sucker! Good-by!

CABOT Go afore I . . . !

PETER Whoop! (*He picks a stone from the road.* SIMEON *does the same*).

SIMEON Maw'll be in the parlor.

PETER Ay-eh! One! Two!

CABOT (*frightened*) What air ye . . . ?

PETER Three! (*They both throw, the stones hitting the parlor window with a crash of glass, tearing the shade*).

SIMEON Whoop!

PETER Whoop!

CABOT (*in a fury now, rushing toward them*) If I kin lay hands on ye—I'll break yer bones fur ye! (*But they beat a capering retreat before him,* SIMEON *with the gate still under his arm.* CABOT *comes back, panting with impotent rage. Their voices as they go off take up the song of the gold-seekers to the old tune of "Oh, Susannah!"*

"I jumped aboard the Liza ship,
And traveled on the sea,
And every time I thought of home
I wished it wasn't me!
Oh! Californi-a,
That's the land fur me!
I'm off to Californi-a!
With my wash bowl on my knee."

(*In the meantime, the window of the upper bedroom on right is raised and* ABBIE *sticks her head out. She looks down at* CABOT*—with a sigh of relief*).

ABBIE Waal—that's the last o' them two, hain't it? (*He doesn't answer. Then in possessive tones*) This here's a nice bedroom, Ephraim. It's a r'al nice bed. Is it my room, Ephraim?

CABOT (*grimly—without looking up*) Our'n! (*She cannot control a grimace of aversion and pulls back her head slowly and shuts the window. A sudden horrible thought seems to enter* CABOT'S *head*) They been up to somethin'! Mebbe—mebbe they've pizened the stock—'r somethin'! (*He almost runs off down toward the barn. A moment later the kitchen door is slowly pushed open and* ABBIE *enters. For a moment she stands looking at* EBEN. *He does not notice her at first. Her eyes take him in penetratingly with a calculating appraisal of his strength as against hers. But under this her desire is dimly awakened by his youth and good looks. Suddenly he becomes conscious of her presence and looks up. Their eyes meet. He leaps to his feet, glowering at her speechlessly*).

ABBIE (*in her most seductive tones which she uses all through this scene*) Be you—Eben? I'm Abbie— (*She laughs*) I mean, I'm yer new Maw.

EBEN (*viciously*) No, damn ye!

ABBIE (*as if she hadn't heard—with a queer smile*) Yer Paw's spoke a lot o' yew. . . .

EBEN Ha!

ABBIE Ye mustn't mind him. He's an old man. (*A long pause. They stare at each other*) I don't want t' pretend playin' Maw t' ye, Eben. (*Admiringly*) Ye're too big an' too strong fur that. I want t' be frens with ye. Mebbe with me fur a fren ye'd find ye'd like livin' here better. I kin make it easy fur ye with him, mebbe. (*With a scornful sense of power*) I calc'late I kin git him t' do most anythin' fur me.

EBEN (*with bitter scorn*) Ha! (*They stare again,* EBEN *obscurely moved, physically attracted to her—in forced stilted tones*) Yew kin go t' the devil!

ABBIE (*calmly*) If cussin' me does ye good, cuss all ye've a mind t'. I'm all prepared t' have ye agin me—at fust. I don't blame ye nuther. I'd feel the same at any stranger comin' t' take my Maw's place. (*He shudders. She is watching him carefully*) Yew must've cared a lot fur yewr Maw, didn't ye? My Maw died afore I'd growed. I don't remember her none. (*A pause*) But yew won't hate me long, Eben. I'm not the wust in the world—an' yew an' me've got a lot in common. I kin tell that by lookin' at ye. Waal—I've had a hard life, too—oceans o' trouble an' nuthin' but wuk fur reward. I was a orphan early an' had t' wuk fur others in other folks' hums. Then I married an' he turned out a drunken spreer an' so he had to wuk fur others an' me too agen in other folks' hums, an' the baby died, an' my husband got sick an' died too, an' I was glad sayin' now I'm free fur once, on'y I diskivered right away all I was free fur was t' wuk agen in other folks' hums, doin' other folks' wuk till I'd most give up hope o' ever doin' my own wuk in my own hum, an' then your Paw come. . . . (CABOT *appears returning from the barn. He comes to the gate and looks down the road the brothers have gone. A faint strain of their retreating voices is heard: "Oh, Californi-a! That's the place for me." He stands glowering, his fist clenched, his face grim with rage*).

EBEN (*fighting against his growing attraction and sympathy—harshly*) An' bought yew—like a harlot! (*She is stung and flushes angrily. She has been sincerely moved by the recital of her troubles. He adds furiously*) An' the price he's payin' ye—this farm—was my Maw's, damn ye!—an' mine now!

ABBIE (*with a cool laugh of confidence*) Yewr'n? We'll see 'bout that! (*Then strongly*) Waal—what if I did need a hum? What else'd I marry an old man like him fur?

EBEN (*maliciously*) I'll tell him ye said that!

ABBIE (*smiling*) I'll say ye're lyin' a-purpose—an' he'll drive ye off the place!

EBEN Ye devil!

ABBIE (*defying him*) This be my farm—this be my hum—this be my kitchen—!

EBEN (*furiously, as if he were going to attack her*) Shut up, damn ye!

ABBIE (*walks up to him—a queer coarse expression of desire in her face and body—slowly*) An' upstairs—that be my bedroom—an' my bed! (*He stares into her eyes, terribly confused and torn. She adds softly*) I hain't bad nor mean—'ceptin' fur an enemy—but I got t' fight fur what's due me out o' life, if I ever 'spect t' git it. (*Then putting her hand on his arm—seductively*) Let's yew 'n' me be frens, Eben.

EBEN (*stupidly—as if hypnotized*) Ay-eh. (*Then furiously flinging off her arm*) No, ye durned old witch! I hate ye! (*He rushes out the door*).

ABBIE (*looks after him smiling satisfiedly—then half to herself, mouthing the word*) Eben's nice. (*She looks at the table, proudly*) I'll wash up *my* dishes now. (EBEN *appears outside, slamming the door behind him. He comes around corner, stops on seeing his father, and stands staring at him with hate*).

CABOT (*raising his arms to heaven in the fury he can no*

longer control) Lord God o' Hosts, smite the undutiful sons with Thy wust cuss!

EBEN (*breaking in violently*) Yew 'n' yewr God! Allus cussin' folks—allus naggin' 'em!

CABOT (*oblivious to him—summoningly*) God o' the old! God o' the lonesome!

EBEN (*mockingly*) Naggin' His sheep t' sin! T' hell with yewr God! (CABOT *turns. He and* EBEN *glower at each other*).

CABOT (*harshly*) So it's yew. I might've knowed it. (*Shaking his finger threateningly at him*) Blasphemin' fool! (*Then quickly*) Why hain't ye t' wuk?

EBEN Why hain't yew? They've went. I can't wuk it all alone.

CABOT (*contemptuously*) Nor noways! I'm wuth ten o' ye yit, old's I be! Ye'll never be more'n half a man! (*Then, matter-of-factly*) Waal—let's git t' the barn. (*They go. A last faint note of the "Californi-a" song is heard from the distance.* ABBIE *is washing her dishes*).

CURTAIN

PART TWO · SCENE ONE

The exterior of the farmhouse, as in Part One—a hot Sunday afternoon two months later. ABBIE, *dressed in her best, is discovered sitting in a rocker at the end of the porch. She rocks listlessly, enervated by the heat, staring in front of her with bored, half-closed eyes.*

EBEN *sticks his head out of his bedroom window. He looks around furtively and tries to see—or hear—if anyone is on the porch, but although he has been careful to make no noise,* ABBIE *has sensed his movement. She stops rocking, her face grows animated and eager, she waits attentively.* EBEN *seems to feel her presence, he scowls back his thoughts of her and spits with exaggerated disdain—then withdraws back into the room.* ABBIE *waits, holding her breath as she listens with passionate eagerness for every sound within the house.*

EBEN *comes out. Their eyes meet. His falter, he is confused, he turns away and slams the door resentfully. At this gesture,* ABBIE *laughs tantalizingly, amused but at the same time piqued and irritated. He scowls, strides off the porch to the path and starts to walk past her to the road with a grand swagger of ignoring her existence. He is dressed in his store suit, spruced up, his face shines from soap and water.* ABBIE *leans forward on her chair, her eyes hard and angry now, and, as he passes her, gives a sneering, taunting chuckle.*

EBEN (*stung—turns on her furiously*) What air yew cacklin' 'bout?

ABBIE (*triumphant*) Yew!

EBEN What about me?

ABBIE Ye look all slicked up like a prize bull.

EBEN (*with a sneer*) Waal—ye hain't so durned purty yerself, be ye? (*They stare into each other's eyes, his held by hers in spite of himself, hers glowingly possessive. Their physical attraction becomes a palpable force quivering in the hot air*).

ABBIE (*softly*) Ye don't mean that, Eben. Ye may think ye mean it, mebbe, but ye don't. Ye can't. It's agin nature, Eben. Ye been fightin' yer nature ever since the day I come—tryin' t' tell yerself I hain't purty t'ye. (*She laughs a low humid laugh without taking her eyes from his. A pause—her body squirms desirously—she murmurs languorously*) Hain't the sun strong an' hot? Ye kin feel it burnin' into the earth—Nature—makin' thin's grow—bigger 'n' bigger—burnin' inside ye—makin' ye want t' grow—into somethin' else—till ye're jined with it—an' it's your'n—but it owns ye, too—an' makes ye grow bigger—like a tree—like them elums— (*She laughs again softly, holding his eyes. He takes a step toward her, compelled against his will*) Nature'll beat ye, Eben. Ye might's well own up t' it fust 's last.

EBEN (*trying to break from her spell—confusedly*) If Paw'd hear ye goin' on. . . . (*Resentfully*) But ye've made such a damned idjit out o' the old devil . . . ! (ABBIE *laughs*).

ABBIE Waal—hain't it easier fur yew with him changed softer?

EBEN (*defiantly*) No. I'm fightin' him—fightin' yew—fightin' fur Maw's rights t' her hum! (*This breaks her spell for him. He glowers at her*) An' I'm onto ye. Ye hain't foolin' me a mite. Ye're aimin' t' swaller up everythin' an' make it your'n. Waal, you'll find I'm a heap sight bigger hunk nor yew kin chew! (*He turns from her with a sneer*).

ABBIE (*trying to regain her ascendancy—seductively*) Eben!

EBEN Leave me be! (*He starts to walk away*).

ABBIE (*more commandingly*) Eben!

EBEN (*stops—resentfully*) What d'ye want?

ABBIE (*trying to conceal a growing excitement*) Whar air ye goin'?

EBEN (*with malicious nonchalance*) Oh—up the road a spell.

ABBIE T' the village?

EBEN (*airily*) Mebbe.

ABBIE (*excitedly*) T' see that Min, I s'pose?

EBEN Mebbe.

ABBIE (*weakly*) What d'ye want t' waste time on her fur?

EBEN (*revenging himself now—grinning at her*) Ye can't beat Nature, didn't ye say? (*He laughs and again starts to walk away*).

ABBIE (*bursting out*) An ugly old hake!

EBEN (*with a tantalizing sneer*) She's purtier'n yew be!

ABBIE That every wuthless drunk in the country has. . . .

EBEN (*tauntingly*) Mebbe—but she's better'n yew. She owns up fa'r 'n' squar' t' her doin's.

ABBIE (*furiously*) Don't ye dare compare. . . .

EBEN She don't go sneakin' an' stealin'—what's mine.

ABBIE (*savagely seizing on his weak point*) Your'n? Yew mean—my farm?

EBEN I mean the farm yew sold yerself fur like any other old whore—my farm!

ABBIE (*stung—fiercely*) Ye'll never live t' see the day when even a stinkin' weed on it 'll belong t' ye! (*Then in a scream*) Git out o' my sight! Go on t' yer slut—disgracin' yer Paw 'n' me! I'll git yer Paw t' horsewhip ye off the place if I want t'! Ye're only livin' here 'cause I tolerate ye! Git along! I hate the sight o' ye! (*She stops panting and glaring at him*).

EBEN (*returning her glance in kind*) An' I hate the sight o' yew! (*He turns and strides off up the road. She follows his retreating figure with concentrated hate. Old* CABOT *appears coming up from the barn. The hard, grim expression of his face has changed. He seems in some queer way softened, mellowed. His eyes have taken on a strange, incongruous dreamy quality. Yet there is not hint of physical weakness about him—rather he looks more robust and younger.* ABBIE *sees him and turns away quickly with unconcealed aversion. He comes slowly up to her*).

CABOT (*mildly*) War yew an' Eben quarrelin' agen?

ABBIE (*shortly*) No.

CABOT Ye was talkin' a'mighty loud. (*He sits down on the edge of porch*).

ABBIE (*snappishly*) If ye heerd us they hain't no need askin' questions.

CABOT I didn't hear what ye said.

ABBIE (*relieved*) Waal—it wa'n't nothin' t' speak on.

CABOT (*after a pause*) Eben's queer.

ABBIE (*bitterly*) He's the dead spit 'n' image o' yew!

CABOT (*queerly interested*) D'ye think so, Abbie? (*After a pause, ruminatingly*) Me 'n' Eben's allus fit 'n' fit. I never could b'ar him noways. He's so thunderin' soft—like his Maw.

ABBIE (*scornfully*) Ay-eh! 'Bout as soft as yew be!

CABOT (*as if he hadn't heard*) Mebbe I been too hard on him.

ABBIE (*jeeringly*) Waal—ye're gittin' soft now—soft as slop! That's what Eben was sayin'.

CABOT (*his face instantly grim and ominous*) Eben was sayin'? Waal, he'd best not do nothin' t' try me 'r he'll soon diskiver. . . . (*A pause. She keeps her face turned away. His gradually softens. He stares up at the sky*) Purty, hain't it?

ABBIE (*crossly*) I don't see nothin' purty.

CABOT The sky. Feels like a wa'm field up thar.

ABBIE (*sarcastically*) Air yew aimin' t' buy up over the farm too? (*She snickers contemptuously*).

CABOT (*strangely*) I'd like t' own my place up thar. (*A pause*) I'm gittin' old, Abbie. I'm gittin' ripe on the bough. (*A pause. She stares at him mystified. He goes on*) It's allus lonesome cold in the house—even when it's bilin' hot outside. Hain't yew noticed?

ABBIE No.

CABOT It's wa'm down t'the barn—nice smellin' an' warm —with the cows. (*A pause*) Cows is queer.

ABBIE Like yew?

CABOT Like Eben. (*A pause*) I'm gittin' t' feel resigned t' Eben—jest as I got t' feel 'bout his Maw. I'm gittin' t' learn to b'ar his softness—jest like her'n. I calc'late I c'd a'most take t' him—if he wa'n't sech a dumb fool! (*A pause*) I s'pose it's old age a-creepin' in my bones.

ABBIE (*indifferently*) Waal—ye hain't dead yet.

CABOT (*roused*) No, I hain't, yew bet—not by a hell of a sight—I'm sound 'n' tough as hickory! (*Then moodily*) But arter three score and ten the Lord warns ye t' prepare. (*A pause*) That's why Eben's come in my head. Now that his cussed sinful brothers is gone their path t' hell, they's no one left but Eben.

ABBIE (*resentfully*) They's me, hain't they? (*Agitatedly*) What's all this sudden likin' ye've tuk to Eben? Why don't ye say nothin' 'bout me? Hain't I yer lawful wife?

CABOT (*simply*) Ay-eh. Ye be. (*A pause—he stares at her desirously—his eyes grow avid—then with a sudden movement he seizes her hands and squeezes them, declaiming in a queer camp-meeting preacher's tempo*) Yew air my Rose o' Sharon! Behold, yew air fair; yer eyes air doves; yer lips air like scarlet; yer two breasts air like two fawns; yer navel be like a round goblet; yer belly be like a heap o' wheat. . . . (*He covers her hand with kisses. She does not seem to notice. She stares before her with hard angry eyes*).

ABBIE (*jerking her hands away—harshly*) So ye're plannin' t' leave the farm t' Eben, air ye?

CABOT (*dazedly*) Leave . . . ? (*Then with resentful obstinacy*) I hain't a-givin' it t' no one!

ABBIE (*remorselessly*) Ye can't take it with ye.

CABOT (*thinks a moment—then reluctantly*) No, I calc'late

not. (*After a pause—with a strange passion*) But if I could, I would, by the Etarnal! 'R if I could, in my dyin' hour, I'd set it afire an' watch it burn—this house an' every ear o' corn an' every tree down t' the last blade o' hay! I'd sit an' know it was all a-dying with me an' no one else'd ever own what was mine, what I'd made out o' nothin' with my own sweat 'n' blood! (*A pause—then he adds with a queer affection*) 'Ceptin' the cows. Them I'd turn free.

ABBIE (*harshly*) An' me?

CABOT (*with a queer smile*) Ye'd be turned free, too.

ABBIE (*furiously*) So that's the thanks I git fur marryin' ye—t' have ye change kind to Eben who hates ye, an' talk o' turnin' me out in the road.

CABOT (*hastily*) Abbie! Ye know I wa'n't. . . .

ABBIE (*vengefully*) Just let me tell ye a thing or two 'bout Eben! Whar's he gone? T' see that harlot, Min! I tried fur t' stop him. Disgracin' yew an' me—on the Sabbath, too!

CABOT (*rather guiltily*) He's a sinner—nateral-born. It's lust eatin' his heart.

ABBIE (*enraged beyond endurance—wildly vindictive*) An' his lust fur me! Kin ye find excuses fur that?

CABOT (*stares at her—after a dead pause*) Lust—fur yew?

ABBIE (*defiantly*) He was tryin' t' make love t' me—when ye heerd us quarrelin'.

CABOT (*stares at her—then a terrible expression of rage comes over his face—he springs to his feet shaking all over*) By the A'mighty God—I'll end him!

ABBIE (*frightened now for* EBEN) No! Don't ye!

CABOT (*violently*) I'll git the shotgun an' blow his soft brains t' the top o' them elums!

ABBIE (*throwing her arms around him*) No, Ephraim!

CABOT (*pushing her away violently*) I will, by God!

ABBIE (*in a quieting tone*) Listen, Ephraim. 'Twa'n't nothin' bad—on'y a boy's foolin'—'twa'n't meant serious—jest jokin' an' teasin'. . . .

CABOT Then why did ye say—lust?

ABBIE It must hev sounded wusser'n I meant. An' I was mad at thinkin'—ye'd leave him the farm.

CABOT (*quieter but still grim and cruel*) Waal then, I'll horsewhip him off the place if that much'll content ye.

ABBIE (*reaching out and taking his hand*) No. Don't think o' me! Ye mustn't drive him off. 'Tain't sensible. Who'll ye get to help ye on the farm? They's no one hereabouts.

CABOT (*considers this—then nodding his appreciation*) Ye got a head on ye. (*Then irritably*) Waal, let him stay. (*He sits down on the edge of the porch. She sits beside him. He murmurs contemptuously*) I oughtn't t' git riled so—at that 'ere fool calf. (*A pause*) But har's the p'int. What son o' mine'll keep on here t' the farm—when the Lord does call me? Simeon an' Peter air gone t' hell—an' Eben's follerin' 'em.

ABBIE They's me.

CABOT Ye're on'y a woman.

ABBIE I'm yewr wife.

CABOT That hain't me. A son is me—my blood—mine. Mine ought t' git mine. An' then it's still mine—even though I be six foot under. D'ye see?

ABBIE (*giving him a look of hatred*) Ay-eh. I see. (*She becomes very thoughtful, her face growing shrewd, her eyes studying* CABOT *craftily*).

CABOT I'm gittin' old—ripe on the bough. (*Then with a sudden forced reassurance*) Not but what I hain't a hard nut t' crack even yet—an' fur many a year t' come! By the Etarnal, I kin break most o' the young fellers' backs at any kind o' work any day o' the year!

ABBIE (*suddenly*) Mebbe the Lord'll give *us* a son.

CABOT (*turns and stares at her eagerly*) Ye mean—a son—t' me 'n' yew?

ABBIE (*with a cajoling smile*) Ye're a strong man yet, hain't ye? 'Tain't noways impossible, be it? We know that. Why d'ye stare so? Hain't ye never thought o' that afore? I been thinkin' o' it all along. Ay-eh—an' I been prayin' it'd happen, too.

CABOT (*his face growing full of joyous pride and a sort of religious ecstasy*) Ye been prayin', Abbie?—fur a son?—t' us?

ABBIE Ay-eh. (*With a grim resolution*) I want a son now.

CABOT (*excitedly clutching both of her hands in his*) It'd be the blessin' o' God, Abbie—the blessin' o' God A'mighty on me—in my old age—in my lonesomeness! They hain't nothin' I wouldn't do fur ye then, Abbie. Ye'd hev on'y t' ask it—anythin' ye'd a mind t'!

ABBIE (*interrupting*) Would ye will the farm t' me then—t' me an' it . . . ?

CABOT (*vehemently*) I'd do anythin' ye axed, I tell ye! I swar it! May I be everlastin' damned t' hell if I wouldn't! (*He sinks to his knees pulling her down with him. He trembles all over with the fervor of his hopes*) Pray t' the Lord agen, Abbie. It's the Sabbath! I'll jine ye! Two prayers air better nor one.

"An' God hearkened unto Rachel"! An' God hearkened unto Abbie! Pray, Abbie! Pray fur him to hearken! (*He bows his head, mumbling. She pretends to do likewise but gives him a side glance of scorn and triumph*).

CURTAIN

SCENE TWO

About eight in the evening. The interior of the two bedrooms on the top floor is shown. EBEN *is sitting on the side of his bed in the room on the left. On account of the heat he has taken off everything but his undershirt and pants. His feet are bare. He faces front, brooding moodily, his chin propped on his hands, a desperate expression on his face.*

In the other room CABOT *and* ABBIE *are sitting side by side on the edge of their bed, an old four-poster with feather mattress. He is in his night shirt, she in her nightdress. He is still in the queer, excited mood into which the notion of a son has thrown him. Both rooms are lighted dimly and flickeringly by tallow candles.*

CABOT The farm needs a son.

ABBIE I need a son.

CABOT Ay-eh. Sometimes ye air the farm an' sometimes the farm be yew. That's why I clove t' ye in my lonesomeness. (*A pause. He pounds his knee with his fist*) Me an' the farm has got t' beget a son!

ABBIE Ye'd best go t' sleep. Ye're gittin' thin's all mixed.

CABOT (*with an impatient gesture*) No, I hain't. My mind's clear's a well. Ye don't know me, that's it. (*He stares hopelessly at the floor*).

ABBIE (*indifferently*) Mebbe. (*In the next room* EBEN *gets up and paces up and down distractedly.* ABBIE *hears him. Her eyes fasten on the intervening wall with concentrated attention.* EBEN *stops and stares. Their hot glances seem to meet through the wall. Unconsciously he stretches out his arms for her and she half rises. Then aware, he mutters a curse at himself and flings himself face downward on the bed, his clenched fists above his head, his face buried in the pillow.* ABBIE *relaxes with a faint sigh but her eyes remain fixed on the wall; she listens with all her attention for some movement from* EBEN).

CABOT (*suddenly raises his head and looks at her—scornfully*) Will ye ever know me—'r will any man 'r woman? (*Shaking his head*) No. I calc'late 't wa'n't t' be. (*He turns away.* ABBIE *looks at the wall. Then, evidently unable to keep silent about his thoughts without looking at his wife, he puts out his hand and clutches her knee. She starts violently, looks at him, sees he is not watching her, concentrates again on the wall and pays no attention to what he says*) Listen, Abbie. When I come here fifty odd year ago—I was jest twenty an' the strongest an' hardest ye ever seen—ten times as strong an' fifty times as hard as Eben. Waal—this place was nothin' but fields o' stones. Folks laughed when I tuk it. They couldn't know what I knowed. When ye kin make corn sprout out o' stones, God's livin' in yew! They wa'n't strong enuf fur that! They reckoned God was easy. They laughed. They don't laugh no more. Some died hereabouts. Some went West an' died. They're all under ground—fur follerin' arter an easy God. God hain't easy. (*He shakes his head slowly*) An' I growed hard. Folks kept allus sayin' he's a hard man like 'twas sinful t' be hard, so's at last I said back at 'em: Waal then, by thunder, ye'll git me hard an' see how ye like it! (*Then suddenly*) But I give in t' weakness once. 'Twas arter I'd been here two year. I got weak—despairful—they was so many stones. They was a party leavin', givin' up, goin' West. I jined 'em. We tracked on 'n' on. We come t' broad medders, plains, whar the soil was black an' rich as gold. Nary a stone. Easy. Ye'd on'y to plow an' sow an' then set an' smoke yer pipe an' watch thin's grow. I could o' been a rich man—but somethin' in me fit me an' fit me—the voice o' God sayin': "This hain't wuth nothin' t' Me. Git ye back t' hum!" I got afeerd o' that voice an' I lit out back t' hum here, leavin' my claim an' crops t' whoever'd a mind t' take 'em. Ay-eh. I actoolly give up what was rightful mine! God's hard, not easy! God's in the stones! Build my church on a rock—out o' stones an' I'll be in them! That's what He meant t' Peter! (*He sighs heavily—a pause*) Stones. I picked 'em up an' piled 'em into walls. Ye kin read the years o' my life in them walls, every day a hefted stone, climbin' over the hills up and down, fencin' in the fields that was mine, whar I'd made thin's grow out o' nothin'—like the will o' God, like the servant o' His hand. It wa'n't easy. It was hard an' He made me hard fur it. (*He pauses*) All the time I kept gittin' lonesomer. I tuk a wife. She bore Simeon an' Peter. She was a good woman. She wuked hard. We was married twenty year. She never knowed me. She helped but she never knowed what she was helpin'. I was allus lonesome. She died. After that it wa'n't so lonesome fur a spell. (*A pause*) I lost count o' the years. I had no time t' fool away countin' 'em. Sim an' Peter helped. The farm growed. It was all mine! When I thought o' that I didn't feel lonesome. (*A pause*) But ye can't hitch yer mind t' one thin' day an' night. I tuk another wife—Eben's Maw. Her folks was contestin' me at law over my deeds t' the farm—my farm! That's why Eben keeps a-talkin' his fool talk o' this bein' his Maw's farm. She bore Eben. She was purty—but soft. She tried t' be hard. She couldn't. She never knowed me nor nothin'. It was lonesomer 'n hell with her. After a matter o' sixteen odd years, she died. (*A pause*) I lived with the boys. They hated me 'cause I was hard. I hated them 'cause they was soft. They coveted the farm without knowin' what it meant. It made me bitter 'n wormwood. It aged me—them coveting what I'd made fur mine. Then this spring the call come—the voice o' God cryin' in my wilderness, in my lonesomeness—t' go out an' seek an' find! (*Turning to her with strange passion*) I sought ye an' I found ye! Yew air my Rose o' Sharon! Yer eyes air like. . . . (*She has turned a blank face, resentful eyes to his. He stares at her for a moment —then harshly*) Air ye any the wiser fur all I've told ye?

ABBIE (*confusedly*) Mebbe.

CABOT (*pushing her away from him—angrily*) Ye don't know nothin'—nor never will. If ye don't hev a son t' redeem ye. . . . (*This in a tone of cold threat*).

ABBIE (*resentfully*) I've prayed, hain't I?

CABOT (*bitterly*) Pray agen—fur understandin'!

ABBIE (*a veiled threat in her tone*) Ye'll have a son out o' me, I promise ye.

CABOT How kin ye promise?

ABBIE I got second-sight mebbe. I kin foretell. (*She gives a queer smile*).

CABOT I believe ye have. Ye give me the chills sometimes. (*He shivers*) It's cold in this house. It's oneasy. They's thin's pokin' about in the dark—in the corners. (*He pulls on his trousers, tucking in his night shirt, and pulls on his boots*).

ABBIE (*surprised*) Whar air ye goin'?

CABOT (*queerly*) Down whar it's restful—whar it's warm down t' the barn. (*Bitterly*) I kin talk t' the cows. They know. They know the farm an' me. They'll give me peace. (*He turns to go out the door*).

ABBIE (*a bit frightenedly*) Air ye ailin' tonight, Ephraim?

CABOT Growin'. Growin' ripe on the bough. (*He turns and goes, his boots clumping down the stairs.* EBEN *sits up with a start, listening.* ABBIE *is conscious of his movement and stares at the wall.* CABOT *comes out of the house around the corner and stands by the gate, blinking at the sky. He stretches up his hands in a tortured gesture*) God A'mighty, call from the dark! (*He listens as if expecting an answer. Then his arms drop, he shakes his head and plods off toward the barn.* EBEN *and* ABBIE *stare at each other through the wall.* EBEN *sighs heavily and* ABBIE *echoes it. Both become terribly nervous, uneasy. Finally* ABBIE *gets up and listens, her ear to the wall. He acts as if he saw every move she was making, he becomes resolutely still. She seems driven into a decision—goes out the door in rear determinedly. His eyes follow her. Then as the door of his room is opened softly, he turns away, waits in an attitude of strained fixity.* ABBIE *stands for a second staring at him, her eyes burning with desire. Then with a little cry she runs over and throws her arms about his neck, she pulls his head back and covers his mouth with kisses. At first, he submits dumbly; then he puts his arms about her neck and returns her kisses, but finally, suddenly aware of his hatred, he hurls her away from him, springing to his feet. They stand speechless and breathless, panting like two animals*).

ABBIE (*at last—painfully*) Ye shouldn't, Eben—ye shouldn't—I'd make ye happy!

EBEN (*harshly*) I don't want t' be happy—from yew!

ABBIE (*helplessly*) Ye do, Eben! Ye do! Why d'ye lie?

EBEN (*viciously*) I don't take t'ye, I tell ye! I hate the sight o' ye!

ABBIE (*with an uncertain troubled laugh*) Waal, I kissed ye anyways—an' ye kissed back—yer lips was burnin'—ye can't lie 'bout that! (*Intensely*) If ye don't care, why did ye kiss me back—why was yer lips burnin'?

EBEN (*wiping his mouth*) It was like pizen on 'em. (*Then tauntingly*) When I kissed ye back, mebbe I thought 'twas someone else.

ABBIE (*wildly*) Min?

EBEN Mebbe.

ABBIE (*torturedly*) Did ye go t' see her? Did ye r'ally go? I thought ye mightn't. Is that why ye throwed me off jest now?

EBEN (*sneeringly*) What if it be?

ABBIE (*raging*) Then ye're a dog, Eben Cabot!

EBEN (*threateningly*) Ye can't talk that way t' me!

ABBIE (*with a shrill laugh*) Can't I? Did ye think I was in love with ye—a weak thin' like yew? Not much! I on'y wanted ye fur a purpose o' my own—an' I'll hev ye fur it yet 'cause I'm stronger'n yew be!

EBEN (*resentfully*) I knowed well it was on'y part o' yer plan t' swaller everythin'!

ABBIE (*tauntingly*) Mebbe!

EBEN (*furious*) Git out o' my room!

ABBIE This air my room an' ye're on'y hired help!

EBEN (*threateningly*) Git out afore I murder ye!

ABBIE (*quite confident now*) I hain't a mite afeerd. Ye want me, don't ye? Yes, ye do! An' yer Paw's son'll never kill what he wants! Look at yer eyes! They's lust fur me in 'em, burnin' 'em up! Look at yer lips now! They're tremblin' an' longin' t' kiss me, an' yer teeth t' bite! (*He is watching her now with a horrible fascination. She laughs a crazy triumphant laugh*) I'm a-goin' t' make all o' this hum my hum! They's one room hain't mine yet, but it's a-goin' t' be tonight. I'm a-goin' down now an' light up! (*She makes him a mocking bow*) Won't ye come courtin' me in the best parlor, Mister Cabot?

EBEN (*staring at her—horribly confused—dully*) Don't ye dare! It hain't been opened since Maw died an' was laid out thar! Don't ye . . . ! (*But her eyes are fixed on his so burningly that his will seems to wither before hers. He stands swaying toward her helplessly*).

ABBIE (*holding his eyes and putting all her will into her words as she backs out the door*) I'll expect ye afore long, Eben.

EBEN (*stares after her for a while, walking toward the door. A light appears in the parlor window. He murmurs*) In the parlor? (*This seems to arouse connotations for he comes back and puts on his white shirt, collar, half ties the tie mechanically, puts on coat, takes his hat, stands barefooted looking about him in bewilderment, mutters wonderingly*) Maw! Whar air yew? (*Then goes slowly toward the door in rear*).

CURTAIN

SCENE THREE

A few minutes later. The interior of the parlor is shown. A grim, repressed room like a tomb in which the family has been interred alive. ABBIE *sits on the edge of the horsehair sofa. She has lighted all the candles and the room is revealed in all its preserved ugliness. A change has come over the woman. She looks awed and frightened now, ready to run away.*

The door is opened and EBEN *appears. His face wears an expression of obsessed confusion. He stands staring at her, his arms hanging disjointedly from his shoulders, his feet bare, his hat in his hand.*

ABBIE (*after a pause—with a nervous, formal politeness*) Won't ye set?

EBEN (*dully*) Ay-eh. (*Mechanically he places his hat carefully on the floor near the door and sits stiffly beside her on the edge of the sofa. A pause. They both remain rigid, looking straight ahead with eyes full of fear*).

ABBIE When I fust come in—in the dark—they seemed somethin' here.

EBEN (*simply*) Maw.

ABBIE I kin still feel—somethin'. . . .

EBEN It's Maw.

ABBIE At fust I was feered o' it. I wanted t' yell an' run. Now—since yew come—seems like it's growin' soft an' kind t' me. (*Addressing the air—queerly*) Thank yew.

EBEN Maw allus loved me.

ABBIE Mebbe it knows I love yew, too. Mebbe that makes it kind t' me.

EBEN (*dully*) I dunno. I should think she'd hate ye.

ABBIE (*with certainty*) No. I kin feel it don't—not no more.

EBEN Hate ye fur stealin' her place—here in her hum—settin' in her parlor whar she was laid— (*He suddenly stops, staring stupidly before him*).

ABBIE What is it, Eben?

EBEN (*in a whisper*) Seems like Maw didn't want me t' remind ye.

ABBIE (*excitedly*) I knowed, Eben! It's kind t' me! It don't b'ar me no grudges fur what I never knowed an' couldn't help!

EBEN Maw b'ars him a grudge.

ABBIE Waal, so does all o' us.

EBEN Ay-eh. (*With passion*) I does, by God!

ABBIE (*taking one of his hands in hers and patting it*) Thar! Don't git riled thinkin' o' him. Think o' yer Maw who's kind t' us. Tell me about yer Maw, Eben.

EBEN They hain't nothin' much. She was kind. She was good.

ABBIE (*putting one arm over his shoulder. He does not seem to notice—passionately*) I'll be kind an' good t' ye!

EBEN Sometimes she used t' sing fur me.

ABBIE I'll sing fur ye!

EBEN This was her hum. This was her farm.

ABBIE This is my hum! This is my farm!

EBEN He married her t' steal 'em. She was soft an' easy. He couldn't 'preciate her.

ABBIE He can't 'preciate me!

EBEN He murdered her with his hardness.

ABBIE He's murderin' me!

EBEN She died. (*A pause*) Sometimes she used to sing fur me. (*He bursts into a fit of sobbing*).

ABBIE (*both her arms around him—with wild passion*) I'll sing fur ye! I'll die fur ye! (*In spite of her overwhelming desire for him, there is a sincere maternal love in her manner and voice—a horribly frank mixture of lust and mother love*) Don't cry, Eben! I'll take yer Maw's place! I'll be everythin' she was t' ye! Let me kiss ye, Eben! (*She pulls his head around. He makes a bewildered pretense of resistance. She is tender*) Don't be afeered! I'll kiss ye pure, Eben—same 's if I was a Maw t' ye—an' ye kin kiss me back 's if yew was my son—my boy—sayin' good-night t' me! Kiss me, Eben. (*They kiss in restrained fashion. Then suddenly wild passion overcomes her. She kisses him lustfully again and again and he flings his arms about her and returns her kisses. Suddenly, as in the bedroom, he frees himself from her violently and springs to his feet. He is trembling all over, in a strange state of terror.* ABBIE *strains her arms toward him with fierce pleading*) Don't ye leave me, Eben! Can't ye see it hain't enuf—lovin' ye like a Maw—can't ye see it's got t' be that an' more—much more—a hundred times more—fur me t' be happy—fur yew t' be happy?

EBEN (*to the presence he feels in the room*) Maw! Maw! What d'ye want? What air ye tellin' me?

ABBIE She's tellin' ye t' love me. She knows I love ye an' I'll be good t' ye. Can't ye feel it? Don't ye know? She's tellin' ye t' love me, Eben!

EBEN Ay-eh. I feel—mebbe she—but—I can't figger out—why—when ye've stole her place—here in her hum—in the parlor whar she was—

ABBIE (*fiercely*) She knows I love ye!

EBEN (*his face suddenly lighting up with a fierce, triumphant grin*) I see it! I see why. It's her vengeance on him—so's she kin rest quiet in her grave!

ABBIE (*wildly*) Vengeance o' God on the hull o' us! What d'we give a durn? I love ye, Eben! God knows I love ye! (*She stretches out her arms for him*).

EBEN (*throws himself on his knees beside the sofa and grabs her in his arms—releasing all his pent-up passion*) An' I love yew, Abbie!—now I kin say it! I been dyin' fur want o' ye—every hour since ye come! I love ye! (*Their lips meet in a fierce, bruising kiss*).

CURTAIN

SCENE FOUR

Exterior of the farmhouse. It is just dawn. The front door at right is opened and EBEN *comes out and walks around to the gate. He is dressed in his working clothes. He seems changed. His face wears a bold and confident expression, he is grinning to himself with evident satisfaction. As he gets near the gate, the window of the parlor is heard opening and the shutters are flung back and* ABBIE *sticks her head out. Her hair tumbles over her shoulders in disarray, her face is flushed, she looks at* EBEN *with tender, languorous eyes and calls softly*).

ABBIE Eben. (*As he turns—playfully*) Jest one more kiss afore ye go. I'm goin' to miss ye fearful all day.

EBEN An' me yew, ye kin bet! (*He goes to her. They kiss several times. He draws away, laughingly*) Thar. That's enuf, hain't it? Ye won't hev none left fur next time.

ABBIE I got a million o' 'em left fur yew! (*Then a bit anxiously*) D'ye r'ally love me, Eben?

EBEN (*emphatically*) I like ye better'n any gal I ever knowed! That's gospel!

ABBIE Likin' hain't lovin'.

EBEN Waal then—I love ye. Now air yew satisfied?

ABBIE Ay-eh, I be. (*She smiles at him adoringly*).

EBEN I better git t' the barn. The old critter's liable t' suspicion an' come sneakin' up.

ABBIE (*with a confident laugh*) Let him! I kin allus pull the wool over his eyes. I'm goin' t' leave the shutters open and let in the sun 'n' air. This room's been dead long enuf. Now it's goin' t' be my room!

EBEN (*frowning*) Ay-eh.

ABBIE (*hastily*) I meant—our room.

EBEN Ay-eh.

ABBIE We made it our'n last night, didn't we? We give it life—our lovin' did. (*A pause*).

EBEN (*with a strange look*) Maw's gone back t' her grave. She kin sleep now.

ABBIE May she rest in peace! (*Then tenderly rebuking*) Ye oughtn't t' talk o' sad thin's—this mornin'.

EBEN It jest come up in my mind o' itself.

ABBIE Don't let it. (*He doesn't answer. She yawns*) Waal, I'm a-goin' t' steal a wink o' sleep. I'll tell the Old Man I hain't feelin' pert. Let him git his own vittles.

EBEN I see him comin' from the barn. Ye better look smart an' git upstairs.

ABBIE Ay-eh. Good-by. Don't ferget me. (*She throws him a kiss. He grins—then squares his shoulders and awaits his father confidently.* CABOT *walks slowly up from the left, staring up at the sky with a vague face*).

EBEN (*jovially*) Mornin', Paw. Star-gazin' in daylight?

CABOT Purty, hain't it?

EBEN (*looking around him possessively*) It's a durned purty farm.

CABOT I mean the sky.

EBEN (*grinning*) How d'ye know? Them eyes o' your'n can't see that fur. (*This tickles his humor and he slaps his thigh and laughs*) Ho-ho! That's a good un!

CABOT (*grimly sarcastic*) Ye're feelin' right chipper, hain't ye? Whar'd ye steal the likker?

EBEN (*good-naturedly*) 'Tain't likker. Jest life. (*Suddenly holding out his hand—soberly*) Yew 'n' me is quits. Let's shake hands.

CABOT (*suspiciously*) What's come over ye?

EBEN Then don't. Mebbe it's jest as well. (*A moment's pause*) What's come over me? (*Queerly*) Didn't ye feel her passin'—goin' back t' her grave?

CABOT (*dully*) Who?

EBEN Maw. She kin rest now an' sleep content. She's quit with ye.

CABOT (*confusedly*) I rested. I slept good—down with the cows. They know how t' sleep. They're teachin' me.

EBEN (*suddenly jovial again*) Good fur the cows! Waal—ye better git t' work.

CABOT (*grimly amused*) Air ye bossin' me, ye calf?

EBEN (*beginning to laugh*) Ay-eh! I'm bossin' yew! Ha-ha-ha! See how ye like it! Ha-ha-ha! I'm the prize rooster o' this roost. Ha-ha-ha! (*He goes off toward the barn laughing*).

CABOT (*looks after him with scornful pity*) Soft-headed. Like his Maw. Dead spit 'n' image. No hope in him! (*He spits with contemptuous disgust*) A born fool! (*Then matter-of-factly*) Waal—I'm gittin' peckish. (*He goes toward door*).

CURTAIN

PART THREE · SCENE ONE

A night in late spring the following year. The kitchen and the two bedrooms upstairs are shown. The two bedrooms are dimly lighted by a tallow candle in each. EBEN *is sitting on the side of the bed in his room, his chin propped on his fists, his face a study of the struggle he is making to understand his conflicting emotions. The noisy laughter and music from below where a kitchen dance is in progress annoy and distract him. He scowls at the floor.*

In the next room a cradle stands beside the double bed.

In the kitchen all is festivity. The stove has been taken down to give more room to the dancers. The chairs, with wooden benches added, have been pushed back against the walls. On these are seated, squeezed in tight against one another, farmers and their wives and their young folks of both sexes from the neighboring farms. They are all chattering and laughing loudly. They evidently have some secret joke in common. There is no end of winking, of nudging, of meaning nods of the head toward CABOT *who, in a state of extreme hilarious excitement increased by the amount he has drunk, is standing near the rear door where there is a small keg of whisky and serving drinks to all the men. In the left corner, front, dividing the attention with her husband,* ABBIE *is sitting in a rocking chair, a shawl wrapped about her shoulders. She is very pale, her face is thin and drawn, her eyes are fixed anxiously on the open door in rear as if waiting for someone.*

The musician is tuning up his fiddle, seated in the far right corner. He is a lanky young fellow with a long, weak face. His pale eyes blink incessantly and he grins about him slyly with a greedy malice.

ABBIE (*suddenly turning to a young girl on her right*) Whar's Eben?

YOUNG GIRL (*eying her scornfully*) I dunno, Mrs. Cabot. I hain't seen Eben in ages. (*Meaningly*) Seems like he's spent most o' his time t' hum since yew come.

ABBIE (*vaguely*) I tuk his Maw's place.

YOUNG GIRL Ay-eh. So I've heerd. (*She turns away to retail this bit of gossip to her mother sitting next to her.* ABBIE *turns to her left to a big stoutish middle-aged man whose flushed face and starting eyes show the amount of "likker" he has consumed).*

ABBIE Ye hain't seen Eben, hev ye?

MAN No, I hain't. (*Then he adds with a wink*) If yew hain't, who would?

ABBIE He's the best dancer in the county. He'd ought t' come an' dance.

MAN (*with a wink*) Mebbe he's doin' the dutiful an' walkin' the kid t' sleep. It's a boy, hain't it?

ABBIE (*nodding vaguely*) Ay-eh—born two weeks back—purty's a picter.

MAN They all is—t' their Maws. (*Then in a whisper, with a nudge and a leer*) Listen, Abbie—if ye ever git tired o' Eben, remember me! Don't fergit now! (*He looks at her uncomprehending face for a second—then grunts disgustedly*) Waal—guess I'll likker agin. (*He goes over and joins* CABOT *who is arguing noisily with an old farmer over cows. They all drink*).

ABBIE (*this time appealing to nobody in particular*) Wonder what Eben's a-doin'? (*Her remark is repeated down the line with many a guffaw and titter until it reaches the fiddler. He fastens his blinking eyes on* ABBIE).

FIDDLER (*raising his voice*) Bet I kin tell ye, Abbie, what Eben's doin'! He's down t' the church offerin' up prayers o' thanksgivin'. (*They all titter expectantly*).

A MAN What fur? (*Another titter*).

FIDDLER 'Cause unto him a— (*He hesitates just long enough*) brother is born! (*A roar of laughter. They all look from* ABBIE *to* CABOT. *She is oblivious, staring at the door.* CABOT, *although he hasn't heard the words, is irritated by the laughter and steps forward, glaring about him. There is an immediate silence*).

CABOT What're ye all bleatin' about—like a flock o' goats? Why don't ye dance, damn ye? I axed ye here t' dance—t' eat, drink an' be merry—an' thar ye set cacklin' like a lot o' wet hens with the pip! Ye've swilled my likker an' guzzled my vittles like hogs, hain't ye? Then dance fur me, can't ye? That's fa'r an' squar', hain't it? (*A grumble of resentment goes around but they are all evidently in too much awe of him to express it openly*).

FIDDLER (*slyly*) We're waitin' fur Eben. (*A suppressed laugh*).

CABOT (*with a fierce exultation*) T'hell with Eben! Eben's

done fur now! I got a new son! (*His mood switching with drunken suddenness*) But ye needn't t' laugh at Eben, none o' ye! He's my blood, if he be a dumb fool. He's better nor any o' yew! He kin do a day's work a'most up t' what I kin—an' that'd put any o' yew pore critters t' shame!

FIDDLER An' he kin do a good night's work too! (*A roar of laughter*).

CABOT Laugh, ye damn fools! Ye're right jist the same, Fiddler. He kin work day an' night too, like I kin, if need be!

OLD FARMER (*from behind the keg where he is weaving drunkenly back and forth—with great simplicity*) They hain't many t' touch ye, Ephraim—a son at seventy-six. That's a hard man fur ye! I be on'y sixty-eight an' I couldn't do it. (*A roar of laughter in which* CABOT *joins uproariously*).

CABOT (*slapping him on the back*) I'm sorry fur ye, Hi. I'd never suspicion sech weakneess from a boy like yew!

OLD FARMER An' I never reckoned yew had it in ye nuther, Ephraim. (*There is another laugh*).

CABOT (*suddenly grim*) I got a lot in me—a hell of a lot—folks don't know on. (*Turning to the fiddler*) Fiddle 'er up, durn ye! Give 'em somethin' t' dance t'! What air ye, an ornament? Hain't this a celebration? Then grease yer elbow an' go it!

FIDDLER (*seizes a drink which the* OLD FARMER *holds out to him and downs it*) Here goes! (*He starts to fiddle "Lady of the Lake." Four young fellows and four girls form in two lines and dance a square dance. The* FIDDLER *shouts directions for the different movements, keeping his words in the rhythm of the music and interspersing them with jocular personal remarks to the dancers themselves. The people seated along the walls stamp their feet and clap their hands in unison.* CABOT *is especially active in this respect. Only* ABBIE *remains apathetic, staring at the door as if she were alone in a silent room*).

FIDDLER Swing your partner t' the right! That's it, Jim! Give her a b'ar hug! Her Maw hain't lookin'. (*Laughter*) Change partners! That suits ye, don't it, Essie, now ye got Reub afore ye? Look at her redden up, will ye? Waal, life is short an' so's love, as the feller says. (*Laughter*).

CABOT (*excitedly, stamping his foot*) Go it, boys! Go it, gals!

FIDDLER (*with a wink at the others*) Ye're the spryest seventy-six ever I sees, Ephraim! Now if ye'd on'y good eyesight . . . ! (*Suppressed laughter. He gives* CABOT *no chance to retort but roars*) Promenade! Ye're walkin' like a bride down the aisle, Sarah! Waal, while they's life they's allus hope, I've heerd tell. Swing your partner to the left! Gosh A'mighty, look at Johnny Cook high-steppin'! They hain't goin' t'be much strength left fur howin' in the corn lot t'morrow. (*Laughter*).

CABOT Go it! Go it! (*Then suddenly, unable to restrain himself any longer, he prances into the midst of the dancers, scattering them, waving his arms about wildly*) Ye're all hoofs! Git out o' my road! Give me room! I'll show ye dancin'. Ye're all too soft! (*He pushes them roughly away. They crowd back toward the walls, muttering, looking at him resentfully*).

FIDDLER (*jeeringly*) Go it, Ephraim! Go it! (*He starts "Pop Goes the Weasel," increasing the tempo with every verse until at the end he is fiddling crazily as fast as he can go*).

CABOT (*starts to dance, which he does very well and with tremendous vigor. Then he begins to improvise, cuts incredibly grotesque capers, leaping up and cracking his heels together, prancing around in a circle with body bent in an Indian war dance, then suddenly straightening up and kicking as high as he can with both legs. He is like a monkey on a string. And all the while he intersperses his antics with shouts and derisive comments*) Whoop! Here's dancin' fur ye! Whoop! See that! Seventy-six, if I'm a day! Hard as iron yet! Beatin' the young 'uns like I allus done! Look at me! I'd invite ye t' dance on my hundredth birthday on'y ye'll all be dead by then. Ye're a sickly generation! Yer hearts air pink, not red! Yer veins is full o' mud an' water! I be the on'y man in the county! Whoop! See that! I'm a Injun! I've killed Injuns in the West afore ye was born—an' skulped 'em too! They's a arrer wound on my backside I c'd show ye! The hull tribe chased me. I outrun 'em all—with the arrer stuck in me! An' I tuk vengeance on 'em. Ten eyes fur an eye, that was my motter! Whoop! Look at me! I kin kick the ceilin' off the room! Whoop!

FIDDLER (*stops playing—exhaustedly*) God A'mighty, I got enuf. Ye got the devil's strength in ye.

CABOT (*delightedly*) Did I beat yew, too? Wa'al, ye played smart. Hev a swig. (*He pours whisky for himself and* FIDDLER. *They drink. The others watch* CABOT *silently with cold, hostile eyes. There is a dead pause. The* FIDDLER *rests.* CABOT *leans against the keg, panting, glaring around him confusedly. In the room above,* EBEN *gets to his feet and tiptoes out the door in rear, appearing a moment later in the other bedroom. He moves silently, even frightenedly, toward the cradle and stands there looking down at the baby. His face is as vague as his reactions are confused, but there is a trace of tenderness, of interested discovery. At the same moment that he reaches the cradle,* ABBIE *seems to sense something. She gets up weakly and goes to* CABOT).

ABBIE I'm goin' up t' the baby.

CABOT (*with real solicitation*) Air ye able fur the stairs? D'ye want me t' help ye, Abbie?

ABBIE No. I'm able. I'll be down agen soon.

CABOT Don't ye git wore out! He needs ye, remember—our son does! (*He grins affectionately, patting her on the back. She shrinks from his touch*).

ABBIE (*dully*) Don't—tech me. I'm goin'—up. (*She goes.* CABOT *looks after her. A whisper goes around the room.* CABOT *turns. It ceases. He wipes his forehead streaming with sweat. He is breathing pantingly*).

CABOT I'm a-goin' out t' git fresh air. I'm feelin' a mite dizzy. Fiddle up thar! Dance, all o' ye! Here's likker fur them as wants it. Enjoy yerselves. I'll be back. (*He goes, closing the door behind him*).

FIDDLER (*sarcastically*) Don't hurry none on our account! (*A suppressed laugh. He imitates* ABBIE) Whar's Eben? (*More laughter*).

A WOMAN (*loudly*) What's happened in this house is plain as the nose on yer face! (ABBIE *appears in the doorway upstairs and stands looking in surprise and adoration at* EBEN *who does not see her*).

A MAN Ssshh! He's li-ble t' be listenin' at the door. That'd be like him. (*Their voices die to an intensive whispering. Their faces are concentrated on this gossip. A noise as of dead leaves in the wind comes from the room.* CABOT *has come out from the porch and stands by the gate, leaning on it, staring at the sky blinkingly.* ABBIE *comes across the room silently.* EBEN *does not notice her until quite near*).

EBEN (*starting*) Abbie!

ABBIE Ssshh! (*She throws her arms around him. They kiss —then bend over the cradle together*) Ain't he purty?—dead spit 'n' image o' yew!

EBEN (*pleased*) Air he? I can't tell none.

ABBIE E-zactly like!

EBEN (*frowningly*) I don't like this. I don't like lettin' on what's mine's his'n. I been doin' that all my life. I'm gittin' t' the end o' b'arin' it!

ABBIE (*putting her finger on his lips*) We're doin' the best we kin. We got t' wait. Somethin's bound t' happen. (*She puts her arms around him*) I got t' go back.

EBEN I'm goin' out. I can't b'ar it with the fiddle playin' an' the laughin'.

ABBIE Don't git feelin' low. I love ye, Eben. Kiss me. (*He kisses her. They remain in each other's arms*).

CABOT (*at the gate, confusedly*) Even the music can't drive it out—somethin'. Ye kin feel it droppin' off the elums, climbin' up the roof, sneakin' down the chimney, pokin' in the corners! They's no peace in houses, they's no rest livin' with folks. Somethin's always livin' with ye. (*With a deep sigh*) I'll go t' the barn an' rest a spell. (*He goes wearily toward the barn*).

FIDDLER (*tuning up*) Let's celebrate the old skunk gittin' fooled! We kin have some fun now he's went. (*He starts to fiddle "Turkey in the Straw." There is real merriment now. The young folks get up to dance*).

CURTAIN

SCENE TWO

*A half-hour later—Exterior—*EBEN *is standing by the gate looking up at the sky, an expression of dumb pain bewildered by itself on his face.* CABOT *appears, returning from the barn, walking wearily, his eyes on the ground. He sees* EBEN *and his whole mood immediately changes. He becomes excited, a cruel, triumphant grin comes to his lips, he strides up and slaps* EBEN *on the back. From within comes the whining of the fiddle and the noise of stamping feet and laughing voices.*

CABOT So har ye be!

EBEN (*startled, stares at him with hatred for a moment—then dully*) Ay-eh.

CABOT (*surveying him jeeringly*) Why hain't ye been in t' dance? They was all axin' fur ye.

EBEN Let 'em ax!

CABOT They's a hull passel o' purty gals.

EBEN T' hell with 'em!

CABOT Ye'd ought t' be marryin' one o' 'em soon.

EBEN I hain't marryin' no one.

CABOT Ye might 'arn a share o' a farm that way.

EBEN (*with a sneer*) Like yew did, ye mean? I hain't that kind.

CABOT (*stung*) Ye lie! 'Twas yer Maw's folks aimed t' steal my farm from me.

EBEN Other folks don't say so. (*After a pause—defiantly*) An' I got a farm, anyways!

CABOT (*derisively*) Whar?

EBEN (*stamps a foot on the ground*) Har!

CABOT (*throws his head back and laughs coarsely*) Ho-ho! Ye hev, hev ye? Waal, that's a good un!

EBEN (*controlling himself—grimly*) Ye'll see!

CABOT (*stares at him suspiciously, trying to make him out—a pause—then with scornful confidence*) Ay-eh. I'll see. So'll ye. It's ye that's blind—blind as a mole underground. (EBEN *suddenly laughs, one short sardonic bark: "Ha." A pause.* CABOT *peers at him with renewed suspicion*) Whar air ye hawin' 'bout? (EBEN *turns away without answering.* CABOT *grows angry*) God A'mighty, yew air a dumb dunce! They's nothin' in that thick skull o' your'n but noise—like a empty keg it be! (EBEN *doesn't seem to hear.* CABOT'S *rage grows*) Yewr farm! God A'mighty! If ye wa'n't a born donkey ye'd know ye'll never own stick nor stone on it, specially now arter him bein' born. It's his'n, I tell ye—his'n arter I die—but I'll live a hundred jest t' fool ye all—an' he'll be growed then—yewr age a'most! (EBEN *laughs again his sardonic "Ha." This drives* CABOT *into a fury*) Ha? Ye think ye kin git 'round that someways, do ye? Waal, it'll be her'n, too—Abbie's—ye won't git 'round her—she knows yer tricks—she'll be too much fur ye—she wants the farm her'n—she was afeerd o' ye—she told me ye was sneakin' 'round tryin' t' make love t' her t' git her on yer side . . . ye . . . ye mad fool, ye! (*He raises his clenched fists threateningly*).

EBEN (*is confronting him choking with rage*) Ye lie, ye old skunk! Abbie never said no sech thing!

CABOT (*suddenly triumphant when he sees how shaken* EBEN *is*) She did. An' I says, I'll blow his brains t' the top o' them elums—an' she says no, that hain't sense, who'll ye git t'help ye on the farm in his place—an' then she says yew'n me ought t' have a son—I know we kin, she says—an' I says, if we do, ye kin have anythin' I've got ye've a mind t'. An' she says, I wants Eben cut off so's this farm'll be mine when ye die! (*With terrible gloating*) An' that's what's happened, hain't it? An' the farm's her'n! An' the dust o' the road—that's your'n! Ha! Now who's hawin'?

EBEN (*has been listening, petrified with grief and rage—suddenly laughs wildly and brokenly*) Ha-ha-ha! So that's her sneakin' game—all along!—like I suspicioned at fust—t' swaller it all—an' me, too . . . ! (*Madly*) I'll murder her! (*He springs toward the porch but* CABOT *is quicker and gets in between*).

CABOT No, ye don't!

EBEN Git out o' my road! (*He tries to throw* CABOT *aside. They grapple in what becomes immediately a murderous struggle. The old man's concentrated strength is too much for* EBEN. CABOT *gets one hand on his throat and presses him back across the stone well. At the same moment,* ABBIE *comes out on the porch. With a stifled cry she runs toward them*).

ABBIE Eben! Ephraim! (*She tugs at the hand on* EBEN'S *throat*) Let go, Ephraim! Ye're chokin' him!

CABOT (*removes his hand and flings* EBEN *sideways full length on the grass, gasping and choking. With a cry,* ABBIE *kneels beside him, trying to take his head on her lap, but he pushes her away.* CABOT *stands looking down with fierce triumph*) Ye needn't t've fret, Abbie, I wa'n't aimin' t' kill him. He hain't wuth hangin' fur—not by a hell of a sight! (*More and more triumphantly*) Seventy-six an' him not thirty yit—an' look whar he be fur thinkin' his Paw was easy! No, by God, I hain't easy! An' him upstairs, I'll raise him t' be like me! (*He turns to leave them*) I'm goin' in an' dance!—sing an' celebrate! (*He walks to the porch—then turns with a great grin*) I don't calc'late it's left in him, but if he gits pesky, Abbie, ye jest sing out. I'll come a-runnin' an' by the Etarnal, I'll put him across my knee an' birch him! Ha-ha-ha! (*He goes into the house laughing. A moment later his loud "whoop" is heard*).

ABBIE (*tenderly*) Eben. Air ye hurt? (*She tries to kiss him but he pushes her violently away and struggles to a sitting position*).

EBEN (*gaspingly*) T' hell—with ye!

ABBIE (*not believing her ears*) It's me, Eben—Abbie—don't ye know me?

EBEN (*glowering at her with hatred*) Ay-eh—I know ye—now! (*He suddenly breaks down, sobbing weakly*).

ABBIE (*fearfully*) Eben—what's happened t' ye—why did ye look at me 's if ye hated me?

EBEN (*violently, between sobs and gasps*) I do hate ye! Ye're a whore—a damn trickin' whore!

ABBIE (*shrinking back horrified*) Eben! Ye don't know what ye're sayin'!

EBEN (*scrambling to his feet and following her—accusingly*) Ye're nothin' but a stinkin' passel o' lies! Ye've been lyin' t' me every word ye spoke, day an' night, since we fust—done it. Ye've kept sayin' ye loved me. . . .

ABBIE (*frantically*) I do love ye! (*She takes his hand but he flings hers away*).

EBEN (*unheeding*) Ye've made a fool o' me—a sick, dumb fool—a-purpose! Ye've been on'y playin' yer sneakin', stealin' game all along—gittin' me t' lie with ye so's ye'd hev a son he'd think was his'n, an' makin' him promise he'd give ye the farm and let me eat dust, if ye did git him a son! (*Staring at her with anguished, bewildered eyes*) They must be a devil livin' in ye! T'ain't human t' be as bad as that be!

ABBIE (*stunned—dully*) He told yew . . . ?

EBEN Hain't it true? It hain't no good in yew lyin'.

ABBIE (*pleadingly*) Eben, listen—ye must listen—it was long ago—afore we done nothin'—yew was scornin' me—goin' t' see Min—when I was lovin' ye—an' I said it t' him t' git vengeance on ye!

EBEN (*unheedingly. With tortured passion*) I wish ye was dead! I wish I was dead along with ye afore this come! (*Ragingly*) But I'll git my vengeance too! I'll pray Maw t' come back t' help me—t' put her cuss on yew an' him!

ABBIE (*brokenly*) Don't ye, Eben! Don't ye! (*She throws herself on her knees before him, weeping*) I didn't mean t' do bad t' ye! Fergive me, won't ye?

EBEN (*not seeming to hear her—fiercely*) I'll git squar' with the old skunk—an' yew! I'll tell him the truth 'bout the son he's so proud o'! Then I'll leave ye here t' pizen each other—with Maw comin' out o' her grave at nights—an' I'll go t' the gold fields o' Californi-a whar Sim an' Peter be!

ABBIE (*terrified*) Ye won't—leave me? Ye can't!

EBEN (*with fierce determination*) I'm a-goin', I tell ye! I'll git rich thar an' come back an' fight him fur the farm he stole—an' I'll kick ye both out in the road—t' beg an' sleep in the woods—an' yer son along with ye—t' starve an' die! (*He is hysterical at the end*).

ABBIE (*with a shudder—humbly*) He's yewr son, too, Eben.

EBEN (*torturedly*) I wish he never was born! I wish he'd die this minit! I wish I'd never sot eyes on him! It's him—yew havin' him—a-purpose t' steal—that's changed everythin'!

ABBIE (*gently*) Did ye believe I loved ye—afore he come?

EBEN Ay-eh—like a dumb ox!

ABBIE An' ye don't believe no more?

EBEN B'lieve a lyin' thief! Ha!

ABBIE (*shudders—then humbly*) An' did ye r'ally love me afore?

EBEN (*brokenly*) Ay-eh—an' ye was trickin' me!

ABBIE An' ye don't love me now!

EBEN (*violently*) I hate ye, I tell ye!

ABBIE An' ye're truly goin' West—goin' t' leave me—all account o' him being born?

EBEN I'm a-goin' in the mornin'—or may God strike me t' hell!

ABBIE (*after a pause—with a dreadful cold intensity—slowly*) If that's what his comin 's done t' me—killin' yewr love—takin' yew away—my on'y joy—the on'y joy I ever knowed—like heaven t' me—purtier'n heaven—then I hate him, too, even if I be his Maw!

EBEN (*bitterly*) Lies! Ye love him! He'll steal the farm fur ye! (*Brokenly*) But t'ain't the farm so much—not no more—it's yew foolin' me—gittin' me t' love ye—lyin' yew loved me—jest t' git a son t' steal!

ABBIE (*distractedly*) He won't steal! I'd kill him fust! I do love ye! I'll prove t' ye . . . !

EBEN (*harshly*) T'ain't no use lyin' no more. I'm deaf t' ye! (*He turns away*) I hain't seein' ye agen. Good-by!

ABBIE (*pale with anguish*) Hain't ye even goin' t' kiss me—not once—arter all we loved?

EBEN (*in a hard voice*) I hain't wantin' t' kiss ye never agen! I'm wantin' t' forgit I ever sot eyes on ye!

ABBIE Eben!—ye mustn't—wait a spell—I want t' tell ye. . . .

EBEN I'm a-goin' in t' git drunk. I'm a-goin' t' dance.

ABBIE (*clinging to his arm—with passionate earnestness*) If I could make it—'s if he'd never come up between us—if I could prove t' ye I wa'n't schemin' t' steal from ye—so's everythin' could be jest the same with us, lovin' each other jest the same, kissin' an' happy the same's we've been happy afore he come—if I could do it—ye'd love me agen, wouldn't ye? Ye'd kiss me agen? Ye wouldn't never leave me, would ye?

EBEN (*moved*) I calc'late not. (*Then shaking her hand off his arm—with a bitter smile*) But ye hain't God, be ye?

ABBIE (*exultantly*) Remember ye've promised! (*Then with*

strange intensity) Mebbe I kin take back one thin' God does!

EBEN (*peering at her*) Ye're gittin' cracked, hain't ye? (*Then going towards door*) I'm a-goin' t' dance.

ABBIE (*calls after him intensely*) I'll prove t' ye! I'll prove I love ye better'n. . . . (*He goes in the door, not seeming to hear. She remains standing where she is, looking after him—then she finishes desperately*) Better'n everythin' else in the world!

CURTAIN

SCENE THREE

Just before dawn in the morning—shows the kitchen and CABOT'S *bedroom. In the kitchen, by the light of a tallow candle on the table,* EBEN *is sitting, his chin propped on his hands, his drawn face blank and expressionless. His carpetbag is on the floor beside him. In the bedroom, dimly lighted by a small whale-oil lamp,* CABOT *lies asleep.* ABBIE *is bending over the cradle, listening, her face full of terror yet with an undercurrent of desperate triumph. Suddenly, she breaks down and sobs, appears about to throw herself on her knees beside the cradle; but the old man turns restlessly, groaning in his sleep, and she controls herself, and, shrinking away from the cradle with a gesture of horror, backs swiftly toward the door in rear and goes out. A moment later she comes into the kitchen and, running to* EBEN, *flings her arms about his neck and kisses him wildly. He hardens himself, he remains unmoved and cold, he keeps his eyes straight ahead.*

ABBIE (*hysterically*) I done it, Eben! I told ye I'd do it! I've proved I love ye—better'n everythin'—so's ye can't never doubt me no more!

EBEN (*dully*) Whatever ye done, it hain't no good now.

ABBIE (*wildly*) Don't ye say that! Kiss me, Eben, won't ye? I need ye t' kiss me arter what I done! I need ye t' say ye love me!

EBEN (*kisses her without emotion—dully*) That's fur good-by. I'm a-goin' soon.

ABBIE No! No! Ye won't go—not now!

EBEN (*going on with his own thoughts*) I been a-thinkin'—an' I hain't goin' t' tell Paw nothin'. I'll leave Maw t' take vengeance on ye. If I told him, the old skunk'd jest be stinkin' mean enuf to take it out on that baby. (*His voice showing emotion in spite of him*) An' I don't want nothin' bad t' happen t' him. He hain't t' blame fur yew. (*He adds with a certain queer pride*) An' he looks like me! An' by God, he's mine! An' some day I'll be a-comin' back an' . . . !

ABBIE (*too absorbed in her own thoughts to listen to him—pleadingly*) They's no cause fur ye t' go now—they's no sense—it's all the same's it was—they's nothin' come b'tween us now—arter what I done!

EBEN (*something in her voice arouses him. He stares at her a bit frightenedly*) Ye look mad, Abbie. What did ye do?

ABBIE I—I killed him, Eben.

EBEN (*amazed*) Ye killed him?

ABBIE (*dully*) Ay-eh.

EBEN (*recovering from his astonishment—savagely*) An' serves him right! But we got t' do somethin' quick t' make it look 's if the old skunk'd killed himself when he was drunk. We kin prove by 'em all how drunk he got.

ABBIE (*wildly*) No! No! Not him! (*Laughing distractedly*) But that's what I ought t' done, hain't it? I oughter killed him instead! Why didn't ye tell me?

EBEN (*appalled*) Instead? What d'ye mean?

ABBIE Not him.

EBEN (*his face grown ghastly*) Not—not that baby!

ABBIE (*dully*) Ay-eh?

EBEN (*falls to his knees as if he'd been struck—his voice trembling with horror*) Oh, God A'mighty! A'mighty God! Maw, whar was ye, why didn't ye stop her?

ABBIE (*simply*) She went back t' her grave that night we fust done it, remember? I hain't felt her about since. (*A pause.* EBEN *hides his head in his hands, trembling all over as if he had the ague. She goes on dully*) I left the piller over his little face. Then he killed himself. He stopped breathin'. (*She begins to weep softly*).

EBEN (*rage beginning to mingle with grief*) He looked like me. He was mine, damn ye!

ABBIE (*slowly and brokenly*) I didn't want t' do it. I hated myself fur doin' it. I loved him. He was so purty—dead spit 'n' image o' yew. But I loved yew more—an' yew was goin' away—far off whar I'd never see ye agen, never kiss ye, never feel ye pressed agin me agen—an' ye said ye hated me fur havin' him—ye said ye hated him an' wished he was dead—ye said if it hadn't been fur him comin' it'd be the same's afore between us.

EBEN (*unable to endure this, springs to his feet in a fury, threatening her, his twitching fingers seeming to reach out for her throat*) Ye lie! I never said—I never dreamed ye'd—I'd cut off my head afore I'd hurt his finger!

ABBIE (*piteously, sinking on her knees*) Eben, don't ye look at me like that—hatin' me—not after what I done fur ye—fur us—so's we could be happy agen—

EBEN (*furiously now*) Shut up, or I'll kill ye! I see yer game now—the same old sneakin' trick—ye're aimin' t' blame me fur the murder ye done!

ABBIE (*moaning—putting her hands over her ears*) Don't ye, Eben! Don't ye! (*She grasps his legs*).

EBEN (*his mood suddenly changing to horror, shrinks away from her*) Don't ye tech me! Ye're pizen! How could ye—t' murder a pore little critter— Ye must've swapped yer soul t' hell! (*Suddenly raging*) Ha! I kin see why ye done it! Not the lies ye jest told—but 'cause ye wanted t' steal agen—steal the last thin' ye'd left me—my part o' him—no, the hull o' him—ye saw he looked like me—ye knowed he was all mine—an' ye couldn't b'ar it—I know ye! Ye killed him fur bein' mine! (*All this has driven him almost insane. He makes a rush past her for the door—then turns—shaking both fists at her, violently*) But I'll take vengeance now! I'll git the Sheriff! I'll tell him everythin'! Then I'll sing "I'm off to Californi-a!" an' go—gold—Golden Gate—gold sun—fields o' gold in the West! (*This last he half shouts, half croons incoherently, suddenly breaking off passionately*) I'm a-goin' fur the Sheriff t' come an' git ye! I want ye tuk away, locked up from me! I can't stand t' luk at ye! Murderer an' thief 'r not, ye still tempt me! I'll give ye up t' the Sheriff (*He turns and runs out, around the corner of house, panting and sobbing, and breaks into a swerving sprint down the road*).

ABBIE (*struggling to her feet, runs to the door, calling after him*) I love ye, Eben! I love ye! (*She stops at the door weakly, swaying, about to fall*) I don't care what ye do—if ye'll on'y love me agen—(*She falls limply to the floor in a faint*).

CURTAIN

SCENE FOUR

About an hour later. Same as Scene Three. Shows the kitchen and CABOT'S *bedroom. It is after dawn. The sky is brilliant with the sunrise. In the kitchen,* ABBIE *sits at the table, her body limp and exhausted, her head bowed down over her arms, her face hidden. Upstairs,* CABOT *is still asleep but awakens with a start. He looks toward the window and gives a snort of surprise and irritation—throws back the covers and begins hurriedly pulling on his clothes. Without looking behind him, he begins talking to* ABBIE *whom he supposes beside him.*

CABOT Thunder 'n' lightin', Abbie! I hain't slept this late in fifty year! Looks 's if the sun was full riz a'most. Must've been the dancin' an' likker. Must be gittin' old. I hope Eben's t' wuk. Ye might've tuk the trouble t' rouse me, Abbie. (*He turns—sees no one there—surprised*) Waal—whar air she? Gittin' vittles, I calc'late. (*He tiptoes to the cradle and peers down—proudly*) Mornin', sonny. Purty's a picture! Sleepin' sound. He don't beller all night like most o' 'em. (*He goes quietly out the door in rear—a few moments later enters kitchen—sees* ABBIE*—with satisfaction*) So thar ye be. Ye got any vittles cooked?

ABBIE (*without moving*) No.

CABOT (*coming to her, almost sympathetically*) Ye feelin' sick?

ABBIE No.

CABOT (*pats her on shoulder. She shudders*) Ye'd best lie down a spell. (*Half jocularly*) Yer son'll be needin' ye soon. He'd ought t' wake up with a gnashin' appetite, the sound way he's sleepin'.

ABBIE (*shudders—then in a dead voice*) He hain't never goin' t' wake up.

CABOT (*jokingly*) Takes after me this mornin'. I hain't slept so late in . . .

ABBIE He's dead.

CABOT (*stares at her—bewilderedly*) What. . . .

ABBIE I killed him.

CABOT (*stepping back from her—aghast*) Air ye drunk—'r crazy—'r . . . !

ABBIE (*suddenly lifts her head and turns on him—wildly*) I killed him, I tell ye! I smothered him. Go up an' see if ye don't b'lieve me! (CABOT *stares at her a second, then bolts out the rear door—can be heard bounding up the stairs—and rushes into the bedroom and over to the cradle.* ABBIE *has sunk back lifelessly into her former position.* CABOT *puts his hand down on the body in the crib. An expression of fear and horror comes over his face*).

CABOT (*shrinking away—tremblingly*) God A'mighty! God A'mighty. (*He stumbles out the door—in a short while returns to the kitchen—comes to* ABBIE, *the stunned expression still on his face—hoarsely*) Why did ye do it? Why? (*As she doesn't answer, he grabs her violently by the shoulder and shakes her*) I ax ye why ye done it! Ye'd better tell me 'r . . . !

ABBIE (*gives him a furious push which sends him staggering back and springs to her feet—with wild rage and hatred*) Don't ye dare tech me! What right hev ye t' question me 'bout him? He wa'n't yewr son! Think I'd have a son by yew? I'd die fust! I hate the sight o' ye an' allus did! It's yew I should've murdered, if I'd had good sense! I hate ye! I love Eben. I did from the fust. An' he was Eben's son—mine an' Eben's—not your'n!

CABOT (*stands looking at her dazedly—a pause—finding his words with an effort—dully*) That was it—what I felt—pokin' round the corners—while ye lied—holdin' yerself from me—sayin' ye'd a'ready conceived— (*He lapses into crushed silence—then with a strange emotion*) He's dead, sart'n. I felt his heart. Pore little critter! (*He blinks back one tear, wiping his sleeve across his nose*).

ABBIE (*hysterically*) Don't ye! Don't ye! (*She sobs unrestrainedly*).

CABOT (*with a concentrated effort that stiffens his body into a rigid line and hardens his face into a stony mask—through his teeth to himself*) I got t' be—like a stone—a rock o' jedgment! (*A pause. He gets complete control over himself—harshly*) If he was Eben's, I be glad he air gone! An' mebbe I suspicioned it all along. I felt they was somethin' onnateral—somewhars—the house got so lonesome—an' cold—drivin' me down t' the barn—t' the beasts o' the field. . . . Ay-eh. I must've suspicioned—somethin'. Ye didn't fool me—not altogether, leastways—I'm too old a bird—growin' ripe on the bough. . . . (*He becomes aware he is wandering, straightens again, looks at* ABBIE *with a cruel grin*) So ye'd like t' hev murdered me 'stead o' him, would ye? Waal, I'll live to a hundred! I'll live t' see ye hung! I'll deliver ye up t' the jedgment o' God an' the law! I'll git the Sheriff now. (*Starts for the door*).

ABBIE (*dully*) Ye needn't. Eben's gone fur him.

CABOT (*amazed*) Eben—gone fur the Sheriff?

ABBIE Ay-eh.

CABOT T' inform agen ye?

ABBIE Ay-eh.

CABOT (*considers this—a pause—then in a hard voice*) Waal, I'm thankful fur him savin' me the trouble. I'll git t' wuk. (*He goes to the door—then turns—in a voice full of strange emotion*) He'd ought t' been my son, Abbie. Ye'd ought t' loved me. I'm a man. If ye'd loved me, I'd never told no Sheriff on ye no matter what ye did, if they was t' brile me alive!

ABBIE (*defensively*) They's more to it nor yew know, makes him tell.

CABOT (*dryly*) Fur yewr sake, I hope they be. (*He goes out—comes around to the gate—stares up at the sky. His control relaxes. For a moment he is old and weary. He murmurs despairingly*) God A'mighty, I be lonesomer'n ever! (*He hears running footsteps from the left, immediately is himself again.* EBEN *runs in, panting exhaustedly, wild-eyed and mad looking. He lurches through the gate.* CABOT *grabs him by the shoulder.* EBEN *stares at him dumbly*) Did ye tell the Sheriff?

EBEN (*nodding stupidly*) Ay-eh.

CABOT (*gives him a push away that sends him sprawling—laughing with withering contempt*) Good fur ye! A prime chip o' yer Maw ye be! (*He goes toward the barn, laughing harshly.* EBEN *scrambles to his feet. Suddenly* CABOT *turns—grimly threatening*) Git off this farm when the Sheriff takes her—or, by God, he'll have t' come back an' git me fur murder, too! (*He stalks off.* EBEN *does not appear to have heard him. He runs to the door and comes into the kitchen.* ABBIE *looks up with a cry of anguished joy.* EBEN *stumbles over and throws himself on his knees beside her—sobbing brokenly*).

EBEN Fergive me!

ABBIE (*happily*) Eben! (*She kisses him and pulls his head over against her breast*).

EBEN I love ye! Fergive me!

ABBIE (*ecstatically*) I'd fergive ye all the sins in hell fur sayin' that! (*She kisses his head, pressing it to her with a fierce passion of possession*).

EBEN (*brokenly*) But I told the Sheriff. He's comin' fur ye!

ABBIE I kin b'ar what happens t' me—now!

EBEN I woke him up. I told him. He says, wait 'til I git dressed. I was waiting. I got to thinkin' o' yew. I got to thinkin' how I'd loved ye. It hurt like somethin' was bustin' in my chest an' head. I got t' cryin'. I knowed sudden I loved ye yet, an' allus would love ye!

ABBIE (*caressing his hair—tenderly*) My boy, hain't ye?

EBEN I begun t' run back. I cut across the fields an' through the woods. I thought ye might have time t' run away—with me—an' . . .

ABBIE (*shaking her head*) I got t' take my punishment—t' pay fur my sin.

EBEN Then I want t' share it with ye.

ABBIE Ye didn't do nothin'.

EBEN I put it in yer head. I wisht he was dead! I as much as urged ye t' do it!

ABBIE No. It was me alone!

EBEN I'm as guilty as yew be! He was the child o' our sin.

ABBIE (*lifting her head as if defying God*) I don't repent that sin! I hain't askin' God t' fergive that!

EBEN Nor me—but it led up t' the other—an' the murder ye did, ye did 'count o' me—an' it's my murder, too, I'll tell the Sheriff—an' if ye deny it, I'll say we planned it t'gether—an' they'll all b'lieve me, fur they suspicion everythin' we've done, an' it'll seem likely an' true to 'em. An' it is true—way down. I did help ye—somehow.

ABBIE (*laying her head on his—sobbing*) No! I don't want yew t' suffer!

EBEN I got t' pay fur my part o' the sin! An' I'd suffer wust leavin' ye, goin' West, thinkin' o' ye day an' night, bein' out when yew was in— (*Lowering his voice*) 'r bein' alive when yew was dead. (*A pause*) I want t' share with ye, Abbie—prison 'r death 'r hell 'r anythin'! (*He looks into her eyes and forces a trembling smile*) If I'm sharin' with ye, I won't feel lonesome, leastways.

ABBIE (*weakly*) Eben! I won't let ye! I can't let ye!

EBEN (*kissing her—tenderly*) Ye can't he'p yerself. I got ye beat fur once!

ABBIE (*forcing a smile—adoringly*) I hain't beat—s'long's I got ye!

EBEN (*hears the sound of feet outside*) Ssshh! Listen! They've come t' take us!

ABBIE No, it's him. Don't give him no chance to fight ye, Eben. Don't say nothin'—no matter what he says. An' I won't neither. (*It is* CABOT. *He comes up from the barn in a great state of excitement and strides into the house and then into the kitchen.* EBEN *is kneeling beside* ABBIE, *his arm around her, hers around him. They stare straight ahead*).

CABOT (*stares at them, his face hard. A long pause—vindictively*) Ye make a slick pair o' murderin' turtle doves! Ye'd ought t' be both hung on the same limb an' left thar t' swing in the breeze an' rot—a warnin' t' old fools like me t' b'ar their lonesomeness alone—an' fur young fools like ye t' hobble their lust. (*A pause. The excitement returns to his face, his eyes snap, he looks a bit crazy*) I couldn't work today. I couldn't take no interest. T' hell with the farm! I'm leavin' it! I've turned the cows an' other stock loose! I've druv 'em into the woods whar they kin be free! By freein' 'em, I'm freein' myself! I'm quittin' here today! I'll set fire t' house an' barn an' watch 'em burn, an' I'll leave yer Maw t' haunt the ashes, an' I'll will the fields back t' God, so that nothin' human kin never touch 'em! I'll be a-goin' to Californi-a—t' jine Simeon an' Peter—true sons o' mine if they be dumb fools—an' the Cabots'll find Solomon's Mines t'gether! (*He suddenly cuts a mad caper*) Whoop! What was the song they sung? "Oh, Californi-a! That's the land fur me." (*He sings this—then gets on his knees by the floor-board under which the money was hid*) An' I'll sail thar on one o' the finest clippers I kin find! I've got the money! Pity ye didn't know whar this was hidden so's ye could steal. . . . (*He has pulled up the board. He stares—feels—stares again. A pause of dead silence. He slowly turns, slumping into a sitting position on the floor, his eyes like those of a dead fish, his face the sickly green of an attack of nausea. He swallows painfully several times—forces a weak smile at last*) So—ye did steal it!

EBEN (*emotionlessly*) I swapped it t' Sim an' Peter fur their share o' the farm—t' pay their passage t' Californi-a.

CABOT (*with one sardonic*) Ha! (*He begins to recover. Gets slowly to his feet—strangely*) I calc'late God give it to 'em—not yew! God's hard, not easy! Mebbe they's easy gold in the West but it hain't God's gold. It hain't fur me. I kin hear His voice warnin' me agen t' be hard an' stay on my farm. I kin see his hand usin' Eben t' steal t' keep me from weakness. I kin feel I be in the palm o' His hand, His fingers guidin' me. (*A pause—then he mutters sadly*) It's a-goin' t' be lonesomer now than ever it war afore—an' I'm gittin' old, Lord—ripe on the bough. . . . (*Then stiffening*) Waal—what d'ye want? God's lonesome, hain't He? God's hard an' lonesome! (*A pause. The Sheriff with two men comes up the road from the left. They move cautiously to the door. The Sheriff knocks on it with the butt of his pistol*).

SHERIFF Open in the name o' the law! (*They start*).

CABOT They've come fur ye. (*He goes to the rear door*) Come in, Jim! (*The three men enter.* CABOT *meets them in doorway*) Jest a minit, Jim. I got 'em safe here. (*The Sheriff nods. He and his companions remain in the doorway*).

EBEN (*suddenly calls*) I lied this mornin', Jim. I helped her to do it. Ye kin take me, too.

ABBIE (*brokenly*) No!

CABOT Take 'em both. (*He comes forward—stares at* EBEN *with a trace of grudging admiration*) Purty good—fur yew! Waal, I got t' round up the stock. Good-by.

EBEN Good-by.

ABBIE Good-by. (CABOT *turns and strides past the men—comes out and around the corner of the house, his shoulders squared, his face stony, and stalks grimly toward the barn. In the meantime the Sheriff and men have come into the room*).

SHERIFF (*embarrassedly*) Wall—we'd best start.

ABBIE Wait. (*Turns to* EBEN) I love ye, Eben.

EBEN I love ye, Abbie. (*They kiss. The three men grin and shuffle embarrassedly.* EBEN *takes* ABBIE'S *hand. They go out the door in rear, the men following, and come from the house, walking hand in hand to the gate.* EBEN *stops there and points to the sunrise sky*) Sun's a-rizin'. Purty, hain't it?

ABBIE Ay-eh. (*They both stand for a moment looking up raptly in attitudes strangely aloof and devout*).

SHERIFF (*looking around at the farm enviously—to his companion*) It's a jim-dandy farm, no denyin'. Wished I owned it!

CURTAIN

Strange Interlude

CHARACTERS

CHARLES MARSDEN

PROFESSOR HENRY LEEDS

NINA LEEDS, *his daughter*

EDMUND DARRELL

SAM EVANS

MRS. AMOS EVANS, *Sam's mother*

GORDON EVANS

MADELINE ARNOLD

FIRST PART

ACT ONE: Library, the Leeds' home in a small university town of New England—an afternoon in late summer.

ACT TWO: The same. Fall of the following year. Night.

ACT THREE: Dining room of the Evans' homestead in northern New York state—late spring of the next year. Morning.

ACT FOUR: The same as Acts One and Two. Fall of the same year. Evening.

ACT FIVE: Sitting room of small house Evans has rented in a seashore suburb near New York. The following April. Morning.

SECOND PART

ACT SIX: The same. A little over a year later. Evening.

ACT SEVEN: Sitting room of the Evans' apartment on Park Avenue. Nearly eleven years later. Early afternoon.

ACT EIGHT: Section of afterdeck of the Evans' cruiser anchored near the finish line at Poughkeepsie. Ten years later. Afternoon.

ACT NINE: A terrace on the Evans' estate on Long Island. Several months later. Late afternoon.

Strange Interlude

FIRST PART · ACT ONE

SCENE: *The library of* PROFESSOR LEEDS' *home in a small university town in New England. This room is at the front part of his house with windows opening on the strip of lawn between the house and the quiet residential street. It is a small room with a low ceiling. The furniture has been selected with a love for old New England pieces. The walls are lined almost to the ceiling with glassed-in bookshelves. These are packed with books, principally editions, many of them old and rare, of the ancient classics in the original Greek and Latin, of the later classics in French and German and Italian, of all the English authors who wrote while* s *was still like an* f *and a few since then, the most modern probably being Thackeray. The atmosphere of the room is that of a cosy, cultured retreat, sedulously built as a sanctuary where, secure with the culture of the past at his back, a fugitive from reality can view the present safely from a distance, as a superior with condescending disdain, pity, and even amusement.*

There is a fair-sized table, a heavy armchair, a rocker, and an old bench made comfortable with cushions. The table, with the Professor's armchair at its left, is arranged toward the left of the room, the rocker is at center, the bench at right.

There is one entrance, a door in the right wall, rear.

It is late afternoon of a day in August. Sunshine, cooled and dimmed in the shade of trees, fills the room with a soothing light.

The sound of a MAID'S VOICE*—a middle-aged woman—explaining familiarly but respectfully from the right, and* MARSDEN *enters. He is a tall thin man of thirty-five, meticulously well-dressed in tweeds of distinctly English tailoring, his appearance that of an Anglicized New England gentleman. His face is too long for its width, his nose is high and narrow, his* *forehead broad, his mild blue eyes those of a dreamy self-analyst, his thin lips ironical and a bit sad. There is an indefinable feminine quality about him, but it is nothing apparent in either appearance or act. His manner is cool and poised. He speaks with a careful ease as one who listens to his own conversation. He has long fragile hands, and the stoop to his shoulders of a man weak muscularly, who has never liked athletics and has always been regarded as of delicate constitution. The main point about his personality is a quiet charm, a quality of appealing, inquisitive friendliness, always willing to listen, eager to sympathize, to like and to be liked.*

MARSDEN (*standing just inside the door, his tall, stooped figure leaning back against the books—nodding back at the* MAID *and smiling kindly*) I'll wait in here, Mary. (*His eyes follow her for a second, then return to gaze around the room slowly with an appreciative relish for the familiar significance of the books. He smiles affectionately and his amused voice recites the words with a rhetorical resonance*) Sanctum Sanctorum! (*His voice takes on a monotonous musing quality, his eyes stare idly at his drifting thoughts*)

How perfectly the Professor's unique haven! . . .

(*He smiles*)

Primly classical . . . when New Englander meets Greek! . . .

(*Looking at the books now*)

He hasn't added one book in years . . . how old was I when I first came here? . . . six . . . with my father . . . father . . . how dim his face has grown! . . . he wanted to speak to me just before he died . . . the hospital . . . smell of iodoform in the cool halls . . . hot summer . . . I bent down . . . his voice had withdrawn so far away . . . I couldn't understand him . . . what son can ever understand? . . . always too near, too soon, too distant or too late! . . .

(*His face has become sad with a memory of the bewildered suffering of the adolescent boy he had been at the time of his father's death. Then he shakes his head, flinging off his thoughts, and makes himself walk about the room*)

What memories on such a smiling afternoon! . . . this pleasant old town after three months . . . I won't go to Europe again . . . couldn't write a line there . . . how answer the fierce question of all those dead and maimed? . . . too big a job for me! . . .

(*He sighs—then self-mockingly*)

But back here . . . it is the interlude that gently questions . . .

in this town dozing . . . decorous bodies moving with circumspection through the afternoons . . . their habits affectionately chronicled . . . an excuse for weaving amusing words . . . my novels . . . not of cosmic importance, hardly . . .

(*Then self-reassuringly*)

but there is a public to cherish them, evidently . . . and I can write! . . . more than one can say of these modern sex-yahoos! . . . I must start work tomorrow . . . I'd like to use the Professor in a novel sometime . . . and his wife . . . seems impossible she's been dead six years . . . so aggressively his wife! . . . poor Professor! now it's Nina who bosses him . . . but that's different . . . she has bossed me, too, ever since she was a baby . . . she's a woman now . . . known love and death . . . Gordon brought down in flames . . . two days before the armistice . . . what fiendish irony! . . . his wonderful athlete's body . . . her lover . . . charred bones in a cage of twisted steel . . . no wonder she broke down . . . Mother said she's become quite queer lately . . . Mother seemed jealous of my concern . . . why have I never fallen in love with Nina? . . . could I? . . . that way . . . used to dance her on my knee . . . sit her on my lap . . . even now she'd never think anything about it . . . but sometimes the scent of her hair and skin . . . like a dreamy drug . . . dreamy! . . . there's the rub! . . . all dreams with me! . . . my sex life among the phantoms! . . .

(*He grins torturedly*)

Why? . . . oh, this digging in gets nowhere . . . to the devil with sex! . . . our impotent pose of today to beat the loud drum on fornication! . . . boasters . . . eunuchs parading with the phallus! . . . giving themselves away . . . whom do they fool? . . . not even themselves! . . .

(*His face suddenly full of an intense pain and disgust*)

Ugh! . . . always that memory! . . . why can't I ever forget? . . . as sickeningly clear as if it were yesterday . . . prep school . . . Easter vacation . . . Fatty Boggs and Jack Frazer . . . that house of cheap vice . . . one dollar! . . . why did I go? . . . Jack, the dead game sport . . . how I admired him! . . . afraid of his taunts . . . he pointed to the Italian girl . . . "Take her!" . . . daring me . . . I went . . . miserably frightened . . . what a pig she was! . . . pretty vicious face under caked powder and rouge . . . surly and contemptuous . . . lumpy body . . . short legs and thick ankles . . . slums of Naples . . . "What you gawkin' about? Git a move on, kid" . . . kid! . . . I *was* only a kid! . . . sixteen . . . test of manhood . . . ashamed to face Jack again unless . . . fool! . . . I might have lied to him! . . . but I honestly thought that wench would feel humiliated if I . . . oh, stupid kid! . . . back at the hotel I waited till they were asleep . . . then sobbed . . . thinking of Mother . . . feeling I had defiled her . . . and myself . . . forever! . . .

(*Mocking bitterly*)

(*He gets to his feet impatiently*)

Why does my mind always have to dwell on that? . . . too silly . . . no importance really . . . an incident such as any boy of my age . . .

(*He hears someone coming quickly from the right and turns expectantly.* PROFESSOR LEEDS *enters, a pleased relieved expression fighting the flurried worry on his face. He is a small, slender man of fifty-five, his hair gray, the top of his head bald. His face, prepossessing in spite of its too-small, over-refined features, is that of a retiring, studious nature. He has intelligent eyes and a smile that can be ironical. Temperamentally timid, his defense is an assumption of his complacent, superior manner of the classroom toward the world at large. This defense is strengthened by a natural tendency toward a prim provincialism where practical present-day considerations are concerned (though he is most liberal—even radical—in his tolerant understanding of the manners and morals of Greece and Imperial Rome!). This classroom poise of his, however, he cannot quite carry off outside the classroom. There is an unconvincing quality about it that leaves his larger audience—and particularly the* PROFESSOR *himself—subtly embarrassed. As* MARSDEN *is one of his old students, whom, in addition, he has known from childhood, he is perfectly at ease with him*).

MARSDEN (*holding out his hand—with unmistakable liking*) Here I am again, Professor!

PROFESSOR LEEDS (*shaking his hand and patting him on the back—with genuine affection*) So glad to see you, Charlie! A surprise too! We didn't expect you back so soon! (*He sits in his chair on the left of the table while* MARSDEN *sits in the rocker. Looking away from* MARSDEN *a moment, his face now full of selfish relief as he thinks*)

Fortunate, his coming back . . . always calming influence on Nina . . .

MARSDEN And I never dreamed of returning so soon. But Europe, Professor, is the big casualty they were afraid to set down on the list.

PROFESSOR LEEDS (*his face clouding*) Yes, I suppose you found everything completely changed since before the war. (*He thinks resentfully*)

The war . . . Gordon! . . .

MARSDEN Europe has "gone west"—(*He smiles whimsically*) to America, let's hope! (*Then frowningly*) I couldn't stand it. There were millions sitting up with the corpse already, who had a family right to be there— (*Then matter-of-factly*) I was wasting my time too. I couldn't write a line. (*Then gaily*) But where's Nina? I must see Nina!

PROFESSOR LEEDS She'll be right in. She said she wanted to finish thinking something out— You'll find Nina changed, Charlie, greatly changed! (*He sighs—thinking with a trace of guilty alarm*)

> The first thing she said at breakfast . . . "I dreamed of Gordon" . . . as if she wanted to taunt me! . . . how absurd! . . . her eyes positively glared! . . .

(*Suddenly blurting out resentfully*) She dreams about Gordon.

MARSDEN (*looking at him with amused surprise*) Well, I'd hardly call that a change, would you?

PROFESSOR LEEDS (*thinking, oblivious to this remark*)

> But I must constantly bear in mind that she's not herself . . . that she's a sick girl . . .

MARSDEN (*thinking*)

> The morning news of Gordon's death came . . . her face like gray putty . . . beauty gone . . . no face can afford intense grief . . . it's only later when sorrow . . .

(*With concern*) Just what do you mean by changed, Professor? Before I left she seemed to be coming out of that horrible numbed calm.

PROFESSOR LEEDS (*slowly and carefully*) Yes, she has played a lot of golf and tennis this summer, motored around with her friends, and even danced a good deal. And she eats with a ravenous appetite. (*Thinking frightenedly*)

> Breakfast . . . "dreamed of Gordon" . . . what a look of hate for me in her eyes! . . .

MARSDEN But that sounds splendid! When I left she wouldn't see anyone or go anywhere. (*Thinking pityingly*)

> Wandering from room to room . . . her thin body and pale lost face . . . gutted, love-abandoned eyes! . . .

PROFESSOR LEEDS Well, now she's gone to the opposite extreme! Sees everyone—bores, fools—as if she'd lost all discrimination or wish to discriminate. And she talks interminably, Charlie—intentional nonsense, one would say! Refuses to be serious! Jeers at everything!

MARSDEN (*consolingly*) Oh, that's all undoubtedly part of the effort she's making to forget.

PROFESSOR LEEDS (*absent-mindedly*) Yes. (*Arguing with himself*)

Shall I tell him? . . . no . . . it might sound silly . . . but it's terrible to be so alone in this . . . if Nina's mother had lived . . . my wife . . . dead! . . . and for a time I actually felt released! . . . wife! . . . help-meet! . . . now I need help! . . . no use! . . . she's gone! . . .

MARSDEN (*watching him—thinking with a condescending affection*)

Good little man . . . he looks worried . . . always fussing about something . . . he must get on Nina's nerves. . . .

(*Reassuringly*) No girl could forget Gordon in a hurry, especially after the shock of his tragic death.

PROFESSOR LEEDS (*irritably*) I realize that. (*Thinking resentfully*)

Gordon . . . always Gordon with everyone! . . .

MARSDEN By the way, I located the spot near Sedan where Gordon's machine fell. Nina asked me to, you know.

PROFESSOR LEEDS (*irritated—expostulatingly*) For heaven's sake, don't remind her! Give her a chance to forget if you want to see her well again. After all, Charlie, life must be lived and Nina can't live with a corpse forever! (*Trying to control his irritation and talk in an objective tone*) You see, I'm trying to see things through clearly and unsentimentally. If you'll remember, I was as broken up as anyone over Gordon's death. I'd become so reconciled to Nina's love for him—although, as you know, I was opposed at first, and for fair reasons, I think, for the boy, for all his good looks and prowess in sport and his courses, really came of common people and had no money of his own except as he made a career for himself.

MARSDEN (*a trifle defensively*) I'm sure he would have had a brilliant career.

PROFESSOR LEEDS (*impatiently*) No doubt. Although you must acknowledge, Charlie, that college heroes rarely shine brilliantly in after life. Unfortunately, the tendency to spoil them in the university is a poor training—

MARSDEN But Gordon was absolutely unspoiled, I should say.

PROFESSOR LEEDS (*heatedly*) Don't misunderstand me, Charlie! I'd be the first to acknowledge— (*A bit pathetically*) It isn't Gordon, Charlie. It's his memory, his ghost, you might call it, haunting Nina, whose influence I have come to dread because of the terrible change in her attitude toward me. (*His *face twitches as if he were on the verge of tears—he thinks desperately*)

I've got to tell him . . . he will see that I acted for the best . . . that I was justified. . . .

(*He hesitates—then blurts out*) It may sound incredible, but Nina has begun to act as if she hated me!

MARSDEN (*startled*) Oh, come now!

PROFESSOR LEEDS (*insistently*) Absolutely! I haven't wanted to admit it. I've refused to believe it, until it's become too appallingly obvious in her whole attitude toward me! (*His voice trembles*).

MARSDEN (*moved—expostulating*) Oh, now you're becoming morbid! Why, Nina has always idolized you! What possible reason—?

PROFESSOR LEEDS (*quickly*) I can answer that, I think. She has a reason. But why she should blame me when she must know I acted for the best— You probably don't know, but just before he sailed for the front Gordon wanted their marriage to take place, and Nina consented. In fact, from the insinuations she lets drop now, she must have been most eager, but at the time— However, I felt it was ill-advised and I took Gordon aside and pointed out to him that such a precipitate marriage would be unfair to Nina, and scarcely honorable on his part.

MARSDEN (*staring at him wonderingly*) You said that to Gordon? (*Thinking cynically*)

A shrewd move! . . . Gordon's proud spot, fairness and honor! . . . but was it honorable of you? . . .

PROFESSOR LEEDS (*with a touch of asperity*) Yes, I said it, and I gave him my reason. There *was* the possibility he might be killed, in the flying service rather more than a possibility, which needless to say, I did not point out, but which Gordon undoubtedly realized, poor boy! If he were killed, he would be leaving Nina a widow, perhaps with a baby, with no resources, since he was penniless, except what pension she might get from the government; and all this while she was still at an age when a girl, especially one of Nina's charm and beauty, should have all of life before her. Decidedly, I told him, in justice to Nina, they must wait until he had come back and begun to establish his position in the world. That was the square thing. And Gordon was quick to agree with me!

MARSDEN (*thinking*)

The square thing! . . . but we must all be crooks where happiness is concerned! . . . steal or starve! . . .

(*Then rather ironically*) And so Gordon told Nina he'd suddenly realized it wouldn't be fair to her. But I gather he didn't tell her it was your scruple originally?

PROFESSOR LEEDS No, I asked him to keep what I said strictly confidential.

MARSDEN (*thinking ironically*)

Trusted to his honor again! . . . old fox! . . . poor Gordon! . . .

But Nina suspects now that you—?

PROFESSOR LEEDS (*startled*) Yes. That's exactly it. She knows in some queer way. And she acts toward me exactly as if she thought I had deliberately destroyed her happiness, that I had hoped for Gordon's death and been secretly overjoyed when the news came! (*His voice is shaking with emotion*) And there you have it, Charlie—the whole absurd mess! (*Thinking with a strident accusation*)

And it's true, you contemptible . . . !

(*Then miserably defending himself*)

No! . . . I acted unselfishly . . . for her sake! . . .

MARSDEN (*wonderingly*) You don't mean to tell me she has accused you of all this?

PROFESSOR LEEDS Oh, no, Charlie! Only by hints—looks—innuendos. She knows she has no real grounds, but in the present state of her mind the real and the unreal become confused—

MARSDEN (*thinking cynically*)

As always in all minds . . . or how could men live? . . .

(*Soothingly*) That's just what you ought to bear in your mind—the state of hers—and not get so worked up over what I should say is a combination of imagination on both your parts. (*He gets to his feet as he hears voices from the right*) Buck up! This must be Nina coming. (*The* PROFESSOR *gets to his feet, hastily composing his features into his bland, cultured expression*).

MARSDEN (*thinking self-mockingly but a bit worried about himself*)

My heart pounding! . . . seeing Nina again! . . . how sentimental . . . how she'd laugh if she knew! . . . and quite rightly . . . absurd for me to react as if I loved . . . that way . . . her dear old Charlie . . . ha! . . .

(*He smiles with bitter self-mockery*)

PROFESSOR LEEDS (*thinking worriedly*)

I hope she won't make a scene . . . she's seemed on the verge all day . . . thank God, Charlie's like one of the family . . . but what a life for me! . . . with the opening of the new term only a few weeks off! . . . I can't do it . . . I'll have to call in a nerve specialist . . . but the last one did her no good . . . his outrageous fee . . . he can take it to court . . . I absolutely refuse . . . but if he should bring suit? . . . what a scandal . . . no, I'll have to pay . . . somehow . . . borrow . . . he has me in a corner, the robber! . . .

NINA (*enters and stands just inside the doorway looking directly at her father with defiant eyes, her face set in an expression of stubborn resolve. She is twenty, tall with broad square shoulders, slim strong hips and long beautifully developed legs—a fine athletic girl of the swimmer, tennis player, golfer type. Her straw-blond hair framing her sunburned face, is bobbed. Her face is striking, handsome rather than pretty, the bone structure prominent, the forehead high, the lips of her rather large mouth clearly modelled above the firm jaw. Her eyes are beautiful and bewildering, extraordinarily large and a deep greenish blue. Since* GORDON'S *death they have a quality of continually shuddering before some terrible enigma, of being wounded to their depths and made defiant and resentful by their pain. Her whole manner, the charged atmosphere she gives off, is totally at variance with her healthy outdoor physique. It is strained, nerve-racked, hectic, a terrible tension of will alone maintaining self-possession. She is dressed in smart sport clothes. Too preoccupied with her resolve to remember or see* MARSDEN, *she speaks directly to her father in a voice tensely cold and calm*) I have made up my mind, Father.

PROFESSOR LEEDS (*thinking distractedly*)

(*Flustered—hastily*) Don't you see Charlie, Nina?

MARSDEN (*troubled—thinking*)

(*He comes forward toward her—a bit embarrassed but affectionately using his pet name for her*) Hello, Nina Cara Nina! Are you trying to cut me dead, young lady?

NINA (*turning her eyes to* MARSDEN, *holding out her hand for him to shake, in her cool, preoccupied voice*) Hello, Charlie. (*Her eyes immediately return to her father*) Listen, Father!

MARSDEN (*standing near her, concealing his chagrin*)

That hurts! . . . I mean nothing! . . . but she's a sick girl . . . I must make allowance . . .

PROFESSOR LEEDS (*thinking distractedly*)

That look in her eyes! . . . hate! . . .

(*With a silly giggle*) Really, Nina, you're absolutely rude! What has Charlie done?

NINA (*in her cool tone*) Why, nothing. Nothing at all. (*She goes to him with a detached, friendly manner*) Did I seem rude, Charlie? I didn't mean to be. (*She kisses him with a cool, friendly smile*) Welcome home. (*Thinking wearily*)

What has Charlie done? . . . nothing . . . and never will . . . Charlie sits beside the fierce river, immaculately timid, cool and clothed, watching the burning, frozen naked swimmers drown at last. . . .

MARSDEN (*thinking torturedly*)

Cold lips . . . the kiss of contempt! . . . for dear old Charlie! . . .

(*Forcing a good-natured laugh*) Rude? Not a bit! (*Banteringly*) As I've often reminded you, what can I expect when the first word you ever spoke in this world was an insult to me. "Dog" you said, looking right at me—at the age of one! (*He laughs. The* PROFESSOR *laughs nervously.* NINA *smiles perfunctorily*).

NINA (*thinking wearily*)

The fathers laugh at little daughter Nina . . . I must get away! nice Charlie doggy . . . faithful . . . fetch and carry . . . bark softly in books at the deep night. . . .

PROFESSOR LEEDS (*thinking*)

(*Giggle gone to a twitching grin*) You are a cool one, Nina! You'd think you'd just seen Charlie yesterday!

NINA (*slowly—coolly and reflectively*) Well, the war is over. Coming back safe from Europe isn't such an unusual feat now, is it?

MARSDEN (*thinking bitterly*)

A taunt . . . I didn't fight . . . physically unfit . . . not like Gordon . . . Gordon in flames . . . how she must resent my living! . . . thinking of me, scribbling in press bureau . . . louder and louder lies . . . drown the guns and the screams . . . deafen the world with lies . . . hired choir of liars! . . .

(*Forcing a joking tone*) Little you know the deadly risks I ran, Nina! If you'd eaten some of the food they gave me on my renovated transport, you'd shower me with congratulations! (*The* PROFESSOR *forces a snicker*).

NINA (*coolly*) Well, you're here, and that's that. (*Then suddenly expanding in a sweet, genuinely affectionate smile*) And I *am* glad, Charlie, always glad you're here! You know that.

MARSDEN (*delighted and embarrassed*) I hope so, Nina!

NINA (*turning on her father—determinedly*) I must finish what I started to say, Father. I've thought it all out and decided that I simply must get away from here at once—or go crazy! And I'm going on the nine-forty tonight. (*She turns to* MARS-

DEN *with a quick smile*) You'll have to help me pack, Charlie! (*Thinking with weary relief*)

Now that's said . . . I'm going . . . never come back . . . oh, how I loathe this room! . . .

MARSDEN (*thinking with alarm*)

What's this? . . . going? . . . going to whom? . . .

PROFESSOR LEEDS (*thinking—terrified*)

Going? . . . never come back to me? . . . no! . . .

(*Desperately putting on his prim severe manner toward an unruly pupil*) This is rather a sudden decision, isn't it? You haven't mentioned before that you were considering—in fact, you've led me to believe that you were quite contented here—that is, of course, I mean for the time being, and I really think—

MARSDEN (*looking at* NINA*—thinking with alarm*)

Going away to whom? . . .

(*Then watching the* PROFESSOR *with a pitying shudder*)

He's on the wrong tack with his professor's manner . . . her eyes seeing cruelly through him . . . with what terrible recognition! . . . God, never bless me with children! . . .

NINA (*thinking with weary scorn*)

The Professor of Dead Languages is talking again . . . a dead man lectures on the past of living . . . since I was born I have been in his class, loving-attentive, pupil-daughter Nina . . . my ears numb with spiritless messages from the dead . . . dead words droning on . . . listening because he is my cultured father . . . a little more inclined to deafness than the rest (let me be just) because he is my father . . . father? . . . what is father? . . .

PROFESSOR LEEDS (*thinking—terrified*)

I must talk her out of it! . . . find the right words! . . . oh, I know she won't hear me! . . . oh, wife, why did you die, you would have talked to her, she would have listened to you! . . .

(*Continuing in his professor's superior manner*) —and I really think, in justice to yourself above all, you ought to consider this step with great care before you definitely commit yourself. First and foremost, there is your health to be taken into consideration. You've been very ill, Nina, how perilously so perhaps you're not completely aware, but I assure you, and Charlie can corroborate my statement, that six months ago the doctors thought it might be years before—and yet, by staying home and resting and finding healthy outdoor recreation among your old friends, and keeping your mind occupied with the routine of managing the household— (*He forces a prim playful smile*) and managing me, I might add!—you have wonderfully improved and I think it most ill-advised in the hottest part of August, while you're really still a convalescent—

NINA (*thinking*)

Talking! . . . his voice like a fatiguing dying tune droned on a beggar's organ . . . his words arising from the tomb of a soul in puffs of ashes . . .

(*Torturedly*)

Ashes! . . . oh, Gordon, my dear one! . . . oh, lips on my lips, oh, strong arms around me, oh, spirit so brave and generous and gay! . . . ashes dissolving into mud! . . . mud and ashes! . . . that's all! . . . gone! . . . gone forever from me! . . .

PROFESSOR LEEDS (*thinking angrily*)

Her eyes . . . I know that look . . . tender, loving . . . not for me . . . damn Gordon! . . . I'm glad he's dead! . . .

(*A touch of asperity in his voice*) And at a couple of hours' notice to leave everything in the air, as it were— (*Then judicially*) No, Nina, frankly, I can't see it. You know I'd gladly consent to anything in the world to benefit you, but—surely, you can't have reflected!

NINA (*thinking torturedly*)

Gordon darling, I must go away where I can think of you in silence! . . .

(*She turns on her father, her voice trembling with the effort to keep it in control—icily*) It's no use talking, Father. I *have* reflected and I am going!

PROFESSOR LEEDS (*with asperity*) But I tell you it's quite impossible! I don't like to bring up the money consideration but I couldn't possibly afford— And how will you support yourself, if I may ask? Two years in the University, I am sorry to say, won't be much use to you when applying for a job. And even if you had completely recovered from your nervous breakdown, which it's obvious to anyone you haven't, then I most decidedly think you should finish out your science course and take your degree before you attempt—

(*Thinking desperately*)

No use! . . . she doesn't hear . . . thinking of Gordon . . . she'll defy me . . .

NINA (*thinking desperately*)

I must keep calm . . . I mustn't let go or I'll tell him everything . . . and I mustn't tell him . . . he's my father . . .

(*With the same cold calculating finality*) I've already had six months' training for a nurse. I will finish my training. There's a doctor I know at a sanitarium for crippled soldiers—a friend of Gordon's. I wrote to him and he answered that he'll gladly arrange it.

PROFESSOR LEEDS (*thinking furiously*)

Gordon's friend . . . Gordon again! . . .

(*Severely*) You seriously mean to tell me you, in your condition, want to nurse in a soldiers' hospital! Absurd!

MARSDEN (*thinking with indignant revulsion*)

Quite right, Professor! . . . her beauty . . . all those men . . . in their beds . . . it's too revolting! . . .

(*With a persuasive quizzing tone*) Yes, I must say I can't see you as a peace-time Florence Nightingale, Nina!

NINA (*coolly, struggling to keep control, ignoring these remarks*) So you see, Father, I've thought of everything and there's not the slightest reason to worry about me. And I've been teaching Mary how to take care of you. So you won't need me at all. You can go along as if nothing had happened—and really, nothing will have happened that hasn't already happened.

PROFESSOR LEEDS Why, even the manner in which you address me—the tone you take—proves conclusively that you're not yourself!

NINA (*her voice becoming a bit uncanny, her thoughts breaking through*) No, I'm not myself yet. That's just it. Not all myself. But I've been becoming myself. And I must finish!

PROFESSOR LEEDS (*with angry significance—to* MARSDEN) You hear her, Charlie? She's a sick girl!

NINA (*slowly and strangely*) I'm not sick. I'm too well. But they are sick and I must give my health to help them to live on, and to live on myself. (*With a sudden intensity in her tone*) I must pay for my cowardly treachery to Gordon! You should understand this, Father, you who— (*She swallows hard, catching her breath*)

(*Thinking desperately*)

I'm beginning to tell him! . . . I mustn't! . . . he's my father! . . .

PROFESSOR LEEDS (*in a panic of guilty fear, but defiantly*) What do you mean? I am afraid you're not responsible for what you're saying.

NINA (*again with the strange intensity*) I must pay! It's my plain duty! Gordon is dead! What use is my life to me or anyone? But I must make it of use—by giving it! (*Fiercely*) I must learn to give myself, do you hear—give and give until I can make that gift of myself for a man's happiness without scruple, without fear, without joy except in his joy! When I've accomplished this I'll have found myself, I'll know how to start in living my own life again! (*Appealing to them with a desperate impatience*) Don't you see? In the name of the commonest decency and honor, I owe it to Gordon!

PROFESSOR LEEDS (*sharply*) No, I can't see—nor anyone else! (*Thinking savagely*)

I hope Gordon is in hell! . . .

MARSDEN (*thinking*)

Give herself? . . . can she mean her body? . . . beautiful body . . . to cripples? . . . for Gordon's sake? . . . damn Gordon! . . .

(*Coldly*) What do you mean, you owe it to Gordon, Nina?

PROFESSOR LEEDS (*bitterly*) Yes, how ridiculous! It seems to me when you gave him your love, he got more than he could ever have hoped—

NINA (*with fierce self-contempt*) I gave him? What did I give him? It's what I didn't give! That last night before he sailed—in his arms until my body ached—kisses until my lips were numb—knowing all that night—something in me knowing he would die, that he would never kiss me again—knowing this so surely yet with my cowardly brain lying, no, he'll come back and marry you, you'll be happy ever after and feel his children at your breast looking up with eyes so much like his, possessing eyes so happy in possessing you! (*Then violently*) But Gordon never possessed me! I'm still Gordon's silly virgin! And Gordon is muddy ashes! And I've lost my happiness forever! All that last night I knew he wanted me. I knew it was only the honorable code-bound Gordon, who kept commanding from his brain, no, you mustn't, you must respect her, you must wait till you have a marriage license! (*She gives a mocking laugh*).

PROFESSOR LEEDS (*shocked*) Nina! This is really going too far!

MARSDEN (*repelled—with a superior sneer*) Oh, come now, Nina! You've been reading books. Those don't sound like your thoughts.

NINA (*without looking at him, her eyes on her father's—intensely*) Gordon wanted me! I wanted Gordon! I should have made him take me! I knew he would die and I would have no children, that there would be no big Gordon or little Gordon left to me, that happiness was calling me, never to call again if I refused! And yet I did refuse! I didn't make him take me! I lost him forever! And now I am lonely and not pregnant with anything at all, but—but loathing! (*She hurls this last at her *father—fiercely*) Why did I refuse? What was that cowardly something in me that cried, no, you mustn't, what would your father say?

PROFESSOR LEEDS (*thinking—furiously*)

> What an animal! . . . and my daughter! . . . she doesn't get it from me! . . . was her mother like that? . . .

(*Distractedly*) Nina! I really can't listen!

NINA (*savagely*) And that's exactly what my father did say! Wait, he told Gordon! Wait for Nina till the war's over, and you've got a good job and can afford a marriage license!

PROFESSOR LEEDS (*crumbling pitifully*) Nina! I—!

MARSDEN (*flurriedly—going to him*) Don't take her seriously, Professor! (*Thinking with nervous repulsion*)

> Nina has changed . . . all flesh now . . . lust . . . who would dream she was so sensual? . . . I wish I were out of this! . . . I wish I hadn't come here today! . . .

NINA (*coldly and deliberately*) Don't lie any more, Father! Today I've made up my mind to face things. I know now why Gordon suddenly dropped all idea of marriage before he left, how unfair to me he suddenly decided it would be! Unfair to me! Oh, that's humorous! To think I might have had happiness, Gordon, and now Gordon's child— (*Then directly accusing him*) You told him it'd be unfair, you put him on his honor, didn't you?

PROFESSOR LEEDS (*collecting himself—woodenly*) Yes. I did it for your sake, Nina.

NINA (*in the same voice as before*) It's too late for lies!

PROFESSOR LEEDS (*woodenly*) Let us say then that I *persuaded* myself it was for your sake. That may be true. You are young. You think one can live with truth. Very well. It is also true I was jealous of Gordon. I was alone and I wanted to keep your love. I hated him as one hates a thief one may not accuse nor punish. I did my best to prevent your marriage. I was glad when he died. There. Is that what you wish me to say?

NINA Yes. Now I begin to forget I've hated you. You were braver than I, at least.

PROFESSOR LEEDS I wanted to live comforted by your love until the end. In short, I am a man who happens to be your father. (*He hides his face in his hands and weeps softly*) Forgive that man!

MARSDEN (*thinking timidly*)

> In short, forgive us our possessing as we forgive those who possessed before us . . . Mother must be wondering what

keeps me so long . . . it's time for tea . . . I must go home . . .

NINA (*sadly*) Oh, I forgive you. But do you understand now that I must somehow find a way to give myself to Gordon still, that I must pay my debt and learn to forgive myself?

PROFESSOR LEEDS Yes.

NINA Mary will look after you.

PROFESSOR LEEDS Mary will do very well, I'm sure.

MARSDEN (*thinking*)

Nina has changed . . . this is no place for me . . . Mother is waiting tea. . . .

(*Then venturing on an uncertain tone of pleasantry*) Quite so, you two. But isn't this all nonsense? Nina will be back with us in a month, Professor, what with the depressing heat and humidity, and the more depressing halt and the lame!

PROFESSOR LEEDS (*sharply*) She must stay away until she gets well. This time I do speak for her sake.

NINA I'll take the nine-forty. (*Turning to* MARSDEN—*with a sudden girlishness*) Come on upstairs, Charlie, and help me pack. (*She grabs him by the hand and starts to pull him away*).

MARSDEN (*shrugging his shoulders—confusedly*) Well—I don't understand this!

NINA (*with a strange smile*) But some day I'll read it all in one of your books, Charlie, and it'll be so simple and easy to understand that I won't be able to recognize it, Charlie, let alone understand it! (*She laughs teasingly*) Dear old Charlie!

MARSDEN (*thinking in agony*)

God damn in hell . . . dear old Charlie! . . .

(*Then with a genial grin*) I'll have to propose, Nina, if you continue to be my severest critic! I'm a stickler for these little literary conventions, you know!

NINA All right. Propose while we pack. (*She leads him off, right*).

PROFESSOR LEEDS (*blows his nose, wipes his eyes, sighs, clears his throat, squares his shoulders, pulls his coat down in front, sets his tie straight, and starts to take a brisk turn about the room. His face is washed blandly clean of all emotion*)

Three weeks now . . . new term . . . I will have to be looking over my notes. . . .

(*He looks out of window, front*)

Grass parched in the middle . . . Tom forgotten the sprinkler . . . careless . . . ah, there goes Mr. Davis of the bank . . . bank . . . my salary will go farther now . . . books I really need . . . all bosh two can live as cheaply as one . . . there are worse things than being a trained nurse . . . good background of discipline . . . she needs it . . . she may meet rich fellow there . . . mature . . . only students here for her . . . and their fathers never approve if they have anything. . . .

(*He sits down with a forced sigh of peace*)

I am glad we had it out . . . his ghost will be gone now . . . no more Gordon, Gordon, Gordon, love and praise and tears, all for Gordon! . . . Mary will do very well by me . . . I will have more leisure and peace of mind . . . and Nina will come back home . . . when she is well again . . . the old Nina! . . . my little Nina! . . . she knows and she forgave me . . . she said so . . . said! . . . but could she really? . . . don't you imagine? . . . deep in her heart? . . . She still must hate? . . . oh, God! . . . I feel cold! . . . alone! . . . this home is abandoned! . . . the house is empty and full of death! . . . there is a pain about my heart! . . .

(*He calls hoarsely, getting to his feet*) Nina!

NINA'S VOICE (*her voice, fresh and girlish, calls from upstairs*) Yes, Father. Do you want me?

PROFESSOR LEEDS (*struggling with himself—goes to door and calls with affectionate blandness*) No. Never mind. Just wanted to remind you to call for a taxi in good time.

NINA'S VOICE I won't forget.

PROFESSOR LEEDS (*looks at his watch*)

Five-thirty just . . . nine-forty, the train . . . then . . . Nina no more! . . . four hours more . . . she'll be packing . . . then good-bye . . . a kiss . . . nothing more ever to say to each other . . . and I'll die in here some day . . . alone . . . gasp, cry out for help . . . the president will speak at the funeral . . . Nina will be here again . . . Nina in black . . . too late! . . .

(*He calls hoarsely*) Nina! (*There is no answer*)

(*He turns to the bookcase and pulls out the first volume his hands come on and opens it at random and begins to read aloud sonorously like a child whistling to keep up his courage in the dark*)

"Stetit unus in arcem
Erectus capitis victorque ad sidera mittit
Sidereos oculos propiusque adspectat Olympum
Inquiritque Iovem;" . . .

CURTAIN

ACT TWO

SCENE: *The same as Scene One,* PROFESSOR LEEDS' *study. It is about nine o'clock of a night in early fall, over a year later. The appearance of the room is unchanged except that all the shades, of the color of pale flesh, are drawn down, giving the windows a suggestion of lifeless closed eyes and making the room seem more withdrawn from life than before. The reading lamp on the table is lit. Everything on the table, papers, pencils, pens, etc., is arranged in meticulous order.*

MARSDEN *is seated on the chair at center. He is dressed carefully in an English made suit of blue serge so dark as to seem black, and which, combined with the gloomy brooding expression of his face, strongly suggests one in mourning. His tall, thin body sags wearily in the chair, his head is sunk forward, the chin almost touching his chest, his eyes stare sadly at nothing.*

MARSDEN (*his thoughts at ebb, without emphasis, sluggish and melancholy*)

Prophetic Professor! . . . I remember he once said . . . shortly after Nina went away . . . "some day, in here, you'll find me" . . . did he foresee? . . . no . . . everything in life is so contemptuously accidental! . . . God's sneer at our self-importance! . . .

(*Smiling grimly*)

Poor Professor! he was horribly lonely . . . tried to hide it . . . always telling you how beneficial the training at the hospital would be for her . . . poor old chap! . . .

(*His voice grows husky and uncertain—he controls it—straightens himself*)

What time is it? . . .

(*He takes out his watch mechanically and looks at it*)

Ten after nine. . . . Nina ought to be here. . . .

(*Then with sudden bitterness*)

Will she feel any real grief over his death, I wonder? . . . I doubt it! . . . but why am I so resentful? . . . the two times I've visited the hospital she's been pleasant enough . . . pleasantly evasive! . . . perhaps she thought her father had sent me to spy on her . . . poor Professor! . . . at least she answered his letters . . . he used to show them to me . . . pathetically overjoyed . . . newsy, loveless scripts, telling nothing whatever about herself . . . well, she won't have to compose them any more . . . she never answered mine . . . she might at least have acknowledged them. . . . Mother thinks she's behaved quite inexcusably . . .

(*Then jealously*)

I suppose every single damned inmate has fallen in love with her! . . . her eyes seemed cynical . . . sick with men . . . as though I'd looked into the eyes of a prostitute . . . not that I ever have . . . except that once . . . the dollar house . . . hers were like patent leather buttons in a saucer of blue milk! . . .

(*Getting up with a movement of impatience*)

The devil! . . . what beastly incidents our memories insist on cherishing! . . . the ugly and disgusting . . . the beautiful things we have to keep diaries to remember! . . .

(*He smiles with a wry amusement for a second—then bitterly*)

That last night Nina was here . . . she talked so brazenly about giving herself . . . I wish I knew the truth of what she's been doing in that house full of men . . . particularly that self-important young ass of a doctor! . . . Gordon's friend! . . .

(*He frowns at himself, determinedly puts an end to his train of thought and comes and sits down again in the chair—in sneering, conversational tones as if he were this time actually addressing another person*)

Really, it's hardly a decent time, is it, for that kind of speculation . . . with her father lying dead upstairs? . . .

(*A silence as if he had respectably squelched himself—then he pulls out his watch mechanically and stares at it. As he does so a noise of a car is heard approaching, stopping at the curb beyond the garden. He jumps to his feet and starts to go to door—then hesitates confusedly*)

No, let Mary go . . . I wouldn't know what to do . . . take her in my arms? . . . kiss her? . . . right now? . . . or wait until she? . . .

(*A bell rings insistently from the back of the house. From the front voices are heard, first* NINA'S, *then a man's.* MARSDEN *starts, his face suddenly angry and dejected*)

Someone with her! . . . a man! . . . I thought she'd be alone! . . .

(MARY *is heard shuffling to the front door which is opened. Immediately, as* MARY *sees* NINA, *she breaks down and there is the sound of her uncontrolled sobbing and choking, incoherent words drowning out* NINA'S *voice, soothing her*).

NINA (*as* MARY'S *grief subsides a trifle, her voice is heard, flat and toneless*) Isn't Mr. Marsden here, Mary? (*She calls*) Charlie!

MARSDEN (*confused—huskily*) In here—I'm in the study, Nina. (*He moves uncertainly toward the door*).

NINA (*comes in and stands just inside the doorway. She is dressed in a nurse's uniform with cap, a raglan coat over it. She appears older than in the previous scene, her face is pale and much thinner, her cheekbones stand out, her mouth is taut in hard lines of a cynical scorn. Her eyes try to armor her wounded spirit with a defensive stare of disillusionment. Her training has also tended to coarsen her fiber a trifle, to make her insensitive to suffering, to give her the nurse's professionally callous attitude. In her fight to regain control of her nerves she has over-striven after the cool and efficient poise, but she is really in a more highly strung, disorganized state than ever, although she is now more capable of suppressing and concealing it. She remains strikingly handsome and her physical appeal is enhanced by her pallor and the mysterious suggestion about her of hidden experience. She stares at* MARSDEN *blankly and speaks in queer flat tones*) Hello, Charlie. He's dead, Mary says.

MARSDEN (*nodding his head several times—stupidly*) Yes.

NINA (*in same tones*) It's too bad. I brought Doctor Darrell. I thought there might be a chance. (*She pauses and looks about the room—thinking confusedly*)

> His books . . . his chair . . . he always sat there . . . there's his table . . . little Nina was never allowed to touch anything . . . she used to sit on his lap . . . cuddle against him . . . dreaming into the dark beyond the windows . . . warm in his arms before the fireplace . . . dreams like sparks soaring up to die in the cold dark . . . warm in his love, safe-drifting into sleep . . . "Daddy's girl, aren't you?" . . .

(*She looks around and then up and down*)

> His home . . . my home . . . he was my father . . . he's dead . . .

(*She shakes her head*)

> Yes, I hear you, little Nina, but I don't understand one word of it. . . .

(*She smiles with a cynical self-contempt*)

> I'm sorry, Father! . . . you see you've been dead for me a long time . . . when Gordon died, all men died . . . what did you feel for me then? . . . nothing . . . and now I feel nothing . . . it's too bad . . .

MARSDEN (*thinking woundedly*)

> I hoped she would throw herself in my arms . . . weeping . . .

hide her face on my shoulder . . . "Oh, Charlie, you're all I've got left in the world . . ."

(*Then angrily*)

Why did she have to bring that Darrell with her?

NINA (*flatly*) When I said good-bye that night I had a premonition I'd never see him again.

MARSDEN (*glad of this opening for moral indignation*) You've never tried to see him, Nina! (*Then overcome by disgust with himself—contritely*) Forgive me! It was rotten of me to say that!

NINA (*shaking her head—flatly*) I didn't want him to see what he would have thought was me. (*Ironically*) That's the other side of it you couldn't dissect into words from here, Charlie! (*Then suddenly asking a necessary question in her nurse's cool, efficient tones*) Is he upstairs? (MARSDEN *nods stupidly*) I'll take Ned up. I might as well. (*She turns and walks out briskly*).

MARSDEN (*staring after her—dully*)

That isn't Nina. . . .

(*Indignantly*)

They've killed her soul down there! . . .

(*Tears come to his eyes suddenly and he pulls out his handkerchief and wipes them, muttering huskily*)

Poor old Professor! . . .

(*Then suddenly jeering at himself*)

For God's sake, stop acting! . . . it isn't the Professor! . . . dear old Charlie is crying because she didn't weep on his shoulder . . . as he had hoped! . . .

(*He laughs harshly—then suddenly sees a man outside the doorway and stares—then calls sharply*) Who's that?

EVANS (*his voice embarrassed and hesitating comes from the hall*) It's all right. (*He appears in the doorway, grinning bashfully*) It's me—I, I mean—Miss Leeds told me to come in here. (*He stretches out his hand awkwardly*) Guess you don't remember me, Mr. Marsden. Miss Leeds introduced us one day at the hospital. You were leaving just as I came in. Evans is my name.

MARSDEN (*who has been regarding him with waning resentment, forces a cordial smile and shakes hands*) Oh, yes. At first I couldn't place you.

EVANS (*awkwardly*) I sort of feel I'm butting in.

MARSDEN (*beginning to be taken by his likable boyish

quality) Not at all. Sit down. (*He sits in the rocker at center as* EVANS *goes to the bench at right.* EVANS *sits uncomfortably hunched forward, twiddling his hat in his hands. He is above the medium height, very blond, with guileless, diffident blue eyes, his figure inclined to immature lumbering outlines. His face is fresh and red-cheeked, handsome in a boyish fashion. His manner is bashful with women or older men, coltishly playful with his friends. There is a lack of self-confidence, a lost and strayed appealing air about him, yet with a hint of some unawakened obstinate force beneath his apparent weakness. Although he is twenty-five and has been out of college three years, he still wears the latest in collegiate clothes and as he looks younger than he is, he is always mistaken for an undergraduate and likes to be. It keeps him placed in life for himself*).

MARSDEN (*studying him keenly—amused*)

> This is certainly no giant intellect . . . overgrown boy . . . likable quality though . . .

EVANS (*uneasy under* MARSDEN'S *eyes*)

> Giving me the once-over . . . seems like good egg . . . Nina says he is . . . suppose I ought to say something about his books, but I can't even remember a title of one . . .

(*He suddenly blurts out*) You've known Nina—Miss Leeds—ever since she was a kid, haven't you?

MARSDEN (*a bit shortly*) Yes. How long have you known her?

EVANS Well—really only since she's been at the hospital, although I met her once years ago at a Prom with Gordon Shaw.

MARSDEN (*indifferently*) Oh, you knew Gordon?

EVANS (*proudly*) Sure thing! I was in his class! (*With admiration amounting to hero-worship*) He sure was a wonder, wasn't he?

MARSDEN (*cynically*)

> Gordon über alles and forever! . . . I begin to appreciate the Professor's viewpoint . . .

(*Casually*) A fine boy! Did you know him well?

EVANS No. The crowd he went with were mostly fellows who were good at sports—and I always was a dud. (*Forcing a smile*) I was always one of the first to get bounced off the squad in any sport. (*Then with a flash of humble pride*) But I never quit trying, anyway!

MARSDEN (*consolingly*) Well, the sport hero usually doesn't star after college.

EVANS Gordon did! (*Eagerly—with intense admiration*) In the war! He was an ace! And he always fought just as cleanly as he'd played football! Even the Huns respected him!

MARSDEN (*thinking cynically*)

This Gordon worshipper must be the apple of Nina's eye!

(*Casually*) Were you in the army?

EVANS (*shamefacedly*) Yes—infantry—but I never got to the front—never saw anything exciting. (*Thinking glumly*)

Won't tell him I tried for flying service . . . wanted to get in Gordon's outfit . . . couldn't make the physical exam. . . . never made anything I wanted . . . suppose I'll lose out with Nina, too . . .

(*Then rallying himself*)

Hey, you! . . . what's the matter with you? . . . don't quit! . . .

MARSDEN (*who has been staring at him inquisitively*) How did you happen to come out here tonight?

EVANS I was calling on Nina when your wire came. Ned thought I better come along, too—might be of some use.

MARSDEN (*frowning*) You mean Doctor Darrell? (EVANS *nods*) Is he a close friend of yours?

EVANS (*hesitatingly*) Well, sort of. Roomed in the same dorm with me at college. He was a senior when I was a freshman. Used to help me along in lots of ways. Took pity on me, I was so green. Then about a year ago when I went to the hospital to visit a fellow who'd been in my outfit I ran into him again. (*Then with a grin*) But I wouldn't say Ned was close to anyone. He's a dyed-in-the-wool doc. He's only close to whatever's the matter with you! (*He chuckles—then hastily*) But don't get me wrong about him. He's the best egg ever! You know him, don't you?

MARSDEN (*stiffly*) Barely. Nina introduced us once. (*Thinking bitterly*)

He's upstairs alone with her . . . I hoped it would be I who . . .

EVANS

Don't want him to get the wrong idea of Ned . . . Ned's my best friend . . . doing all he can to help me with Nina . . . he thinks she'll marry me in the end . . . God, if she only would! . . . I wouldn't expect her to love me at first . . . be happy only to take care of her . . . cook her breakfast . . . bring it up to her in bed . . . tuck the pillows behind her . . . comb her hair for her . . . I'd be happy just to kiss her hair! . . .

MARSDEN (*agitated—thinking suspiciously*)

What are Darrell's relations with Nina? . . . close to what's the matter with her? . . . damned thoughts! . . . why should I care? . . . I'll ask this Evans . . . pump him while I have a chance . . .

(*With forced indifference*) Is your friend, the Doctor, "close" to Miss Leeds? She's had quite a lot the matter with her since her breakdown, if that's what interests him! (*He smiles casually*).

EVANS (*gives a start, awakening from his dream*) Oh—er—yes. He's always trying to bully her into taking better care of herself, but she only laughs at him. (*Soberly*) It'd be much better if she'd take his advice.

MARSDEN (*suspiciously*) No doubt.

EVANS (*pronounces with boyish solemnity*) She isn't herself, Mr. Marsden. And I think nursing all those poor guys keeps the war before her when she ought to forget it. She ought to give up nursing and be nursed for a change, that's my idea.

MARSDEN (*struck by this—eagerly*) Exactly my opinion. (*Thinking*)

If she'd settle down here . . . I could come over every day . . . I'd nurse her . . . Mother home . . . Nina here . . . how I could work then! . . .

EVANS (*thinking*)

He certainly seems all for me . . . so far! . . .

(*Then in a sudden flurry*)

Shall I tell him? . . . he'll be like her guardian now . . . I've got to know how he stands . . .

(*He starts with a solemn earnestness*) Mr. Marsden, I—there's something I ought to tell you, I think. You see, Nina's talked a lot about you. I know how much she thinks of you. And now her old man— (*He hesitates in confusion*) I mean, her father's dead—

MARSDEN (*in a sort of panic—thinking*)

What's this? . . . proposal? . . . in form? . . . for her hand? . . . to me? . . . Father Charlie now, eh? . . . ha! . . . God, what a fool! . . . does he imagine she'd ever love him? . . . but she might . . . not bad looking . . . likable, innocent . . . something to mother . . .

EVANS (*blundering on regardless now*) I know it's hardly the proper time—

MARSDEN (*interrupting—dryly*) Perhaps I can anticipate. You want to tell me you're in love with Nina?

EVANS Yes, sir, and I've asked her to marry me.

MARSDEN What did she say?

EVANS (*sheepishly*) Nothing. She just smiled.

MARSDEN (*with relief*) Ah. (*Then harshly*) Well, what could you expect? Surely you must know she still loves Gordon?

EVANS (*manfully*) Sure I know it—and I admire her for it! Most girls forget too easily. She ought to love Gordon for a long time yet. And I know I'm an awful wash-out compared to him—but I love her as much as he did, or anyone could! And I'll work my way up for her—I know I can!—so I can give her everything she wants. And I wouldn't ask for anything in return except the right to take care of her. (*Blurts out confusedly*) I never think of her—that way—she's too beautiful and wonderful—not that I don't hope she'd come to love me in time—

MARSDEN (*sharply*) And just what do you expect me to do about all this?

EVANS (*taken aback*) Why—er—nothing, sir. I just thought you ought to know. (*Sheepishly he glances up at ceiling, then down at floor, twiddling his hat*).

MARSDEN (*thinking—at first with a grudging appreciation and envy*)

> He thinks he means that . . . pure love! . . . it's easy to talk . . . he doesn't know life . . . but he might be good for Nina . . . if she were married to this simpleton would she be faithful! . . . and then I? . . . what a vile thought! . . . I don't mean that! . . .

(*Then forcing a kindly tone*) You see, there's really nothing I can do about it. (*With a smile*) If Nina will, she will—and if she won't, she won't. But I can wish you good luck.

EVANS (*immediately all boyish gratitude*) Thanks! That's darn fine of you, Mr. Marsden!

MARSDEN But I think we'd better let the subject drop, don't you? We're forgetting that her father—

EVANS (*guiltily embarrassed*) Yes—sure—I'm a damn fool! Excuse me! (*There is the noise of steps from the hall and* DOCTOR EDMUND DARRELL *enters. He is twenty-seven, short, dark, wiry, his movements rapid and sure, his manner cool and observant, his dark eyes analytical. His head is handsome and intelligent. There is a quality about him, provoking and disturbing to women, of intense passion which he has rigidly trained himself to control and set free only for the objective satisfaction of studying his own and their reactions; and so he has come to consider himself as immune to love through his scientific understanding of its real sexual nature. He sees* EVANS *and* MARSDEN, *nods at* MARSDEN *silently, who returns it coldly, goes to the table and taking a prescription pad from his pocket, hastily scratches on it*).

MARSDEN (*thinking sneeringly*)

Amusing, these young doctors! . . . perspire with the effort to appear cool! . . . writing a prescription . . . cough medicine for the corpse, perhaps! . . . good-looking? . . . more or less . . . attractive to women, I dare say. . . .

DARRELL (*tears it off—hands it to* EVANS) Here, Sam. Run along up the street and get this filled.

EVANS (*with relief*) Sure. Glad of the chance for a walk. (*He goes out, rear*).

DARRELL (*turning to* MARSDEN) It's for Nina. She's got to get some sleep tonight. (*He sits down abruptly in the chair at center.* MARSDEN *unconsciously takes the* PROFESSOR'S *place behind the table. The two men stare at each other for a moment,* DARRELL *with a frank probing, examining look that ruffles* MARSDEN *and makes him all the more resentful toward him*)

This Marsden doesn't like me . . . that's evident . . . but he interests me . . . read his books . . . wanted to know his bearing on Nina's case . . . his novels just well-written surface . . . no depth, no digging underneath . . . why? . . . has the talent but doesn't dare . . . afraid he'll meet himself somewhere . . . one of those poor devils who spend their lives trying not to discover which sex they belong to! . . .

MARSDEN

Giving me the fishy, diagnosing eye they practice at medical school . . . like freshmen from Ioway cultivating broad A's at Harvard! . . . what is his specialty? . . . neurologist, I think . . . I hope not psychoanalyst . . . a lot to account for, Herr Freud! . . . punishment to fit his crimes, be forced to listen eternally during breakfast while innumerable plain ones tell him dreams about snakes . . . pah, what an easy cure-all! . . . sex the philosopher's stone . . . "O Oedipus, O my king! The world is adopting you!" . . .

DARRELL

Must pitch into him about Nina . . . have to have his help . . . damn little time to convince him . . . he's the kind you have to explode a bomb under to get them to move . . . but not too big a bomb . . . they blow to pieces easily . . .

(*Brusquely*) Nina's gone to pot again! Not that her father's death is a shock in the usual sense of grief. I wish to God it were! No, it's a shock because it's finally convinced her she can't feel anything any more. That's what she's doing upstairs now—trying to goad herself into feeling something!

MARSDEN (*resentfully*) I think you're mistaken. She loved her father—

DARRELL (*shortly and dryly*) We can't waste time being sentimental, Marsden! She'll be down any minute, and I've got a lot to talk over with you. (*As* MARSDEN *seems again about to protest*) Nina has a real affection for you and I imagine you have for her. Then you'll want as much as I do to get her straightened out. She's a corking girl. She ought to have every chance for a happy life. (*Then sharply driving his words in*) But the way she's conditioned now, there's no chance. She's piled on too many destructive experiences. A few more and she'll dive for the gutter just to get the security that comes from knowing she's touched bottom and there's no farther to go!

MARSDEN (*revolted and angry, half-springs to his feet*) Look here, Darrell, I'll be damned if I'll listen to such a ridiculous statement!

DARRELL (*curtly—with authority*) How do you know it's ridiculous? What do you know of Nina since she left home? But she hadn't been nursing with us three days before I saw she really ought to be a patient; and ever since then I've studied her case. So I think it's up to you to listen.

MARSDEN (*freezingly*) I'm listening. (*With apprehensive terror*)

> Gutter . . . has she . . . I wish he wouldn't tell me! . . .

DARRELL (*thinking*)

> How much need I tell him? . . . can't tell him the raw truth about her promiscuity . . . he isn't built to face reality . . . no writer is outside of his books . . . have to tone it down for him . . . but not too much! . . .

Nina has been giving way more and more to a morbid longing for martyrdom. The reason for it is obvious. Gordon went away without—well, let's say marrying her. The war killed him. She was left suspended. Then she began to blame herself and to want to sacrifice herself and at the same time give happiness to various fellow war-victims by pretending to love them. It's a pretty idea but it hasn't worked out. Nina's a bad actress. She hasn't convinced the men of her love—or herself of her good intentions. And each experience of this kind has only left her more a prey to a guilty conscience than before and more determined to punish herself!

MARSDEN (*thinking*)

What does he mean? . . . how far did she? . . . how many? . . . (*Coldly and sneeringly*) May I ask on what specific actions of hers this theory of yours is based?

DARRELL (*coldly in turn*) On her evident craving to make an exhibition of kissing, necking, petting—whatever you call it—spooning in general—with any patient in the institution who got a case on her! (*Ironically—thinking*)

Spooning! . . . rather a mild word for her affairs . . . but strong enough for this ladylike soul. . . .

MARSDEN (*bitterly*)

He's lying! . . . what's he trying to hide? . . . was he one of them? . . . her lover? . . . I must get her away from him . . . get her to marry Evans! . . .

(*With authority*) Then she mustn't go back to your hospital, that's certain!

DARRELL (*quickly*) You're quite right. And that brings me to what I want you to urge her to do.

MARSDEN (*thinking suspiciously*)

He doesn't want her back . . . I must have been wrong . . . but there might be many reasons why he'd wish to get rid of her . . .

(*Coldly*) I think you exaggerate my influence.

DARRELL (*eagerly*) Not a bit. You're the last link connecting her with the girl she used to be before Gordon's death. You're closely associated in her mind with that period of happy security, of health and peace of mind. I know that from the way she talks about you. You're the only person she still respects—and really loves. (*As* MARSDEN *starts guiltily and glances at him in confusion—with a laugh*) Oh, you needn't look frightened. I mean the sort of love she'd feel for an uncle.

MARSDEN (*thinking in agony*)

Frightened? . . . was I? . . . only person she loves . . . and then he said "love she'd feel for an uncle" . . . Uncle Charlie now! . . . God damn him! . . .

DARRELL (*eyeing him*)

Looks damnably upset . . . wants to evade all responsibility for her, I suppose . . . he's that kind . . . all the better! . . . he'll be only too anxious to get her safely married. . . .

(*Bluntly*) And that's why I've done all this talking. You've got to help snap her out of this.

MARSDEN (*bitterly*) And how, if I may ask?

DARRELL There's only one way I can see. Get her to marry Sam Evans.

MARSDEN (*astonished*) Evans? (*He makes a silly gesture toward the door—thinking confusedly*)

Wrong again . . . why does he want her married to . . . it's some trick. . . .

DARRELL Yes, Evans. He's in love with her. And it's one of those unselfish loves you read about. And she is fond of him. In a maternal way, of course—but that's just what she needs now, someone she cares about to mother and boss and keep her occupied. And still more important, this would give her a chance to have children. She's got to find normal outlets for her craving for sacrifice. She needs normal love objects for the emotional life Gordon's death blocked up in her. Now marrying Sam ought to do the trick. Ought to. Naturally, no one can say for certain. But I think his unselfish love, combined with her real liking for him, will gradually give her back a sense of security and a feeling of being worth something to life again, and once she's got that, she'll be saved! (*He has spoken with persuasive feeling. He asks anxiously*) Doesn't that seem good sense to you?

MARSDEN (*suspicious—dryly non-committal*) I'm sorry but I'm in no position to say. I don't know anything about Evans, for one thing.

DARRELL (*emphatically*) Well, I do. He's a fine healthy boy, clean and unspoiled. You can take my word for that. And I'm convinced he's got the right stuff in him to succeed, once he grows up and buckles down to work. He's only a big kid now, but all he needs is a little self-confidence and a sense of responsibility. He's holding down a fair job, too, considering he's just started in the advertising game—enough to keep them living. (*With a slight smile*) I'm prescribing for Sam, too, when I boost this wedding.

MARSDEN (*his snobbery coming out*) Do you know his family—what sort of people?—

DARRELL (*bitingly*) I'm not acquainted with their social qualifications, if that's what you mean! They're upstate country folks—fruit growers and farmers, well off, I believe. Simple, healthy people, I'm sure of that although I've never met them.

MARSDEN (*a bit shamefacedly—changing the subject hastily*) Have you suggested this match to Nina?

DARRELL Yes, a good many times lately in a half-joking way. If I were serious she wouldn't listen, she'd say I was prescribing. But I think what I've said has planted it in her mind as a possibility.

MARSDEN (*thinking suspiciously*)

Is this doctor her lover? . . . trying to pull the wool over my eyes? . . . use me to arrange a convenient triangle for him? . . .

(*Harshly—but trying to force a joking tone*) Do you know what I'm inclined to suspect, Doctor? That you may be in love with Nina yourself!

DARRELL (*astonished*) The deuce you do! What in the devil makes you think that? Not that any man mightn't fall in love with Nina. Most of them do. But I didn't happen to. And what's more I never could. In my mind she always belongs to Gordon. It's probably a reflection of her own silly fixed idea about him. (*Suddenly, dryly and harshly*) And I couldn't share a woman—even with a ghost! (*Thinking cynically*)

Not to mention the living who have had her! . . . Sam doesn't know about them . . . and I'll bet he couldn't believe it of her even if she confessed! . . .

MARSDEN (*thinking baffledly*)

Wrong again! . . . he isn't lying . . . but I feel he's hiding something . . . why does he speak so resentfully of Gordon's memory? . . . why do I sympathize? . . .

(*In a strange mocking ironic tone*) I can quite appreciate your feeling about Gordon. I wouldn't care to share with a ghost-lover myself. That species of dead is so invulnerably alive! Even a doctor couldn't kill one, eh? (*He forces a laugh—then in a friendly confidential tone*) Gordon is too egregious for a ghost. That was the way Nina's father felt about him, too. (*Suddenly reminded of the dead man—in penitently sad tones*) You didn't know her father, did you? A charming old fellow!

DARRELL (*hearing a noise from the hall—warningly*) Sstt! (NINA *enters slowly. She looks from one to the other with a queer, quick, inquisitive stare, but her face is a pale expressionless mask drained of all emotional response to human contacts. It is as if her eyes were acting on their own account as restless, prying, recording instruments. The two men have risen and stare at her anxiously.* DARRELL *moves back and to one side until he is standing in relatively the same place as* MARSDEN *had occupied in the previous scene while* MARSDEN *is in her father's place and she stops where she had been. There is a pause. Then just as each of the men is about to speak she answers as if they had asked a question*).

NINA (*in a queer flat voice*) Yes, he's dead—my father—whose passion created me—who began me—he is ended. There is only his end living—his death. It lives now to draw nearer me, to draw me nearer, to become my end! (*Then with a strange twisted smile*) How we poor monkeys hide from ourselves behind the sounds called words!

MARSDEN (*thinking frightenedly*)

How terrible she is! . . . who is she? . . . not my Nina! . . .

(*As if to reassure himself—timidly*) Nina! (DARRELL *makes an impatient gesture for him to let her go on. What she is saying interests him and he feels talking it out will do her good. She looks at* MARSDEN *for a moment startledly as if she couldn't recognize him*).

NINA What? (*Then placing him—with real affection that is like a galling goad to him*) Dear old Charlie!

MARSDEN

Dear damned Charlie! . . . She loves to torture! . . .

(*Then forcing a smile—soothingly*) Yes, Nina Cara Nina! Right here!

NINA (*forcing a smile*) You look frightened, Charlie. Do I seem queer? It's because I've suddenly seen the lies in the sounds called words. You know—grief, sorrow, love, father—those sounds our lips make and our hands write. You ought to know what I mean. You work with them. Have you written another novel lately? But, stop to think, you're just the one who couldn't know what I mean. With you the lies have become the only truthful things. And I suppose that's the logical conclusion to the whole evasive mess, isn't it? Do you understand me, Charlie? Say lie— (*She says it, drawing it out*) L-i-i-e! Now say life. L-i-i-f-e! You see! Life is just a long drawn out lie with a sniffling sigh at the end! (*She laughs*).

MARSDEN (*in strange agony*)

She's hard! . . . like a whore! . . . tearing your heart with dirty finger nails! . . . my Nina! . . . cruel bitch! . . . some day I won't bear it! . . . I'll scream out the truth about every woman! no kinder at heart than dollar tarts! . . .

(*Then in a passion of remorse*)

Forgive me, Mother! . . . I didn't mean all! . . .

DARRELL (*a bit worried himself now—persuasively*) Why not sit down, Nina, and let us two gentlemen sit down?

NINA (*smiling at him swiftly and mechanically*) Oh, all right, Ned. (*She sits at center. He comes and sits on the bench.* MARSDEN *sits by the table. She continues sarcastically*) Are you prescribing for me again, Ned? This is my pet doctor, Charlie. He couldn't be happy in heaven unless God called him in because He'd caught something! Did you ever know a young scientist, Charlie? He believes if you pick a lie to pieces, the pieces are the truth! I like him because he's so inhuman. But once he kissed me—in a moment of carnal weakness! I was as startled as if a mummy had done it! And then he looked so disgusted with himself! I had to laugh! (*She smiles at him with a pitying scorn*).

DARRELL (*good-naturedly smiling*) That's right! Rub it in! (*Ruffled but amused in spite of it*)

> I'd forgotten about that kiss . . . I was sore at myself afterwards . . . she was so damned indifferent! . . .

NINA (*wanderingly*) Do you know what I was doing upstairs? I was trying to pray. I tried hard to pray to the modern science God. I thought of a million light years to a spiral nebula—one other universe among innumerable others. But how could that God care about our trifling misery of death-born-of-birth? I couldn't believe in Him, and I wouldn't if I could! I'd rather imitate His indifference and prove I had that one trait at least in common!

MARSDEN (*worriedly*) Nina, why don't you lie down?

NINA (*jeeringly*) Oh, let me talk, Charlie! They're only words, remember! So many many words have jammed up into thoughts in my poor head! You'd better let them overflow or they'll burst the dam! I wanted to believe in any God at any price—a heap of stones, a mud image, a drawing on a wall, a bird, a fish, a snake, a baboon—or even a good man preaching the simple platitudes of truth, those Gospel words we love the sound of but whose meaning we pass on to spooks to live by!

MARSDEN (*again—half-rising—frightenedly*) Nina! You ought to stop talking. You'll work yourself into— (*He glances angrily at* DARRELL *as if demanding that, as a doctor, he do something*).

NINA (*with bitter hopelessness*) Oh, all right!

DARRELL (*answering his look—thinking*)

> You poor fool! . . . it'll do her good to talk this out of her system . . . and then it'll be up to you to bring her around to Sam . . .

(*Starts toward the door*) Think I'll go out and stretch my legs.

MARSDEN (*thinking—in a panic*)

> I don't want to be alone with her! . . . I don't know her! . . . I'm afraid! . . .

(*Protestingly*) Well—but—hold on—I'm sure Nina would rather—

NINA (*dully*) Let him go. I've said everything I can ever

say—to him. I want to talk to you, Charlie. (DARRELL *goes out noiselessly with a meaning look at* MARSDEN—*a pause*).

MARSDEN (*thinking tremblingly*)

Here . . . now . . . what I hoped . . . she and I alone . . . she will cry . . . I will comfort her . . . why am I so afraid? . . . whom do I fear? . . . is it she? . . . or I? . . .

NINA (*suddenly, with pity yet with scorn*) Why have you always been so timid, Charlie? Why are you always afraid? What are you afraid of?

MARSDEN (*thinking in a panic*)

She sneaked into my soul to spy! . . .

(*Then boldly*)

Well then, a little truth for once in a way! . . .

(*Timidly*) I'm afraid of—of life, Nina.

NINA (*nodding slowly*) I know. (*After a pause—queerly*) The mistake began when God was created in a male image. Of course, women would see Him that way, but men should have been gentlemen enough, remembering their mothers, to make God a woman! But the God of Gods—the Boss—has always been a man. That makes life so perverted, and death so unnatural. We should have imagined life as created in the birth-pain of God the Mother. Then we would understand why we, Her children, have inherited pain, for we would know that our life's rhythm beats from Her great heart, torn with the agony of love and birth. And we would feel that death meant reunion with Her, a passing back into Her substance, blood of Her blood again, peace of Her peace! (MARSDEN *has been listening to her fascinatedly. She gives a strange little laugh*) Now wouldn't that be more logical and satisfying than having God a male whose chest thunders with egotism and is too hard for tired heads and thoroughly comfortless? Wouldn't it, Charlie?

MARSDEN (*with a strange passionate eagerness*) Yes! It would, indeed! It would, Nina!

NINA (*suddenly jumping to her feet and going to him—with a horrible moaning desolation*) Oh, God, Charlie, I want to believe in something! I want to believe so I can feel! I want to feel that he is dead—my father! And I can't feel anything, Charlie! I can't feel anything at all! (*She throws herself on her knees beside him and hides her face in her hands on his knees and begins to sob—stifled torn sounds*).

MARSDEN (*bends down, pats her head with trembling hands, soothes her with uncertain trembling words*) There—there—

don't—Nina, please—don't cry—you'll make yourself sick—come now—get up—do! (*His hands grasping her arms he half raises her to her feet, but, her face still hidden in her hands, sobbing, she slips on to his lap like a little girl and hides her face on his shoulder. His expression becomes transported with a great happiness—in an ecstatic whisper*)

As I dreamed . . . with a deeper sweetness! . . .

(*He kisses her hair with a great reverence*)

There . . . this is all my desire . . . I am this kind of lover . . . this is my love . . . she is my girl . . . not woman . . . my little girl . . . and I am brave because of her little girl's pure love . . . and I am proud . . . no more afraid . . . no more ashamed of being pure! . . .

(*He kisses her hair again tenderly and smiles at himself—then soothingly with a teasing incongruous gaiety*) This will never do, Nina Cara Nina—never, never do, you know—I can't permit it!

NINA (*in a muffled voice, her sobbing beginning to ebb away into sighs—in a young girl's voice*) Oh, Charlie, you're so kind and comforting! I've wanted you so!

MARSDEN (*immediately disturbed*)

Wanted? . . . wanted? . . . not that kind of wanted . . . can she mean? . . .

(*Questioning hesitatingly*) You've wanted me, Nina?

NINA Yes,—awfully! I've been so homesick. I've wanted to run home and 'fess up, tell how bad I've been, and be punished! Oh, I've got to be punished, Charlie, out of mercy for me, so I can forgive myself! And now Father dead, there's only you. You will, won't you—or tell me how to punish myself? You've simply got to, if you love me!

MARSDEN (*thinking intensely*)

If I love her! . . . oh, I do love her! . . .

(*Eagerly*) Anything you wish, Nina—anything!

NINA (*with a comforted smile, closing her eyes and cuddling up against him*) I knew you would. Dear old Charlie! (*As he gives a wincing start*) What is it? (*She looks up into his face*).

MARSDEN (*forcing a smile—ironically*) Twinge—rheumatics—getting old, Nina. (*Thinking with wild agony*)

Dear old Charlie! . . . descended again into hell! . . .

(*Then in a flat voice*) What do you want to be punished for, Nina?

NINA (*in a strange, far-away tone, looking up not at him

but at the ceiling) For playing the silly slut, Charlie. For giving my cool clean body to men with hot hands and greedy eyes which they called love! Ugh! (*A shiver runs over her body*).

MARSDEN (*thinking with sudden agony*)

Then she did! . . . the little filth! . . .

(*In his flat voice*) You mean you— (*Then pleadingly*) But not—Darrell?

NINA (*with simple surprise*) Ned? No, how could I? The war hadn't maimed him. There would have been no point in that. But I did with others—oh, four or five or six or seven men, Charlie. I forget—and it doesn't matter. They were all the same. Count them all as one, and that one a ghost of nothing. That is, to me. They were important to themselves, if I remember rightly. But I forget.

MARSDEN (*thinking in agony*)

But why? . . . the dirty little trollop! . . . why? . . .

(*In his flat voice*) Why did you do this, Nina?

NINA (*with a sad little laugh*) God knows, Charlie! Perhaps I knew at the time but I've forgotten. It's all mixed up. There was a desire to be kind. But it's horribly hard to give anything, and frightful to receive! And to give love—oneself—not in this world! And men are difficult to please, Charlie. I seemed to feel Gordon standing against a wall with eyes bandaged and these men were a firing squad whose eyes were also bandaged—and only I could see! No, I was the blindest! I would not see! I knew it was a stupid, morbid business, that I was more maimed than they were, really, that the war had blown my heart and insides out! And I knew too that I was torturing these tortured men, morbidly super-sensitive already, that they loathed the cruel mockery of my gift! Yet I kept on, from one to one, like a stupid, driven animal until one night not long ago I had a dream of Gordon diving down out of the sky in flames and he looked at me with such sad burning eyes, and all my poor maimed men, too, seemed staring out of his eyes with a burning pain, and I woke up crying, my own eyes burning. Then I saw what a fool I'd been—a guilty fool! So be kind and punish me!

MARSDEN (*thinking with bitter confusion*)

I wish she hadn't told me this . . . it has upset me terribly! . . . I positively must run home at once . . . Mother is waiting up . . . oh, how I'd love to hate this little whore! . . . then I could punish! . . . I wish her father were alive . . . "now he's dead there's only you," she said . . . "I've wanted you," . . .

(*With intense bitterness*)

Dear old Father Charlie now! . . . ha! . . . that's how she wants me! . . .

(*Then suddenly in a matter-of-fact tone that is mockingly like her father's*) Then, under the circumstances, having weighed the pros and cons, so to speak, I should say that decidedly the most desirable course—

NINA (*drowsily—her eyes shut*) You sound so like Father, Charlie.

MARSDEN (*in the tone like her father's*) —is for you to marry that young Evans. He is a splendid chap, clean and boyish, with real stuff in him, too, to make a career for himself if he finds a help-meet who will inspire him to his best efforts and bring his latent ability to the surface.

NINA (*drowsily*) Sam is a nice boy. Yes, it would be a career for me to bring a career to his surface. I would be busy—surface life—no more depths, please God! But I don't love him, Father.

MARSDEN (*blandly—in the tone like her father's*) But you like him, Nina. And he loves you devotedly. And it's time you were having children—and when children come, love comes, you know.

NINA (*drowsily*) I want children. I must become a mother so I can give myself. I am sick of sickness.

MARSDEN (*briskly*) Then it's all settled?

NINA (*drowsily*) Yes. (*Very sleepily*) Thank you, Father. You've been so kind. You've let me off too easily. I don't feel as if you'd punished me hardly at all. But I'll never, never do it again, I promise—never, never!— (*She falls asleep and gives a soft little snore*).

MARSDEN (*still in her father's tones—very paternally—looking down*) She's had a hard day of it, poor child! I'll carry her up to her room. (*He rises to his feet with* NINA *sleeping peacefully in his arms. At this moment* SAM EVANS *enters from the right with the package of medicine in his hand*).

EVANS (*grinning respectfully*) Here's the— (*As he sees* NINA) Oh! (*Then excitedly*) Did she faint?

MARSDEN (*smiling kindly at* EVANS*—still in her father's tones*) Sssh! She's asleep. She cried and then she fell asleep—like a little girl. (*Then benignantly*) But first we spoke a word about you, Evans, and I'm sure you have every reason to hope.

EVANS (*overcome, his eyes on his shuffling feet and twiddling cap*) Thanks—I—I really don't know how to thank—

MARSDEN (*going to door—in his own voice now*) I've got to go home. My mother is waiting up for me. I'll just carry Nina upstairs and put her on her bed and throw something over her.

EVANS Can't I help you, Mr. Marsden?

MARSDEN (*dully*) No. I cannot help myself. (*As* EVANS *looks puzzled and startled he adds with an ironical, self-mocking geniality*) You'd better call me just Charlie after this. (*He smiles bitterly to himself as he goes out*).

EVANS (*looks after him for a moment—then cannot restrain a joyful, coltish caper—gleefully*) Good egg! Good old Charlie! (*As if he had heard or guessed,* MARSDEN'S *bitter laugh comes back from the end of the hallway*).

CURTAIN

ACT THREE

SCENE: *Seven months or so later—the dining room of the* EVANS' *homestead in northern New York state—about nine o'clock in the morning of a day in late spring of the following year.*

The room is one of those big, misproportioned dining rooms that are found in the large, jigsaw country houses scattered around the country as a result of the rural taste for grandeur in the eighties. There is a cumbersome hanging lamp suspended from chains over the exact center of the ugly table with its set of straightbacked chairs set back at spaced intervals against the walls. The wall paper, a repulsive brown, is stained at the ceiling line with damp blotches of mildew, and here and there has started to peel back where the strips join. The floor is carpeted in a smeary brown with a dark red design blurred into it. In the left wall is one window, with starched white curtains, looking out on a covered side-porch, so that no sunlight ever gets to this room and the light from the window, although it is a beautiful warm day in the flower garden beyond the porch, is cheerless and sickly. There is a door in the rear, to left of center, that leads to a hall opening on the same porch. To the right of door a heavy sideboard, a part of the set, displaying some "company" china and glassware. In the right wall, a door leading to the kitchen. NINA *is seated at the foot of the table, her back to the window, writing a letter. Her whole personality seems changed, her face has a contented expression, there is an inner calm about her. And her personal appearance has changed in kind, her face and figure have filled out, she is prettier in a conventional way and less striking and unusual; nothing remains of the strange fascination of her face except her unchangeably mysterious eyes.*

NINA (*reading what she has just written over to herself*) It's a queer house, Ned. There is something wrong with its psyche, I'm sure. Therefore you'd simply adore it. It's a hideous old place, a faded gingerbread with orange fixin's and numerous lightning rods. Around it are acres and acres of apple trees in full bloom, all white and pinkish and beautiful, like brides just tripping out of church with the bridegroom, Spring, by the arm.

Which reminds me, Ned, that it's over six months since Sam and I were married and we haven't seen hide nor hair of you since the ceremony. Do you think that is any nice way to act? You might at least drop me a line. But I'm only joking. I know how busy you must be now that you've got the chance you've always wanted to do research work. Did you get our joint letter of congratulation written after we read of your appointment?

But to get back to this house. I feel it has lost its soul and grown resigned to doing without it. It isn't haunted by anything at all—and ghosts of some sort are the only normal life a house has—like our minds, you know. So although last evening when we got here at first I said "obviously haunted" to myself, now that I've spent one night in it I know that whatever spooks there may once have been have packed up their manifestations a long time ago and drifted away over the grass, wisps of mist between the apple trees, without one backward glance of regret or recollection. It's incredible to think Sam was born and spent his childhood here. I'm glad he doesn't show it! We slept last night in the room he was born in. Or rather he slept, I couldn't. I lay awake and found it difficult to breathe, as if all the life in the air had long since been exhausted in keeping the dying living a little longer. It was hard to believe anyone had ever been born alive there. I know you're saying crossly "She's still morbid" but I'm not. I've never been more normal. I feel contented and placid.

(*Looking up from the letter, thinking embarrassedly*)

Should I have told him? . . . no . . . my own secret . . . tell no one . . . not even Sam . . . why haven't I told Sam? . . . it'd do him so much good . . . he'd feel so proud of himself, poor dear . . . no . . . I want to keep it just my baby . . . only mine . . . as long as I can . . . and it will be time enough to let Ned know when I go to New York . . . he can suggest a good obstetrician . . . how delighted he'll be when he hears! . . . he always said it would be the best thing for me . . . well, I do feel happy when I think . . . and I love Sam now . . . in a way . . . it will be his baby too . . .

(*Then with a happy sigh, turns back to letter*)

But speaking of Sam's birth, you really must meet his mother sometime. It's amazing how little she is like him, a strange woman from the bit I saw of her last night. She has been writing Sam regularly once a week ever since she's known we were married, the most urgent invitations to visit her. They were really more like commands, or prayers. I suspect she is terribly lonely all by herself in this big house. Sam's feeling toward her puzzles me. I don't believe he ever mentioned her until her letters began coming or that he'd ever have come to see the poor woman if I hadn't insisted. His attitude rather shocked me. It was just as though he'd forgotten he had a mother. And yet as soon as he saw her he was sweet enough. She seemed dreadfully upset to see Charlie with us, until we'd explained it was thanks to his kindness and in his car we were taking this deferred honeymoon. Charlie's like a fussy old woman about his car, he's afraid to let Sam or me drive it—

MARSDEN (*enters from the rear. He is spruce, dressed immaculately, his face a bit tired and resigned, but smiling kindly. He has a letter in his hand*) Good morning. (*She gives a start and instinctively covers the letter with her hand*).

NINA Good morning. (*Thinking amusedly*)

If he knew what I'd just written . . . poor old Charlie! . . .

(*Then indicating the letter he carries*) I see you're an early correspondent, too.

MARSDEN (*with sudden jealous suspicion*)

Why did she cover it up like that? . . . whom is she writing to? . . .

(*Coming toward her*) Just a line to Mother to let her know we've not all been murdered by rum-bandits. You know how she worries.

NINA (*thinking with a trace of pitying contempt*)

Apron strings . . . still his devotion to her is touching . . . I hope if mine is a boy he will love me as much . . . oh, I hope it is a boy . . . healthy and strong and beautiful . . . like Gordon! . . .

(*Then suddenly sensing* MARSDEN'S *curiosity—perfunctorily*) I'm writing to Ned Darrell. I've owed him one for ages. (*She folds it up and puts it aside*).

MARSDEN (*thinking glumly*)

I thought she'd forgotten him . . . still I suppose it's just friendly . . . and it's none of my business now she's married. . . .

(*Perfunctorily*) How did you sleep?

NINA Not a wink. I had the strangest feeling.

MARSDEN Sleeping in a strange bed, I suppose. (*Jokingly*) Did you see any ghosts?

NINA (*with a sad smile*) No, I got the feeling the ghosts had all deserted the house and left it without a soul—as the dead so often leave the living— (*She forces a little laugh*) if you get what I mean.

MARSDEN (*thinking worriedly*)

Slipping back into that morbid tone . . . first time in a long while . . .

(*Teasingly*) Hello! Do I hear graveyards yawning from their sleep—and yet I observe it's a gorgeous morning without, the flowers are flowering, the trees are treeing with one another, and you, if I mistake not, are on your honeymoon!

NINA (*immediately gaily mocking*) Oh, very well, old thing! "God's in His heaven, all's right with the world!" And Pippa's cured of the pip! (*She dances up to him*).

MARSDEN (*gallantly*) Pippa is certainly a pippin this morning!

NINA (*kisses him quickly*) You deserve one for that! All I meant was that ghosts remind me of men's smart crack about women, you can't live with them and can't live without them. (*Stands still and looks at him teasingly*) But there you stand proving me a liar by every breath you draw! You're ghostless and womanless—and as sleek and satisfied as a pet seal! (*She sticks out her tongue at him and makes a face of superior scorn*) Bah! That for you, 'Fraid-cat Charlie, you slacker bachelor! (*She runs to the kitchen door*) I'm going to bum some more coffee! How about you?

MARSDEN (*with a forced smile*) No, thank you. (*She disappears into the kitchen—thinking with bitter pain*)

Ghostless! . . . if she only knew . . . that joking tone hides her real contempt! . . .

(*Self-mockingly*)

"But when the girls began to play 'Fraid-cat Charlie ran away!"

(*Then rallying himself*)

Bosh! . . . I haven't had such thoughts . . . not since their marriage . . . happy in her happiness . . . but is she happy? . . . in the first few months she was obviously playing a part . . . kissed him too much . . . as if she'd determined to make herself a loving wife . . . and then all of a sudden she became contented . . . her face filled out . . . her eyes lazily examined peace . . . pregnant . . . yes, she must be . . . I hope so. . . . Why? . . . for her sake . . . my own, too . . . when she has a child I know I can entirely accept . . . forget I have lost her . . . lost her? . . . silly ass! . . . how can you lose what you never possessed? . . . except in dreams! . . .

(*Shaking his head exasperatedly*)

Round and round . . . thoughts . . . damn pests! . . . mosquitoes of the soul . . . whine, sting, suck one's blood . . . why did I invite Nina and Sam on this tour . . . it's a business trip with me, really . . . I need a new setting for my next novel . . . "Mr. Marsden departs a bit from his familiar field" . . . well, there they were stuck in the Professor's house . . . couldn't afford a vacation . . . never had a honeymoon . . . I've pretended to be done up every night so they could . . . I've gone to bed right after dinner so they could be alone and . . . I wonder if she can really like him . . . that way? . . .

(*The sound of* EVANS' *voice and his mother's is heard from the garden.* MARSDEN *goes over and carefully peers out*)

Sam with his mother . . . peculiar woman . . . strong . . . good character for a novel . . . no, she's too somber . . . her eyes are the saddest . . . and, at the same time, the grimmest . . . they're coming in . . . I'll drive around the country a bit . . . give them a chance for a family conference . . . discuss Nina's pregnancy, I suppose . . . does Sam know? . . . he gives no indication . . . why do wives hide it from their husbands? . . . ancient shame . . . guilty of continuing life, of bringing fresh pain into the world . . .

(*He goes out, rear. The outside door in the hall is heard being opened and* EVANS *and his mother evidently meet* MARSDEN *as he is about to go out. Their voices, his voice explaining, are heard, then the outer door being opened and shut again as* MARSDEN *departs. A moment later* EVANS *and his mother enter the dining room.* SAM *looks timorously happy, as if he could not quite believe in his good fortune and had constantly to reassure himself about it, yet he is riding the crest of the wave, he radiates love and devotion and boyish adoration. He is a charming-looking fresh boy now. He wears a sweater and linen knickers, collegiate to the last degree. His mother is a tiny woman with a frail figure, her head and face, framed in iron-gray hair, seeming much too large for her body, so that at first glance she gives one the impression of a wonderfully made, lifelike doll. She is only about forty-five but she looks at least sixty. Her face with its delicate features must have once been of a romantic, tender, clinging-vine beauty, but what has happened to her has compressed its defenseless curves into planes, its mouth into the thin line around a locked door, its gentle chin has been forced out agressively by a long reliance on clenched teeth. She is very pale. Her big dark eyes are grim with the prisoner-pain of a walled-in soul. Yet a sweet loving-kindness, the ghost of an old faith and trust in life's goodness, hovers girlishly, fleetingly, about the corners of her mouth and softens into deep sorrow the shadowy grimness of her eyes. Her voice jumps startlingly in tone from a caressing gentleness to a blunted flat assertiveness, as if what she said then was merely a voice on its own without human emotion to inspire it*).

EVANS (*as they come in—rattling on in the cocksure boastful way of a boy showing off his prowess before his mother, confident of thrilled adulation*) In a few years you won't have to worry one way or another about the darned old apple crop. I'll be able to take care of you then. Wait and see! Of course, I'm not making so much now. I couldn't expect to. I've only just started. But I'm making good, all right, all right—since I got married—and it's only a question of time when— Why, to show you, Cole—he's the manager and the best egg ever—called me into his office and told me he'd had his eye on me, that my stuff was exactly what they wanted, and he thought I had the makings of a real find. (*Proudly*) How's that? That's certainly fair enough, isn't it?

MRS. EVANS (*vaguely—she has evidently not heard much of what he said*) That's fine, Sammy. (*Thinking apprehensively*)

> I do hope I'm wrong! . . . but that old shiver of dread took me the minute she stepped in the door! . . . I don't think she's told Sammy but I got to make sure. . . .

EVANS (*seeing her preoccupation now—deeply hurt—testily*) I'll bet you didn't hear a word I said! Are you still worrying about how the darn old apples are going to turn out?

MRS. EVANS (*with a guilty start—protestingly*) Yes, I did hear you, Sammy—every word! That's just what I was thinking about—how proud I am you're doing so wonderful well!

EVANS (*mollified but still grumbling*) You'd never guess it from the gloomy way you looked! (*But encouraged to go on*) And Cole asked me if I was married—seemed to take a real personal interest—said he was glad to hear it because marriage was what put the right kind of ambition into a fellow—unselfish ambition—working for his wife and not just himself— (*Then embarrassedly*) He even asked me if we were expecting an addition to the family.

MRS. EVANS (*seeing this is her chance—quickly—forcing a smile*) I've been meaning to ask you that myself, Sammy. (*Blurts out apprehensively*) She—Nina—she isn't going to have a baby, is she?

EVANS (*with an indefinable guilty air—as if he were reluctant to admit it*) I—why—you mean, is she now? I don't think so, Mother (*He strolls over to the window whistling with an exaggeratedly casual air, and looks out*).

MRS. EVANS (*thinking with grim relief*)

He don't know . . . there's that much to be thankful for, anyway. . . .

EVANS (*thinking with intense longing*)

If that'd only happen! . . . soon! . . . Nina's begun to love me . . . a little . . . I've felt it the last two months . . . God, it's made me happy! . . . before that she didn't . . . only liked me . . . that was all I asked . . . never dared hope she'd come to love me . . . even a little . . . so soon . . . sometimes I feel it's too good to be true . . . don't deserve it . . . and now . . . if that'd happen . . . then I'd feel sure . . . it'd be there . . . half Nina, half me . . . living proof! . . .

(*Then an apprehensive note creeping in*)

And I know she wants a baby so much . . . one reason why she married me . . . and I know she's felt right along that then she'd love me . . . really love me . . .

(*Gloomily*)

I wonder why . . . ought to have happened before this . . . hope it's nothing wrong . . . with me! . . .

(*He starts, flinging off his thoughts—then suddenly clutching at a straw, turns hopefully to his mother*) Why did you ask me that, Mother? D'you think—?

MRS. EVANS (*hastily*) No, indeed! I don't think she is! I wouldn't say so at all!

EVANS (*dejectedly*) Oh—I thought perhaps— (*Then changing the subject*) I suppose I ought to go up and say hello to Aunt Bessie.

MRS. EVANS (*her face becoming defensive—in blunted tones, a trifle pleadingly*) I wouldn't, Sammy. She hasn't seen you since you were eight. She wouldn't know you. And you're on your honeymoon, and old age is always sad to young folks. Be happy while you can! (*Then pushing him toward door*) Look here! You catch that friend, he's just getting his car out. You drive to town with him, give me a chance to get to know my daughter-in-law, and call her to account for how she's taking care of you! (*She laughs forcedly*).

EVANS (*bursting out passionately*) Better than I deserve! She's an angel, Mother! I know you'll love her!

MRS. EVANS (*gently*) I do already, Sammy! She's so pretty and sweet!

EVANS (*kisses her—joyously*) I'll tell her that. I'm going

out this way and kiss her good-bye. (*He runs out through the kitchen door*).

MRS. EVANS (*looking after him—passionately*)

He loves her! . . . he's happy! . . . that's all that counts! . . . being happy! . . .

(*Thinking apprehensively*)

If only she isn't going to have a baby . . . if only she doesn't care so much about having one . . . I got to have it out with her . . . got to! . . . no other way . . . in mercy . . . in justice . . . this has got to end with my boy . . . and he's got to live happy! . . .

(*At the sound of steps from the kitchen she straightens up in her chair stiffly*).

NINA (*comes in from the kitchen, a cup of coffee in her hand, smiling happily*) Good morning— (*She hesitates—then shyly*) Mother. (*She comes over and kisses her—slips down and sits on the floor beside her*).

MRS. EVANS (*flusteredly—hurriedly*) Good morning! It's a real fine day, isn't it? I ought to have been here and got your breakfast, but I was out gallivanting round the place with Sammy. I hope you found everything you wanted.

NINA Indeed I did! And I ate so much I'm ashamed of myself! (*She nods at the cup of coffee and laughs*) See. I'm still at it.

MRS. EVANS Good for you!

NINA I ought to apologize for coming down so late. Sam should have called me. But I wasn't able to get to sleep until after daylight somehow.

MRS. EVANS (*strangely*) You couldn't sleep? Why? Did you feel anything funny—about this house?

NINA (*struck by her tone—looks up*) No. Why? (*Thinking*)

How her face changes! . . . what sad eyes! . . .

MRS. EVANS (*thinking in an agony of apprehension*)

Got to start in to tell her . . . got to . . .

NINA (*apprehensive herself now*)

That sick dead feeling . . . when something is going to happen . . . I felt it before I got the cable about Gordon . . .

(*Then taking a sip of coffee, and trying to be pleasantly casual*) Sam said you wanted to talk to me.

MRS. EVANS (*dully*) Yes. You love my boy, don't you?

NINA (*startled—forcing a smile, quickly*) Why, of course! (*Reassuring herself*)

No, it isn't a lie . . . I do love him . . . the father of my baby . . .

MRS. EVANS (*blurts out*) Are you going to have a baby, Nina?

NINA (*she presses* MRS. EVANS' *hand—simply*) Yes, Mother.

MRS. EVANS (*in her blunt flat tones—with a mechanical rapidity to her words*) Don't you think it's too soon? Don't you think you better wait until Sammy's making more money? Don't you think it'll be a drag on him and you? Why don't you just go on being happy together, just you two?

NINA (*thinking frightenedly*)

What is behind what she's saying? . . . that feeling of death again! . . .

(*Moving away from her—repulsed*) No, I don't think any of those things, Mrs. Evans. I want a baby—beyond everything! We both do!

MRS. EVANS (*hopelessly*) I know. (*Then grimly*) But you can't! You've got to make up your mind you can't! (*Thinking fiercely—even with satisfaction*)

Tell her! . . . make her suffer what I was made to suffer! . . . I've been too lonely! . . .

NINA (*thinking with terrified foreboding*)

I knew it! . . . Out of a blue sky . . . black! . . .

(*Springing to her feet—bewilderedly*) What do you mean? How can you say a thing like that?

MRS. EVANS (*reaching out her hand tenderly, trying to touch* NINA) It's because I want Sammy—and you, too, child—to be happy. (*Then as* NINA *shrinks away from her hand—in her blunted tones*) You just can't.

NINA (*defiantly*) But I can! I have already! I mean—I am, didn't you understand me?

MRS. EVANS (*gently*) I know it's hard. (*Then inexorably*) But you can't go on!

NINA (*violently*) I don't believe you know what you're saying! It's too terrible for you—Sam's own mother—how would you have felt if someone—when you were going to have Sam—came to you and said—?

MRS. EVANS (*thinking fiercely*)

Now's my chance! . . .

(*Tonelessly*) They did say it! Sam's own father did—my husband! And I said it to myself! And I did all I could, all my husband could think of, so's I wouldn't—but we didn't know enough. And right to the time the pains come on, I prayed Sammy'd be born dead, and Sammy's father prayed, but Sammy was born healthy and smiling, and we just had to love him, and live in fear. He doubled the torment of fear we lived in. And that's what you'd be in for. And Sammy, he'd go the way his father went. And your baby, you'd be bringing it into torment. (*A bit violently*) I tell you it'd be a crime—a crime worse than murder! (*Then recovering—commiseratingly*) So you just can't, Nina!

NINA (*who has been listening distractedly—thinking*)

Don't listen to her! . . . feeling of death! . . . what is it? . . . she's trying to kill my baby! . . . oh, I hate her! . . .

(*Hysterically resentful*) What do you mean? Why don't you speak plainly? (*Violently*) I think you're horrible! Praying your baby would be born dead! That's a lie! You couldn't!

MRS. EVANS (*thinking*)

I know what she's doing now . . . just what I did . . . trying not to believe . . .

(*Fiercely*)

But I'll make her! . . . she's got to suffer, too! . . . I been too lonely! . . . she's got to share and help me save my Sammy! . . .

(*With an even more blunted flat relentless tonelessness*) I thought I was plain, but I'll be plainer. Only remember it's a family secret and now you're one of the family. It's the curse on the Evanses. My husband's mother—she was an only child—died in an asylum and her father before her. I know that for a fact. And my husband's sister, Sammy's aunt, she's out of her mind. She lives on the top floor of this house, hasn't been out of her room in years, I've taken care of her. She just sits, doesn't say a word, but she's happy, she laughs to herself a lot, she hasn't a care in the world. But I remember when she was all right, she was always unhappy, she never got married, most people around here were afraid of the Evanses in spite of their being rich for hereabouts. They knew about the craziness going back, I guess, for heaven knows how long. I didn't know about the Evanses until after I'd married my husband. He came to the town I lived in, no one there knew about the Evanses. He didn't tell me until after we were married. He asked me to forgive him, he said he loved me so much he'd have gone mad without me, said I was his only hope of salvation. So I forgave him. I loved him an awful lot. I said to myself, I'll be his salvation—and maybe I could have been if we hadn't had Sammy born. My husband kept real well up to then. We'd swore we'd never have children, we never forgot to be careful for two whole years. Then one night we'd both gone to a dance, we'd both had a little punch to drink, just enough—to forget—driving home in the moonlight—that moonlight!—such little things at the back of big things!

NINA (*in a dull moan*) I don't believe you! I won't believe you!

MRS. EVANS (*drones on*) My husband, Sammy's father, in spite of all he and I fought against it, he finally gave in to it when Sammy was only eight, he couldn't keep up any more living in fear for Sammy, thinking any minute the curse might get him, every time he was sick, or had a headache, or bumped his head, or started crying, or had a nightmare and screamed, or said something queer like children do naturally. (*A bit stridently*) Living like that with that fear is awful torment! I know that! I went through it by his side! It nearly drove me crazy, too—but I didn't have it in my blood! And that's why I'm telling you! You got to see you can't, Nina!

NINA (*suddenly breaking out—frenziedly*) I don't believe you! I don't believe Sam would ever have married me if he knew—!

MRS. EVANS (*sharply*) Who said Sammy knew? He don't know a single thing about it! That's been the work of my life, keeping him from knowing. When his father gave up and went off into it I sent Sammy right off to boarding school. I told him his father was sick, and a little while after I sent word his father was dead, and from then on until his father did really die during Sammy's second year to college, I kept him away at school in winter and camp in summers and I went to see him, I never let him come home. (*With a sigh*) It was hard, giving up Sammy, knowing I was making him forget he had a mother. I was glad taking care of them two kept me so busy I didn't get much chance to think then. But here's what I've come to think since, Nina: I'm certain sure my husband might have kept his mind with the help of my love if I hadn't had Sammy. And if I'd never had Sammy I'd never have loved Sammy—or missed him, would I?—and I'd have kept my husband.

NINA (*not heeding this last—with wild mockery*) And I thought Sam was so normal—so healthy and sane—not like me! I thought he'd give me such healthy, happy children and I'd forget myself in them and learn to love him!

MRS. EVANS (*horrified, jumping to her feet*) Learn to? You told me you did love Sammy!

NINA No! Maybe I almost have—lately—but only when I thought of his baby! Now I hate him! (*She begins to weep hysterically.* MRS. EVANS *goes to her and puts her arms around her.* NINA *sobs out)* Don't touch me! I hate you, too! Why didn't you tell him he must never marry!

MRS. EVANS What reason could I give, without telling him everything? And I never heard about you till after you were married. Then I wanted to write to you but I was scared he might read it. And I couldn't leave her upstairs to come away to see you. I kept writing Sammy to bring you here right off, although having him come frightened me to death for fear he might get to suspect something. You got to get him right away from here, Nina! I just kept hoping you wouldn't want children right away—young folks don't nowadays—until I'd seen you and told you everything. And I thought you'd love him like I did his father, and be satisfied with him alone.

NINA (*lifting her head—wildly*) No! I don't! I won't! I'll leave him!

MRS. EVANS (*shaking her, fiercely*) You can't! He'd go crazy sure then! You'd be a devil! Don't you see how he loves you?

NINA (*breaking away from her—harshly*) Well, I don't love him! I only married him because he needed me—and I needed children! And now you tell me I've got to kill my—oh, yes, I see I've got to, you needn't argue any more! I love it too much to make it run that chance! And I hate it too, now, because it's sick, it's not my baby, it's his! (*With terrible ironic bitterness*) And still you can dare to tell me I can't even leave Sam!

MRS. EVANS (*very sadly and bitterly*) You just said you married him because he needed you. Don't he need you now—more'n ever? But I can't tell you not to leave him, not if you don't love him. But you oughtn't to have married him when you didn't love him. And it'll be your fault, what'll happen.

NINA (*torturedly*) What will happen?—what do you mean? —Sam will be all right—just as he was before—and it's not my fault anyway!—it's not my fault! (*Then thinking conscience-strickenly*)

> Poor Sam . . . she's right . . . it's not his fault . . . it's mine . . . I wanted to use him to save myself . . . I acted the coward again . . . as I did with Gordon . . .

MRS. EVANS (grimly) You know what'll happen to him if you leave him—after all I've told you! (*Then breaking into intense pleading*) Oh, I'd get down on my knees to you, don't make my boy run that risk! You got to give one Evans, the last one, a chance to live in this world! And you'll learn to love him, if you give up enough for him! (*Then with a grim smile*) Why, I even love that idiot upstairs, I've taken care of her so many years, lived her life for her with my life, you might say. You give your life to Sammy, then you'll love him same as you love yourself. You'll have to! That's sure as death! (*She laughs a queer gentle laugh full of amused bitterness*).

NINA (*with a sort of dull stupid wonderment*) And you've found peace?—

MRS. EVANS (*sardonically*) There's peace in the green fields of Eden, they say! You got to die to find out! (*Then proudly*) But I can say I feel proud of having lived fair to them that gave me love and trusted in me!

NINA (*struck—confusedly*) Yes—that's true, isn't it? (*Thinking strangely*)

> Lived fair . . . pride . . . trust . . . play the game! . . . who is speaking to me . . . Gordon! . . . oh, Gordon, do you mean I must give Sam the life I didn't give you? . . . Sam loved you too . . . he said, if we have a boy, we'll call him Gordon in Gordon's honor . . . Gordon's honor! . . . what must I do now in your honor, Gordon? . . . yes! . . . I know! . . .

(*Speaking mechanically in a dull voice*) All right, Mother. I'll stay with Sam. There's nothing else I can do, is there, when it isn't his fault, poor boy! (*Then suddenly snapping and bursting out in a despairing cry*) But I'll be so lonely! I'll have lost my baby! (*She sinks down on her knees at* MRS. EVANS' *feet—piteously*) Oh, Mother, how can I keep on living?

MRS. EVANS (*thinking miserably*)

> Now she knows my suffering . . . now I got to help her . . . she's got a right to have a baby . . . another baby . . . sometime . . . somehow . . . she's giving her life to have my Sammy . . . I got to save her! . . .

(*Stammeringly*) Maybe, Nina—

NINA (*dully and resentfully again now*) And how about Sam? You want him to be happy, don't you? It's just as important for him as it is for me that I should have a baby! If you know anything at all about him, you ought to see that!

MRS. EVANS (*sadly*) I know that. I see that in him, Nina. (*Gropingly*) There must be a way—somehow. I remember when I was carrying Sam, sometimes I'd forget I was a wife, I'd only remember the child in me. And then I used to wish I'd gone out deliberate in our first year, without my husband knowing, and picked a man, a healthy male to breed by, same's we do with stock, to give the man I loved a healthy child. And if I didn't love that other man nor him me where would be the harm? Then God would whisper: "It'd be a sin, adultery, the worst sin!" But after He'd gone I'd argue back again to myself, then we'd have a healthy child, I needn't be afraid! And maybe my husband would feel without ever knowing how he felt it, that I wasn't afraid and that child wasn't cursed and so he needn't fear and I could save him. (*Then scornfully*) But I was too afraid of God then to have ever done it! (*Then very simply*) He loved children so, my poor husband did, and the way they took to him, you never saw anything like it, he was a natural born father. And Sammy's the same.

NINA (*as from a distance—strangely*) Yes, Sammy's the same. But I'm not the same as you. (*Defiantly*) I don't believe in God the Father!

MRS. EVANS (*strangely*) Then it'd be easy for you. (*With a grim smile*) And I don't believe in Him, neither, not any more. I used to be a great one for worrying about what's God and what's devil, but I got richly over it living here with poor folks that was being punished for no sins of their own, and me being punished with them for no sin but loving much. (*With decision*) Being happy, that's the nearest we can ever come to knowing what's good! Being happy, that's good! The rest is just talk! (*She pauses—then with a strange austere sternness*) I love my boy, Sammy. I could see how much he wants you to have a baby. Sammy's got to feel sure you love him—to be happy. Whatever you can do to make him happy is good—is good, Nina! I don't care what! You've got to have a healthy baby—sometime—so's you can both be happy! It's your rightful duty!

NINA (*confusedly—in a half-whisper*) Yes, Mother. (*Thinking longingly*)

> I want to be happy! . . . it's my right . . . and my duty! . . .

(*Then suddenly in guilty agony*)

> Oh, my baby . . . my poor baby . . . I'm forgetting you . . . desiring another after you are dead! . . . I feel you beating against my heart for mercy . . . oh! . . .

(*She weeps with bitter anguish*).

MRS. EVANS (*gently and with deep sympathy*) I know what you're suffering. And I wouldn't say what I just said now only I know us two mustn't see each other ever again. You and Sammy have got to forget me. (*As* NINA *makes a motion of protest—grimly and inexorably*) Oh, yes, you will—easy. People forget everything. They got to, poor people! And I'm saying what I said about a healthy baby so's you will remember it when you need to, after you've forgotten—this one.

NINA (*sobbing pitifully*) Don't! Please, Mother!

MRS. EVANS (*with sudden tenderness—gathering* NINA *up in her arms, brokenly*) You poor child! You're like the daughter of my sorrow! You're closer to me now than ever Sammy could be! I want you to be happy! (*She begins to sob, too, kissing* NINA'S *bowed head*).

CURTAIN

ACT FOUR

SCENE: *An evening early in the following winter about seven months later. The* PROFESSOR'S *study again. The books in the cases have never been touched, their austere array shows no gaps, but the glass separating them from the world is gray with dust, giving them a blurred ghostly quality. The table, although it is the same, is no longer the* PROFESSOR'S *table, just as the other furniture in the room, by its disarrangement, betrays that the* PROFESSOR'S *well-ordered mind no longer trims it to his personality. The table has become neurotic. Volumes of the* Encyclopaedia Britannica *mixed up with popular treatises on mind training for success, etc., looking startlingly modern and disturbing against the background of classics in the original, are slapped helter-skelter on top of each other on it. The titles of these books face in all directions, no one volume is placed with any relation to the one beneath it—the effect is that they have no connected meaning. The rest of the table is littered with an ink bottle, pens, pencils, erasers, a box of typewriting paper, and a typewriter at the center before the chair, which is pushed back, setting the rug askew. On the floor beside the table are an overflowing wastepaper basket, a few sheets of paper and the rubber cover for the typewriter like a collapsed tent. The rocking chair is no longer at center but has been pulled nearer the table, directly faces it with its back to the bench. This bench in turn has been drawn much closer, but is now placed more to the rear and half faces front, its back squarely to the door in the corner.*

EVANS *is seated in the* PROFESSOR'S *old chair. He has evidently been typing, or is about to type, for a sheet of paper can be seen in the machine. He smokes a pipe, which he is always relighting whether it needs it or not, and which he bites and shifts about and pulls in and out and puffs at nervously. His expression is dispirited, his eyes shift about, his shoulders are collapsed submissively. He seems much thinner, his face drawn and sallow. The collegiate clothes are no longer natty, they need pressing and look too big for him.*

EVANS (*turns to his typewriter and pounds out a few words with a sort of aimless desperation—then tears the sheet out of the machine with an exclamation of disgust, crumples it up and throws it violently on the floor, pushing his chair back and jumping to his feet*) Hell! (*He begins pacing up and down the room, puffing at his pipe, thinking tormentedly*)

No use . . . can't think of a darn thing . . . well, who could dope out a novel ad on another powdered milk, anyway? . . . all the stuff been used already . . . Tartars conquering on dried mares' milk . . . Metchnikoff, eminent scientist . . . been done to death . . . but simply got to work out something or . . . Cole said, what's been the matter with you lately? . . . you started off so well . . . I thought you were a real find, but your work's fallen off to nothing . . .

(*He sits down on the edge of the bench nearby, his shoulders hunched—despondently*)

Couldn't deny it . . . been going stale ever since we came back from that trip home . . . no ideas . . . I'll get fired . . . sterile . . .

(*With a guilty terror*)

in more ways than one, I guess! . . .

(*He springs to his feet as if this idea were a pin stuck in him—lighting his already lighted pipe, walks up and down again, forcing his thoughts into other channels*)

Bet the old man turns over in his grave at my writing ads in his study . . . maybe that's why I can't . . . bum influence . . . try tomorrow in my bedroom . . . sleeping alone . . . since Nina got sick . . . some woman's sickness . . . wouldn't tell me . . . too modest . . . still, there are some things a husband has a right to know . . . especially when we haven't . . . in five months . . . doctor told her she mustn't, she said . . . what doctor? . . . she's never said . . . what the hell's the matter with you, do you think Nina's lying? . . . no . . . but . . .

(*Desperately*)

If I was only sure it was because she's really sick . . . not just sick of me! . . .

(*He sinks down in the rocking chair despondently*)

Certainly been a big change in her . . . since that visit home . . . what happened between Mother and her? . . . she says nothing . . . they seemed to like each other . . . both of them cried when we left . . . still, Nina insisted on going that same day and Mother seemed anxious to get rid of us . . . can't make it out . . . next few weeks Nina couldn't be loving enough . . . I never was so happy . . . then she crashed . . . strain of waiting and hoping she'd get pregnant . . . and nothing happening . . . that's what did it . . . my fault! . . . how d'you know? . . . you can't tell that! . . .

(*He jumps to his feet again—walks up and down again distractedly*)

God, if we'd only have a kid! . . . then I'd show them all what I could do! . . . Cole always used to say I had the stuff, and Ned certainly thought so. . . .

(*With sudden relieved excitement*)

By gosh, I was forgetting! . . . Ned's coming out tonight . . . forgot to tell Nina . . . mustn't let her get wise I got him to come to look her over . . . she'd hate me for swallowing my pride after he's never been to see us . . . but I had to . . . this has got my goat . . . I've got to know what's wrong . . . and Ned's the only one I can trust . . .

(*He flings himself on chair in front of desk and, picking up a fresh sheet of paper, jams it into the machine*)

Gosh, I ought to try and get a new start on this before it's time . . .

(*He types a sentence or two, a strained frown of concentration on his face.* NINA *comes silently through the door and stands just inside it looking at him. She has grown thin again, her face is pale and drawn, her movements are those of extreme nervous tension*).

NINA (*before she can stifle her immediate reaction of contempt and dislike*)

How weak he is! . . . he'll never do anything . . . never give me my desire . . . if he'd only fall in love with someone else . . . go away . . . not be here in my father's room . . . I even have to give him a home . . . if he'd disappear . . . leave me free . . . if he'd die . . .

(*Checking herself—remorsefully*)

I must stop such thoughts . . . I don't mean it . . . poor Sam! . . . trying so hard . . . loving me so much . . . I give so little in return . . . he feels I'm always watching him with scorn . . . I can't tell him it's with pity . . . how can I help watching him? . . . help worrying over his worry because of what it might lead to . . . after what his mother . . . how horrible life is! . . . he's worried now . . . he doesn't sleep . . . I hear him tossing about . . . I must sleep with him again soon . . . he's only home two nights a week . . . it isn't fair of me . . . I must try . . . I must! . . . he suspects my revulsion . . . it's hurting him . . . oh, poor dead baby I dared not bear, how I might have loved your father for your sake! . . .

EVANS (*suddenly feeling her presence, jerks himself to his feet—with a diffident guilty air which is noticeable about him now whenever he is in her presence*) Hello, dear. I thought you were lying down. (*Guiltily*) Did the noise of my typing bother you? I'm terribly sorry!

NINA (*irritated in spite of herself*)

Why is he always cringing? . . .

(*She comes forward to the chair at center and sits down—forcing a smile*) But there's nothing to be terribly sorry about! (*As he stands awkward and confused, like a schoolboy who has been called on to recite and cannot and is being "bawled out" before the class, she forces a playful tone*) Goodness, Sam, how tragic you can get about nothing at all!

EVANS (*still forced to justify himself—contritely*) I know it isn't pleasant for you having me drag my work out here, trying to pound out rotten ads. (*With a short laugh*) Trying to is right! (*Blurts out*) I wouldn't do it except that Cole gave me a warning to buck up—or get out.

NINA (*stares at him, more annoyed, her eyes hardening, thinking*)

Yes! . . . he'll always be losing one job, getting another, starting with a burst of confidence each time, then . . .

(*Cutting him with a careless sneering tone*) Well, it isn't a job to worry much about losing, is it?

EVANS (*wincing pitiably*) No, not much money. But I used to think there was a fine chance to rise there—but of course that's my fault, I haven't made good— (*He finishes miserably*) somehow.

NINA (*her antagonism giving way to remorseful pity*)

What makes me so cruel? . . . he's so defenseless . . . his mother's baby . . . poor sick baby! . . . poor Sam!

(*She jumps to her feet and goes over to him*).

EVANS (*as she comes—with a defensive, boastful bravery*) Oh, I can get another job just as good, all right—maybe a lot better.

NINA (*reassuringly*) Certainly, you can! And I'm sure you're not going to lose this one. You're always anticipating trouble. (*She kisses him and sits on the arm of his chair, putting an arm around his neck and pulling his head on to her breast*) And it isn't your fault, you big goose, you! It's mine. I know how hard it makes everything for you, being tied to a wife who's too sick to be a wife. You ought to have married a big strapping, motherly—

EVANS (*in the seventh heaven now—passionately*) Bunk! All the other women in the world aren't worth your little finger! It's you who ought to have married someone worth while, not a poor fish like me! But no one could love you more than I do, no matter what he was!

NINA (*presses his head on her breast, avoiding his eyes, kisses him on the forehead*) And I love you, Sam. (*Staring out over his head—with loving pity, thinking*)

I almost do . . . poor unfortunate boy! . . . at these moments . . . as his mother loves him . . . but that isn't enough for him . . . I can hear his mother saying, "Sammy's got to feel sure you love him . . . to be happy." . . . I must try to make him feel sure . . .

(*Speaking gently*) I want you to be happy, Sam.

EVANS (*his face transformed with happiness*) I am—a hundred times more than I deserve!

NINA (*presses his head down on her breast so he cannot see her eyes—gently*) Ssshh. (*Thinking sadly*)

I promised her . . . but I couldn't see how hard it would be to let him love me . . . after his baby . . . was gone . . . it was hard even to keep on living . . . after that operation . . . Gordon's spirit followed me from room to room . . . poor reproachful ghost! . . .

(*With bitter mockery*)

Oh, Gordon, I'm afraid this is a deeper point of honor than any that was ever shot down in flames! . . . what would your honor say now? . . . "Stick to him! . . . play the game!" . . . oh, yes, I know . . . I'm sticking . . . but he isn't happy . . . I'm trying to play the game . . . then why do I keep myself from him? . . . but I was really sick . . . for a time after . . . since then, I couldn't . . . but . . . oh, I'll try . . . I'll try soon . . .

(*Tenderly—but having to force herself to say it*) Doesn't my boy want to sleep with me again—sometime soon?

EVANS (*passionately—hardly able to believe his ears*) Oh, it'd be wonderful, Nina! But are you sure you really want me to—that you'll feel well enough?

NINA (*repeats his words as if she were memorizing a lesson*) Yes, I want you to. Yes, I'll feel well enough. (*He seizes her hand and kisses it in a passionately grateful silence—she thinks with resigned finality*)

There, Sammy's mother and Gordon . . . I'll play the game . . . it will make him happy for a while . . . as he was in those weeks after we'd left his mother . . . when I gave myself with a mad pleasure in torturing myself for his pleasure! . . .

(*Then with weary hopelessness*)

He'll be happy until he begins to feel guilty again because I'm not pregnant . . .

(*With a grim bitter smile*)

Poor Sam, if he only knew the precautions . . . as if I wouldn't die rather than take the slightest chance of that happening! . . . ever again . . . what a tragic joke it was on both of us! . . . I wanted my baby so! . . . oh, God! . . . his mother said . . . "You've got to have a healthy baby . . . sometime . . . it's your rightful duty" . . . that seemed right then . . . but now . . . it seems cowardly . . . to betray poor Sam . . . and vile to give myself . . . without love or desire . . . and yet I've given myself to men before without a thought just to give them a moment's happiness . . . can't I do that again? . . . when it's a case of Sam's happiness? . . . and my own? . . .

(*She gets up from beside him with a hunted movement*) It must be half past eight. Charlie's coming to bring his suggestions on my outline for Gordon's biography.

EVANS (*his bliss shattered—dejectedly*)

Always happens . . . just as we get close . . . something comes between . . .

(*Then confusedly*) Say, I forgot to tell you Ned's coming out tonight.

NINA (*astonished*) Ned Darrell?

EVANS Sure. I happened to run into him the other day and invited him and he said Saturday evening. He couldn't tell what train. Said never mind meeting him.

NINA (*excitedly*) Why didn't you tell me before, you big booby! (*She kisses him*) There, don't mind. But it's just like you. Now someone'll have to go down to the store. And I'll have to get the spare room ready. (*She hurries to the doorway. He follows her*).

EVANS I'll help you.

NINA You'll do nothing of the kind! You'll stay right downstairs and bring them in here and cover up my absence. Thank heavens, Charlie won't stay long if Ned is here. (*The doorbell rings—excitedly*) There's one of them now. I'll run upstairs. Come up and tell me if it's Ned—and get rid of Charlie. (*She kisses him playfully and hurries out*).

EVANS (*looking after her—thinks*)

She seems better tonight . . . happier . . . she seems to love me . . . if she'll only get all well again, then everything will . . .

(*The bell rings again*)

I must give Ned a good chance to talk to her . . .

(*He goes out to the outer door—returns a moment later with* MARSDEN. *The latter's manner is preoccupied and nervous. His face has an expression of anxiety which he tries to conceal. He seems a prey to some inner fear he is trying to hide even from himself and is resolutely warding off from his consciousness. His tall, thin body stoops as if a part of its sustaining will had been removed).*

EVANS (*with a rather forced welcoming note*) Come on in, Charlie. Nina's upstairs lying down.

MARSDEN (*with marked relief*) Then by all means don't disturb her. I just dropped in to bring back her outline with the suggestions I've made. (*He has taken some papers out of his pocket and hands them to* EVANS) I couldn't have stayed but a minute in any event. Mother is a bit under the weather these days.

EVANS (*perfunctorily*) Too bad. (*Thinking vindictively*)

Serve her right, the old scandal-monger, after the way she's gossiped about Nina! . . .

MARSDEN (*with assumed carelessness*) Just a little indigestion. Nothing serious but it annoys her terribly. (*Thinking frightenedly*)

That dull pain she complains of . . . I don't like it . . . and she won't see anyone but old Doctor Tibbetts . . . she's sixty-eight . . . I can't help fearing . . . no! . . .

EVANS (*bored—vaguely*) Well, I suppose you've got to be careful of every little thing when you get to her age.

MARSDEN (*positively bristling*) Her age? Mother isn't so old!

EVANS (*surprised*) Over sixty five, isn't she?

MARSDEN (*indignantly*) You're quite out there! She's still under sixty-five—and in health and spirits she isn't more than fifty! Every one remarks that! (*Annoyed at himself*)

Why did I lie to him about her age? . . . I must be on edge . . . Mother is rather difficult to live with these days, getting me worried to death, when it's probably nothing . . .

EVANS (*annoyed in his turn—thinking*)

Why all the fuss? . . . as if I gave a damn if the old girl was a million! . . .

(*Indicating the papers*) I'll give these to Nina first thing in the morning.

MARSDEN (*mechanically*) Righto. Thank you. (*He starts to go toward door—then turns—fussily*) But you'd better take a look while I'm here and see if it's clear. I've written on the margins. See if there's anything you can't make out. (EVANS *nods helplessly and begins reading the sheets, going back beneath the lamp).*

MARSDEN (*looking around him with squeamish disapproval*)

What a mess they've made of this study . . . poor Professor! . . . dead and forgotten . . . and his tomb desecrated . . . does Sam write his ads here of a week-end now? . . . the last touch! . . . and Nina labors with love at Gordon's biography . . . whom the Professor hated! . . . "life is so full of a number of things!" . . . why does everyone in the world think they can write? . . . but I've only myself to blame . . . why in the devil did I ever suggest it to her? . . . because I hoped my helping her while Sam was in the city would bring us alone together? . . . but I made the suggestion before she had that abortion performed! . . . how do you know she did? . . . because I know! . . . there are psychic affinities . . . her body confessed . . . and since then, I've felt an aversion . . . as if she were a criminal . . . she is! . . . how could she? . . . why? . . . I thought she wanted a child . . . but evidently I don't know her . . . I suppose, afraid it would spoil her figure . . . her flesh . . . her power to enslave men's senses . . . mine . . . and I had hoped . . . looked forward to her becoming a mother . . . for my peace of mind. . . .

(*Catching himself—violently*)

Shut up! . . . what a base creature I'm becoming! . . . to have such thoughts when Mother is sick and I ought to be thinking only of her! . . . and it's none of my damn business, anyway! . . .

(*Glaring at* EVANS *resentfully as if he were to blame*)

Look at him! . . . he'll never suspect anything! . . . what a simple-simon! . . . he adored Gordon as a newsboy does a champion pugilist! . . . and Nina writes of Gordon as if he had been a demi-god! . . . when actually he came from the commonest people! . . .

(*He suddenly speaks to* EVANS *with a really savage satisfaction*) Did I tell you I once looked up Gordon's family in Beachampton? A truly deplorable lot! When I remembered Gordon and looked at his father I had either to suspect a lover in the wood pile or to believe in an immaculate conception . . . that is, until I saw his mother! Then a stork became the only conceivable explanation!

EVANS (*who has only half-heard and hasn't understood, says vaguely*) I never saw his folks. (*Indicating the papers*) I can make this all out all right.

MARSDEN (*sarcastically*) I'm glad it's understandable!

EVANS (*blunderingly*) I'll give it to Nina—and I hope your mother is feeling better tomorrow.

MARSDEN (*piqued*) Oh, I'm going. Why didn't you tell me if I was interrupting—your writing!

EVANS (*immediately guilty*) Oh, come on, Charlie, don't get peevish, you know I didn't mean— (*The bell rings.* EVANS *stammers in confusion, trying at a nonchalant air*) Hello! That must be Ned. You remember Darrell. He's coming out for a little visit. Excuse me. (He blunders out of the door).

MARSDEN (*looking after him with anger mixed with alarmed suspicion and surprise*)

> Darrell? . . . what's he doing here? . . . have they been meeting? . . . perhaps he was the one who performed the . . . no, his idea was she ought to have a child . . . but if she came and begged him? . . . but why should Nina beg not to have a baby? . . .

(*Distractedly*)

> Oh, I don't know! . . . it's all a sordid mess! . . . I ought to be going home! . . . I don't want to see Darrell! . . .

(*He starts for the door—then struck by a sudden thought, stops*)

> Wait . . . I could ask him about Mother . . . yes . . . good idea . . .

(*He comes back to the middle of the room, front, and is standing there when* DARRELL *enters, followed by* EVANS. DARRELL *has not changed in appearance except that his expression is graver and more thoughtful. His manner is more convincingly authoritative, more mature. He takes in* MARSDEN *from head to foot with one comprehensive glance*).

EVANS (*awkwardly*) Ned, you remember Charlie Marsden?

MARSDEN (*holding out his hand, urbanely polite*) How are you, Doctor?

DARRELL (*shaking his hand—briefly*) Hello.

EVANS I'll go up and tell Nina you're here, Ned. (*He goes, casting a resentful glance at* MARSDEN).

MARSDEN (*awkwardly, as* DARRELL *sits down in the chair at center, goes over and stands by the table*) I was on the point of leaving when you rang. Then I decided to stop and renew our acquaintance. (*He stoops and picks up one sheet of paper, and puts it back carefully on the table*).

DARRELL (*watching him—thinking*)

> Neat . . . suspiciously neat . . . he's an old maid who seduces himself in his novels . . . so I suspect . . . I'd like a chance to study him more closely . . . .

MARSDEN (*thinking resentfully*)

What a boor! . . . he might say something! . . .

(*Forcing a smile*) And I wanted to ask a favor of you, a word of advice as to the best specialist, the very best, it would be possible to consult—

DARRELL (*sharply*) On what?

MARSDEN (*almost naïvely*) My mother has a pain in her stomach.

DARRELL (*amused—dryly*) Possibly she eats too much.

MARSDEN (*as he bends and carefully picks another sheet from the floor to place it as carefully on the table*) She doesn't eat enough to keep a canary alive. It's a dull, constant pain, she says. She's terribly worried. She's terrified by the idea of cancer. But, of course, that's perfect rot, she's never been sick a day in her life and—

DARRELL (*sharply*) She's showing more intelligence about her pain than you are.

MARSDEN (*bending down for another sheet, his voice trembling with terror*) I don't understand—quite. Do you mean to say you think—?

DARRELL (*brutally*) It's possible.

(*He has pulled out his pen and a card and is writing. Thinking grimly*)

Explode a bomb under him, as I did once before . . . only way to get him started doing anything. . . .

MARSDEN (*angrily*) But—that's nonsense!

DARRELL (*with satisfaction—unruffledly*) People who are afraid to face unpleasant possibilities until it's too late commit more murders and suicides than— (*Holds out card*) Doctor Schultz is your man. Take her to see him—tomorrow!

MARSDEN (*bursting out in anger and misery*) Damn it, you're condemning her without—! (*He breaks down chokingly*) You've no damn right!— (*He bends down, trembling all over, to pick up another piece of paper*).

DARRELL (*genuinely astonished and contrite*)

And I thought he was so ingrown he didn't care a damn about anyone! . . . his mother . . . now I begin to see him . . .

(*He jumps from his chair and going to* MARSDEN *puts a hand on his shoulder—kindly*) I beg your pardon, Marsden. I only wanted to drive it in that all delay is dangerous. Your mother's pain may be due to any number of harmless causes, but you owe it to her to make sure. Here. (*He hands out the card*).

MARSDEN (*straightens up and takes it, his eyes grateful

now—humbly) Thank you. I'll take her to see him tomorrow. (EVANS *comes in*).

EVANS (*to* MARSDEN, *blunderingly*) Say, Charlie, I don't want to hurry you but Nina wants some things at the store before it closes, and if you'd give me a lift—

MARSDEN (*dully*) Of course. Come along. (*He shakes hands with* DARRELL) Good night, Doctor—and thank you.

DARRELL Good night. (MARSDEN *goes, followed by* EVANS).

EVANS (*turns in the doorway and says meaningly*) Nina'll be right down. For Pete's sake, have a good heart-to-heart talk with her, Ned!

DARRELL (*frowning—impatiently*) Oh—all right! Run along. (EVANS *goes.* DARRELL *remains standing near the table looking after them, thinking about* MARSDEN)

> Queer fellow, Marsden . . . mother's boy still . . . if she dies what will he do? . . .

(*Then dismissing* MARSDEN *with a shrug of his shoulders. He moves around the table examining its disorder critically, then sits down in armchair—amused*)

> Evidences of authorship . . . Sam's ads? . . . isn't making good, he said . . . was I wrong in thinking he had stuff in him? . . . hope not . . . always liked Sam, don't know why exactly . . . said Nina'd gotten into a bad state again . . . what's happened to their marriage? . . . I felt a bit sorry for myself at their wedding . . . not that I'd ever fallen . . . but I did envy him in a way . . . she always had strong physical attraction for me . . . that time I kissed her . . . one reason I've steered clear since . . . take no chances on emotional Didos . . . need all my mind on my work . . . got rid of even that slight suspicion . . . I'd forgotten all about her . . . she's a strange girl . . . interesting case . . . I should have kept in touch on that account . . . hope she'll tell me about herself . . . can't understand her not having child . . . it's so obviously the sensible thing . . .

(*Cynically*)

> Probably why . . . to expect common sense of people proves you're lacking in it yourself! . . .

NINA (*enters silently. She has fixed herself up, put on her best dress, arranged her hair, rouged, etc.—but it is principally her mood that has changed her, making her appear a younger, prettier person for the moment.* DARRELL *immediately senses her presence, and, looking up, gets to his feet with a smile of affectionate admiration. She comes quickly over to him saying with frank pleasure*) Hello, Ned. I'm certainly glad to see you again—after all these years!

DARRELL (*as they shake hands—smiling*) Not as long as all that, is it? (*Thinking admiringly*)

Wonderful-looking as ever . . . Sam is a lucky devil! . . .

NINA (*thinking*)

Strong hands like Gordon's . . . take hold of you . . . not like Sam's . . . yielding fingers that let you fall back into yourself . . .

(*Teasingly*) I ought to cut you dead after the shameful way you've ignored us!

DARRELL (*a bit embarrassedly*) I've really meant to write. (*His eyes examining her keenly*)

Been through a lot since I saw her . . . face shows it . . . nervous tension pronounced . . . hiding behind her smile . . .

NINA (*uneasy under his glance*)

I hate that professional look in his eyes . . . watching symptoms . . . without seeing me . . .

(*With resentful mockery*) Well, what do you suspect is wrong with the patient now, Doctor? (*She laughs nervously*) Sit down, Ned. I suppose you can't help your diagnosing stare. (*She turns from him and sits down in the rocker at center*).

DARRELL (*quickly averting his eyes—sits down—jokingly*) Same old unjust accusation! You were always reading diagnosis into me, when what I was really thinking was what fine eyes you had, or what a becoming gown, or—

NINA (*smiling*) Or what a becoming alibi you could cook up! Oh, I know you! (*With a sudden change of mood she laughs gaily and naturally*) But you're forgiven—that is, if you can explain why you've never been to see us.

DARRELL Honestly, Nina, I've been so rushed with work I haven't had a chance to go anywhere.

NINA Or an inclination!

DARRELL (*smiling*) Well—maybe.

NINA Do you like the Institute so much? (*He nods gravely*) Is it the big opportunity you wanted?

DARRELL (*simply*) I think it is.

NINA (*with a smile*) Well, you're the taking kind for whom opportunities are made!

DARRELL (*smiling*) I hope so.

NINA (*sighing*) I wish that could be said of more of us— (*Then quickly*) —meaning myself.

DARRELL (*thinking with a certain satisfaction*)

Meaning Sam . . . that doesn't look hopeful for future wedded bliss! . . .

(*Teasingly*) But I heard you were "taking an opportunity" to go in for literature—collaborating with Marsden.

NINA No, Charlie is only going to advise. He'd never deign to appear as co-author. And besides, he never appreciated the real Gordon. No one did except me.

DARRELL (*thinking caustically*)

Gordon myth strong as ever . . . root of her trouble still . . .

(*Keenly inquisitive*) Sam certainly appreciated him, didn't he?

NINA (*not remembering to hide her contempt*) Sam? Why, he's the exact opposite in every way!

DARRELL (*caustically thinking*)

These heroes die hard . . . but perhaps she can write him out of her system. . . .

(*Persuasively*) Well, you're going ahead with the biography, aren't you? I think you ought to.

NINA (*dryly*) For my soul, Doctor? (*Listlessly*) I suppose I will. I don't know. I haven't much time. The duties of a wife— (*Teasingly*) By the way, if it isn't too rude to inquire, aren't you getting yourself engaged to some fair lady or other?

DARRELL (*smiling—but emphatically*) Not on your life! Not until after I'm thirty-five, at least!

NINA (*sarcastically*) Then you don't believe in taking your own medicine? Why, Doctor! Think of how much good it would do you!— (*Excitedly with a hectic sarcasm*) —if you had a nice girl to love—or was it learn to love?—and take care of—whose character you could shape and whose life you could guide and make what you pleased, in whose unselfish devotion you could find peace! (*More and more bitterly sarcastic*) And you ought to have a baby, Doctor! You will never know what life is, you'll never be really happy until you've had a baby, Doctor—a fine, healthy baby! (*She laughs a bitter, sneering laugh*).

DARRELL (*after a quick, keen glance, thinking*)

Good! . . . she's going to tell . . .

(*Meekly*) I recognize my arguments. Was I really wrong on every point, Nina?

NINA (*harshly*) On every single point, Doctor!

DARRELL (*glancing at her keenly*) But how? You haven't given the baby end of it a chance yet, have you?

NINA (*bitterly*) Oh, haven't I? (*Then bursts out with intense bitterness*) I'll have you know I'm not destined to bear babies, Doctor!

DARRELL (*startledly*)

What's that . . . why not? . . .

(*Again with a certain satisfaction*)

Can she mean Sam? . . . that he . . .

(*Soothingly—but plainly disturbed*) Why don't you begin at the beginning and tell me all about it? I feel responsible.

NINA (*fiercely*) You are! (*Then wearily*) And you're not. No one is. You didn't know. No one could know.

DARRELL (*in same tone*) Know what? (*Thinking with the same eagerness to believe something he hopes*)

She must mean no one could know that Sam wasn't . . . but I might have guessed it . . . from his general weakness . . . poor unlucky devil . . .

(*Then as she remains silent—urgingly*) Tell me. I want to help you, Nina.

NINA (*touched*) It's too late, Ned. (*Then suddenly*) I've just thought—Sam said he happened to run into you. That isn't so, is it? He went to see you and told you how worried he was about me and asked you out to see me, didn't he? (*As* DARRELL *nods*) Oh, I don't mind! It's even rather touching. (*Then mockingly*) Well, since you're out here professionally, and my husband wants me to consult you, I might as well give you the whole case history! (*Wearily*) I warn you it isn't pretty, Doctor! But then life doesn't seem to be pretty, does it? And, after all, you aided and abetted God the Father in making this mess. I hope it'll teach you not to be so cocksure in future. (*More and more bitterly*) I must say you proceeded very unscientifically, Doctor! (*Then suddenly starts her story in a dull monotonous tone recalling that of* EVANS' *mother in the previous act*) When we went to visit Sam's mother I'd known for two months that I was going to have a baby.

DARRELL (*startled—unable to hide a trace of disappointment*) Oh, then you actually were? (*Thinking disappointedly and ashamed of himself for being disappointed*)

All wrong, what I thought . . . she was going to . . . then why didn't she? . . .

NINA (*with a strange happy intensity*) Oh, Ned, I loved it more than I've ever loved anything in my life—even Gordon! I loved it so it seemed at times that Gordon must be its real father, that Gordon must have come to me in a dream while I was lying asleep beside Sam! And I was happy! I almost loved Sam then! I felt he was a good husband!

DARRELL (*instantly repelled—thinking with scornful jealousy*)

Ha! . . . the hero again! . . . comes to her bed! . . . puts horns on poor Sam! . . . becomes the father of his child! . . . I'll be damned if hers isn't the most idiotic obsession I ever . . .

NINA (*her voice suddenly becoming flat and lifeless*) And then Sam's mother told me I couldn't have my baby. You see, Doctor, Sam's great-grandfather was insane, and Sam's grandmother died in an asylum, and Sam's father had lost his mind for years before he died, and an aunt who is still alive is crazy. So of course I had to agree it would be wrong—and I had an operation.

DARRELL (*who has listened with amazed horror—profoundly shocked and stunned*) Good God! Are you crazy, Nina? I simply can't believe! It would be too hellish! Poor Sam, of all people! (*Bewilderedly*) Nina! Are you absolutely sure?

NINA (*immediately defensive and mocking*) Absolutely, Doctor! Why? Do you think it's I who am crazy? Sam looks so healthy and sane, doesn't he? He fooled you completely, didn't he? You thought he'd be an ideal husband for me! And poor Sam's fooling himself too because he doesn't know anything about all this—so you can't blame him, Doctor!

DARRELL (*thinking in a real panic of horror—and a flood of protective affection for her*)

God, this is too awful! . . . on top of all the rest! . . . how did she ever stand it! . . . she'll lose her mind too! . . . and it's my fault! . . .

(*Getting up, comes to her and puts his hands on her shoulders, standing behind her—tenderly*) Nina! I'm so damn sorry! There's only one possible thing to do now. You'll have to make Sam give you a divorce.

NINA (*bitterly*) Yes? Then what do you suppose would be his finish? No, I've enough guilt in my memory now, thank you! I've got to stick to Sam! (*Then with a strange monotonous insistence*) I've promised Sam's mother I'd make him happy! He's unhappy now because he thinks he isn't able to give me a child. And I'm unhappy because I've lost my child. So I must have another baby—somehow—don't you think, Doctor?—to make us both happy? (*She looks up at him pleadingly. For a moment they stare into each other's eyes—then both turn away in guilty confusion*).

DARRELL (*bewilderedly thinking*)

That look in her eyes . . . what does she want me to think?

. . . why does she talk so much about being happy? . . . am I happy? . . . I don't know . . . what is happiness? . . .

(*Confusedly*) Nina, I don't know what to think.

NINA (*thinking strangely*)

That look in his eyes . . .what did he mean? . . .

(*With the same monotonous insistence*) You must know what to think. I can't think it out myself any more. I need your advice—your *scientific* advice this time, if you please, Doctor. I've thought and thought about it. I've told myself it's what I ought to do. Sam's own mother urged me to do it. It's sensible and kind and just and good. I've told myself this a thousand times and yet I can't quite convince something in me that's afraid of something. I need the courage of someone who can stand outside and reason it out as if Sam and I were no more than guinea pigs. You've got to help me, Doctor! You've got to show me what's the sane—the truly sane, you understand!—thing I must do for Sam's sake, and my own.

DARRELL (*thinking confusedly*)

What do I have to do? . . . this was all my fault . . . I owe her something in return . . . I owe Sam something . . . I owe them happiness! . . .

(*Irritably*)

Damn it, there's a humming in my ears! . . . I've caught some fever . . . I swore to live coolly . . . let me see. . . .

(*In a cold, emotionless professional voice, his face like a mask of a doctor*) A doctor must be in full possession of the facts, if he is to advise. What is it precisely that Sam's wife has thought so much of doing?

NINA (*in the same insistent tone*) Of picking out a healthy male about whom she cared nothing and having a child by him that Sam would believe was his child, whose life would give him confidence in his own living, who would be for him a living proof that his wife loved him. (*Confusedly, strangely and purposefully*)

This doctor is healthy. . . .

DARRELL (*in his ultra-professional manner—like an automaton of a doctor*) I see. But this needs a lot of thinking over. It isn't easy to prescribe— (*Thinking*)

I have a friend who has a wife . . . I was envious at his wedding . . . but what has that to do with it? . . . damn it, my mind won't work! . . . it keeps running away to her . . . it wants to mate with her mind . . . in the interest of science? . . . what damned rot I'm thinking! . . .

NINA (*thinking as before*)

This doctor is nothing to me but a healthy male . . . when he was Ned he once kissed me . . . but I cared nothing about him . . . so that's all right, isn't it, Sam's Mother?

DARRELL (*thinking*)

Let me see. . . . I am in the laboratory and they are guinea pigs . . . in fact, in the interest of science, I can be for the purpose of this experiment, a healthy guinea pig myself and still remain an observer . . . I observe my pulse is high, for example, and that's obviously because I am stricken with a recurrence of an old desire . . . desire is a natural male reaction to the beauty of the female . . . her husband is my friend. . . . I have always tried to help him . . .

(*Coldly*) I've been considering what Sam's wife told me and her reasoning is quite sound. The child can't be her husband's.

NINA Then you agree with Sam's mother? She said: "Being happy is the nearest we can ever come to knowing what good is!"

DARRELL I agree with her decidedly. Sam's wife should find a healthy father for Sam's child at once. It is her sane duty to her husband. (*Worriedly thinking*)

Have I ever been happy? . . . I have studied to cure the body's unhappiness . . . I have watched happy smiles form on the lips of the dying . . . I have experienced pleasure with a number of women I desired but never loved . . . I have known a bit of honor and a trifle of self-satisfaction . . . this talk of happiness seems to me extraneous . . .

NINA (*beginning to adopt a timid, diffident, guilty tone*) This will have to be hidden from Sam so he can never know! Oh, Doctor, Sam's wife is afraid!

DARRELL (*sharply professional*) Nonsense! This is no time for timidity! Happiness hates the timid! So does science! Certainly Sam's wife must conceal her action! To let Sam know would be insanely cruel of her—and stupid, for then no one could be the happier for her act! (*Anxiously thinking*)

Am I right to advise this? . . . yes, it is clearly the rational thing to do . . . but this advice betrays my friend! . . . no, it saves him! . . . it saves his wife . . . and if a third party should know a little happiness . . . is he any poorer, am I any the less his friend because I saved him? . . . no, my duty to him is plain . . . and my duty as an experimental searcher after truth . . . to observe these three guinea pigs, of which I am one . . .

NINA (*thinking determinedly*)

I must have my baby! . . .

(*Timidly—gets from her chair and half-turns toward him—*

pleadingly) You must give his wife courage, Doctor. You must free her from her feeling of guilt.

DARRELL There can only be guilt when one deliberately neglects one's manifest duty to life. Anything else is rot! This woman's duty is to save her husband and herself by begetting a healthy child! (*Thinking guiltily and instinctively moving away from her*)

I am healthy . . . but he is my friend . . . there is such a thing as honor! . . .

NINA (*determinedly*)

I must take my happiness! . . .

(*Frightenedly—comes after him*) But she is ashamed. It's adultery. It's wrong.

DARRELL (*moving away again—with a cold sneering laugh of impatience*) Wrong! Would she rather see her husband wind up in an asylum? Would she rather face the prospect of going to pot mentally, morally, physically herself through year after year of devilling herself and him? Really, Madame, if you can't throw overboard all such irrelevant moral ideas, I'll have to give up this case here and now! (*Thinking frightenedly*)

Who is talking? . . . is he suggesting me? . . . but you know very well I can't be the one, Doctor! . . . why not, you're healthy and it's a friendly act for all concerned . . .

NINA (*thinking determinedly*)

I must have my baby! . . .

(*Going further toward him—she can now touch him with her hand*) Please, Doctor, you must give her strength to do this right thing that seems to her so right and then so wrong! (*She puts out her hand and takes one of his*).

DARRELL (*thinking frightenedly*)

Whose hand is this? . . . it burns me . . . I kissed her once . . . her lips were cold . . . now they would burn with happiness for me! . . .

NINA (*taking his other hand and slowly pulling him around to face her, although he does not look at her—pleadingly*) Now she feels your strength. It gives her the courage to ask you, Doctor, to suggest the father. She has changed, Doctor, since she became Sam's wife. She can't bear the thought now of giving herself to any man she could neither desire nor respect. So each time her thoughts come to the man she must select they are afraid to go on! She needs your courage to choose!

DARRELL (*as if listening to himself*)

Sam is my friend . . . well, and isn't she your friend? . . . her two hands are so warm! . . . I must not even hint at my desire! . . .

(*Judicially calm*) Well, the man must be someone who is not unattractive to her physically, of course.

NINA Ned always attracted her.

DARRELL (*thinking frightenedly*)

What's that she said? . . . Ned? . . . attracts? . . .

(*In same tone*) And the man should have a mind that can truly understand—a scientific mind superior to the moral scruples that cause so much human blundering and unhappiness.

NINA She always thought Ned had a superior mind.

DARRELL (*thinking frightenedly*)

Did she say Ned? . . . she thinks Ned . . . ?

(*In same tone*) The man should like and admire her, he should be her good friend and want to help her, but he should not love her—although he might, without harm to anyone, desire her.

NINA Ned does not love her—but he used to like her and, I think, desire her. Does he now, Doctor?

DARRELL (*thinking*)

Does he? . . . who is he? . . . he is Ned! . . . Ned is I! . . . I desire her! . . . I desire happiness! . . .

(*Tremblingly now—gently*) But, Madame, I must confess the Ned you are speaking of is I, and I am Ned.

NINA (*gently*) And I am Nina, who wants her baby. (*Then she reaches out and turns his head until his face faces hers but he keeps his eyes down—she bends her head meekly and submissively softly*) I should be so grateful, Ned. (*He starts, looks up at her wildly, makes a motion as though to take her in his arms, then remains fixed for a moment in that attitude, staring at her bowed head as she repeats submissively*) I should be so humbly grateful.

DARRELL (*suddenly falling on his knees and taking her hand in both of his and kissing it humbly—with a sob*) Yes—yes, Nina—yes—for your happiness—in that spirit! (*Thinking—fiercely triumphant*)

I shall be happy for a while! . . .

NINA (*raising her head—thinking—proudly triumphant*)

I shall be happy! . . . I shall make my husband happy!

CURTAIN

ACT FIVE

SCENE: *The sitting room of a small house* EVANS *has rented in a seashore suburb near New York. It is a bright morning in the following April.*

The room is a typical sitting room of the quantity-production bungalow type. Windows on the left look out on a broad porch. A double doorway in rear leads into the hall. A door on right, to the dining room. NINA *has tried to take the curse of offensive, banal newness off the room with some of her own things from her old home but the attempt has been half-hearted in the face of such overpowering commonness, and the result is a room as disorganized in character as was the* PROFESSOR'S *study in the last Act.*

The arrangement of the furniture follows the same pattern as in preceding scenes. There is a Morris chair and a round golden oak table at left of center, an upholstered chair, covered with bright chintz at center, a sofa covered with the same chintz at right.

NINA *is sitting in the chair at center. She has been trying to read a book but has let this drop listlessly on her lap. A great change is noticeable in her face and bearing. She is again the pregnant woman of Act Three but this time there is a triumphant strength about her expression, a ruthless self-confidence in her eyes. She has grown stouter, her face has filled out. One gets no impression of neurotic strain from her now, she seems nerveless and deeply calm.*

NINA (*as if listening for something within her—joyfully*) There! . . . that can't be my imagination . . . I felt it plainly . . . life . . . my baby . . . my only baby . . . the other never really lived . . . this is the child of my love! . . . I love Ned! . . . I've loved him since that first afternoon . . . when I went to him . . . so scientifically! . . .

(*She laughs at herself*)

Oh, what a goose I was! . . . then love came to me . . . in his arms . . . happiness! . . . I hid it from him . . . I saw he was frightened . . . his own joy frightened him . . . I could feel him fighting with himself . . . during all those afternoons . . . our wonderful afternoons of happiness! . . . and I said nothing . . . I made myself be calculating . . . so when he finally said . . .

dreadfully disturbed . . . "Look here, Nina, we've done all that is necessary, playing with fire is dangerous" . . . I said, "You're quite right, Ned, of all things I don't want to fall in love with you!" . . .

(*She laughs*)

He didn't like that! . . . he looked angry . . . and afraid . . . then for weeks he never even phoned . . . I waited . . . it was prudent to wait . . . but every day I grew more terrified . . . then just as my will was breaking, his broke . . . he suddenly appeared again . . . but I held him to his aloof doctor's pose and sent him away, proud of his will power . . . and sick of himself with desire for me! . . . every week since then he's been coming out here . . . as my doctor . . . we've talked about our child wisely, dispassionately . . . as if it were Sam's child . . . we've never given in to our desire . . . and I've watched love grow in him until I'm sure . . .

(*With sudden alarm*)

But am I? . . . he's never once mentioned love . . . perhaps I've been a fool to play the part I've played . . . it may have turned him against me . . .

(*Suddenly with calm confidence*)

No . . . he does . . . I feel it . . . it's only when I start thinking, I begin to doubt . . .

(*She settles back and stares dreamily before her—a pause*)

There . . . again . . . his child! . . . my child moving in my life . . . my life moving in my child . . . the world is whole and perfect . . . all things are each other's . . . life is . . . and the is is beyond reason . . . questions die in the silence of this peace . . . I am living a dream within the great dream of the tide . . . breathing in the tide I dream and breathe back my dream into the tide . . . suspended in the movement of the tide, I feel life move in me, suspended in me . . . no whys matter . . . there is no why . . . I am a mother . . . God is a Mother . . .

(*She sighs happily, closing her eyes. A pause.* EVANS *enters from the hallway in rear. He is dressed carefully but his clothes are old ones—shabby collegiate gentility—and he has forgotten to shave. His eyes look pitiably harried, his manner has become a distressingly obvious attempt to cover up a chronic state of nervous panic and guilty conscience. He stops inside the doorway and looks at her with a pitiable furtiveness, arguing with himself, trying to get up his courage*)

Tell her! . . . go on! . . . you made up your mind to, didn't you? . . . don't quit now! . . . tell her you've decided . . . for her sake . . . to face the truth . . . that she can't love you . . .

she's tried . . . she's acted like a good sport . . . but she's beginning to hate you . . . and you can't blame her . . . she wanted children . . . and you haven't been able . . .

(*Protesting feebly*)

But I don't know for certain . . . that that's my fault . . .

(*Then bitterly*)

Aw, don't kid yourself, if she'd married someone else . . . if Gordon had lived and married her . . . I'll bet in the first month she'd . . . you'd better resign from the whole game . . . with a gun! . . .

(*He swallows hard as if he were choking back a sob—then savagely*)

Stop whining! . . . go on and wake her up! . . . say you're willing to give her a divorce so she can marry some real guy who can give her what she ought to have! . . .

(*Then with sudden terror*)

And if she says yes? . . . I couldn't bear it! . . . I'd die without her! . . .

(*Then with a somber alien forcefulness*)

All right . . . good riddance! . . . I'd have the guts to bump off then, all right! . . . that'd set her free . . . come on now! . . . ask her! . . .

(*But his voice begins to tremble uncertainly again as he calls*) Nina!

NINA (*opens her eyes and gazes calmly, indifferently at him*) Yes?

EVANS (*immediately terrified and beaten—thinking*) (*Stammering*) I hate to wake you up but—it's about time for Ned to come, isn't it?

NINA (*calmly*) I wasn't asleep.

(*Thinking as if she found it hard to concentrate on him, to realize his existence*)

This man is my husband . . . it's hard to remember that . . . people will say he's the father of my child. . . .

(*With revulsion*)

That's shameful! . . . and yet that's exactly what I wanted! . . . wanted! . . . not now! . . . now I love Ned! . . . I won't lose him! . . . Sam must give me a divorce . . . I've sacrificed enough of my life . . what has he given me? . . . not even a home . . . I had to sell my father's home to get money so we could move near his job . . . and then he lost his job! . . . now he's depending on Ned to help him get another! . . . my love! . . . how shameless! . . .

(*Then contritely*)

Oh, I'm unjust . . . poor Sam doesn't know about Ned . . .

and it was I who wanted to sell the place . . . I was lonely there . . . I wanted to be near Ned. . . .

EVANS (*thinking in agony*)

What's she thinking? . . . probably lucky for me I don't know! . . .

(*Forcing a brisk air as he turns away from her*) I hope Ned brings that letter he promised me to the manager of the Globe Company. I'm keen to get on the job again.

NINA (*with scornful pity*) Oh, I guess Ned will bring the letter. I asked him not to forget.

EVANS I hope they'll have an opening right off. We can use the money. (*Hanging his head*) I feel rotten, living on you when you've got so little.

NINA (*indifferently but with authority, like a governess to a small boy*) Now, now!

EVANS (*relieved*) Well, it's true. (*Then coming to her—humbly ingratiating*) You've felt a lot better lately, haven't you, Nina?

NINA (*with a start—sharply*) Why?

EVANS You look ever so much better. You're getting fat. (*He forces a grin*).

NINA (*curtly*) Don't be absurd, please! As a matter of fact, I don't feel a bit better.

EVANS (*thinking despondently*)

Lately, she jumps on me every chance she gets . . . as if everything I did disgusted her! . . .

(*He strays over to the window and looks out listlessly*) I thought we'd get some word from Charlie this morning saying if he was coming down or not. But I suppose he's still too broken up over his mother's death to write.

NINA (*indifferently*) He'll probably come without bothering to write. (*Vaguely—wonderingly*)

Charlie . . . dear old Charlie . . . I've forgotten him, too. . . .

EVANS I think that's Ned's car now. Yes. It's stopping. I'll go out and meet him. (*He starts for the door in rear*).

NINA (*sharply, before she can restrain the impulse*) Don't be such a fool!

EVANS (*stops—stammers confusedly*) What—what's the matter?

NINA (*controlling herself—but irritably*) Don't mind me. I'm nervous. (*Thinking guiltily*)

One minute I feel ashamed of him for making such a fool of

himself over my lover . . . the next minute something hateful urges me to drive him into doing it! . . .

(*The maid has answered the ring and opened the outer door.* NED DARRELL *comes in from the rear. His face looks older. There is an expression of defensive bitterness and self-resentment about his mouth and eyes. This vanishes into one of desire and joy as he sees* NINA. *He starts toward her impulsively*) Nina! (*Then stops short as he sees* EVANS).

NINA (*forgetting* EVANS, *gets to her feet as if to receive* DARRELL *in her arms—with love*) Ned!

EVANS (*affectionately and gratefully*) Hello, Ned! (*He holds out his hand which* DARRELL *takes mechanically*).

DARRELL (*trying to overcome his guilty embarrassment*) Hello, Sam. Didn't see you. (*Hurriedly reaching in his coat pocket*) Before I forget, here's that letter. I had a talk over the phone with Appleby yesterday. He's pretty sure there's an opening— (*With a condescension he can't help*) —but you'll have to get your nose on the grindstone to make good with him.

EVANS (*flushing guiltily—forcing a confident tone*) You bet I will! (*Then gratefully and humbly*) Gosh, Ned, I can't tell you how grateful I am!

DARRELL (*brusquely, to hide his embarrassment*) Oh, shut up! I'm only too glad.

NINA (*watching* EVANS *with a contempt that is almost gloating—in a tone of curt dismissal*) You'd better go and shave, hadn't you if you're going to town?

EVANS (*guiltily, passing his hand over his face—forcing a brisk purposeful air*) Yes, of course. I forgot I hadn't. Excuse me, will you? (*This to* DARRELL, EVANS *hurries out, rear*).

DARRELL (*as soon as he is out of earshot—turning on* NINA *accusingly*) How can you treat him that way? It makes me feel—like a swine!

NINA (*flushing guiltily—protestingly*) What way? (*Then inconsequentially*) He's always forgetting to shave lately.

DARRELL You know what I mean, Nina! (*Turns away from her—thinking bitterly*)

What a rotten liar I've become! . . . and he trusts me absolutely! . . .

NINA (*thinking frightenedly*)

Why doesn't he take me in his arms? . . . oh, I feel he doesn't love me now! . . . he's so bitter! . . .

(*Trying to be matter-of-fact*) I'm sorry, Ned. I don't mean to be cross but Sam does get on my nerves.

DARRELL (*thinking bitterly*)

Sometimes I almost hate her! . . . if it wasn't for her I'd have kept my peace of mind . . . no good for anything lately, damn it! . . . but it's idiotic to feel guilty . . . if Sam only didn't trust me! . . .

(*Then impatiently*)

Bosh! . . . sentimental nonsense! . . . end justifies means! . . . this will have a good end for Sam, I swear to that! . . . why doesn't she tell him she's pregnant? . . . what's she waiting for? . . .

NINA (*thinking passionately, looking at him*)

Oh, my lover, why don't you kiss me? . . .

(*Imploringly*) Ned! Don't be cross with me, please!

DARRELL (*fighting to control himself—coldly*) I'm not cross, Nina. Only you must admit these triangular scenes are, to say the least, humiliating. (*Resentfully*) I won't come out here again!

NINA (*with a cry of pain*) Ned!

DARRELL (*thinking exultingly at first*)

She loves me! . . . she's forgotten Gordon! . . . I'm happy! . . . do I love her? . . . no! . . I won't! . . . I can't! . . . think what it would mean to Sam! . . to my career! . . . be objective about it! . . . you guinea pig! . . . I'm her doctor . . . and Sam's . . . I prescribed a child for them . . . that's all there is to it! . . .

NINA (*torn between hope and fear*)

What is he thinking? . . . he's fighting his love . . . oh, my lover! . . .

(*Again with longing*) Ned!

DARRELL (*putting on his best professional air, going to her*) How do you feel today? You look as if you might have a little fever. (*He takes her hand as if to feel her pulse. Her hand closes over his. She looks up into his face. He keeps his turned away*).

NINA (*straining up toward him—with intense longing—thinking*)

I love you! . . . take me! . . . what do I care for anything in the world but you! . . . let Sam die! . . .

DARRELL (*fighting himself—thinking*)

Christ! . . . touch of her skin! . . . her nakedness! . . . those afternoons in her arms! happiness! . . . what do I care for anything else? . . . to hell with Sam! . . .

NINA (*breaking out passionately*) Ned! I love you! I can't hide it any more! I won't! I love you, Ned!

DARRELL (*suddenly taking her in his arms and kissing her frantically*) Nina! Beautiful!

NINA (*triumphantly—between kisses*) You love me, don't you? Say you do, Ned!

DARRELL (*passionately*) Yes! Yes!

NINA (*with a cry of triumph*) Thank God! At last you've told me! You've confessed it to yourself! Oh, Ned, you've made me so happy! (*There is a ring from the front doorbell.* DARRELL *hears it. It acts like an electric shock on him. He tears himself away from her. Instinctively she gets up too and moves to the lounge at right*).

DARRELL (*stupidly*) Someone—at the door. (*He sinks down in the chair by the table at left. Thinking torturedly*)

> I said I loved her! . . . she won! . . . she used my desire! . . . but I don't love her! . . . I won't! . . . she can't own my life! . . .

(*Violently—almost shouts at her*) I don't, Nina! I tell you I don't!

NINA (*the maid has just gone to the front door*) Sshh! (*Then in a triumphant whisper*) You do, Ned! You do!

DARRELL (*with dogged stupidity*) I don't! (*The front door has been opened.* MARSDEN *appears in the rear, walks slowly and woodenly like a man in a trance into the room. He is dressed immaculately in deep mourning. His face is pale, drawn, haggard with loneliness and grief. His eyes have a dazed look as if he were still too stunned to comprehend clearly what has happened to him. He does not seem conscious of* DARRELL'S *presence at first. His shoulders are bowed, his whole figure droops*).

NINA (*thinking—in a strange superstitious panic*)

> Black . . . in the midst of happiness . . . black comes . . . again . . . death . . . my father . . . comes between me and happiness! . . .

(*Then recovering herself, scornfully*)

> You silly coward! . . . it's only Charlie! . . .

(*Then with furious resentment*)

> The old fool! . . . what does he mean coming in on us without warning? . . .

MARSDEN (*forcing a pitiful smile to his lips*) Hello, Nina. I know it's an imposition—but—I've been in such a terrible state since Mother— (*He falters, his face becomes distorted into an ugly mask of grief, his eyes water*).

NINA (*immediately sympathetic, gets up and goes to him impulsively*) There's no question of imposition, Charlie. We were expecting you. (*She has come to him and put her arms around him. He gives way and sobs, his head against her shoulder*).

MARSDEN (*brokenly*) You don't know, Nina—how terrible—it's terrible!—

NINA (*leading him to the chair at center, soothingly*) I know, Charlie.

(*Thinking with helpless annoyance*)

Oh, dear, what can I say? . . . his mother hated me . . .
I'm not glad she's dead . . . but neither am I sorry . . .

(*With a trace of contempt*)

Poor Charlie . . . he was so tied to her apron strings . . .

(*Then kindly but condescendingly, comforting him*) Poor old Charlie!

MARSDEN (*the words and the tone shock his pride to life. He raises his head and half pushes her away—resentfully, thinking*)

Poor old Charlie! . . . damn it, what am I to her? . . . her old dog who's lost his mother? . . . Mother hated her . . . no, poor dear Mother was so sweet, she never hated anyone . . . she simply disapproved . . .

(*Coldly*) I'm all right, Nina. Quite all right now, thank you. I apologize for making a scene.

DARRELL (*has gotten up from his chair—with relief—thinking*)

Thank God for Marsden . . . I feel sane again . . .

(*He comes to* MARSDEN*—cordially*) How are you, Marsden? (*Then offering conventional consolation, pats* MARSDEN'S *shoulder*) I'm sorry, Marsden.

MARSDEN (*startled, looks up at him in amazement*) Darrell! (*Then with instant hostility*) There's nothing to be sorry about that I can discover! (*Then as they both look at him in surprise he realizes what he has said—stammeringly*) I mean—sorry—is hardly the right word—hardly—is it?

NINA (*worriedly*) Sit down, Charlie. You look so tired. (*He slumps down in the chair at center mechanically.* NINA *and* DARRELL *return to their chairs.* NINA *looks across him at* DARRELL*—triumphantly—thinking*)

You do love me, Ned! . . .

DARRELL (*thinking—answering her look—defiantly*)

I don't love you! . . .

MARSDEN (*stares intensely before him. Thinking suspiciously—morbidly agitated*)

Darrell! . . . and Nina! . . . there's something in this room! something disgusting! . . . like a brutal, hairy hand, raw and red, at my throat! . . . stench of human life! . . . heavy and rank! . . . outside it's April . . . green buds on the slim trees . . . the sadness of spring . . . my loss at peace in Nature . . . her sorrow of birth consoling my sorrow of death . . . something human and unnatural in this room! . . . love and hate and passion and possession! . . . cruelly indifferent to my loss! . . . mocking my loneliness! . . . no longer any love for me in any room! . . . lust in this room! . . . lust with a loathsome jeer taunting my sensitive timidities! . . . my purity! . . . purity? . . . ha! yes, if you say prurient purity! . . . lust ogling me for a dollar with oily shoe button Italian eyes! . . .

(*In terror*)

What thoughts! . . . what a low scoundrel you are! . . . and your mother dead only two weeks! . . . I hate Nina! . . . that Darrell in this room! . . . I feel their desires! . . . where is Sam? . . . I'll tell him! . . . no, he wouldn't believe . . . he's such a trusting fool . . . I must punish her some other way . . .

(*Remorsefully*)

What? . . . punish Nina? . . . my little Nina? . . . why, I want her to be happy! . . . even with Darrell? . . it's all so confused! . . . I must stop thinking! . . . I must talk! . . . forget! . . . say something! . . forget everything . . .

(*He suddenly bursts into a flood of garrulity*) Mother asked for you, Nina—three days before the end. She said, "Where is Nina Leeds now, Charlie? When is she going to marry Gordon Shaw?" Her mind was wandering, poor woman! You remember how fond she always was of Gordon. She used to love to watch the football games when he was playing. He was so handsome and graceful, she always thought. She always loved a strong, healthy body. She took such strict care of her own, she walked miles every day, she loved bathing and boating in the summer even after she was sixty, she was never sick a day in her life until— (*He turns on* DARRELL*—coldly*) You were right, Doctor Darrell. It was cancer. (*Then angrily*) But the doctor you sent me to, and the others he called in could do nothing for her—absolutely nothing! I might just as well have imported some witch doctors from the Solomon Islands! They at least would have diverted her in her last hours with their singing and dancing, but your specialists were at total loss! (*Suddenly with an insulting, ugly sneer, raising his voice*) I think you doctors are a pack of God-damned ignorant liars and hypocrites!

NINA (*sharply*) Charlie!

MARSDEN (*coming to himself—with a groan—shamefacedly*) Don't mind me. I'm not myself, Nina. I've been through hell! (*He seems about to sob—then abruptly springs to his feet, wildly*) It's this room! I can't stand this room! There's something repulsive about it!

NINA (*soothingly*) I know it's ugly, Charlie. I haven't had a chance to fix it up yet. We've been too broke.

MARSDEN (*confusedly*) Oh, it's all right. I'm ugly, too! Where's Sam?

NINA (*eagerly*) Right upstairs. Go on up. He'll be delighted to see you.

MARSDEN (*vaguely*) Very well. (*He goes to the door, then stops mournfully*) But from what I saw on that visit to his home, he doesn't love his mother much. I don't think he'll understand, Nina. He never writes to her, does he?

NINA (*uneasily*) No—I don't know.

MARSDEN She seemed lonely. He'll be sorry for it some day after she— (*He gulps*) Well— (*He goes*).

NINA (*in a sudden panic—thinking*)

I can't remember her now! . . . I won't! . . . I've got to be happy! . . .

(*Then resolutely*)

DARRELL (*uneasily trying to force a casual conversation*) Poor Marsden is completely knocked off balance, isn't he? (*A pause*) My mother died when I was away at school. I hadn't seen her in some time, so her death was never very real to me; but in Marsden's case—

NINA (*with a possessive smile of tolerance*) Never mind Charlie, Ned. What do I care about Charlie? I love you! And you love me!

DARRELL (*apprehensively, forcing a tone of annoyed rebuke*) But I don't! And you don't! You're simply letting your romantic imagination run away with you— (*Showing his jealous resentment in spite of himself*) —as you did once before with Gordon Shaw!

NINA (*thinking*)

He is jealous of Gordon! . . . how wonderful that is! . . .

(*With provoking calm*) I loved Gordon.

DARRELL (*irritably ignoring this as if he didn't want to hear it*) Romantic imagination! It has ruined more lives than all the diseases! Other diseases, I should say! It's a form of insanity! (*He gets up forcefully and begins to pace about the room. Thinking uneasily*)

Mustn't look at her . . . find an excuse and get away . . . and this time never come back! . . .

(*Avoiding looking at her, trying to argue reasonably—coldly*) You're acting foolishly, Nina—and very unfairly. The agreement we made has no more to do with love than a contract for building a house. In fact, you know we agreed it was essential that love mustn't enter into it. And it hasn't in spite of what you say. (*A pause. He walks about. She watches him. He thinks*)

She's got to come back to earth! . . . I've got to break with her! . . . bad enough now! . . . but to go on with it! . . . what a mess it'd make of all our lives! . . .

NINA (*thinking tenderly*)

Let his pride put all the blame on me! . . . I'll accept it gladly! . . .

DARRELL (*irritably*) Of course, I realize I've been to blame, too. I haven't been able to be as impersonal as I thought I could be. The trouble is there's been a dangerous physical attraction. Since I first met you, I've always desired you physically. I admit that now.

NINA (*smiling tenderly—thinking*)

Oh, he admits that, does he? . . . poor darling! . . .

(*Enticingly*) And you still do desire me, don't you, Ned?

DARRELL (*keeping his back turned to her—roughly*) No! That part of it is finished! (NINA *laughs softly, possessively. He whirls around to face her—angrily*) Look here! You're going to have the child you wanted, aren't you?

NINA (*implacably*) My child wants its father!

DARRELL (*coming a little toward her—desperately*) But you're crazy! You're forgetting Sam! It may be stupid but I've got a guilty conscience! I'm beginning to think we've wronged the very one we were trying to help!

NINA You were trying to help me, too, Ned!

DARRELL (*stammering*) Well—all right—let's say that part of it was all right then. But it's got to stop! It can't go on!

NINA (*implacably*) Only your love can make me happy now! Sam must give me a divorce so I can marry you.

DARRELL (*thinking suspiciously*)

Look out! . . . there it is! . . . marry! . . . own me! . . . ruin my career! . . .

(*Scornfully*) Marry? Do you think I'm a fool? Get that out of your head quick! I wouldn't marry anyone—no matter what! (*As she continues to look at him with unmoved determination—pleadingly*) Be sensible, for God's sake! We're absolutely unsuited to each other! I don't admire your character! I don't respect you! I know too much about your past! (*Then indignantly*) And how about Sam? Divorce him? Have you forgotten all his mother told you? Do you mean to say you'd deliberately—? And you expect me to—? What do you think I am?

NINA (*inflexibly*) You're my lover! Nothing else matters. Yes, I remember what Sam's mother said. She said, "being happy is the nearest we can come to knowing what good is." And I'm going to be happy! I've lost everything in life so far because I didn't have the courage to take it—and I've hurt everyone around me. There's no use trying to think of others. One human being can't think of another. It's impossible. (*Gently and caressingly*) But this time I'm going to think of my own happiness—and that means you—and our child! That's quite enough for one human being to think of, dear, isn't it? (*She reaches out and takes his hand. A pause. With her other hand she gently pulls him around until he is forced to look into her eyes*).

DARRELL (*thinking fascinatedly*)

> I see my happiness in her eyes . . . the touch of her soft skin! . . . those afternoons! . . . God, I was happy! . . .

(*In a strange dazed voice—as if it were forced out of him by an impulse stronger than his will*) Yes, Nina.

NINA (*in a determined voice*) I've given Sam enough of my life! And it hasn't made him happy, not the least bit! So what's the good? And how can we really know that his thinking our child was his would do him any good? We can't! It's all guesswork. The only thing sure is that we love each other.

DARRELL (*dazedly*) Yes. (*A noise from the hall and* EVANS *comes in from the rear. He sees their two hands together but mistakes their meaning*).

EVANS (*genially—with a forced self-confident air*) Well, Doc, how's the patient? I think she's much better, don't you—although she won't admit it.

DARRELL (*at the first sound of* EVANS' *voice, pulls his hand from* NINA'S *as if it were a hot coal—avoiding* EVANS' *eyes, moving away from her jerkily and self-consciously*) Yes. Much better.

EVANS Good! (*He pats* NINA *on the back. She shrinks*

away. His confidence vanishes in a flash. Thinking miserably)

Why does she shrink away . . . if I even touch her? . . .

NINA (*matter-of-factly*) I must see how lunch is coming on. You'll stay, of course, Ned?

DARRELL (*struggling—shakenly*) No, I think I'd better— (*Thinking desperately*)

Got to go! . . . can't go! . . . got to go! . . .

EVANS Oh, come on, old man!

NINA (*thinking*)

He must stay . . . and after lunch we'll tell Sam . . .

(*With certainty*) He'll stay. (*Meaningly*) And we want to have a long talk with you after lunch, Sam—don't we, Ned? (DARRELL *does not answer. She goes out, right*).

EVANS (*vaguely making talk*) I got Charlie to lie down. He's all in, poor guy. (*Then trying to face* DARRELL *who keeps looking away from him*) What did Nina mean, you want a long talk with me? Or is it a secret, Ned?

DARRELL (*controlling an impulse toward hysterical laughter*) A secret? Yes, you bet it's a secret! (*He flings himself in the chair at left, keeping his face averted. His thoughts bitter and desperate like a cornered fugitive's*)

This is horrible! . . . Sam thinks I'm finest fellow in world . . . and I do this to him! . . . as if he hadn't enough! . . . born under a curse! . . . I finish him! . . . a doctor! . . . God damn it! . . . I can see his end! . . . never forgive myself . . never forget! . . . break me! . . . ruin my career! . . .

(*More desperately*)

Got to stop this! . . . while there's time! . . . she said . . . after lunch, talk . . . she meant, tell him . . . that means kill him . . . then she'll marry me! . . .

(*Beginning to be angry*)

By God, I won't! . . . she'll find out! . . . smiling! . . . got me where she wants me! . . . then be as cruel to me as she is to him! . . . love me? . . . liar! . . . still loves Gordon! . . . her body is a trap! . . . I'm caught in it! . . . she touches my hand, her eyes get in mine, I lose my will! . . .

(*Furiously*)

By God, she can't make a fool of me that way! . . . I'll go away some place! . . . go to Europe! . . . study! . . . forget her in work! . . . keep hidden until boat sails so she can't reach me! . . .

(*He is in a state of strange elation by this time*)

Go now! . . . no! . . . got to spike her guns with Sam! . . . by God, I see! . . . tell him about baby! . . . that'll stop her! . . . when she knows I've told him that, she'll see it's hopeless! . . .

she'll stick to him! . . . poor Nina! . . . I'm sorry! . . . she does love me! . . . hell! . . . she'll forget! . . . she'll have her child! . . . she'll be happy! . . . and Sam'll be happy! . . .

(*He suddenly turns to* EVANS *who has been staring at him, puzzledly—in a whisper*) Look here, Sam. I can't stay to lunch. I haven't time, I've got a million things to do. I'm sailing for Europe in a few days.

EVANS (*surprised*) You're sailing?

DARRELL (*very hurriedly*) Yes—going to study over there for a year or so. I haven't told anyone. I came out today to say good-bye. You won't be able to reach me again. I'll be out of town visiting. (*Then elatedly*) And now for your secret! It ought to make you very happy, Sam. I know how much you've wished for it, so I'm going to tell you although Nina'll be furious with me. She was saving it to surprise you with at her own proper time— (*Still more elatedly*) —but I'm selfish enough to want to see you happy before I go!

EVANS (*not daring to believe what he hopes—stammering*) What—what is it, Ned?

DARRELL (*clapping him on the back—with strange joviality*) You're going to be a father, old scout, that's the secret! (*Then as* EVANS *just stares at him dumbly in a blissful satisfaction, he rattles on*) And now I've got to run. See you again in a year or so. I've said good-bye to Nina. Good-bye, Sam. (*He takes his hand and clasps it*) Good luck! Buckle down to work now! You've got the stuff in you! When I get back I'll expect to hear you're on the high road to success! And tell Nina I'll expect to find you both happy in your child—both of you, tell her!—happy in your child! Tell her that, Sam! (*He turns and goes to the door. Thinking as he goes*)

That does it! . . . honorably! . . . I'm free! . . .

(*He goes out—then out the front door—a moment later his motor is heard starting—dies away*).

EVANS (*stares after him dumbly in the same state of happy stupefaction—mumbles*) Thank you—Ned. (*Thinking disjointedly*)

Why did I doubt myself? . . . now she loves me . . . she's loved me right along . . . I've been a fool . . .

(*He suddenly falls on his knees*)

Oh, God, I thank you!

(NINA *comes in from the kitchen. She stops in amazement when she sees him on his knees. He jumps to his feet and takes her in his arms with confident happiness and kisses her*) Oh,

Nina, I love you so! And now I know you love me! I'll never be afraid of anything again!

NINA (*bewildered and terror-stricken, trying feebly to push him away—thinking*)

Has he . . . has he gone crazy? . . .

(*Weakly*) Sam! What's come over you, Sam?

EVANS (*tenderly*) Ned told me—the secret—and I'm so happy, dear! (*He kisses her again*).

NINA (*stammering*) Ned told you—what?

EVANS (*tenderly*) That we're going to have a child, dear. You mustn't be sore at him. Why did you want to keep it a secret from me? Didn't you know how happy it would make me, Nina?

NINA He told you we—we—you, the father—? (*Then suddenly breaking from him—wildly*) Ned! Where is Ned?

EVANS He left a moment ago.

NINA (*stupidly*) Left? Call him back. Lunch is ready.

EVANS He's gone. He couldn't stay. He's got so much to do getting ready to sail.

NINA Sail?

EVANS Didn't he tell you he was sailing for Europe? He's going over for a year or so to study.

NINA A year or so! (*Wildly*) I've got to call him up! No, I'll go in and see him right now! (*She takes a wavering step toward the door. Thinking in anguish*)

Go! . . . go to him! . . . find him! . . . my lover! . . .

EVANS He won't be there, I'm afraid. He said we couldn't reach him, that he'd be visiting friends out of town until he sailed. (*Solicitously*) Why, do you have to see him about something important, Nina? Perhaps I could locate—

NINA (*stammering and swaying*) No. (*She stifles an hysterical laugh*) No, nothing—nothing important—nothing is important—ha—! (*She stifles another laugh—then on the verge of fainting, weakly*) Sam! Help me—

EVANS (*rushes to her, supports her to sofa at right*) Poor darling! Lie down and rest. (*She remains in a sitting position, staring blankly before her. He chafes her wrists*) Poor darling! (*Thinking jubilantly*)

Her condition . . . this weakness comes from her condition! . . .

NINA (*thinking in anguish*)

Ned doesn't love me! . . . he's gone! . . . gone forever! . . . like Gordon! . . . no, not like Gordon! . . . like a sneak, a coward! . . . a liar! . . . oh, I hate him! . . . O Mother God, please let me hate him! . . . he must have been planning this! . . . he must have known today when he said he loved me! . . .

(*Thinking frenziedly*)

I won't bear it! . . . he thinks he has palmed me off on Sam forever! . . . and his child! . . . he can't! . . . I'll tell Sam he was lying! . . . I'll make Sam hate him! . . . I'll make Sam kill him! . . . I'll promise to love Sam if he kills him! . . .

(*Suddenly turns to* EVANS—*savagely*) He lied to you!

EVANS (*letting her wrists drop—appalled—stammers*) You mean—Ned lied about—?

NINA (*in same tone*) Ned lied to you!

EVANS (*stammers*) You're not—going to have a child—

NINA (*savagely*) Oh, yes! Oh, yes, I am! Nothing can keep me from that! But you're—you're—I mean, you . . . (*Thinking in anguish*)

I can't say that to him! . . . I can't tell him without Ned to help me! . . . I can't! . . . look at his face! . . . oh, poor Sammy! . . . poor little boy! . . . poor little boy! . . .

(*She takes his head and presses it to her breast and begins to weep. Weeping*) I mean, you weren't to know about it, Sammy.

EVANS (*immediately on the crest again—tenderly*) Why? Don't you want me to be happy, Nina?

NINA Yes—yes, I do, Sammy. (*Thinking strangely*)

Little boy! . . . little boy! . . . one gives birth to little boys! . . . one doesn't drive them mad and kill them! . . .

EVANS (*thinking*)

She's never called me Sammy before . . . someone used to . . . oh, yes, Mother. . . .

(*Tenderly and boyishly*) And I'm going to make you happy from now on, Nina. I tell you, the moment Ned told me, something happened to me! I can't explain it, but—I'll make good now, Nina! I know I've said that before but I was only boasting. I was only trying to make myself think so. But now I say it knowing I can do it! (*Softly*) It's because we're going to have a child, Nina. I knew that you'd never come to really love me without that. That's what I was down on my knees for when you came in. I was thanking God—for our baby!

NINA (*tremblingly*) Sammy! Poor boy!

EVANS Ned said when he came back he'd expect to find us both happy—in our baby. He said to tell you that. You will be happy now, won't you, Nina?

NINA (*brokenly and exhaustedly*) I'll try to make you happy, Sammy. (*He kisses her, then hides his head on her *breast. She stares out over his head. She seems to grow older. Thinking as if she were repeating the words of some inner voice of life*)

Not Ned's child! . . . not Sam's child! . . . mine! . . . there! . . . again! . . . I feel my child live . . . moving in my life . . . my life moving in my child . . . breathing in the tide I dream and breathe my dream back into the tide . . . God is a Mother. . . .

(*Then with sudden anguish*)

Oh, afternoons . . . dear wonderful afternoons of love with you, my lover . . . you are lost . . . gone from me forever! . . .

CURTAIN

SECOND PART · ACT SIX

SCENE: *The same—an evening a little over a year later. The room has undergone a significant change. There is a comfortable, homey atmosphere as though now it definitely belonged to the type of person it was built for. It has a proud air of modest prosperity.*

It is soon after dinner—about eight o'clock. EVANS *is sitting by the table at left, glancing through a newspaper at headlines and reading an article here and there.* NINA *is in the chair at center, knitting a tiny sweater.* MARSDEN *is sitting on the sofa at right, holding a book which he pretends to be looking through, but glancing wonderingly at* EVANS *and* NINA.

There is a startling change in EVANS. *He is stouter, the haggard look of worry and self-conscious inferiority has gone from his face, it is full and healthy and satisfied. There is also, what is more remarkable, a decided look of solidity about him, of a determination moving toward ends it is confident it can achieve. He has matured; found his place in the world.*

The change in NINA *is also perceptible. She looks noticeably older, the traces of former suffering are marked on her face, but there is also an expression of present contentment and calm.*

MARSDEN *has aged greatly. His hair is gray, his expression one of a deep grief that is dying out into a resignation resentful of itself. He is dressed immaculately in dark tweed.*

NINA (*thinking*)
I wonder if there's a draft in the baby's room? . . . maybe I'd better close the window? . . . oh, I guess it's all right . . . he needs lots of fresh air . . . little Gordon . . . he does remind me of Gordon . . . something in his eyes . . . my romantic imagination? . . . Ned said that . . . why hasn't Ned ever written? . . . it's better he hasn't . . . how he made me suffer! but I forgive him . . . he gave me my baby . . . the baby certainly doesn't look like him . . . everyone says he looks like Sam . . . how absurd! . . . but Sam makes a wonderful father . . . he's become a new man in the past year . . . and I've helped him . . . he asks me about everything . . . I have a genuine respect for him now . . . I can give myself without repulsion . . . I am making him happy . . . I've written his mother I'm making him happy . . . I was proud to be able to write her that . . .

how queerly things work out! . . . all for the best . . . and I don't feel wicked . . . I feel good . . .

(*She smiles strangely*)

MARSDEN (*thinking*)

What a change! . . . the last time I was here the air was poisoned . . . Darrell . . . I was sure he was her lover . . . but I was in a morbid state . . . why did Darrell run away? . . . Nina could have got Sam to divorce her if she really loved Darrell . . . then it's evident she couldn't have loved him . . . and she was going to have Sam's baby . . . Darrell's love must have seemed like treachery . . . so she sent him away . . . that must be it . . .

(*With satisfaction*)

Yes, I've got it straight now. . . .

(*With contemptuous pity*)

Poor Darrell . . . I have no use for him but I did pity him when I ran across him in Munich . . . he was going the pace . . . looked desperate . . .

(*Then gloomily*)

My running away was about as successful as his . . . as if one could leave one's memory behind! . . . I couldn't forget Mother . . . she haunted me through every city of Europe . . .

(*Then irritatedly*)

I must get back to work! . . . not a line written in over a year! . . . my public will be forgetting me! . . . a plot came to me yesterday . . . my mind is coming around again . . . I am beginning to forget, thank God! . . .

(*Then remorsefully*)

No, I don't want to forget you, Mother! . . . but let me remember . . . without pain! . . .

EVANS (*turning over a page of his paper*) There's going to be the biggest boom before long this country has ever known, or I miss my guess, Nina.

NINA (*with great seriousness*) Do you think so, Sammy?

EVANS (*decidedly*) I'm dead sure of it.

NINA (*with a maternal pride and amusement*)

Dear Sam . . . I can't quite believe in this self-confident business man yet . . . but I have to admit he's proved it . . . he asked for more money and they gave it without question . . . they're anxious to keep him . . . they ought to be . . . how he's slaved! . . . for me and my baby! . . .

EVANS (*has been looking at* MARSDEN *surreptitiously over his paper*)

Charlie's mother must have hoarded up a half-million . . . he'll let it rot in government bonds . . . wonder what he'd say if I proposed that he back me? . . . he's always taken a friendly interest . . . well, it's worth a bet, anyway . . . he'd be an easy partner to handle . . .

MARSDEN (*staring at* EVANS *wonderingly*)

What a changed Sam! I preferred him the old way . . . futile but he had a sensitive quality . . . now he's brash . . . a little success . . . oh, he'll succeed all right . . . his kind are inheriting the earth . . . hogging it, cramming it down their tasteless gullets! . . . and he's happy! . . . actually happy! . . . he has Nina . . . a beautiful baby . . . a comfortable home . . . no sorrow, no tragic memories . . . and I have nothing! . . . but utter loneliness! . . .

(*With grieving self-pity*)

If only Mother had lived! . . . how horribly I miss her! . . . my lonely home . . . who will keep house for me now? . . . it has got to be done sympathetically or I won't be able to work . . . I must write to Jane . . . she'll probably be only too glad . . .

(*Turning to* NINA) I think I'll write to my sister in California and ask her to come on and live with me. She's alone now that her youngest daughter is married, and she has very little money. And my hands are tied as far as sharing the estate with her is concerned. According to Mother's will, I'm cut off too if I give her a penny. Mother never got over her bitter feeling about Jane's marriage. In a way, she was right. Jane's husband wasn't much—no family or position or ability—and I doubt if she was ever happy with him (*Sarcastically*) It was one of those love matches!

NINA (*smiling—teasingly*) There's no danger of your ever making a love match, is there, Charlie?

MARSDEN (*wincing—thinking*)

She can't believe any woman could possibly love me! . . .

(*Caustically*) I trust I'll never make that kind of a fool of my self, Nina!

NINA (*teasingly*) Pooh! Aren't you the superior bachelor! I don't see anything to be so proud of! You're simply shirking, Charlie!

MARSDEN (*wincing but forcing a teasing air*) You were my only true love, Nina. I made a vow of perpetual bachelorhood when you threw me over in Sam's favor!

EVANS (*has listened to this last—jokingly*) Hello! What's this? I never knew you were my hated rival, Charlie!

MARSDEN (*dryly*) Oh—didn't you really? (*But* EVANS *has turned back to his paper. Thinking savagely*)

That fool, too! . . . he jokes about it! . . . as if I were the last one in the world he could imagine . . .

NINA (*teasingly*) Well, if I'm responsible, Charlie, I feel I ought to do something about it. I'll pick out a wife for you—guaranteed to suit! She must be at least ten years older than you, large and matronly and placid, and a wonderful cook and housekeeper—

MARSDEN (*sharply*) Don't be stupid! (*Thinking angrily*)

She picks someone beyond the age! . . . she never imagines sex could enter into it! . . .

NINA (*placatingly—seeing he is really angry*) Why, I was only picking out a type I thought would be good for you, Charlie—and for your work.

MARSDEN (*sneeringly—with a meaning emphasis*) You didn't mention chaste. I couldn't respect a woman who hadn't respected herself!

NINA (*thinking—stung*)

He's thinking of those men in the hospital . . . what a fool I was ever to tell him! . . .

(*Cuttingly*) Oh, so you think you deserve an innocent virgin!

MARSDEN (*coldly—controlling his anger*) Let's drop me, if you please. (*With a look at her that is challenging and malicious*) Did I tell you I ran into Doctor Darrell in Munich?

NINA (*startled—thinking frightenedly and confusedly*)

Ned! . . . he saw Ned! . . . why hasn't he told me before? . . . why did he look at me like that? . . . does he suspect? . . .

MARSDEN (*with savage satisfaction*)

That struck home! . . . look at her! . . . guilty . . . then I was right that day! . . .

(*Casually*) Yes, I chanced to run into him.

NINA (*more calmly now*) Why on earth didn't you tell us before, Charlie?

MARSDEN (*coolly*) Why? Is it such important news? You knew he was there, didn't you? I supposed he'd written you.

EVANS (*looking up from his paper—affectionately*) How was the old scout?

MARSDEN (*maliciously*) He seemed in fine feather—said he was having a gay time. When I saw him he was with a startling looking female—quite beautiful, if you like that type. I gathered they were living together.

NINA (*cannot restrain herself—breaks out*) I don't believe it! (*Then immediately controlling herself and forcing a laugh*) I mean, Ned was always so serious-minded it's hard to imagine him messed up in that sort of thing. (*Thinking in a queer state of jealous confusion*)

Hard to imagine! . . . my lover! . . . oh, pain again! . . . why? . . . I don't love him now . . . be careful! . . . Charlie's staring at me. . . .

MARSDEN (*thinking—jealously*)

Then she did love him! . . . does she still? . . .

(*Hopefully*)

Or is it only pique? . . . no woman likes to lose a man even when she no longer loves him. . . .

(*With malicious insistence*) Why is that hard to imagine, Nina? Darrell never struck me as a Galahad. After all, why shouldn't he have a mistress? (*Meaningly*) He has no tie over here to remain faithful to, has he?

NINA (*struggling with herself—thinking pitiably*)

He's right . . . why shouldn't Ned? . . . is that why he's never written? . . .

(*Airily*) I don't know what ties he has or hasn't got. It's nothing to me if he has fifty mistresses. I suppose he's no better than the rest of you.

EVANS (*looking over at her—tenderly reproachful*) That isn't fair, Nina. (*Thinking proudly*)

I'm proud of that . . . never anyone before her . . .

NINA (*looking at him—with real gratitude*) I didn't mean you, dear. (*Thinking—proudly*)

Thank God for Sammy! . . . I know he's mine . . . no jealousy . . . no fear . . . no pain . . . I've found peace . . .

(*Then distractedly*)

Oh, Ned, why haven't you written? . . . stop it! . . . what a fool I am! . . . Ned's dead for me! . . . oh, I hate Charlie . . . why did he tell me? . . .

MARSDEN (*looking at* EVANS*—contemptuously thinking*)

What a poor simpleton Sam is! . . . boasting of his virtue! . . . as if women loved you for that! . . . they despise it! . . . I don't want Nina to think I've had no experience with women. . . .

(*Mockingly*) So then it's Sam who is the Galahad, eh? Really Nina, you should have him put in the Museum among the prehistoric mammals!

EVANS (*pleased—comes back kiddingly*) Well, I never had your chances, Charlie! I couldn't run over to Europe and get away with murder the way you have!

MARSDEN (*foolishly pleased—admitting while denying*) Oh, I wasn't quite as bad as all that, Sam! (*Scornfully ashamed of himself—thinking*)

Poor sick ass that I am! . . . I want them to think I've been a Don Juan! . . . how pitiful and disgusting! . . . I wouldn't have a mistress if I could! . . . if I could? . . . of course I could! . . . I've simply never cared to degrade myself! . . .

NINA (*thinking—tormentedly*)

The thought of that woman! . . . Ned forgetting our afternoons in nights with her! . . . stop these thoughts! . . . I won't give in to them! . . . why did Charlie want to hurt me? . . . is he jealous of Ned? . . . Charlie has always loved me in some queer way of his own . . . how ridiculous! . . . look at him! . . . he's so proud of being thought a Don Juan! . . . I'm sure he never even dared to kiss a woman except his mother! . . .

(*Mockingly*) Do tell us about all your various mistresses in foreign parts, Charlie!

MARSDEN (*in confusion now*) I—I really don't remember, Nina!

NINA Why, you're the most heartless person I've ever heard of, Charlie! Not remember even one! And I suppose there are little Marsdens—and you've forgotten all about them too! (*She laughs maliciously*—EVANS *laughs with her*).

MARSDEN (*still more confused—with a silly idiotic smirk*) I can't say about that, Nina. It's a wise father who knows his own child, you know!

NINA (*frightenedly—thinking*)

What does he mean? . . . does he suspect about the baby too? . . . I must be terribly careful of Charlie! . . .

EVANS (*looking up from his paper again*) Did Ned say anything about coming back?

NINA (*thinking—longingly*)

Come back? . . . oh, Ned, how I wish! . . .

MARSDEN (*looking at her—meaningly*) No, he didn't say. I gathered he was staying over indefinitely.

EVANS I'd sure like to see him again.

NINA (*thinking*)

He has forgotten me . . . if he did come, he'd probably avoid me. . . .

MARSDEN He spoke of you. He asked if I'd heard whether Nina had had her baby yet or not. I told him I hadn't.

EVANS (*heartily*) Too bad you didn't know. You could have told him what a world-beater we've got! Eh, Nina?

NINA (*mechanically*) Yes. (*Joyfully—thinking*)

Ned asked about my baby! . . . then he hadn't forgotten! . . . if he came back he'd come to see his baby! . . .

EVANS (*solicitously*) Isn't it time to nurse him again?

NINA (*starts to her feet automatically*) Yes, I'm going now. (*She glances at* MARSDEN, *thinking calculatingly*)

I must win Charlie over again . . . I don't feel safe . . .

(*She stops by his chair and takes his hand and looks into his eyes gently and reproachfully*).

MARSDEN (*thinking shamefacedly*)

Why have I been trying to hurt her? . . . my Nina! . . . I am nearer to her than anyone! . . . I'd give my life to make her happy! . . .

NINA (*triumphantly*)

How his hand trembles! . . . what a fool to be afraid of Charlie! . . . I can always twist him round my finger! . . .

(*She runs her hand through his hair, and speaks as though she were hiding a hurt reproach beneath a joking tone*) I shouldn't like you any more, do you know it, after you've practically admitted you've philandered all over Europe! And I thought you were absolutely true to me, Charlie!

MARSDEN (*so pleased he can hardly believe his ears*)

Then she did believe me! . . . she's actually hurt! . . . but I can't let her think . . .

(*With passionate earnestness, clasping her hand in both of his, looking into her eyes*) No, Nina! I swear to you!

NINA (*thinking—cruelly*)

Pah! . . . how limp his hands are! . . . his eyes are so shrinking! . . . is it possible he loves me? . . . like that? . . . what a sickening idea! . . . it seems incestuous somehow! . . . no, it's too absurd! . . .

(*Smiling, gently releases her hand*) All right. I forgive you, Charlie. (*Then matter-of-factly*) Excuse me, please, while I go up and feed my infant, or we're due to hear some lusty howling in a moment. (*She turns away, then impulsively turns back and kisses* MARSDEN *with real affection*) You're an old dear, do you know it, Charlie? I don't know what I'd do without you! (*Thinking*)

It's true, too! . . . he's my only dependable friend . . . I must never lose him . . . never let him suspect about little Gordon . . .

(*She turns to go*).

EVANS (*jumping up, throwing his paper aside*) Wait a second. I'll come with you. I want to say good night to him. (*He comes, puts his arm about her waist, kisses her and they go out together*).

MARSDEN (*thinking excitedly*)

I almost confessed I loved her! . . . a queer expression came over her face . . . what was it? . . . was it satisfaction? . . . she didn't mind? . . . was it pleasure? . . . then I can hope? . . .

(*Then miserably*)

Hope for what? . . . what do I want? . . . If Nina were free, what would I do? . . . would I do anything? . . . would I wish to? . . . what would I offer her? . . . money? . . . she could get that from others . . . myself? . . .

(*Bitterly*)

What a prize! . . . my ugly body . . . there's nothing in me to attract her . . . my fame? . . . God, what a shoddy, pitiful! . . . but I might have done something big . . . I might still . . . if I had the courage to write the truth . . . but I was born afraid . . . afraid of myself . . . I've given my talent to making fools feel pleased with themselves in order that they'd feel pleased with me . . . and like me . . . I'm neither hated nor loved . . . I'm liked . . . women like me . . . Nina likes me! . . .

(*Resentfully*)

She can't help letting the truth escape her! . . . "You're an old dear, do you know it, Charlie?" Oh, yes, I know it . . . too damned well! . . . dear old Charlie! . . .

(*In anguish*)

Dear old Rover, nice old doggie, we've had him for years, he's so affectionate and faithful but he's growing old, he's getting cross, we'll have to get rid of him soon! . . .

(*In a strange rage, threateningly. Then confusedly and shamefacedly*)

Good God, what's the matter with me! . . . since Mother's death I've become a regular idiot! . . .

EVANS (*comes back from the right, a beaming look of proud parenthood on his face*) He was sleeping so soundly an earthquake wouldn't have made him peep! (*He goes back to his chair—earnestly*) He sure is healthy and husky, Charlie. That tickles me more than anything else. I'm going to start in training him as soon as he's old enough—so he'll be a crack athlete when he goes to college—what I wanted to be and couldn't. I want him to justify the name of Gordon and be a bigger star than Gordon ever was, if that's possible.

MARSDEN (*with a sort of pity—thinking*)

His is an adolescent mind . . . he'll never grow up . . . well, in this adolescent country, what greater blessing could he wish for? . . .

(*Forcing a smile*) How about training his mind?

EVANS (*confidently*) Oh, that'll take care of itself. Gordon was always near the top in his studies, wasn't he? And with

Nina for a mother, his namesake ought to inherit a full set of brains.

MARSDEN (*amused*) You're the only genuinely modest person I know, Sam.

EVANS (*embarrassed*) Oh—me—I'm the boob of the family. (*Then hastily*) Except when it comes to business. I'll make the money. (*Confidently*) And you can bet your sweet life I will make it!

MARSDEN I'm quite sure of that.

EVANS (*very seriously—in a confidential tone*) I couldn't have said that two years ago—and believed it. I've changed a hell of a lot! Since the baby was born, I've felt as if I had a shot of dynamite in each arm. They can't pile on the work fast enough. (*He grins—then seriously*) It was about time I got hold of myself. I wasn't much for Nina to feel proud about having around the house in those days. Now—well—at least I've improved. I'm not afraid of my own shadow any more.

MARSDEN (*thinking strangely*)

> Not to be afraid of one's shadow! . . . that must be the highest happiness of heaven! . . .

(*Flatteringly*) Yes, you've done wonders in the past year.

EVANS Oh, I haven't even started yet. Wait till I get my chance! (*Glances at* MARSDEN *sharply, makes up his mind and leans forward toward him confidentially*) And I see my real chance, Charlie—lying right ahead, waiting for me to grab it—an agency that's been allowed to run down and go to seed. Within a year or so they'll be willing to sell out cheap. One of their people who's become a good pal of mine told me in confidence, put it up to me. He'd take it on himself but he's sick of the game. But I'm not! I love it! It's great sport! (*Then putting a brake on this exuberance—matter-of-factly*) But I'll need a hundred thousand—and where will I get it? (*Looking at* MARSDEN *keenly but putting on a joking tone*) Any suggestion you can make, Charlie, will be gratefully received.

MARSDEN (*thinking suspiciously*)

> Does he actually imagine I . . . ? and a hundred thousand, no less! . . . over one-fifth of my entire . . . by Jove, I'll have to throw cold water on that fancy! . . .

(*Shortly*) No, Sam, I can't think of anyone. Sorry.

EVANS (*without losing any confidence—with a grin*)

> Check! . . . That's that! . . . Charlie's out . . . till the next time! . . . but I'll keep after him! . . .

(*Contemplating himself with pride*)

Gee, I have changed all right! I can remember when a refusal like that would have ruined my confidence for six months!

(*Heartily*) Nothing to be sorry about, old man. I only mentioned it on the off chance you might know of someone. (*Trying a bold closing stroke—jokingly*) Why don't you be my partner, Charlie? Never mind the hundred thousand. We'll get that elsewhere. I'll bet you might have darn fine original ideas to contribute. (*Thinking—satisfied*)

There! . . . That'll keep my proposition pinned up in his mind! . . .

(*Then jumping to his feet—briskly*) What do you say to a little stroll down to the shore and back? Come on—do you good. (*Taking his arm and hustling him genially toward the door*) What you need is exercise. You're soft as putty. Why don't you take up golf?

MARSDEN (*with sudden resistance pulls away—determinedly*) No, I won't go, Sam. I want to think out a new plot.

EVANS Oh, all right. If it's a case of work, go to it! See you later. (*He goes out. A moment later the front door is heard closing*).

MARSDEN (*looks after him with a mixture of annoyance and scornful amusement*)

What a fount of meaningless energy he's tapped! . . . always on the go . . . typical terrible child of the age . . . universal slogan, keep moving . . . moving where? never mind that . . . don't think of ends . . . the means are the end . . . keep moving! . . .

(*He laughs scornfully and sits down in* EVANS' *chair, picking up the paper and glancing at it sneeringly*)

It's in every headline of this daily newer testament . . . going . . . going . . . never mind the gone . . . we won't live to see it . . . and we'll be so rich, we can buy off the deluge anyway! . . . even our new God has His price! . . . must have! . . . aren't we made in His image? . . . or vice-versa? . . .

(*He laughs again, letting the paper drop disdainfully—then bitterly*)

But why am I so superior? . . . where am I going? . . . to the same nowhere! . . . worse! . . . I'm not even going! . . . I'm there! . . .

(*He laughs with bitter self-pity—then begins to think with amused curiosity*)

Become Sam's partner? . . . there's a grotesque notion! . . . it might revive my sense of humor about myself, at least . . . I'm the logical one to help him . . . I helped him to Nina

. . . logical partner . . . partner in Nina? . . . what inane thoughts! . . .

(*With a sigh*)

No use trying to think out that plot tonight . . . I'll try to read. . . .

(*He sees the book he has been reading on the couch and gets up to get it. There is a ring from the front door.* MARSDEN *turns toward it uncertainly. A pause. Then* NINA'S *voice calls down the stairs*).

NINA The maid's out. Will you go to the door, Charlie?

MARSDEN Surely. (*He goes out and opens the front door. A pause. Then he can be heard saying resentfully*) Hello, Darrell. (*And someone answering "Hello, Marsden" and coming in and the door closing*).

NINA (*from upstairs, her voice strange and excited*) Who is it, Charlie?

DARRELL (*comes into view in the hall, opposite the doorway, at the foot of the stairs—his voice trembling a little with suppressed emotion*) It's I, Nina—Ned Darrell.

NINA (*with a glad cry*) Ned! (*Then in a voice which shows she is trying to control herself, and is frightened now*) I—make yourself at home. I'll be down—in a minute or two. (DARRELL *remains standing looking up the stairs in a sort of joyous stupor.* MARSDEN *stares at him*).

MARSDEN (*sharply*) Come on in and sit down. (DARRELL *starts, comes into the room, plainly getting a grip on himself.* MARSDEN *follows him, glaring at his back with enmity and suspicion.* DARRELL *moves as far away from him as possible, sitting down on the sofa at right.* MARSDEN *takes* EVANS' *chair by the table.* DARRELL *is pale, thin, nervous, unhealthy looking. There are lines of desperation in his face, puffy shadows of dissipation and sleeplessness under his restless, harried eyes. He is dressed carelessly, almost shabbily. His eyes wander about the room, greedily taking it in*).

DARRELL (*thinking disjointedly*)

Here again! . . . dreamed of this house . . . from here, ran away . . . I've come back . . . my turn to be happy! . . .

MARSDEN (*watching him—savagely*)

Now I know! . . . absolutely! . . . his face! . . . her voice! . . . they did love each other! . . . do now! . . .

(*Sharply*) When did you get back from Europe?

DARRELL (*curtly*) This morning on the *Olympic*. (*Thinking—cautiously*)

Look out for this fellow . . . always had it in for me . . . like a woman . . . smells out love . . . he suspected before . . .

(*Then boldly*)

Well, who gives a damn now? . . . all got to come out! . . . Nina wanted to tell Sam . . . now I'll tell him myself! . . .

MARSDEN (*righteously indignant*)

What has brought him back? . . . what a devilish, cowardly trick to play on poor unsuspecting Sam! . . .

(*Revengefully*)

But I'm not unsuspecting! . . . I'm not their fool! . . .

(*Coldly*) What brought you back so soon? When I saw you in Munich you weren't intending—

DARRELL (*shortly*) My father died three weeks ago. I've had to come back about his estate. (*Thinking*)

Lie . . . Father's death just gave me an excuse to myself . . . wouldn't have come back for that . . . came back because I love her! . . . damn his questions! . . . I want to think . . . before I see her . . . sound of her voice . . . seemed to burn inside my head . . . God, I'm licked! . . . no use fighting it . . . I've done my damnedest . . . work . . . booze . . . other women . . . no use . . . I love her! . . . always! . . . to hell with pride! . . .

MARSDEN (*thinking*)

He has two brothers . . . they'll probably all share equally . . . his father noted Philadelphia surgeon . . . rich, I've heard . . .

(*With a bitter grin*)

Wait till Sam hears that! . . . he'll ask Darrell to back him . . . and Darrell will jump at it . . . chance to avert suspicion . . . conscience money, too! . . . it's my duty to protect Sam . . .

(*As he hears* NINA *coming down the stairs*)

I must watch them . . . it's my duty to protect Nina from herself . . . Sam is a simpleton . . . I'm all she has . . .

DARRELL (*hearing her coming—in a panic—thinking*)

Coming! . . . in a second I'll see her! . . .

(*Terrified*)

Does she still love me? . . . she may have forgotten . . . no, it's my child . . . she can never forget that! . . .

(NINA *comes in from the rear. She has put on a fresh dress, her hair is arranged, her face newly rouged and powdered, she looks extremely pretty and this is heightened by the feverish state of mind she is in—a mixture of love, of triumphant egotism in knowing her lover has come back to her, and of fear and uncertainty in feeling her new peace, her certainties, her contented absorption in her child failing her. She hesitates just inside the door, staring into* DARRELL'S *eyes, thinking a fierce question*).

NINA

Does he still love me? . . .

(*Then triumphantly as she reads him*)

Yes! . . . he does! . . . he does! . . .

DARRELL (*who has jumped to his feet—with a cry of longing*) Nina! (*Thinking with alarm now*)

She's changed! . . . changed! . . . can't tell if she loves! . . .

(*He has started to go to her. Now he hesitates. His voice taking on a pleading uncertain quality*) Nina!

NINA (*thinking triumphantly—with a certain cruelty*)

He loves me! . . . he's mine . . . now more than ever! . . . he'll never dare leave me again! . . .

(*Certain of herself now, she comes to him and speaks with confident pleasure*) Hello, Ned! This is a wonderful surprise! How are you? (*She takes his hand*).

DARRELL (*taken aback—confusedly*) Oh—all right, Nina. (*Thinking in a panic*)

That tone! . . . as if she didn't care! . . . can't believe that! . . . she's playing a game to fool Marsden! . . .

MARSDEN (*who is watching them keenly—thinking*)

She loves his love for her . . . she's cruelly confident . . . much as I hate this man I can't help feeling sorry . . . I know her cruelty . . . it's time I took a hand in this . . . what a plot for a novel! . . .

(*Almost mockingly*) Darrell's father died, Nina. He had to come home to see about the estate.

DARRELL (*with a glare at* MARSDEN*—protestingly*) I was coming home anyway. I only intended to stay a year, and it's over that since— (*Intensely*) I was coming back anyway, Nina!

NINA (*thinking with triumphant happiness*)

You dear, you! . . . as if I didn't know that! . . . oh, how I'd love to take you in my arms! . . .

(*Happily*) I'm awfully glad you've come, Ned. We've missed you terribly.

DARRELL (*thinking—more and more at sea*)

She looks glad . . . but she's changed . . . I don't understand her . . . "we've missed" . . . that means Sam . . . what does that mean? . . .

(*Intensely, pressing her hand*) And I've missed you—terribly!

MARSDEN (*sardonically*) Yes, indeed, Darrell, I can vouch

for their missing you—Sam in particular. He was asking about you only a short while ago—how things were going with you when I saw you in Munich. (*Maliciously*) By the way, who was the lady you were with that day? She was certainly startling looking.

NINA (*thinking—triumphantly mocking*)

A miss, Charlie! . . . he loves me! . . . what do I care about that woman? . . .

(*Gaily*) Yes, who was the mysterious beauty, Ned? Do tell us! (*She moves away from him and sits down at center.* DARRELL *remains standing*)

DARRELL (*glaring at* MARSDEN, *sullenly*) Oh, I don't remember— (*Thinking apprehensively with a bitter resentment*)

She doesn't give a damn! . . . if she loved me she'd be jealous! . . . but she doesn't give a damn! . . .

(*He blurts out resentfully at* NINA) Well, she was my mistress—for a time—I was lonely. (*Then with sudden anger turning on* MARSDEN) But what's all this to you, Marsden?

MARSDEN (*coolly*) Absolutely nothing. Pardon me. It was a tactless question. (*Then with continued open malice*) But I was starting to say how Sam had missed you, Darrell. It's really remarkable. One doesn't encounter such friendship often in these slack days. Why, he'd trust you with anything!

NINA (*wincing—thinking*)

That hurts . . . hurts Ned . . . Charlie is being cruel! . . .

DARRELL (*wincing—in a forced tone*) And I'd trust Sam with anything.

MARSDEN Of course. He is a person one can trust. They are rare. You're going to be amazed at the change in Sam, Darrell. Isn't he, Nina? He's a new man. I never saw such energy. If ever a man was bound for success Sam is. In fact, I'm so confident he is that as soon as he thinks the time is ripe to start his own firm I'm going to furnish the capital and become his silent partner.

DARRELL (*puzzled and irritated—thinking confusedly*)

What's he driving at? . . . why doesn't he get the hell out and leave us alone? . . . but I'm glad Sam is on his feet . . . makes it easier to tell him the truth. . . .

NINA (*thinking—worriedly*)

What's Charlie talking about? . . . it's time I talked to Ned . . . Oh, Ned, I do love you! . . . you can be my lover! . . . we won't hurt Sam! . . . he'll never know! . . .

MARSDEN Yes, ever since the baby was born Sam's been

another man—in fact, ever since he knew there was going to be a baby, isn't it, Nina?

NINA (*agreeing as if she had only half-heard him*) Yes. (*Thinking*)

Ned's baby! . . . I must talk to him about our baby. . . .

MARSDEN Sam is the proudest parent I've ever seen!

NINA (*as before*) Yes, Sam makes a wonderful father, Ned. (*Thinking*)

Ned doesn't care for children . . . I know what you're hoping, Ned . . . but if you think I'm going to take Sam's baby from him, you're mistaken! . . . or if you think I'll run away with you and leave my baby . . .

MARSDEN (*with the same strange driving insistence*) If anything happened to that child I actually believe Sam would lose his reason! Don't you think so, Nina?

NINA (*with emphasis*) I know I'd lose mine! Little Gordon has become my whole life.

DARRELL (*thinking—with a sad bitter irony*)

Sam . . . wonderful father . . . lose his reason . . . little Gordon! . . . Nina called my son after Gordon! . . . romantic imagination! . . . Gordon is still her lover! . . . Gordon, Sam and Nina! . . . and my son! . . . closed corporation! . . . I'm forced out! . . .

(*Then rebelling furiously*)

No! . . . not yet, by God! . . . I'll smash it up! . . . I'll tell Sam the truth no matter what! . . .

NINA (*thinking with a strange calculation*)

I couldn't find a better husband than Sam . . . and I couldn't find a better lover than Ned . . . I need them both to be happy . . .

MARSDEN (*with sudden despairing suspicion*)

Good God . . . after all, is it Sam's child? . . . mightn't it be Darrell's! . . . why have I never thought of that? . . . No! . . . Nina couldn't be so vile! . . . to go on living with Sam, pretending . . . and, after all, why should she, you fool? . . . there's no sense! . . . she could have gone off with Darrell, couldn't she? . . . Sam would have given her a divorce . . . there was no possible reason for her staying with Sam, when she loved Darrell, unless exactly because this was Sam's baby . . . for its sake . . .

(*Hectically relieved*)

Of course! . . . of course! . . . that's all right! . . . I love that poor baby now! . . . I'll fight for its sake against these two! . . .

(*Smilingly gets to his feet—thinking*)

I can leave them alone now . . . for they won't be alone,

thanks to me! . . . I leave Sam and his baby in this room with them . . . and their honor . . .

(*Suddenly raging*)

Their honor! . . . what an obscene joke! . . . the honor of a harlot and a pimp! . . . I hate them! . . . if only God would strike them dead! . . . now! . . . and I could see them die! . . . I would praise His justice! . . . His kindness and mercy to me! . . .

NINA (*thinking—with horrified confusion*)

Why doesn't Charlie go? . . . What is he thinking? . . . I suddenly feel afraid of him! . . .

(*She gets to her feet with a confused pleading cry*) Charlie!

MARSDEN (*immediately urbane and smiling*) It's all right. I'm going out to find Sam. When he knows you're here he'll come on the run, Darrell. (*He goes to the door. They watch him suspiciously*) And you two probably have a lot to talk over. (*He chuckles pleasantly and goes into the hall—mockingly warning*) We'll be back before long. (*The front door is heard slamming.* NINA *and* DARRELL *turn and look at each other guiltily and frightenedly. Then he comes to her and takes both of her hands uncertainly*).

DARRELL (*stammeringly*) Nina—I—I've come back to you—do you—do you still care—Nina?

NINA (*giving way to his love passionately, as if to drown her fears*) I love you, Ned!

DARRELL (*kisses her awkwardly—stammering*) I—I didn't know—you seemed so cold—damn Marsden—he suspects, doesn't he?—but it makes no difference now, does it? (*Then in a flood of words*) Oh, it's been hell, Nina! I couldn't forget you! Other women—they only made me love you more! I hated them and loved you even at the moment when—that's honest! It was always you in my arms—as you used to be—those afternoons—God, how I've thought of them—lying awake—recalling every word you said, each movement, each expression on your face, smelling your hair, feeling your soft body— (*Suddenly taking her in his arms and kissing her again and again—passionately*) Nina! I love you so!

NINA And I've longed for you so much! Do you think I've forgotten those afternoons? (*Then in anguish*) Oh, Ned, why did you run away? I can never forgive that! I can never trust you again!

DARRELL (*violently*) I was a fool! I thought of Sam! And that wasn't all! Oh, I wasn't all noble, I'll confess! I thought of myself and my career! Damn my career! A lot of good that did it! I didn't study! I didn't live! I longed for you—and suffered! I paid in full, believe me, Nina! But I know better now! I've come back. The time for lying is past! You've got to come away with me! (*He kisses her*).

NINA (*letting herself go, kissing him passionately*) Yes! My lover! (*Then suddenly resisting and pushing him away*) No! You're forgetting Sam—and Sam's baby!

DARRELL (*staring at her wildly*) Sam's baby? Are you joking? Ours, you mean! We'll take him with us, of course!

NINA (*sadly*) And Sam?

DARRELL Damn Sam! He's got to give you a divorce! Let him be generous for a change!

NINA (*sadly but determinedly*) He would be. You must be just to Sam. He'd give his life for my happiness. And this would mean his life. Could we be happy then? You know we couldn't! And I've changed, Ned. You've got to realize that. I'm not your old mad Nina. I still love you. I will always love you. But now I love my baby too. His happiness comes first with me!

DARRELL But—he's mine, too!

NINA No! You gave him to Sam to save Sam!

DARRELL To hell with Sam! It was to make you happy!

NINA So I could make Sam happy. That was in it too! I was sincere in that, Ned! If I hadn't been, I could never have gone to you that first day—or if I had, I'd never have forgiven myself. But as it is I don't feel guilty or wicked. I have made Sam happy! And I'm proud! I love Sam's happiness! I love the devoted husband and father in him! And I feel it's his baby—that we've made it his baby!

DARRELL (*distractedly*) Nina! For God's sake! You haven't come to love Sam, have you? Then—I'll go—I'll go away again—I'll never come back—I tried not to this time—but I had to, Nina!

NINA (*taking him in her arms—with sudden alarm*) No, don't go away, Ned—ever again. I don't love Sam! I love you!

DARRELL (*miserably*) But I don't understand! Sam gets everything—and I have nothing!

NINA You have my love. (*With a strange, self-assured smile at him*) It seems to me you're complaining unreasonably!

DARRELL You mean—I can be—your lover again?

NINA (*simply, even matter-of-factly*) Isn't that the nearest we can come to making everyone happy? That's all that counts.

DARRELL (*with a harsh laugh*) And is that what you call playing fair to Sam?

NINA (*simply*) Sam will never know. The happiness I have given him has made him too sure of himself ever to suspect me now. And as long as we can love each other without danger to him, I feel he owes that to us for all we've done for him. (*With finality*) That's the only possible solution, Ned, for all our sakes, now you've come back to me.

DARRELL (*repulsed*) Nina! How can you be so inhuman and calculating!

NINA (*stung—mockingly*) It was you who taught me the scientific approach, Doctor!

DARRELL (*shrinking back from her—threateningly*) Then I'll leave again! I'll go back to Europe! I won't endure—! (*Then in a queer, futile rage*) You think I'll stay—to be your lover—watching Sam with my wife and my child—you think that's what I came back to you for? You can go to hell, Nina!

NINA (*calmly—sure of him*) But what else can I do, Ned? (*Then warningly*) I hear them coming, dear. It's Sam, you know.

DARRELL (*in a frenzy*) What else can you do? Liar! But I can do something else! I can smash your calculating game for you! I can tell Sam—and I will—right now—by God, I will!

NINA (*quietly*) No. You won't, Ned. You can't do that to Sam.

DARRELL (*savagely*) Like hell I can't! (*The front door is opened.* EVANS' *voice is immediately heard, even before he bounds into the room. He rushes up to* DARRELL *hilariously, shakes his hand and pounds his back, oblivious to* DARRELL'S *wild expression*).

EVANS You old son of a gun! Why didn't you let a guy know you were coming? We'd have met you at the dock, and brought the baby. Let me have a look at you! You look thinner. We'll fatten you up, won't we, Nina? Let us do the prescribing this time! Why didn't you let us know where you were, you old bum? We wanted to write you about the baby. And I wanted to boast about how I was getting on! You're the only person in the world—except Nina and Charlie—I would boast about that to.

NINA (*affectionately*) Mercy, Sam, give Ned a chance to get a word in! (*Looking at* DARRELL *pityingly but challengingly*) He wants to tell you something, Sam.

DARRELL (*crushed—stammers*) No—I mean, yes—I want

to tell you how damn glad I am . . . (*He turns away, his face is screwed up in his effort to hold back his tears. Thinking miserably*)

I can't tell him! . . . God damn him, I can't! . . .

NINA (*with a strange triumphant calm*)

There! . . . that's settled for all time! . . . poor Ned! . . . how crushed he looks! . . . I mustn't let Sam look at him! . . .

(*She steps between them protectingly*) Where's Charlie, Sam?

MARSDEN (*appearing from the hall*) Here, Nina. Always here! (*He comes to her, smiling with assurance*).

NINA (*suddenly with a strange unnatural elation—looking from one to the other with triumphant possession*) Yes, you're here, Charlie—always! And you, Sam—and Ned! (*With a strange gaiety*) Sit down, all of you! Make yourselves at home! You are my three men! This is your home with me! (*Then in a strange half-whisper*) Ssshh! I thought I heard the baby. You must all sit down and be very quiet. You must not wake our baby. (*Mechanically, the three sit down, careful to make no noise—*EVANS *in his old place by the table,* MARSDEN *at center,* DARRELL *on the sofa at right. They sit staring before them in silence.* NINA *remains standing, dominating them, a little behind and to the left of* MARSDEN).

DARRELL (*thinking abjectly*)

I couldn't! . . . there are things one may not do and live with oneself afterwards . . . there are things one may not say . . . memory is too full of echoes! . . . there are secrets one must not reveal . . . memory is lined with mirrors! . . . he was too happy! . . . to kill happiness is a worse murder than taking life! . . . I gave him that happiness! . . . Sam deserves my happiness! . . . God bless you, Sam! . . .

(*Then in a strange objective tone—thinking*)

My experiment with the guinea pigs has been a success . . the ailing ones, Sam, and the female, Nina, have been restored to health and normal function . . . only the other male, Ned, seems to have suffered deterioration.

(*Then bitterly humble*)

Nothing left but to accept her terms . . . I love her . . . I can help to make her happy . . . half a loaf is better . . . to a starving man. . . .

(*Glancing over at* EVANS*—bitterly gloating*)

And your child is mine! . . . your wife is mine! . . . your happiness is mine! . . . may you enjoy my happiness, her husband! . . .

EVANS (*looking at* DARRELL *affectionately*)

Sure good to see Ned again . . . a real friend if there ever was one . . . looks blue about something . . . oh, that's right, Charlie said his old man had kicked in . . . his old man was rich . . . that's an idea . . . I'll bet he'd put up that capital . . .

(*Then ashamed of himself*)

Aw hell, what's the matter with me? . . . he's no sooner here than I start . . . he's done enough . . . forget it! . . . now anyway . . . he looks pretty dissipated . . . too many women . . . ought to get married and settle down . . . tell him that if I didn't think he'd laugh at me giving him advice . . . but he'll soon realize I'm not the old Sam he knew . . . I suppose Nina's been boasting about that already . . . she's proud . . . she's helped me . . . she's a wonderful wife and mother . . .

(*Looking up at her—solicitously*)

She acted a bit nervous just now . . . queer . . . like she used to . . . haven't noticed her that way in a long time . . . suppose it's the excitement of Ned turning up . . . mustn't let her get over-excited . . . bad for the baby's milk. . . .

MARSDEN (*glancing furtively over his shoulder at* NINA—*broodingly thinking*)

She's the old queer Nina now . . . the Nina I could never fathom . . . her three men! . . . and we are! . . . I? . . . yes, more deeply than either of the others since I serve for nothing . . . a queer kind of love, maybe . . . I am not ordinary! . . . our child . . . what could she mean by that? . . . child of us three? . . . on the surface, that's insane . . . but I felt when she said it there was something in it . . . she has strange devious intuitions that tap the hidden currents of life . . . dark intermingling currents that become the one stream of desire . . . I feel, with regard to Nina, my life queerly identified with Sam's and Darrell's . . . her child is the child of our three loves for her . . . I would like to believe that . . . I would like to be her husband in a sense . . . and the father of a child, after my fashion . . . I could forgive her everything . . . permit everything . . .

(*Determinedly*)

And I do forgive! . . . and I will not meddle hereafter more than is necessary to guard her happiness, and Sam's and our baby's . . . as for Darrell, I am no longer jealous of him . . . she is only using his love for her own happiness . . . he can never take her away from me! . . .

NINA (*more and more strangely triumphant*)

My three men! . . . I feel their desires converge in me! . . . to form one complete beautiful male desire which I absorb . . . and am whole . . . they dissolve in me, their life is my life . . . I am pregnant with the three! . . . husband! . . . lover!

. . . father! . . . and the fourth man! . . . little man! . . . little Gordon! . . . he is mine too! . . . that makes it perfect! . . .

(*With an extravagant suppressed exultance*)

Why, I should be the proudest woman on earth! . . . I should be the happiest woman in the world! . . .

(*Then suppressing an outbreak of hysterical triumphant laughter only by a tremendous effort*)

Ha-ha . . . only I better knock wood . . .

(*She raps with both knuckles in a fierce tattoo on the table*)

before God the Father hears my happiness! . . .

EVANS (*as the three turn to her—anxiously*) Nina? What's the matter?

NINA (*controlling herself with a great effort, comes to him—forcing a smile—puts her arms around him affectionately*) Nothing, dear. Nerves, that's all. I've gotten over-tired, I guess.

EVANS (*bullying her—with loving authority*) Then you go right to bed, young lady! We'll excuse you.

NINA (*quietly and calmly now*) All right, dear. I guess I do need to rest. (*She kisses him as she might kiss a big brother she loved—affectionately*) Good night, you bossy old thing, you!

EVANS (*with deep tenderness*) Good night, darling.

NINA (*she goes and kisses Charlie dutifully on the cheek as she might her father—affectionately*) Good night, Charlie.

MARSDEN (*with a touch of her father's manner*) That's a good girl! Good night, dear.

NINA (*she goes and kisses* DARRELL *lovingly on the lips as she would kiss her lover*) Good night, Ned.

DARRELL (*looks at her with grateful humility*) Thank you. Good night. (*She turns and walks quietly out of the room. The eyes of the three men follow her*).

CURTAIN

ACT SEVEN

SCENE: *Nearly eleven years later. The sitting room of the* EVANS' *apartment on Park Avenue, New York City—a room that is a tribute to* NINA'S *good taste. It is a large, sunny room, the furniture expensive but extremely simple. The arrangement of the furniture shown is as in previous scenes except there are more pieces. Two chairs are by the table at left. There is a smaller table at center, and a chaise longue. A large, magnificently comfortable sofa is at right.*

It is about one in the afternoon of a day in early fall. NINA *and* DARRELL *and their son,* GORDON, *are in the room.* NINA *is reclining on the chaise longue watching* GORDON *who is sitting on the floor near her, turning over the pages of a book.* DARRELL *is sitting by the table at left, watching* NINA.

NINA *is thirty-five, in the full bloom of her womanhood. She is slimmer than in the previous scene. Her skin still retains a trace of summer tan and she appears in the pink of physical condition. But as in the first act of the play, there is beneath this a sense of great mental strain. One notices the many lines in her face at second glance. Her eyes are tragically sad in repose and her expression is set and masklike.*

GORDON *is eleven—a fine boy with, even at this age, the figure of an athlete. He looks older than he is. There is a grave expression to his face. His eyes are full of a quick-tempered sensitiveness. He does not noticeably resemble his mother. He looks nothing at all like his father. He seems to have sprung from a line distinct from any of the people we have seen.*

DARRELL *has aged greatly. His hair is streaked with gray. He has grown stout. His face is a bit jowly and puffy under the eyes. The features have become blurred. He has the look of a man with no definite aim or ambition to which he can relate his living. His eyes are embittered and they hide his inner self-resentment behind a pose of cynical indifference.*

GORDON (*thinking as he plays—resentfully*)
I wish Darrell'd get out of here! . . . why couldn't Mother let me run my own birthday? . . . I'd never had him here, you bet! . . . what's he always hanging 'round for? . . . why don't he go off on one of his old trips again . . . last time he was

gone more'n a year . . . I was hoping he'd died! . . . what makes Mother like him so much? . . . she makes me sick! . . . I'd think she'd get sick of the old fool and tell him to get out and never come back! . . . I'd kick him out if I was big enough! . . . it's good for him he didn't bring me any birthday present or I'd smash it first chance I got! . . .

NINA (*watching him—brooding with loving tenderness—sadly*)

No longer my baby . . . my little man . . . eleven . . . I can't believe it . . . I'm thirty-five . . . five years more . . . at forty a woman has finished living . . . life passes by her . . . she rots away in peace! . . .

(*Intensely*)

I want to rot away in peace! . . . I'm sick of the fight for happiness! . . .

(*Smiling with a wry amusement at herself*)

What ungrateful thoughts on my son's birthday! . . . my love for him has been happiness . . . how handsome he is! . . . not at all like Ned . . . when I was carrying him I was fighting to forget Ned . . . hoping he might be like Gordon . . . and he is . . . poor Ned, I've made him suffer a great deal! . . .

(*She looks over at* DARRELL*—self-mockingly*)

My lover! . . . so very rarely now, those interludes of passion . . . what has bound us together all these years? . . . love? . . . if he could only have been contented with what I was able to give him! . . . but he has always wanted more . . . yet never had the courage to insist on all or nothing . . . proud without being proud enough! . . . he has shared me for his comfort's sake with a little gratitude and a big bitterness . . . and sharing me has corrupted him! . . .

(*Then bitterly*)

No, I can't blame myself! . . . no woman can make a man happy who has no purpose in life! . . . why did he give up his career? . . . because I had made him weak? . . .

(*With resentful scorn*)

No, it was I who shamed him into taking up biology and starting the station at Antigua . . . if I hadn't he'd simply have hung around me year after year, doing nothing . . .

(*Irritatedly*)

Why does he stay so long? . . . over six months . . . I can't stand having him around me that long any more! . . . why doesn't he go back to the West Indies? . . . I always get a terrible feeling after he's been back a while that he's waiting for Sam to die! . . . or go insane! . . .

DARRELL (*thinking—with an apathetic bitterness*)

What is she thinking? . . . we sit together in silence, thinking

. . . thoughts that never know the other's thoughts . . . our love has become the intimate thinking together of thoughts that are strangers . . . our love! . . . well, whatever it is that has bound us together, it's strong! . . . I've broken with her, run away, tried to forget her . . . running away to come back each time more abject! . . . or, if she saw there was some chance I might break loose, she'd find some way to call me back . . . and I'd forget my longing for freedom, I'd come wagging my tail . . . no, guinea pigs have no tails . . . I hope my experiment has proved something! . . . Sam . . . happy and wealthy . . . and healthy! . . . I used to hope he'd break down . . . I'd watch him and read symptoms of insanity into every move he made . . . despicable? . . . certainly, but love makes one either noble or despicable! . . . he only grew healthier . . . now I've given up watching him . . . almost entirely . . . now I watch him grow fat and I laugh! . . . the huge joke has dawned on me! . . . Sam is the only normal one! . . . we lunatics! . . . Nina and I! . . . have made a sane life for him out of our madness! . . .

(*Watching* NINA—*sadly*)

Always thinking of her son . . . well, I gave him to her . . . Gordon . . . I hate that name . . . why do I continue hanging around here? . . . each time after a few months my love changes to bitterness . . . I blame Nina for the mess I've made of life . . .

NINA (*suddenly turning on him*) When are you going back to the West Indies, Ned?

DARRELL (*determinedly*) Soon!

GORDON (*stops playing to listen—thinking*)

Gosh, I'm glad! . . . How soon, I wonder? . . .

NINA (*with a trace of a sneer*) I don't see how you can afford to leave your work for such long periods. Don't you grow rusty?

DARRELL (*looking at her meaningly*) My life work is to rust—nicely and unobtrusively! (*He smiles mockingly*).

NINA (*sadly—thinking*)

To rot away in peace . . . that's all he wants now, too! . . . and this is what love has done to us! . . .

DARRELL (*bitterly*) My work was finished twelve years ago. As I believe you know, I ended it with an experiment which resulted so successfully that any further meddling with human lives would have been superfluous!

NINA (*pityingly*) Ned!

DARRELL (*indifferent and cynical*) But you meant my present dabbling about. You know better than to call that work. It's merely my hobby. Our backing Sam has made Marsden and me so wealthy that we're forced to take up hobbies. Marsden goes in for his old one of dashing off genteel novels, while I play at biology. Sam argued that golf would be healthier and less nonsensical for me, but you insisted on biology. And give it its due, it has kept me out in the open air and been conducive to travelling and broadening my mind. (*Then forcing a smile*) But I'm exaggerating. I really am interested, or I'd never keep financing the Station. And when I'm down there I do work hard, helping Preston. He's doing remarkable work already, and he's still in his twenties. He'll be a big man—(*His bitterness cropping up again*) at least if he takes my advice and never carries his experiments as far as human lives!

NINA (*in a low voice*) How can you be so bitter, Ned—on Gordon's birthday?

DARRELL (*thinking cynically*)

> She expects me to love the child she deliberately took from me and gave to another man! . . . no, thank you, Nina! . . . I've been hurt enough! . . . I'll not leave myself open there! . . .

(*Regarding his son bitterly*) Every day he gets more like Sam, doesn't he?

GORDON (*thinking*)

> He's talking about me . . . he better look out! . . .

NINA (*resentfully*) I don't think Gordon resembles Sam at all. He reminds me a great deal of his namesake.

DARRELL (*touched on a sore spot—with a nasty laugh—cuttingly*) Gordon Shaw? Not the slightest bit in the world! And you ought to thank God he doesn't! It's the last thing I'd want wished on a boy of mine—to be like that rah-rah hero!

GORDON (*thinking contemptuously*)

> Boy of his! . . . He hasn't got a boy! . . .

NINA (*amused and pleased by his jealousy*)

> Poor Ned! . . . isn't he silly? . . . at his age, after all we've been through, to still feel jealous . . .

DARRELL I'd much rather have him (*Pointing to* GORDON) grow up to be an exact duplicate of the esteemed Samuel!

GORDON (*thinking resentfully*)

> He's always making fun of my father! . . . he better look out! . . .

DARRELL (*more and more mockingly*) And what could be fairer? The good Samuel is an A one success. He has a charming wife and a darling boy, and a Park Avenue apartment and a membership in an expensive golf club. And, above all, he rests so complacently on the proud assurance that he is self-made!

NINA (*sharply*) Ned! You ought to be ashamed! You know how grateful Sam has always been to you!

DARRELL (*bitingly*) Would he be grateful if he knew how much I'd really done for him?

NINA (*sternly*) Ned!

GORDON (*suddenly jumps up and confronts* DARRELL, *his fists clenched, trembling with rage, stammers*) You—shut up —making fun of my father!

NINA (*in dismay*) Gordon!

DARRELL (*mockingly*) My dear boy, I wouldn't make fun of your father for the world!

GORDON (*baffledly—his lips trembling*) You—you did, too! (*Then intensely*) I hate you!

NINA (*shocked and indignant*) Gordon! How dare you talk like that to your Uncle Ned!

GORDON (*rebelliously*) He's not my uncle! He's not my anything!

NINA Not another word or you'll be punished, whether it's your birthday or not! If you can't behave better than that, I'll have to phone to all your friends they mustn't come here this afternoon, that you've been so bad you can't have a party! (*Thinking remorsefully*)

> Is this my fault? . . . I've done my best to get him to love Ned! . . . but it only makes him worse! . . . it makes him turn against me! . . . turn from me to Sam!

GORDON (*sullenly*) I don't care! I'll tell Dad!

NINA (*peremptorily*) Leave the room! And don't come near me again, do you hear, until you've apologized to Uncle Ned! (*Thinking angrily*)

> Dad! . . . It's always Dad with him now! . . .

DARRELL (*boredly*) Oh, never mind, Nina!

GORDON (*going out—mutters*) I won't 'pologize—never! (*Thinking vindictively*)

> I hate her too when she sides with him! . . . I don't care if she is my mother! . . . she has no right! . . .

(*He goes out, rear*).

DARRELL (*irritably*) What if he does hate me? I don't blame him! He suspects what I know—that I've acted like a coward and a weakling toward him! I should have claimed him no matter what happened to other people! Whose fault is it if he hates me, and I dislike him because he loves another father? Ours!

You gave him to Sam and I consented! All right! Then don't blame him for acting like Sam's son!

NINA But he shouldn't say he hates you. (*Thinking bitterly*)

> Sam's! . . . he's becoming all Sam's! . . . I'm getting to mean nothing! . . .

DARRELL (*sardonically*) Perhaps he realizes subconsciously that I am his father, his rival in your love; but I'm not his father ostensibly, there are no taboos, so he can come right out and hate me to his heart's content! (*Bitterly*) If he realized how little you love me any more, he wouldn't bother!

NINA (*exasperatedly*) Oh, Ned, do shut up! I can't stand hearing those same old reproaches I've heard a thousand times before! I can't bear to hear myself making the same old bitter counter-accusations. And then there'll be the same old terrible scene of hate and you'll run away—it used to be to drink and women, now it's to the Station. Or I'll send you away, and then after a time I'll call you back, because I'll have gotten so lonely again living this lonely lie of my life, with no one to speak to except Sam's business friends and their deadly wives. (*She laughs helplessly*) Or else you'll get lonely in your lie a little before I do and come back again of your own desire! And then we'll kiss and cry and love each other again!

DARRELL (*with an ironical grimace*) Or I might cheat myself into believing I'd fallen in love with some nice girl and get myself engaged to be married again as I did once before! And then you'd be jealous again and have to find some way of getting me to break it off!

NINA (*forlornly amused*) Yes—I suppose the thought of a wife taking you away from me would be too much—again! (*Then helplessly*) Oh, Ned, when are we ever going to learn something about each other? We act like such brainless fools—with our love. It's always so wonderful when you first come back, but you always stay too long—or I always keep you too long! You never leave before we've come to the ugly bitter stage when we blame each other! (*Then suddenly forlornly tender*) Is it possible you can still love me, Ned?

DARRELL (*mournfully smiling*) I must, or I'd never act this fool way, would I?

NINA (*smiling back*) And I must love you. (*Then seriously*) After all, I can never forget that Gordon is the child of your love, Ned.

DARRELL (*sadly*) You'd better forget that, for his sake and your own. Children have sure intuitions. He feels cheated of your love—by me. So he's concentrating his affections on Sam whose love he knows is secure, and withdrawing from you.

NINA (*frightened—angrily*) Don't be stupid, Ned! That isn't so at all! I hate you when you talk that way!

DARRELL (*cynically*) Hate me, exactly. As he does! That's what I'm advising you to do if you want to keep his love! (*He smiles grimly*).

NINA (*sharply*) If Gordon doesn't love you it's because you've never made the slightest attempt to be lovable to him! There's no earthly reason why he should like you, when you come right down to it, Ned! Take today, for instance. It's his birthday but you'd forgotten, or didn't care! You never even brought him a present.

DARRELL (*with bitter sadness*) I did bring him a present. It's out in the hall. I bought him a costly delicate one so he could get full satisfaction and yet not strain himself when he smashed it, as he's smashed every present of mine in the past! And I left it out in the hall, to be given to him after I've gone because, after all, he is my son and I'd prefer he didn't smash it before my eyes! (*Trying to mock his own emotion back—with savage bitterness*) I'm selfish, you see! I don't want my son to be too happy at my expense, even on his birthday!

NINA (*tormented by love and pity and remorse*) Ned! For God's sake! How can you torture us like that! Oh, it's too dreadful—what I have done to you! Forgive me, Ned!

DARRELL (*his expression changing to one of pity for her—goes to her and puts his hand on her head—tenderly*) I'm sorry. (*With remorseful tenderness*) Dreadful, what you've done, Nina? Why, you've given me the only happiness I've ever known! And no matter what I may say or do in bitterness, I'm proud—and grateful, Nina!

NINA (*looks up at him with deep tenderness and admiration*) Dearest, it's wonderful of you to say that! (*She gets up and puts her hands on his shoulders and looks into his eyes—tenderly in a sort of pleading*) Can't we be brave enough—for you to go away—now, on this note—sure of our love—with no ugly bitterness for once?

DARRELL (*joyfully*) Yes! I'll go—this minute if you wish!

NINA (*playfully*) Oh, you needn't go this minute! Wait and say good-bye to Sam. He'd be terribly hurt if you didn't. (*Then seriously*) And will you promise to stay away two years—even if I call you back before then—and work this time, really work?

DARRELL I'll try, Nina!

NINA And then—surely come back to me!

DARRELL (*smiling*) Surely—again!

NINA Then good-bye, dear! (*She kisses him*).

DARRELL Again! (*He smiles and she smiles and they kiss again.* GORDON *appears in the doorway at rear and stands for a moment in a passion of jealousy and rage and grief, watching them*).

GORDON (*thinking with a strange tortured shame*)

I mustn't see her! . . . pretend I didn't see her! . . . mustn't never let her know I saw her! . . .

(*He vanishes as silently as he had come*).

NINA (*suddenly moving away from* DARRELL, *looking around her uneasily*) Ned, did you see—? I had the queerest feelings just then that someone—

GORDON (*his voice sounds from the hall with a strained casualness*) Mother! Uncle Charlie's downstairs. Shall he come right up?

NINA (*startled, her own voice straining to be casual*) Yes, dear—of course! (*Then worriedly*) His voice sounded funny. Did it to you? Do you suppose he—?

DARRELL (*with a wry smile*) It's possible. To be on the safe side, you'd better tell him you kissed me good-bye to get rid of me! (*Then angrily*) So Marsden's here again! The damned old woman! I simply can't go him any more, Nina! Why Gordon should take such a fancy to that old sissy is beyond me!

NINA (*suddenly struck—thinking*)

Why, he's jealous of Gordon liking Charlie! . . .

(*Immediately all affectionate pity*)

Then he must love Gordon a little! . . .

(*Letting her pity escape her*) Poor Ned! (*She makes a movement toward him*).

DARRELL (*startled and afraid she may have guessed something he doesn't acknowledge to himself*) What? Why do you say that? (*Then rudely defensive*) Don't be silly! (*Resentfully*) You know well enough what I've always held against him! I wanted to put up all the money to back Sam when he started. I wanted to do it for Sam's sake—but especially for my child's sake. Why did Marsden absolutely insist on Sam letting him in equally? It isn't that I begrudge him the money he's made, but I know there was something queer in his mind and that he did it intentionally to spite me! (*From the hallway comes the sound of* MARSDEN'S *voice and* GORDON'S *greeting him vociferously as he lets him into the apartment. As* DARRELL *listens his expression becomes furious again. He bursts out angrily*) You're letting that old ass spoil Gordon, you fool, you! (MARSDEN *comes in from the rear, smiling, immaculately dressed as usual. He looks hardly any older except that his hair is grayer and his tall figure more stooped. His expression and the general atmosphere he gives out are more nearly like those of Act One. If not happy, he is at least living in comparative peace with himself and his environment*).

MARSDEN (*comes straight to* NINA) Hello, Nina Cara Nina! Congratulations on your son's birthday! (*He kisses her*) He's grown so much bigger and stronger in the two months since I've seen him. (*He turns and shakes hands with* DARRELL *coldly —with a trace of a patronizing air*) Hello, Darrell. Last time I was here you were leaving for the West Indies in a week but I see you're still around.

DARRELL (*furious—with a mocking air*) And here you are around again yourself! You're looking comfortable these days, Marsden. I hope your sister is well. It must be a great comfort, having her to take your mother's place! (*Then with a harsh laugh*) Yes, we're two bad pennies, eh, Marsden?—counterfeits—fakes—Sam's silent partners!

NINA (*thinking irritably*)

> Ned's getting hateful again! . . . Poor Charlie! . . . I won't have him insulted! . . . he's become such a comfort . . . he understands so much . . . without my having to tell him . . .

(*Looking rebukingly at* DARRELL) Ned is sailing this week, Charlie.

MARSDEN (*thinking triumphantly*)

> He's trying to insult me . . . I know all he means . . . but what do I care what he says . . . she's sending him away! . . . intentionally before me! . . . it means he's finished! . . .

DARRELL (*thinking resentfully*)

> Is she trying to humiliate me before him? . . . I'll teach her! . . .

(*Then struggling with himself—remorsefully*)

> No . . . not this time . . . I promised . . . no quarrel . . . remember . . .

(*Acquiescing—with a pleasant nod to* MARSDEN) Yes, I'm going this week and I expect to be gone at least two years this time—two years of hard work.

MARSDEN (*thinking with scornful pity*)

His work! . . . what a pretense! . . . a scientific dilettante! . . . could anything be more pitiable? . . . poor chap! . . .

(*Perfunctorily*) Biology must be an interesting study. I wish I knew more about it.

DARRELL (*stung yet amused by the other's tone—ironically*) Yes, so do I wish you did, Marsden! Then you might write more about life and less about dear old ladies and devilish bachelors! Why don't you write a novel about life sometime, Marsden? (*He turns his back on* MARSDEN *with a glance of repulsion and walks to the window and stares out*).

MARSDEN (*confusedly*) Yes—decidedly—but hardly in my line— (*Thinking in anguish—picking up a magazine and turning over the pages aimlessly*)

That . . . is . . . true! . . . he's full of poison! . . . I've never married the word to life! . . . I've been a timid bachelor of arts, not an artist! . . . my poor pleasant books! . . . all is well! . . . is this well, the three of us? . . . Darrell has become less and less her lover . . . Nina has turned more and more to me . . . we have built up a secret life of subtle sympathies and confidences . . . she has known I have understood about her mere physical passion for Darrell . . . what woman could be expected to love Sam passionately? . . . some day she'll confide all about Darrell to me . . . now that he's finished . . . she knows that I love her without my telling . . . she even knows the sort of love it is. . . .

(*Passionately—thinking*)

My love is finer than any she has known! . . . I do not lust for her! . . . I would be content if our marriage should be purely the placing of our ashes in the same tomb . . . our urn side by side and touching one another . . . could the others say as much, could they love so deeply? . . .

(*Then suddenly miserably self-contemptuous*)

What! . . . platonic heroic at my age! . . . do I believe a word of that? . . . look at her beautiful eyes! . . . wouldn't I give anything in life to see them desire me? . . . and the intimacy I'm boasting about, what more does it mean than that I've been playing the dear old Charlie of her girlhood again? . . .

(*Thinking in anguish*)

Damned coward and weakling! . . .

NINA (*looking at him—pityingly—thinking*)

What does he always want of me? . . . me? . . . I am the only one who senses his deep hurt . . . I feel how life has wounded him . . . is that partly my fault, too? . . . I have wounded everyone . . . poor Charlie, what can I do for you? . . . if giving myself to you would bring you a moment's happiness, could I? . . . the idea used to be revolting . . . now, nothing about love seems important enough to be revolting . . . poor Charlie, he only thinks he ought to desire me! . . . dear Charlie, what a perfect lover he would make for one's old age! . . . what a perfect lover when one was past passion! . . .

(*Then with sudden scornful revulsion*)

These men make me sick! . . . I hate all three of them! . . . they disgust me! . . . the wife and mistress in me has been killed by them! . . . thank God, I am only a mother now! . . . Gordon is my little man, my only man! . . .

(*Suddenly*) I've got a job for you, Charlie—make the salad dressing for lunch. You know, the one I'm so crazy about.

MARSDEN (*springs to his feet*) Righto! (*He puts his arm about her waist and they go out together laughingly, without a glance at* DARRELL).

DARRELL (*thinking dully*)

I mustn't stay to lunch . . . ghost at my son's feast! . . . I better go now . . . why wait for Sam? . . . what is there to say to him I can say? . . . and there's nothing about him I want to see . . . he's as healthy as a pig . . . and as sane . . . I was afraid once his mother had lied to Nina . . . I went upstate and investigated . . . true, every word of it . . . his great-grandfather, his grandmother, his father, were all insane . . .

(*Moving uneasily*)

Stop it! . . . time to go when those thoughts come . . . sail on Saturday . . . not come here again . . . Nina will soon be fighting Sam for my son's love! . . . I'm better out of that! . . . Oh Christ, what a mess it all is! . . .

GORDON (*appears in the doorway in rear. He carries a small, expensive yacht's model of a sloop with the sails set. He is in a terrific state of conflicting emotions, on the verge of tears yet stubbornly determined*)

I got to do it! . . . Gosh, it's awful . . . this boat is so pretty . . . why did it have to come from him? . . . I can get Dad to buy me another boat . . . but now I love this one . . . but he kissed Mother . . . she kissed him . . .

(*He walks up defiantly and confronts* DARRELL *who turns to him in surprise*) Hey—Darrell—did you—? (*He stops chokingly*).

DARRELL (*immediately realizing what is coming—thinking with somber anguish*)

So this has to happen! . . . what I dreaded! . . . my fate is merciless, it seems! . . .

(*With strained kindliness*) Did what?

GORDON (*growing hard—stammers angrily*) I found this—

out in the hall. It can't be from anybody else. Is this—your present?

DARRELL (*hard and defiant himself*) Yes.

GORDON (*in a rage—tremblingly*) Then—here's what—I think of you! (*Beginning to cry, he breaks off the mast, bowsprit, breaks the mast in two, tears the rigging off and throws the dismantled hull at* DARRELL'S *feet*) There! You can keep it!

DARRELL (*his anger overcoming him for an instant*) You —you mean little devil, you! You don't get that from me— (*He has taken a threatening step forward.* GORDON *stands white-faced, defying him.* DARRELL *pulls himself up short—then in a trembling voice of deeply wounded affection*) You shouldn't have done that, son. What difference do I make? It was never my boat. But it was your boat. You should consider the boat, not me. Don't you like boats for themselves? It was a beautiful little boat, I thought. That's why I—

GORDON (*sobbing miserably*) It was awful pretty! I didn't want to do it! (*He kneels down and gathers up the boat into his arms again*) Honest I didn't. I love boats! But I hate you! (*This last with passionate intensity*).

DARRELL (*dryly*) So I've observed. (*Thinking with angry anguish*)

He hurts, damn him! . . .

GORDON No, you don't know! More'n ever now! More'n ever! (*The secret escaping him*) I saw you kissing Mother! I saw Mother, too!

DARRELL (*startled, but immediately forcing a smile*) But I was saying good-bye. We're old friends. You know that.

GORDON You can't fool me! This was different! (*Explosively*) It would serve you good and right—and Mother, too— if I was to tell Dad on you!

DARRELL Why, I'm Sam's oldest friend. Don't make a little fool of yourself!

GORDON You are not his friend. You've always been hanging around cheating him—hanging around Mother!

DARRELL Keep still! What do you mean cheating him?

GORDON I don't know. But I know you aren't his friend. And sometime I'm going to tell him I saw you—

DARRELL (*with great seriousness now—deeply moved*) Listen! There are things a man of honor doesn't tell anyone— not even his mother or father. You want to be a man of honor, don't you? (*Intensely*) There are things we don't tell, you and

I! (*He has put his hand around* GORDON'S *shoulder impulsively*)

This is my son! . . . I love him! . . .

GORDON (*thinking—terribly torn*)

Why do I like him now? . . . I like him awful! . . .

(*Crying*) We?—who d'you mean?—I've got honor!—more'n you!—you don't have to tell me!—I wasn't going to tell Dad anyway, honest I wasn't! We?—what d'you mean, we?—I'm not like you! I don't want to be ever like you! (*There is the sound of a door being flung open and shut and* EVANS' *hearty voice*).

EVANS (*from the entrance hall*) Hello, everybody!

DARRELL (*slapping* GORDON *on the back*) Buck up, son! Here he is! Hide that boat or he'll ask questions. (GORDON *runs and hides the boat under the sofa. When* EVANS *enters,* GORDON *is entirely composed and runs to him joyfully.* EVANS *has grown stouter, his face is heavy now, he has grown executive and used to command, he automatically takes charge wherever he is. He does not look his age except that his hair has grown scanty and there is a perceptible bald spot on top. He is expensively tailored*).

EVANS (*hugging* GORDON *to him—lovingly*) How's the old son? How's the birthday coming along?

GORDON Fine, Dad!

EVANS Hello, Ned! Isn't this kid of mine a whopper for his age, though!

DARRELL (*smiling strainedly*) Yes. (*Writhing—thinking*)

It hurts now! . . . to see my son his son! . . . I've had enough! . . . get out! . . . any excuse! . . . I can phone afterwards! . . . I'll yell out the whole business if I stay! . . .

I was just going, Sam. I've got to step around and see a fellow who lives near—biologist. (*He has gone to the door*).

EVANS (*disappointedly*) Then you won't be here for lunch?

DARRELL (*thinking*)

I'll yell the truth into your ears if I stay a second longer . . . you damned lunatic! . . .

Can't stay. Sorry. This is important. I'm sailing in a few days—lots to do—see you later, Sam. So long—Gordon.

GORDON (*as he goes out with awkward haste*) Good-bye—Uncle Ned. (*Thinking confusedly*)

Why did I call him that when I said I never would? . . . I know . . . must be because he said he's sailing and I'm glad . . .

EVANS So long, Ned. (*Thinking—good-naturedly superior*)

Ned and his biology! . . . He takes his hobby pretty seriously! . . .

(*With satisfaction*)

Well, he can afford to have hobbies now! . . . his investment with me has made him a pile. . . .

Where's Mother, son?

GORDON Out in the kitchen with Uncle Charlie. (*Thinking*)

I hope he never comes back! . . . why did I like him then? . . . it was only for a second . . . I didn't really . . . I never could! . . . why does he always call me Gordon as if he hated to? . . .

EVANS (*sitting down at left*) I hope lunch is ready soon. I'm hungry as the devil, aren't you?

GORDON (*absent-mindedly*) Yes, Dad.

EVANS Come over here and tell me about your birthday. (GORDON *comes over.* EVANS *pulls him up on his lap*) How'd you like your presents? What'd you get from Uncle Ned?

GORDON (*evasively*) They were all dandy. (*Suddenly*) Why was I named Gordon?

EVANS Oh, you know all about that—all about Gordon Shaw. I've told you time and again.

GORDON You told me once he was Mother's beau—when she was a girl.

EVANS (*teasingly*) What do you know about beaus? You're growing up!

GORDON Did Mother love him a lot?

EVANS (*embarrassedly*) I guess so.

GORDON (*thinking keenly*)

That's why Darrell hates me being called Gordon . . . he knows Mother loved Gordon better'n she does him . . . now I know how to get back at him . . . I'll be just like Gordon was and Mother'll love me better'n him! . . .

And then that Gordon was killed, wasn't he? Am I anything like him?

EVANS I hope you are. If when you go to college you can play football or row like Gordon did, I'll—I'll give you anything you ask for! I mean that!

GORDON (*dreamily*) Tell me about him again, will you, Dad—about the time he was stroking the crew and the fellow who was Number Seven began to crack, and he couldn't see him but he felt him cracking somehow, and he began talking back to him all the time and sort of gave him his strength so that when the race was over and they'd won Gordon fainted and the other fellow didn't.

EVANS (*with a fond laugh*) Why, you know it all by heart! What's the use of my telling you?

NINA (*comes in from the rear while they are talking. She comes forward slowly—thinking resentfully*)

Does he love Sam more than he does me? . . . oh, no, he can't! . . . but he trusts him more! . . . he confides in him more! . . .

GORDON Did you ever used to fight fellows, Dad?

EVANS (*embarrassedly*) Oh, a little—when I had to.

GORDON Could you lick Darrell?

NINA (*thinking frightenedly*)

Why does he ask that? . . .

EVANS (*surprised*) Your Uncle Ned? What for? We've always been friends.

GORDON I mean, if you weren't friends, could you?

EVANS (*boastfully*) Oh, yes, I guess so. Ned was never as strong as I was.

NINA (*thinking contemptuously*)

Ned is weak. . . .

(*Then apprehensively*)

But you're getting too strong, Sam. . . .

GORDON But Gordon could have licked you, couldn't he?

EVANS You bet he could!

GORDON (*thinking*)

She must have loved Gordon better'n Dad even! . . .

NINA (*she comes forward to the chair at center, forcing a smile*) What's all this talk about fighting? That's not nice. For heaven's sake, Sam, don't encourage him—

EVANS (*grinning*) Never mind the women, Gordon. You've got to know how to fight to get on in this world.

NINA (*thinking pityingly*)

You poor booby! . . . how brave you are now! . . .

(*Softly*) Perhaps you're right, dear. (*Looking around*) Has Ned gone?

GORDON (*defiantly*) Yes—and he's not coming back—and he's sailing soon!

NINA (*with a shudder*)

Why does he challenge me that way? . . . and cling to Sam? . . . he must have seen Ned and me . . . he doesn't offer to come to my lap . . . he used to . . . Ned was right . . . I've got to lie to him . . . get him back . . . here . . . on my lap! . . .

(*With a sneer—to* EVANS) I'm glad Ned's gone. I was afraid he was going to be on our hands all day.

GORDON (*eagerly, half-getting down from his father's lap*) You're glad—? (*Then cautiously thinking*)

She's cheating . . . I saw her kiss him. . . .

NINA Ned's getting to be an awful bore. He's so weak. He can't get started on anything unless he's pushed.

GORDON (*moving a little nearer—searching her face—thinking*)

She doesn't seem to like him so much . . . but I saw her kiss him! . . .

EVANS (*surprised*) Oh, come now, Nina, aren't you being a little hard on Ned? It's true he's sort of lost his grip in a way but he's our best friend.

GORDON (*moving away from his father again—resentfully—thinking*)

What's Dad standing up for him to her for? . . .

NINA (*thinking triumphantly*)

That's right, Sam . . . just what I wanted you to say! . . .

(*Boredly*) Oh, I know he is but he gets on my nerves hanging around all the time. Without being too rude, I urged him to get back to his work, and made him promise me he wouldn't return for two years. Finally he promised—and then he became silly and sentimental and asked me to kiss him good-bye for good luck! So I kissed him to get rid of him! The silly fool!

GORDON (*thinking—overjoyed*)

Then! . . . that's why! . . . that's why! . . . and he'll be gone two years! . . . oh, I'm so glad! . . .

(*He goes to her and looks up into her face with shining eyes*) Mother!

NINA Dear! (*She takes him up on her lap and hugs him in her arms*).

GORDON (*kisses her*) There! (*Triumphantly thinking*)

That makes up for his kiss! . . . That takes it off her mouth. . . .

EVANS (*grinning*) Ned must be falling for you—in his old age! (*Then sentimentally*) Poor guy! He's never married, that's the trouble. He's lonely. I know how he feels. A fellow needs a little feminine encouragement to help him keep his head up.

NINA (*snuggling* GORDON'S *head against hers—laughing teasingly*) I think your hard-headed Dad is getting mushy and silly! What do you think, Gordon?

GORDON (*laughing with her*) Yes, he's mushy, Mother! He's silly! (*He kisses her and whispers*) I'm going to be like Gordon Shaw, Mother! (*She hugs him fiercely to her, triumphantly happy*).

EVANS (*grinning*) You two are getting too hard-boiled for me. (*He laughs. They all laugh happily together*).

NINA (*suddenly overcome by a wave of conscience-stricken remorse and pity*)

Oh, I am hard on Ned! . . . poor dear generous Ned! . . . you told me to lie to your son against you . . . for my sake . . . I'm not worthy of your love! . . . I'm low and selfish! . . . but I do love you! . . . this is the son of our love in my arms! . . . oh, Mother God, grant my prayer that some day we may tell our son the truth and he may love his father! . . .

GORDON (*sensing her thoughts, sits up in her lap and stares into her face, while she guiltily avoids his eyes—in fear and resentment. Thinking*)

She's thinking about that Darrell now! . . . I know! . . . she likes him too! . . . she can't fool me! . . . I saw her kissing! . . . she didn't think he was a silly fool then! . . . she was lying to Dad and me! . . .

(*He pushes off her lap and backs away from her*).

NINA (*thinking frightenedly*)

He read my thoughts! . . . I mustn't even think of Ned when he's around! . . . poor Ned! . . . no, don't think of him! . . .

(*Leaning forward toward* GORDON *with her arms stretched out entreatingly but adopting a playful tone*) Why, Gordon, what's come over you? You jumped off my lap as though you'd sat on a tack! (*She forces a laugh*).

GORDON (*his eyes on the floor—evasively*) I'm hungry. I want to see if lunch is nearly ready. (*He turns abruptly and runs out*).

EVANS (*in a tone of superior manly understanding, kindly but laying down the law to womanly weakness*) He's sick of being babied, Nina. You forget he's getting to be a big boy. And we want him to grow up a real he-man and not an old lady like Charlie. (*Sagaciously*) That's what's made Charlie like he is, I'll bet. His mother never stopped babying him.

NINA (*submissively—but with a look of bitter scorn at him*) Perhaps you're right, Sam.

EVANS (*confidently*) I know I am!

NINA (*thinking with a look of intense hatred*)

Oh, Mother God, grant that I may some day tell this fool the truth! . . .

CURTAIN

ACT EIGHT

SCENE: *Late afternoon in late June, ten years later—the afterdeck of the* EVANS' *motor cruiser anchored in the lane of yachts near the finish line at Poughkeepsie. The bow and amidship of the cruiser are off right, pointed upstream. The portside rail is in the rear, the curve of the stern at left, the rear of the cabin with broad windows and a door is at right. Two wicker chairs are at left and a chaise longue at right. A wicker table with another chair is at center. The afterdeck is in cool shade, contrasted with the soft golden haze of late afternoon sunlight that glows on the river.*

NINA *is sitting by the table at center,* DARRELL *in the chair farthest left,* MARSDEN *in the chaise longue at right.* EVANS *is leaning over the rail directly back of* NINA, *looking up the river through a pair of binoculars.* MADELINE ARNOLD *is standing by his side.*

NINA'S *hair has turned completely white. She is desperately trying to conceal the obvious inroads of time by an over-emphasis on makeup that defeats its end by drawing attention to what it would conceal. Her face is thin, her cheeks taut, her mouth drawn with forced smiling. There is little left of her face's charm except her eyes which now seem larger and more deeply mysterious than ever. But she has kept her beautiful figure. It has the tragic effect of making her face seem older and more worn-out by contrast. Her general manner recalls instantly the* NINA *of Act Four, neurotic, passionately embittered and torn. She is dressed in a white yachting costume.*

DARRELL *seems to have "thrown back" to the young doctor we had seen at the house of* NINA'S *father in Act Two. He has again the air of the cool, detached scientist regarding himself and the people around him as interesting phenomena. In appearance, he is once more sharply defined, his face and body have grown lean and well-conditioned, the puffiness and jowls of the previous Act are gone. His skin is tanned almost black by his years in the tropics. His thick hair is iron-gray. He wears flannel pants, a blue coat, white buckskin shoes. He looks his fifty-one years, perhaps, but not a day more.* MARSDEN *has aged greatly. The stoop of his tall figure is accentuated, his hair has grown whitish. He is an older image of the* MARSDEN *of Act Five, who was so prostrated by his mother's death. Now it is his sister's death two months before that has plunged him into despair. His present grief, however, is more resigned to its fate than the old. He is dressed immaculately in black, as in Act Five.*

EVANS *is simply* EVANS, *his type logically developed by ten years of continued success and accumulating wealth, jovial and simple and good-natured as ever, but increasingly stubborn and self-opinionated. He has grown very stout. His jowly broad face has a heavy, flushed, apoplectic look. His head has grown quite bald on top. He is wearing a yachting cap, blue yachting coat, white flannel pants, buckskin shoes.*

MADELINE ARNOLD *is a pretty girl of nineteen, with dark hair and eyes. Her skin is deeply tanned, her figure tall and athletic, reminding one of* NINA'S *when we first saw her. Her personality is direct and frank. She gives the impression of a person who always knows exactly what she is after and generally gets it, but is also generous and a good loser, a good sport who is popular with her own sex as well as sought after by men. She is dressed in a bright-colored sport costume.*

EVANS (*nervous and excited—on pins and needles—lowering his binoculars impatiently*) Can't see anything up there! There's a damned haze on the river! (*Handing the binoculars to* MADELINE) Here, Madeline. You've got young eyes.

MADELINE (*eagerly*) Thank you. (*She looks up the river through the glasses*).

NINA (*thinking—bitterly*)

Young eyes! . . . they look into Gordon's eyes! . . . he sees love in her young eyes! . . . mine are old now! . . .

EVANS (*pulling out his watch*) Soon be time for the start. (*Comes forward—exasperatedly*) Of course, the damned radio has to pick out this time to go dead! Brand new one I had installed especially for this race, too! Just my luck! (*Coming to* NINA *and putting his hand on her shoulder*) Gosh, I'll bet Gordon's some keyed-up right at this moment, Nina!

MADELINE (*without lowering the glasses*) Poor kid! I'll bet he is!

NINA (*thinking with intense bitterness*)

That tone in her voice! . . . her love already possesses him! . . . my son! . . .

(*Vindictively*)

But she won't! . . . as long as I live! . . .

(*Flatly*) Yes, he must be nervous.

EVANS (*taking his hand away, sharply*) I didn't mean nervous. He doesn't know what it is to have nerves. Nothing's ever got him rattled yet. (*This last with a resentful look down at her as he moves back to the rail*).

MADELINE (*with the calm confidence of one who knows*) Yes, you can bank on Gordon never losing his nerve.

NINA (*coldly*) I'm quite aware my son isn't a weakling— (*Meaningly, with a glance at* MADELINE) even though he does do weak things sometimes.

MADELINE (*without lowering the glasses from her eyes— thinking good-naturedly*)

Ouch! . . . that was meant for me! . . .

(*Then hurt*)

Why does she dislike me so? . . . I've done my best, for Gordon's sake, to be nice to her. . . .

EVANS (*looking back at* NINA *resentfully—thinking*)

Another nasty crack at Madeline! . . . Nina's certainly become the prize bum sport! . . . I thought once her change of life was over she'd be ashamed of her crazy jealousy . . . instead of that it's got worse . . . but I'm not going to let her come between Gordon and Madeline . . . he loves her and she loves him . . . and her folks have got money and position, too . . . and I like her a lot . . . and, by God, I'm going to see to it their marriage goes through on schedule, no matter how much Nina kicks up! . . .

DARRELL (*keenly observant—thinking*)

Nina hates this young lady . . . of course! . . . Gordon's girl . . . she'll smash their engagement if she can . . . as she did mine once . . . once! . . . thank God my slavery is over! . . . how did she know I was back in town? . . . I wasn't going to see her again . . . but her invitation was so imploring . . . my duty to Gordon, she wrote . . . what duty? . . . pretty late in the day! . . . that's better left dead, too! . . .

EVANS (*looking at his watch again*) They ought to be lined up at the start any minute now. (*Pounding his fist on the rail— letting his pent-up feelings explode*) Come on, Gordon!

NINA (*startled—with nervous irritation*) Sam! I told you I have a splitting headache! (*Thinking intensely*)

You vulgar boor! . . . Gordon's engagement to her is all your fault! . . .

EVANS (*Resentfully*) I'm sorry. Why don't you take some aspirin? (*Thinking irritably*)

Nina in the dumps! . . . Charlie in mourning! . . . what a pair of killjoys! . . . I wanted to bring Gordon and his friends on board to celebrate . . . no chance! . . . have to take Madeline . . . stage a party in New York . . . leave this outfit flat . . . Nina'll be sore as the devil but she'll have to like it . . .

DARRELL (*examining* NINA *critically—thinking*)

She's gotten into a fine neurotic state . . . reminds me of when I first knew her . . .

(*Then exultantly*)

Thank God, I can watch her objectively again . . . these last three years away have finally done it . . . complete cure! . . .

(*Then remorsefully*)

Poor Nina! . . . we're all deserting her . . .

(*Then glancing at* MARSDEN—*with a trace of a sneer*)

Even Marsden seems to have left her for the dead! . . .

MARSDEN (*vaguely irritated—thinking*)

What am I doing here? . . . what do I care about this stupid race? . . . why did I let Nina bully me into coming? . . . I ought to be alone . . . with my memories of dear Jane . . . it will be two months ago Saturday she died . . .

(*His lips tremble, tears come to his eyes*)

MADELINE (*with an impatient sigh, lowering the glasses*) It's no use, Mr. Evans, I can't see a thing.

EVANS (*with angry disgust*) If only that damned radio was working!

NINA (*exasperatedly*) For heaven's sake, stop swearing so much!

EVANS (*hurt—indignantly*) What about it if I am excited? Seems to me you could show a little more interest without it hurting you, when it's Gordon's last race, his last appearance on a varsity! (*He turns away from her*).

MADELINE (*thinking*)

He's right . . . she's acting rotten . . . if I were Gordon's mother, I certainly wouldn't . . .

EVANS (*turning back to* NINA—*resentfully*) You used to cheer loud enough for Gordon Shaw! And our Gordon's got him beat a mile, as an oarsman, at least! (*Turning to* DARRELL) And that isn't father stuff either, Ned! All the experts say so!

DARRELL (*cynically*) Oh, come on, Sam! Surely no one could ever touch Shaw in anything! (*He glances at* NINA *with a sneer. Immediately angry at himself*)

What an idiot! . . . that popped out of me! . . . old habit! . . . I haven't loved her in years! . . .

NINA (*thinking indifferently*)

Ned still feels jealous . . . that no longer pleases me . . . I don't feel anything . . . except that I must get him to help me. . . .

(*She turns to* DARRELL *bitterly*) Sam said "our" Gordon. He means his. Gordon's become so like Sam, Ned, you won't recognize him!

MADELINE (*thinking indignantly*)

She's crazy! . . . he's nothing like his father! . . . he's so strong and handsome! . . .

EVANS (*good-naturedly, with a trace of pride*) You flatter me, Nina. I wish I thought that. But he isn't a bit like me, luckily for him. He's a dead ringer for Gordon Shaw at his best.

MADELINE (*thinking*)

Shaw . . . I've seen his picture in the gym . . . my Gordon is better looking . . . he once told me Shaw was an old beau of his mother's . . . they say she was beautiful once . . .

NINA (*shaking her head—scornfully*) Don't be modest, Sam. Gordon *is* you. He may be a fine athlete like Gordon Shaw, because you've held that out to him as your ideal, but there the resemblance ceases. He isn't really like him at all, not the slightest bit!

EVANS (*restraining his anger with difficulty—thinking*)

I'm getting sick of this! . . . she's carrying her jealous grouch too far! . . .

(*Suddenly exploding, pounds his fist on the rail*) Damn it, Nina, if you had any feeling you couldn't—right at the moment when he's probably getting into the shell— (*He stops, trying to control himself, panting, his face red*).

NINA (*staring at him with repulsion—with cool disdain*) I didn't say anything so dire, did I—merely that Gordon resembles you in character. (*With malice*) Don't get so excited. It's bad for your high blood pressure. Ask Ned if it isn't. (*Intensely—thinking*)

If he'd only die! . . .

(*Thinking—immediately*)

Oh, I don't mean that . . . I mustn't . . .

DARRELL (*thinking keenly*)

There's a death wish . . . things have gone pretty far . . . Sam does look as if he might have a bad pressure . . . what hope that would have given me at one time! . . . no more, thank God! . . .

(*In a joking tone*) Oh, I guess Sam's all right, Nina.

EVANS (*gruffly*) I never felt better. (*He jerks out his watch again*) Time for the start. Come on in the cabin, Ned, and shoot a drink. We'll see if McCabe's getting the damned radio fixed. (*Passing by* MARSDEN *he claps him on the shoulder exasperatedly*) Come on, Charlie! Snap out of it!

MARSDEN (*startled out of his trance—bewilderdly*) Eh?—what is it?—are they coming?

EVANS (*recovering his good nature—with a grin, taking his arm*) You're coming to shoot a drink. You need about ten, I think, to get you in the right spirit to see the finish! (*To* DARRELL *who has gotten up but is still standing by his chair*) Come on, Ned.

NINA (*quickly*) No, leave Ned with me. I want to talk to him. Take Madeline—and Charlie.

MARSDEN (*looking at her appealingly*) But I'm perfectly contented sitting— (*Then after a look in her eyes—thinking*)

She wants to be alone with Darrell . . . all right . . . doesn't matter now . . . their love is dead . . . but there's still some secret between them she's never told me . . . never mind . . . she'll tell me sometime . . . I'm all she will have left . . . soon. . . .

(*Then stricken with guilt*)

Poor dear Jane! . . . how can I think of anyone but you! . . . God, I'm contemptible! . . . I'll get drunk with that fool! . . . that's all I'm good for! . . .

MADELINE (*thinking resentfully*)

She takes a fine do-this-little-girl tone toward me! . . . I'll give in to her now . . . but once I'm married! . . .

EVANS Come on then, Madeline. We'll give you a small one. (*Impatiently*) Charlie! Head up!

MARSDEN (*with hectic joviality*) I hope it's strong poison!

EVANS (*laughing*) That's the spirit! We'll make a sport out of you yet!

MADELINE (*laughing, goes and takes* MARSDEN'S *arm*) I'll see you get home safe, Mr. Marsden! (*They go into the cabin,* EVANS *following them.* NINA *and* DARRELL *turn and look at each other wonderingly, inquisitively, for a long moment.* DARRELL *remains standing and seems to be a little uneasy*).

DARRELL (*thinking with melancholy interest*)

And now? . . . what? . . . I can look into her eyes . . . strange eyes that will never grow old . . . without desire or jealousy or bitterness . . . was she ever my mistress? . . . can she be the mother of my child? . . . is there such a person as my son? . . . I can't think of these things as real any more . . . they must have happened in another life. . . .

NINA (*thinking sadly*)

My old lover . . . how well and young he looks . . . now we

no longer love each other at all . . . our account with God the Father is settled . . . afternoons of happiness paid for with years of pain . . . love, passion, ecstasy . . . in what a far-off life were they alive! . . . the only living life is in the past and future . . . the present is an interlude . . . strange interlude in which we call on past and future to bear witness we are living! . . .

(*With a sad smile*) Sit down, Ned. When I heard you were back I wrote you because I need a friend. It has been so long since we loved each other we can now be friends again. Don't you feel that?

DARRELL (*gratefully*) Yes. I do. (*He sits down in one of the chairs at left, drawing it up closer to her. Thinking cautiously*)

I want to be her friend . . . but I will never . . .

NINA (*thinking cautiously*)

I must keep very cool and sensible or he won't help me . . .

(*With a friendly smile*) I haven't seen you look so young and handsome since I first knew you. Tell me your secret. (*Bitterly*) I need it! I'm old! Look at me! And I was actually looking forward to being old! I thought it would mean peace. I've been sadly disillusioned! (*Then forcing a smile*) So tell me what fountain of youth you've found.

DARRELL (*proudly*) That's easy. Work! I've become as interested in biology as I once was in medicine. And not selfishly interested, that's the difference. There's no chance of my becoming a famous biologist and I know it. I'm very much a worker in the ranks. But our Station is a "huge success," as Sam would say. We've made some damned important discoveries. I say "we." I really mean Preston. You may remember I used to write you about him with enthusiasm. He's justified it. He *is* making his name world-famous. He's what I might have been—I did have the brains, Nina!—if I'd had more guts and less vanity, if I'd hewn to the line! (*Then forcing a smile*) But I'm not lamenting. I've found myself in helping him. In that way I feel I've paid my debt—that his work is partly my work. And he acknowledges it. He possesses the rare virtue of gratitude. (*With proud affection*) He's a fine boy, Nina! I suppose I should say man now he's in his thirties.

NINA (*thinking with bitter sorrow*)

So, Ned . . . you remember our love . . . with bitterness! . . . as a stupid mistake! . . . the proof of a gutless vanity that ruined your career! . . . oh! . . .

(*Then controlling herself—thinking cynically*)

Well, after all, how do I remember our love? . . . with no emotion at all, not even bitterness! . . .

(*Then with sudden alarm*)

He's forgotten Gordon for this Preston! . . .

(*Thinking desperately*)

I must make him remember Gordon is his child or I can never persuade him to help me! . . .

(*Reproachfully*) So you have found a son while I was losing mine—who is yours, too!

DARRELL (*struck by this—impersonally interested*) That's never occurred to me but now I think of it—(*Smiling*) Yes, perhaps unconsciously Preston is a compensating substitute. Well, it's done both of us good and hasn't harmed anyone.

NINA (*with bitter emphasis*) Except your real son—and me—but we don't count, I suppose!

DARRELL (*coolly*) Harmed Gordon? How? He's all right, isn't he? (*With a sneer*) I should say from all I've been hearing that he was your ideal of college hero—like his never-to-be-forgotten namesake!

NINA (*thinking resentfully*)

He's sneering at his own son! . . .

(*Then trying to be calculating*)

But I mustn't get angry . . . I must make him help me. . . .

(*Speaking with gentle reproach*) And am I the ideal of a happy mother, Ned?

DARRELL (*immediately moved by pity and ashamed of himself*) Forgive me, Nina. I haven't quite buried all my bitterness, I'm afraid. (*Gently*) I'm sorry you're unhappy, Nina.

NINA (*thinking with satisfaction*)

He means that . . . he still does care a little . . . if only it's enough to . . . !

(*Speaking sadly*) I've lost my son, Ned! Sam has made him all his. And it was done so gradually that, although I realized what was happening, there was never any way I could interfere. What Sam advised seemed always the best thing for Gordon's future. And it was always what Gordon himself wanted, to escape from me to boarding school and then to college, to become Sam's athletic hero—

DARRELL (*impatiently*) Oh, come now, Nina, you know you've always longed for him to be like Gordon Shaw!

NINA (*bursting out in spite of herself—violently*) He's not like Gordon! He's forgotten me for that—! (*Trying to be more reasonable*) What do I care whether he's an athlete or not? It's such nonsense, all this fuss! I'm not the slightest bit interested in this race today, for example! I wouldn't care if he came in last! (*Stopping herself—thinking frightenedly*)

Oh, if he should ever guess I said that! . . .

DARRELL (*thinking keenly*)

Hello! . . . she said that as if she'd like to see him come last! . . . why? . . .

(*Then vindictively*)

Well, so would I! . . . it's time these Gordons took a good licking from life! . . .

MADELINE (*suddenly appears in the door from the cabin, her face flushed with excitement*) They're off! Mr. Evans is getting something—it's terribly faint but—Navy and Washington are leading—Gordon's third! (*She disappears back in the cabin*).

NINA (*looking after her with hatred*)

Her Gordon! . . . she is so sure! . . . how I've come to detest her pretty face! . . .

DARRELL (*thinking with a sneer*)

"Gordon's third"! . . . you might think there was no one else pulling the shell! . . . what idiots women make of themselves about these Gordons! . . . she's pretty, that Madeline! . . . she's got a figure like Nina's when I first loved her . . . those afternoons . . . age is beginning to tell on Nina's face . . . but she's kept her wonderful body! . . .

(*With a trace of malice—dryly*) There's a young lady who seems to care a lot whether Gordon comes in last or not!

NINA (*trying to be sorrowful and appealing*) Yes. Gordon is hers now, Ned. (*But she cannot bear this thought—vindictively*) That is, they're engaged. But, of course, that doesn't necessarily mean— Can you imagine him throwing himself away on a little fool like that? I simply can't believe he really loves her! Why, she's hardly even pretty and she's deadly stupid. I thought he was only flirting with her—or merely indulging in a passing physical affair. (*She winces*) At his age, one has to expect—even a mother must face nature. But for Gordon to take her seriously, and propose marriage—it's too idiotic for words!

DARRELL (*thinking cynically*)

Oh, so you'll compromise on his sleeping with her . . . if you have to . . . but she must have no real claim to dispute your ownership, eh? . . . you'd like to make her the same sort of convenient slave for him that I was for you! . . .

(*Resentfully*) I can't agree with you. I find her quite charming. It seems to me if I were in Gordon's shoes I'd do exactly what he has done. (*In confusion—thinking bitterly*)

In Gordon's shoes! . . . I always was in Gordon Shaw's shoes! . . . and why am I taking this young Gordon's part? . . . what is he to me, for God's sake? . . .

NINA (*unheedingly*) If he marries her, it means he'll forget me! He'll forget me as completely as Sam forgot his mother! She'll keep him away from me! Oh, I know what wives can do! She'll use her body until she persuades him to forget me! My son, Ned! And your son, too! (*She suddenly gets up and goes to him and takes one of his hands in both of hers*) The son of our old love, Ned!

DARRELL (*thinking with a strange shudder of mingled attraction and fear as she touches him*)

Our love . . . old love . . . old touch of her flesh . . . we're old . . . it's silly and indecent . . . does she think she still can own me? . . .

NINA (*in the tone a mother takes in speaking to her husband about their boy*) You'll have to give Gordon a good talking to, Ned.

DARRELL (*still more disturbed—thinking*)

Old . . . but she's kept her wonderful body . . . how many years since? . . . she has the same strange influence over me . . . touch of her flesh . . . it's dangerous . . . bosh, I'm only humoring her as a friend . . . as her doctor . . . and why shouldn't I have a talk with Gordon? . . . a father owes something to his son . . . he ought to advise him. . . .

(*Then alarmed*)

But I was never going to meddle again . . .

(*Sternly*) I swore I'd never again meddle with human lives, Nina!

NINA (*unheedingly*) You must keep him from ruining his life.

DARRELL (*doggedly—struggling with himself*) I won't touch a life that has more than one cell! (*Harshly*) And I wouldn't help you in this, anyway! You've got to give up owning people, meddling in their lives as if you were God and had created them!

NINA (*strangely forlorn*) I don't know what you mean, Ned. Gordon is my son, isn't he?

DARRELL (*with a sudden strange violence*) And mine! Mine, too! (*He stops himself. Thinking*)

Shut up, you fool! . . . is that the way to humor her? . . .

NINA (*with strange quiet*) I think I still love you a little, Ned.

DARRELL (*in her tone*) And I still love you a little, Nina. (*Then sternly*) But I will not meddle in your life again! (*With a harsh laugh*) And you've meddled enough with human love, old lady! Your time for that is over! I'll send you a couple of million cells you can torture without harming yourself! (*Regaining control—shamefacedly*) Nina! Please forgive me!

NINA (*starts as if out of a dream—anxiously*) What were you saying, Ned? (*She lets go of his hand and goes back to her chair*).

DARRELL (*dully*) Nothing.

NINA (*strangely*) We were talking about Sam, weren't we? How do you think he looks?

DARRELL (*confusedly casual*) Fine. A bit too fat, of course. He looks as though his blood pressure might be higher than it ought to be. But that's not unusual in persons of his build and age. It's nothing to hope—I meant, to worry over! (*Then violently*) God damn it, why did you make me say hope?

NINA (*calmly*) It may have been in your mind, too, mayn't it?

DARRELL No! I've nothing against Sam. I've always been his best friend. He owes his happiness to me.

NINA (*strangely*) There are so many curious reasons we dare not think about for thinking things!

DARRELL (*rudely*) Thinking doesn't matter a damn! Life is something in one cell that doesn't need to think!

NINA (*strangely*) I know! God the Mother!

DARRELL (*excitedly*) And all the rest is gutless egotism! But to hell with it! What I started to say was, what possible reason could I have for hoping for Sam's death?

NINA (*strangely*) We're always desiring death for ourselves or others, aren't we—while we while away our lives with the old surface ritual of coveting our neighbor's ass?

DARRELL (*frightenedly*) You're talking like the old Nina now—when I first loved you. Please don't! It isn't decent—at our age! (*thinking in terror*)

The old Nina! . . . am I the old Ned? . . . then that means? . . . but we must not meddle in each other's lives again! . . .

NINA (*strangely*) I am the old Nina! And this time I will not let my Gordon go from me forever!

EVANS (*appears in the doorway of the cabin—excited and irritated*) Madeline's listening in now. It went dead on me.

(*Raising the binoculars as he goes to the rail, he looks up the river*) Last I got, Gordon third, Navy and Washington leading. They're the ones to fear, he said—Navy especially. (*Putting down the glasses—with a groan*) Damned haze! My eyes are getting old. (*Then suddenly with a grin*) You ought to see Charlie! He started throwing Scotch into him as if he were drinking against time. I had to take the bottle away from him. It's hit him an awful wallop. (*Then looking from one to the other—resentfully*) What's the matter with you two? There's a race going on, don't you know it? And you sit like dead clams!

DARRELL (*placatingly*) I thought someone'd better stay out here and let you know when they get in sight.

EVANS (*relieved*) Oh, sure, that's right! Here, take the glasses. You always had good eyes. (DARRELL *gets up and takes the glasses and goes to the rail and begins adjusting them*).

DARRELL Which crew was it you said Gordon feared the most?

EVANS (*has gone back to the cabin doorway*) Navy. (*Then proudly*) Oh, he'll beat them! But it'll be damn close. I'll see if Madeline's getting— (*He goes back in the cabin*).

DARRELL (*looking up the river—with vindictive bitterness—thinking*)

Come on, Navy! . . .

NINA (*thinking bitterly*)

Madeline's Gordon! . . . Sam's Gordon! . . . the thanks I get for saving Sam at the sacrifice of my own happiness! . . . I won't have it! . . . what do I care what happens to Sam now? . . . I hate him! . . . I'll tell him Gordon isn't his child! . . . and threaten to tell Gordon too, unless! . . . he'll be in deadly fear of that! . . . he'll soon find some excuse to break their engagement! . . . he can! . . . he has the strangest influence over Gordon! . . . but Ned must back me up or Sam won't believe me! . . . Ned must tell him too! . . . but will Ned? . . . he'll be afraid of the insanity! . . . I must make him believe Sam's in no danger . . .

(*Intensely*) Listen, Ned, I'm absolutely sure, from things she wrote me before she died, that Sam's mother must have been deliberately lying to me about the insanity that time. She was jealous because Sam loved me and she simply wanted to be revenged, I'm sure.

DARRELL (*without lowering glasses—dryly*) No. She told you the truth. I never mentioned it, but I went up there once and made a thorough investigation of his family.

NINA (*with resentful disappointment*) Oh—I suppose you wanted to make sure so you could hope he'd go insane?

DARRELL (*simply*) I needed to be able to hope that, then. I loved you horribly at that time, Nina—horribly!

NINA (*putting her hands on his arm*) And you don't—any more, Ned? (*Thinking intensely*)

Oh, I must make him love me again . . . enough to make him tell Sam! . . .

DARRELL (*thinking strangely—struggling with himself*)

She'd like to own me again . . . I wish she wouldn't touch me . . . what is this tie of old happiness between our flesh? . . .

(*Harshly—weakly struggling to shake off her hands, without lowering the glasses*) I won't meddle again with human lives, I told you!

NINA (*unheeding, clinging to him*) And I loved you horribly! I still do love you, Ned! I used to hope he'd go insane myself because I loved you so! But look at Sam! He's sane as a pig! There's absolutely no danger now!

DARRELL (*thinking—alarmed*)

What is she after now—what does she want me for? . . .

(*Stiffly*) I'm no longer a doctor but I should say he's a healthy miss of Nature's. It's a thousand to one against it at this late day.

NINA (*with sudden fierce intensity*) Then it's time to tell him the truth, isn't it? We've suffered all our lives for his sake! We've made him rich and happy! It's time he gave us back our son!

DARRELL (*thinking*)

Aha . . . so that's it! . . . tell Sam the truth? . . . at last! . . . by God, I'd like to tell him, at that! . . .

(*With a sneer*) Our son? You mean yours, my dear! Kindly count me out of any further meddling with—

NINA (*unruffledly—obsessed*) But Sam won't believe me if I'm the only one to tell him! He'll think I'm lying for spite, that it's only my crazy jealousy! He'll ask you! You've got to tell him too, Ned!

DARRELL (*thinking*)

I'd like to see his face when I told him his famous oarsman isn't his son but mine! . . . that might pay me back a little for all he's taken from me! . . .

(*Harshly*) I've stopped meddling in Sam's life, I tell you!

NINA (*insistently*) Think of what Sam has made us go through, of how he's made us suffer! You've got to tell him! You still love me a little, don't you, Ned? You must when you remember the happiness we've known in each other's arms! You were the only happiness I've ever known in life!

DARRELL (*struggling weakly—thinking*)

She lies! . . . there was her old lover, Gordon! . . . he was always first! . . . then her son, Gordon! . . .

(*With desperate rancor—thinking*)

Come on, Navy! . . . beat her Gordons for me! . . .

NINA (*intensely*) Oh, if I'd only gone away with you that time when you came back from Europe! How happy we would have been, dear! How our boy would have loved you—if it hadn't been for Sam!

DARRELL (*thinking—weakly*)

Yes, if it hadn't been for Sam I would have been happy! . . . I would have been the world's greatest neurologist! . . . my boy would have loved me and I'd have loved him! . . .

NINA (*with a crowning intensity to break down his last resistance*) You must tell him, Ned! For my sake! Because I love you! Because you remember our afternoons—our mad happiness! Because you love me!

DARRELL (*beaten—dazedly*) Yes—what must I do?—meddle again? (*The noise of* MADELINE'S *excited voice cheering and clapping her hands, of* MARSDEN'S *voice yelling drunkenly, of* EVANS', *all shouting "Gordon! Gordon! Come on, Gordon!" comes from the cabin.* MARSDEN *appears swaying in the cabin doorway yelling "Gordon!" He is hectically tipsy.* DARRELL *gives a violent shudder as if he were coming out of a nightmare and pushes* NINA *away from him*).

DARRELL (*thinking—dazedly still, but in a tone of relief*)

Marsden again! . . . thank God! . . . he's saved me! . . . from her! . . . and her Gordons! . . .

(*Turning on her triumphantly*) No, Nina—sorry—but I can't help you. I told you I'd never meddle again with human lives! (*More and more confidently*) Besides, I'm quite sure Gordon isn't my son, if the real deep core of the truth were known! I was only a body to you. Your first Gordon used to come back to life. I was never more to you than a substitute for your dead lover! Gordon is really Gordon's son! So you see I'd be telling Sam a lie if I boasted that I—And I'm a man of honor! I've proved that, at least! (*He raises his glasses and looks up the river—thinking exultantly*)

I'm free! . . . I've beaten her at last! . . . now come on, Navy! . . . you've got to beat her Gordons for me! . . .

NINA (*after staring at him for a moment—walking away from him—thinking with a dull fatalism*)

I've lost him . . . he'll never tell Sam now . . . is what he said right? . . . is Gordon Gordon's? . . . oh, I hope so! . . . oh, dear, dead Gordon, help me to get back your son! . . . I must find some way. . . .

(*She sits down again*).

MARSDEN (*who has been staring at them with a foolish grin*) Hello, you two! Why do you look so guilty? You don't love each other any more! It's all nonsense! I don't feel the slightest twinge of jealousy. That's proof enough, isn't it? (*Then blandly apologetic*) Pardon me if I sound a bit pipped—a good bit! Sam said ten and then took the bottle away when I'd had only five! But it's enough! I've forgotten sorrow! There's nothing in life worth grieving about, I assure you, Nina! And I've gotten interested in this race now. (*He sings raucously*) Oh, we'll row, row, row, right down the river! And we'll row, row, row—" Remember that old tune—when you were a little girl, Nina? Oh, I'm forgetting Sam said to tell you Gordon was on even terms with the leaders! A gallant spurt did it! Nip and tuck now! I don't care who wins—as long as it isn't Gordon! I don't like him since he's grown up! He thinks I'm an old woman! (*Sings*) "Row, row, row." The field against Gordon!

DARRELL (*hectically*) Right! (*He looks through the glasses—excitedly*) I see a flashing in the water way up there! Must be their oars! They're coming! I'll tell Sam! (*He hurries into the cabin*).

NINA (*thinking dully*)

He'll tell Sam . . . no, he doesn't mean that . . . I must find some other way . . .

MARSDEN (*walks a bit uncertainly to* NINA's *chair*) Gordon really should get beaten today—for the good of his soul, Nina. That Madeline is pretty, isn't she? These Gordons are too infernally lucky—while we others— (*He almost starts to blubber—angrily*) we others have got to beat him today! (*He slumps clumsily down to a sitting position on the deck by her chair and takes her hand and pats it*) There, there, Nina Cara Nina! Don't worry your pretty head! It will all come out all right! We'll only have a little while longer to wait and then you and I'll be quietly married! (*Thinking frightenedly*)

The devil! . . . what am I saying? . . . I'm drunk! . . . all right, all the better! . . . I've wanted all my life to tell her! . . .

Of course, I realize you've got a husband at present but, never mind, I can wait. I've waited a lifetime already; but for a long while now I've had a keen psychic intuition that I wasn't born to die before— (EVANS *and* MADELINE *and* DARRELL *come rushing out of the cabin. They all have binoculars. They run to the rail and train their glasses up the river*).

MADELINE (*excitedly*) I see them! (*Grabbing his arm and pointing*) Look, Mr. Evans—there—don't you see?

EVANS (*excitedly*) No—not yet— Yes! Now I see them! (*Pounding on the rail*) Come on, Gordon boy!

MADELINE Come on, Gordon! (*The whistles and sirens from the yachts up the river begin to be heard. This grows momentarily louder as one after another other yachts join in the chorus as the crews approach nearer and nearer until toward the close of the scene there is a perfect pandemonium of sound*).

NINA (*with bitter hatred—thinking*)

How I hate her! . . .

(*Then suddenly with a deadly calculation—thinking*)

Why not tell her? . . . as Sam's mother told me? . . . of the insanity? . . . she thinks Gordon is Sam's son.

(*With a deadly smile of triumph*)

That will be poetic justice! . . . that will solve everything! . . . she won't marry him! . . . he will turn to me for comfort! . . . but I must plan it out carefully! . . .

MARSDEN (*driven on—extravagantly*) Listen, Nina! After we're married I'm going to write a novel—my first real novel! All the twenty odd books I've written have been long-winded fairy tales for grown-ups—about dear old ladies and witty, cynical bachelors and quaint characters with dialects, and married folk who always admire and respect each other, and lovers who avoid love in hushed whispers! That's what I've been, Nina—a hush-hush whisperer of lies! Now I'm going to give an honest healthy yell—turn on the sun into the shadows of lies—shout "This is life and this is sex, and here are passion and hatred and regret and joy and pain and ecstasy, and these are men and women and sons and daughters whose hearts are weak and strong, whose blood is blood and not a soothing syrup!" Oh, I can do it, Nina! I can write the truth! I've seen it in you, your father, my mother, sister, Gordon, Sam, Darrell and myself. I'll write the book of us! But here I am talking while my last chapters are in the making—right here and now— (*Hurriedly*) You'll excuse me won't you, Nina? I must watch—my duty as an artist! (*He scrambles to his feet and peers about him with a hectic eagerness.* NINA *pays no attention to him*).

EVANS (*exasperatedly, taking down his glasses*) You can't tell a damn thing—which is which or who's ahead—I'm going to listen in again. (*He hurries into the cabin*).

NINA (*with a smile of cruel triumph—thinking*)

I can tell her . . . confidentially . . . I can pretend I'm forced to tell her . . . as Sam's mother did with me . . . because I feel it's due to her happiness and Gordon's . . . it will explain my objection to the engagement . . . oh, it can't help succeeding . . . my Gordon will come back! . . . I'll see he never gets away again! . . .

(*She calls*) Madeline!

MARSDEN (*thinking*)

Why is she calling Madeline? . . . I must watch all this carefully! . . .

EVANS (*comes rushing out in wild alarm*) Bad news! Navy has drawn ahead—half a length—looks like Navy's race, he said— (*Then violently*) But what does he know, the damn fool announcer—some poor boob—!

MADELINE (*excitedly*) He doesn't know Gordon! He's always best when he's pushed to the limit!

NINA (*she calls more sharply*) Madeline!

DARRELL (*turns around to stare at her—thinking*)

Why is she calling Madeline? . . . she's bound she'll meddle in their lives . . . I've got to watch her . . . well, let's see. . . .

(*He touches* MADELINE *on the shoulder*) Mrs. Evans is calling you, Miss Arnold.

MADELINE (*impatiently*) Yes, Mrs. Evans. But they're getting closer. Why don't you come and watch?

NINA (*not heeding—impressively*) There's something I must tell you.

MADELINE (*in hopeless irritation*) But— Oh, all right. (*She hurries over to her, glancing eagerly over her shoulder towards the river*) Yes, Mrs. Evans?

DARRELL (*moves from the rail toward them—thinking keenly*)

I must watch this . . . she's in a desperate meddling mood! . . .

NINA (*impressively*) First, give me your word of honor that you'll never reveal a word of what I'm going to tell you to a living soul—above all not to Gordon!

MADELINE (*looking at her in amazement—soothingly*) Couldn't you tell me later, Mrs. Evans—after the race?

NINA (*sternly—grabbing her by the wrist*) No, now! Do you promise?

MADELINE (*with helpless annoyance*) Yes, Mrs. Evans.

NINA (*sternly*) For the sake of your future happiness and my son's I've got to speak! Your engagement forces me to! You've probably wondered why I objected. It's because the marriage is impossible. You can't marry Gordon! I speak as your friend! You must break your engagement with him at once!

MADELINE (*cannot believe her ears—suddenly panic-stricken*) But why—why?

DARRELL (*who has come closer—resentfully thinking*)
She wants to ruin my son's life as she ruined mine! . . .

NINA (*relentlessly*) Why? Because—

DARRELL (*steps up suddenly beside them—sharply and sternly commanding*) No, Nina! (*He taps* MADELINE *on the shoulder and draws her aside.* NINA *lets go of her wrist and stares after them in a sort of stunned stupor*) Miss Arnold, as a doctor I feel it my duty to tell you that Mrs. Evans isn't herself. Pay no attention to anything she may say to you. She's just passed through a crucial period in a woman's life and she's morbidly jealous of you and subject to queer delusions! (*He smiles kindly at her*) So get back to the race! And God bless you! (*He grips her hand, strangely moved*).

MADELINE (*gratefully*) Thank you. I understand, I think. Poor Mrs. Evans! (*She hurries back to the rail, raising her glasses*).

NINA (*springing to her feet and finding her voice—with despairing accusation*) Ned!

DARRELL (*steps quickly to her side*) I'm sorry, Nina, but I warned you not to meddle. (*Then affectionately*) And Gordon is—well—sort of my stepson, isn't he? I really want him to be happy. (*Then smiling good-naturedly*) All the same, I can't help hoping he'll be beaten in this race. As an oarsman he recalls his father, Gordon Shaw, to me. (*He turns away and raises his glasses, going back to the rail.* NINA *slumps down in her chair again*).

EVANS Damn! They all look even from here! Can you tell which is which, Madeline?

MADELINE No—not yet—oh, dear, this is awful! Gordon!

NINA (*looking about her in the air—with a dazed question*) Gordon?

MARSDEN (*thinking*)
Damn that Darrell! . . . if he hadn't interfered Nina would have told . . . something of infinite importance, I know! . . .
(*He comes and again sits on the deck by her chair and takes

her hand) Because what, Nina—my dear little Nina Cara Nina—because what? Let me help you!

NINA (*staring before her as if she were in a trance—simply, like a young girl*) Yes, Charlie. Yes, Father. Because all of Sam's father's family have been insane. His mother told me that time so I wouldn't have his baby. I was going to tell Madeline that so she wouldn't marry Gordon. But it would have been a lie because Gordon isn't really Sam's child at all, he's Ned's. Ned gave him to me and I gave him to Sam so Sam could have a healthy child and be well and happy. And Sam is well and happy, don't you think? (*Childishly*) So I haven't been such an awfully wicked girl, have I, Father?

MARSDEN (*horrified and completely sobered by what he has heard—stares at her with stunned eyes*) Nina! Good God! Do you know what you're saying?

MADELINE (*excitedly*) There! The one on this side! I saw the color on their blades just now!

EVANS (*anxiously*) Are you sure? Then he's a little behind the other two!

DARRELL (*excitedly*) The one in the middle seems to be ahead! Is that the Navy? (*But the others pay no attention to him. All three are leaning over the rail, their glasses glued to their eyes, looking up the river. The noise from the whistles is now very loud. The cheering from the observation trains can be heard*).

MARSDEN (*stares into her face with great pity now*) Merciful God, Nina! Then you've lived all these years—with this horror! And you and Darrell deliberately—?

NINA (*without looking at him—to the air*) Sam's mother said I had a right to be happy too.

MARSDEN And you didn't love Darrell then—?

NINA (*as before*) I did afterwards. I don't now. Ned is dead, too. (*Softly*) Only you are alive now, Father—and Gordon.

MARSDEN (*gets up and bends over her paternally, stroking her hair with a strange, wild, joyous pity*) Oh, Nina—poor little Nina—my Nina—how you must have suffered! I forgive you! I forgive you everything! I forgive even your trying to tell Madeline—you wanted to keep Gordon—oh, I understand that —and I forgive you!

NINA (*as before—affectionately and strangely*) And I forgive you, Father. It was all your fault in the beginning, wasn't it? You mustn't ever meddle with human lives again!

EVANS (*wildly excited*) Gordon's sprinting, isn't he? He's drawing up on that middle one!

MADELINE Yes! Oh, come on, Gordon!

DARRELL (*exultantly*) Come on, Navy!

EVANS (*who is standing next to* NED, *whirls on him in a furious passion*) What's that? What the hell's the matter with you?

DARRELL (*facing him—with a strange friendliness slaps him on the back*) We've got to beat these Gordons, Sam! We've got to beat—

EVANS (*raging*) You—! (*He draws back his fist—then suddenly horrified at what he is doing but still angry, grabs* DARRELL *by both shoulders and shakes him*) Wake up! What the hell's got into you? Have you gone crazy?

DARRELL (*mockingly*) Probably! It runs in my family! All of my father's people were happy lunatics—not healthy, country folk like yours, Sam! Ha!

EVANS (*staring at him*) Ned, old man, what's the trouble? You said "Navy."

DARRELL (*ironically—with a bitter hopeless laugh*) Slip of the tongue! I meant Gordon! Meant Gordon, of course! Gordon is always meant—meant to win! Come on, Gordon! It's fate!

MADELINE Here they come! They're both spurting! I can see Gordon's back!

EVANS (*forgetting everything else, turns back to the race*) Come on, boy! Come on, son! (*The chorus of noise is now a bedlam as the crews near the finish line. The people have to yell and scream to make themselves heard*).

NINA (*getting up—thinking with a strange, strident, wild passion*)

> I hear the Father laughing! . . . O Mother God, protect my son! . . . let Gordon fly to you in heaven! . . . quick, Gordon . . . love is the Father's lightning! . . . Madeline will bring you down in flames! . . . I hear His screaming laughter! . . . fly back to me! . . .

(*She is looking desperately up into the sky as if some race of life and death were happening there for her*).

EVANS (*holding on to a stanchion and leaning far out at the imminent risk of falling in*) One spurt more will do it! Come on, boy, come on! It took death to beat Gordon Shaw! You can't be beaten either, Gordon! Lift her out of the water, son! Stroke! Stroke! He's gaining now! Over the line, boy! Over with her! Stroke! That's done it! He's won! He's won!

MADELINE (*has been shrieking at the same time*) Gordon! Gordon! He's won! Oh, he's fainted! Poor dear darling! (*She remains standing on the rail, leaning out dangerously, holding on with one hand, looking down longingly toward his shell*).

EVANS (*bounding back to the deck, his face congested and purple with a frenzy of joy, dancing about*) He's won! By God, it was close! Greatest race in the history of rowing! He's the greatest oarsman God ever made! (*Embracing* NINA *and kissing her frantically*) Aren't you happy, Nina? Our Gordon! The greatest ever!

NINA (*torturedly—trying incoherently to force out a last despairing protest*) No!—not yours!—mine!—and Gordon's! —Gordon is Gordon's!—he was my Gordon!—his Gordon is mine!

EVANS (*soothingly, humoring her—kissing her again*) Of course he's yours, dear—and a dead ringer for Gordon Shaw, too! Gordon's body! Gordon's spirit! Your body and spirit, too, Nina! He's not like me, lucky for him! I'm a poor boob! I never could row worth a damn! (*He suddenly staggers as if he were very drunk, leaning on* MARSDEN*—then gives a gasp and collapses inertly to the deck, lying on his back*).

MARSDEN (*stares down at him stupidly—then thinking strangely*)

I knew it! . . . I saw the end beginning! . . .

(*He touches* NINA'S *arm—in a low voice*) Nina—your husband! (*Touching* DARRELL *who has stood staring straight before him with a bitter ironical smile on his lips*) Ned—your friend! Doctor Darrell—a patient!

NINA (*stares down at* EVANS*—slowly, as if trying to bring her mind back to him*) My husband? (*Suddenly with a cry of pain, sinks on her knees beside the body*) Sam!

DARRELL (*looking down at him—thinking yearningly*)

Is her husband dead . . . at last? . . .

(*Then with a shudder at his thoughts*)

No! . . . I don't hope! . . . I don't! . . .

(*He cries*) Sam! (*He kneels down, feels of his heart, pulse, looks into his face—with a change to a strictly professional manner*) He's not dead. Only a bad stroke.

NINA (*with a cry of grief*) Oh, Ned, did all our old secret hopes do this at last?

DARRELL (*professionally, staring at her coldly*) Bosh, Mrs.

Evans! We're not in the Congo that we can believe in evil charms! (*Sternly*) In his condition, Mr. Evans must have absolute quiet and peace of mind or— And perfect care! You must tend him night and day! And I will! We've got to keep him happy!

NINA (*dully*). Again? (*Then sternly in her turn, as if swearing a pledge to herself*) I will never leave his side! I will never tell him anything that might disturb his peace!

MARSDEN (*standing above them—thinking exultantly*)

I will not have long to wait now! . . .

(*Then ashamed*)

How can I think such things . . . poor Sam! . . . he was . . .
I mean he is my friend . . .

(*With assertive loyalty*) A rare spirit! A pure and simple soul! A good man—yes, a good man! God bless him! (*He makes a motion over the body like a priest blessing*).

DARRELL (*his voice suddenly breaking with a sincere human grief*) Sam, old boy! I'm so damned sorry! I will give my life to save you!

NINA (*in dull anguish*) Save—again? (*Then lovingly, kissing* EVANS' *face*) Dear husband, you have tried to make me happy, I will give you my happiness again! I will give you Gordon to give to Madeline!

MADELINE (*still standing on the rail, staring after* GORDON'S *shell*)

Gordon! . . . dear lover . . . how tired . . . but you'll rest in
my arms . . . your head will lie on my breast . . . soon! . . .

CURTAIN

ACT NINE

SCENE: *Several months later. A terrace on the* EVANS' *estate on Long Island. In the rear, the terrace overlooks a small harbor with the ocean beyond. On the right is a side entrance of the pretentious villa. On the left is a hedge with an arched gateway leading to a garden. The terrace is paved with rough stone. There is a stone bench at center, a recliner at right, a wicker table and armchair at left.*

It is late afternoon of a day in early fall. GORDON EVANS *is sitting on the stone bench, his chin propped on his hands,* MADELINE *standing behind him, her arm about his shoulders.* GORDON *is over six feet tall with the figure of a trained athlete. His sun-bronzed face is extremely handsome after the fashion of the magazine cover American collegian. It is a strong face but of a strength wholly material in quality. He has been too thoroughly trained to progress along a certain groove to success ever to question it or be dissatisfied with its rewards. At the same time, although entirely an unimaginative code-bound gentleman of his groove, he is boyish and likable, of an even, modest, sporting disposition. His expression is boyishly forlorn, but he is making a manly effort to conceal his grief.*

MADELINE *is much the same as in the previous Act except that there is now a distinct maternal older feeling in her attitude toward* GORDON *as she endeavors to console him.*

MADELINE (*tenderly, smoothing his hair*) There, dear! I know how horribly hard it is for you. I loved him, too. He was so wonderful and sweet to me.

GORDON (*his voice trembling*) I didn't really realize he was gone—until out at the cemetery— (*His voice breaks*).

MADELINE (*kissing his hair*) Darling! Please don't!

GORDON (*rebelliously*) Damn it, I don't see why he had to die! (*With a groan*) It was that constant grind at the office! I ought to have insisted on his taking better care of himself. But I wasn't home enough, that's the trouble. I couldn't watch him. (*Then bitterly*) But I can't see why Mother didn't!

MADELINE (*reprovingly but showing she shares his feeling*) Now! You mustn't start feeling bitter toward her.

GORDON (*contritely*) I know I shouldn't. (*But returning to his bitter tone*) But I can't help remembering how unreasonably she's acted about our engagement.

MADELINE Not since your father was taken sick, she hasn't, dear. She's been wonderfully nice.

GORDON (*in the same tone*) Nice? Indifferent, you mean! She doesn't seem to care a damn one way or the other any more!

MADELINE You could hardly expect her to think of anyone but your father. She's been with him every minute. I never saw such devotion. (*Thinking*)

> Will Gordon ever get old and sick like that? . . . oh, I hope we'll both die before! . . . but I'd nurse him just as she did his father . . . I'll always love him! . . .

GORDON (*consoled—proudly*) Yes, she sure was wonderful to him, all right! (*Then coming back to his old tone*) But—this may sound rotten of me—I always had a queer feeling she was doing it as a duty. And when he died, I felt her grief was—not from love for him—at least, only the love of a friend, not a wife's love. (*As if under some urgent compulsion from within*) I've never told you, but I've always felt, ever since I was a little kid, that she didn't really love Dad. She liked him and respected him. She was a wonderful wife. But I'm sure she didn't love him. (*Blurting it out as if he couldn't help it*) I'll tell you, Madeline! I've always felt she cared a lot for—Darrell. (*Hastily*) Of course, I might be wrong. (*Then bursting out*) No, I'm not wrong! I've felt it too strongly, ever since I was a kid. And then when I was eleven—something happened. I've been sure of it since then.

MADELINE (*thinking in amazement, but not without a queer satisfaction*)

> Does he mean that she was unfaithful to his father? . . . no, he'd never believe that . . . but what else could he mean? . . .

(*Wonderingly*) Gordon! Do you mean you've been sure that your mother was—

GORDON (*outraged by something in her tone—jumping to his feet and flinging her hand off—roughly*) Was what? What do you mean, Madeline?

MADELINE (*frightened—placatingly puts her arms around him*) I didn't mean anything, dear. I simply thought you meant—

GORDON (*still indignant*) All I meant was that she must have fallen in love with Darrell long after she was married—and then she sent him away for Dad's sake—and mine, too, I suppose. He kept coming back every couple of years. He didn't have guts enough to stay away for good! Oh, I suppose I'm unfair. I suppose it was damned hard on him. He fought it down, too, on account of his friendship for Dad. (*Then with a bitter laugh*) I suppose they'll be getting married now! And I'll have to wish them good luck. Dad would want me to. He was game. (*With a bitter gloomy air*) Life is damn queer, that's all I've got to say!

MADELINE (*thinking with a sort of tender, loving scorn for his boyish naïveté*)

How little he knows her! . . . Mr. Evans was a fine man but . . . Darrell must have been fascinating once . . . if she loved anyone she isn't the kind who would hesitate . . . any more than I have with Gordon . . . oh, I'll never be unfaithful to Gordon . . . I'll love him always! . . .

(*She runs her fingers through his hair caressingly—comfortingly*) You must never blame them, dear. No one can help love. We couldn't, could we? (*She sits beside him. He takes her in his arms. They kiss each other with rising passion.* MARSDEN *comes in noiselessly from the garden, a bunch of roses and a pair of shears in his hands. He looks younger, calm and contented. He is dressed in his all black, meticulous, perfectly tailored mourning costume. He stands looking at the two lovers, a queer agitation coming into his face*).

MARSDEN (*scandalized as an old maid—thinking*)

I must say! . . . his father hardly cold in his grave! . . . it's positively bestial! . . .

(*Then struggling with himself—with a defensive self-mockery*)

Only it wasn't his father . . . what is Sam to Darrell's son? . . . and even if he were Sam's son, what have the living to do with the dead? . . . his duty is to love that life may keep on living . . . and what has their loving to do with me? . . . my life is cool green shade wherein comes no scorching zenith sun of passion and possession to wither the heart with bitter poisons . . . my life gathers roses, coolly crimson, in sheltered gardens, on late afternoons in love with evening . . . roses heavy with after-blooming of the long day, desiring evening . . . my life is an evening . . . Nina is a rose, my rose, exhausted by the long, hot day, leaning wearily toward peace. . . .

(*He kisses one of the roses with a simple sentimental smile—then still smiling, makes a gesture toward the two lovers*)

That is on another planet, called the world . . . Nina and I have moved on to the moon. . . .

MADELINE (*passionately*) Dear one! Sweetheart!

GORDON Madeline! I love you!

MARSDEN (*looking at them—gaily mocking—thinking*)

Once I'd have felt jealous . . . cheated . . . swindled by God out of joy! . . . I would have thought bitterly, "The Gordons have all the luck!" . . . but now I know that dear old Charlie . . . yes, poor dear old Charlie!—passed beyond desire, has all the luck at last! . . .

(*Then matter-of-factly*)

But I'll have to interrupt their biological preparations . . . there are many things still to be done this evening . . . Age's terms of peace, after the long interlude of war with life, have still to be concluded . . . Youth must keep decently away . . . so many old wounds may have to be unbound, and old scars pointed to with pride, to prove to ourselves we have been brave and noble! . . .

(*He lets the shears drop to the ground. They jump startledly and turn around. He smiles quietly*) Sorry to disturb you. I've been picking some roses for your mother, Gordon. Flowers really have the power to soothe grief. I suppose it was that discovery that led to their general use at funerals—and weddings! (*He hands a rose to* MADELINE) Here, Madeline, here's a rose for you. Hail, Love, we who have died, salute you! (*He smiles strangely. She takes the rose automatically, staring at him uncomprehendingly*).

MADELINE (*thinking suspiciously*)

What a queer creature! . . . there's something uncanny! . . . oh, don't be silly! . . . it's only poor old Charlie! . . .

(*She makes him a mocking curtsey*) Thank you, Uncle Charlie!

GORDON (*thinking with sneering pity*)

Poor old guy! . . . he means well . . . Dad liked him. . . .

(*Pretending an interest in the roses*) They're pretty. (*Then suddenly*) Where's Mother—still in the house?

MARSDEN She was trying to get rid of the last of the people. I'm going in. Shall I tell her you want to see her? It would give her an excuse to get away.

GORDON Yes. Will you? (MARSDEN *goes into the house on right*).

MADELINE You'd better see your mother alone. I'll go down to the plane and wait for you. You want to fly back before dark, don't you?

GORDON Yes, and we ought to get started soon. (*Moodily*) Maybe it would be better if you weren't here. There are some things I feel I ought to say to her—and Darrell. I've got to do what I know Dad would have wanted. I've got to be fair. He always was to everyone all his life.

MADELINE You dear, you! You couldn't be unfair to anyone if you tried! (*She kisses him*) Don't be too long.

GORDON (*moodily*) You bet I won't! It won't be so pleasant I'll want to drag it out!

MADELINE Good-bye for a while then.

GORDON So long. (*He looks after her lovingly as she goes out right, rear, around the corner of the house. Thinking*)

Madeline's wonderful! . . . I don't deserve my luck . . . but, God, I sure do love her! . . .

(*He sits down on the bench again, his chin on his hands*)

It seems rotten and selfish to be happy . . . when Dad . . . oh, he understands, he'd want me to be . . . it's funny how I got to care more for Dad than for Mother . . . I suppose it was finding out she loved Darrell . . . I can remember that day seeing her kiss him . . . it did something to me I never got over . . . but she made Dad happy . . . she gave up her own happiness for his sake . . . that was certainly damn fine . . . that was playing the game . . . I'm a hell of a one to criticize . . . my own mother! . . .

(*Changing the subject of his thoughts abruptly*)

Forget it! . . . think of Madeline . . . we'll be married . . . then two months' honeymoon in Europe . . . God, that'll be great! . . . then back and dive into the business . . . Dad relied on me to carry on where he left off . . . I'll have to start at the bottom but I'll get to the top in a hurry, I promise you that, Dad! . . .

(NINA *and* DARRELL *come out of the house on the right. He hears the sound of the door and looks around. Thinking resentfully*)

Funny! . . . I can't stand it even now! . . . when I see him with Mother! . . . I'd like to beat him up! . . .

(*He gets to his feet, his face unconsciously becoming older and cold and severe. He stares accusingly at them as they come slowly toward him in silence.* NINA *looks much older than in the preceding Act. Resignation has come into her face, a resignation that uses no makeup, that has given up the struggle to be sexually attractive and look younger. She is dressed in deep black.* DARRELL'S *deep sunburn of the tropics has faded, leaving his skin a Mongolian yellow. He, too, looks much older. His expression is sad and bitter*).

NINA (*glancing at* GORDON *searchingly—thinking sadly*)

He sent for me to say good-bye . . . really good-bye forever this time . . . he's not my son now, nor Gordon's son, nor Sam's, nor Ned's . . . he has become that stranger, another woman's lover. . . .

DARRELL (*also after a quick keen glance at* GORDON'S *face thinking*)

There's something up . . . some final accounting . . .

(*Thinking resignedly*)

Well, let's get it over . . . then I can go back to work. . . . I've stayed too long up here . . . Preston must be wondering if I've deserted him. . . .

(*Then with a wondering sadness*)

Is that my son? . . . my flesh and blood? . . . staring at me with such cold enmity? . . . how sad and idiotic this all is! . . .

NINA (*putting on a tone of joking annoyance*) Your message was a godsend, Gordon. Those stupid people with their social condolences were killing me. Perhaps I'm morbid but I always have the feeling that they're secretly glad someone is dead—that it flatters their vanity and makes them feel superior because they're living. (*She sits wearily on the bench.* DARRELL *sits on side of the recliner at right*).

GORDON (*repelled by this idea—stiffly*) They were all good friends of Dad's. Why shouldn't they be sincerely sorry? His death ought to be a loss to everyone who knew him. (*His voice trembles. He turns away and walks to the table. Thinking bitterly*)

She doesn't care a damn! . . . she's free to marry Darrell now! . . .

NINA (*thinking sadly, looking at his back*)

He's accusing me because I'm not weeping . . . well, I did weep . . . all I could . . . there aren't many tears left . . . it was too bad Sam had to die . . . living suited him . . . he was so contented with himself . . . but I can't feel guilty . . . I helped him to live . . . I made him believe I loved him . . . his mind was perfectly sane to the end . . . and just before he died, he smiled at me . . . so gratefully and forgivingly, I thought . . . closing our life together with that smile . . . that life is dead . . . it's regrets are dead . . . I am sad but there's comfort in the thought that now I am free at last to rot away in peace . . . I'll go and live in Father's old home . . . Sam bought that back . . . I suppose he left it to me . . . Charlie will come in every day to visit . . . he'll comfort and amuse me . . . we can talk together of the old days . . . when I was a girl . . . when I was happy . . . before I fell in love with Gordon Shaw and all this tangled mess of love and hate and pain and birth began! . . .

DARRELL (*staring at* GORDON'S *back resentfully*)

It gets under my skin to see him act so unfeelingly toward his mother! . . . if he only knew what she's suffered for his sake! . . . the Gordon Shaw ideal passed on through Sam has certainly made my son an insensitive clod! . . .

(*With disgust*)

Bah, what has that young man to do with me? . . . compared to Preston he's only a well-muscled, handsome fool! . . .

(*With a trace of anger*)

But I'd like to jolt his stupid self-complacency! . . . if he knew the facts about himself, he wouldn't be sobbing sentimentally about Sam . . . he'd better change his tune or I'll certainly be tempted to tell him . . . there's no reason for his not knowing now . . .

(*His face is flushed. He has worked himself into a real anger*).

GORDON (*suddenly, having got back his control, turns to them—coldly*) There are certain things connected with Dad's will I thought I ought to— (*With a tinge of satisfied superiority*) I don't believe Dad told you about his will, did he, Mother?

NINA (*indifferently*) No.

GORDON Well, the whole estate goes to you and me, of course. I didn't mean that. (*With a resentful look at* DARRELL) But there is one provision that is peculiar, to say the least. It concerns you, Doctor Darrell—a half-million for your Station to be used in biological research work.

DARRELL (*his face suddenly flushing with anger*) What's that? That's a joke, isn't it? (*Thinking furiously*)

It's worse! . . . it's a deliberate insult! . . . a last sneer of ownership! . . . of my life! . . .

GORDON (*coldly sneering*) I thought it must be a joke myself—but Dad insisted.

DARRELL (*angrily*) Well, I won't accept it—and that's final!

GORDON (*coldly*) It's not left to you but to the Station. Your supervision is mentioned but I suppose if you won't carry on, whoever is in real charge down there will be only too glad to accept it.

DARRELL (*stupefied*) That means Preston! But Sam didn't even know Preston—except from hearing me talk about him! What had Sam to do with Preston? Preston is none of his business! I'll advise Preston to refuse it! (*Thinking torturedly*)

But it's for science! . . . he has no right to refuse! . . . I have no right to ask him to! . . . God damn Sam! . . . wasn't it enough for him to own my wife, my son, in his lifetime? . . .

now in death he reaches out to steal Preston! . . . to steal my work! . . .

NINA (*thinking bitterly*)

Even in death Sam makes people suffer . . .

(*Sympathetically*) It isn't for you—nor for Preston. It's for science, Ned. You must look at it that way.

GORDON (*thinking resentfully*)

What a tender tone she takes toward him! . . . she's forgotten Dad already! . . .

(*With a sneer*) You'd better accept. Half-millions aren't being thrown away for nothing every day.

NINA (*in anguish—thinking*)

How can Gordon insult poor Ned like that! . . . his own father! . . . Ned has suffered too much! . . .

(*Sharply*) I think you've said about enough, Gordon!

GORDON (*bitterly, but trying to control himself—meaningly*) I haven't said all I'm going to say, Mother!

NINA (*thinking—at first frightenedly*)

What does he mean? . . . does he know about Ned being . . . ?

(*Then with a sort of defiant relief*)

Well, what does it matter what he thinks of me? . . . he's hers now, anyway. . . .

DARRELL (*thinking vindictively*)

I hope he knows the truth, for if he doesn't, by God, I'll tell him! . . . if only to get something back from Sam of all he's stolen from me! . . .

(*Authoritatively—as* GORDON *hesitates*) Well, what have you got to say? Your mother and I are waiting.

GORDON (*furiously, taking a threatening step toward him*) Shut up, you! Don't take that tone with me or I'll forget your age— (*Contemptuously*) and give you a spanking!

NINA (*thinking hysterically*)

Spanking! . . . the son spanks the father! . . .

(*Laughing hysterically*) Oh, Gordon, don't make me laugh! It's all so funny!

DARRELL (*jumps from his chair and goes to her—solicitously*) Nina! Don't mind him! He doesn't realize—

GORDON (*maddened, comes closer*) I realize a lot! I realize you've acted like a cur! (*He steps forward and slaps* DARRELL *across the face viciously.* DARRELL *staggers back from the force of the blow, his hands to his face,* NINA *screams and flings herself on* GORDON, *holding his arms*).

NINA (*piteously—hysterically*) For God's sake, Gordon!

What would your father say? You don't know what you're doing! You're hitting your father!

DARRELL (*suddenly breaking down—chokingly*) No—it's all right, son—all right—you didn't know—

GORDON (*crushed, overcome by remorse for his blow*) I'm sorry—sorry—you're right, Mother—Dad would feel as if I'd hit him—just as bad as if I'd hit him!

DARRELL It's nothing, son—nothing!

GORDON (*brokenly*) That's damn fine, Darrell—damn fine and sporting of you! It was a rotten, dirty trick! Accept my apology, Darrell, won't you?

DARRELL (*staring at him stupidly—thinking*)

Darrell? . . . he calls me Darrell! . . . but doesn't he know? . . . I thought she told him. . . .

NINA (*laughing hysterically—thinking*)

I told him he hit his father . . . but he can't understand me! . . . why, of course he can't! . . . how could he? . . .

GORDON (*insistently holding out his hand*) I'm damned sorry! I didn't mean it! Shake hands, won't you?

DARRELL (*doing so mechanically—stupidly*) Only too glad—pleased to meet you—know you by reputation—the famous oarsman—great race you stroked last June—but I was hoping the Navy would give you a beating.

NINA (*thinking in desperate hysterical anguish*)

Oh, I wish Ned would go away and stay away forever! . . . I can't bear to watch him suffer any more! . . . it's too frightful! . . . yes, God the Father, I hear you laughing . . . you see the joke . . . I'm laughing too . . . it's all so crazy, isn't it? . . .

(*Laughing hysterically*) Oh, Ned! Poor Ned! You were born unlucky!

GORDON (*making her sit down again—soothing her*) Mother! Stop laughing! Please! It's all right—all right between us! I've apologized! (*As she has grown calmer*) And now I want to say what I was going to say. It wasn't anything bad. It was just that I wanted you to know how fine I think you've both acted. I've known ever since I was a kid that you and Darrell were in love with each other. I hated the idea on Father's account—that's only natural, isn't it?—but I knew it was unfair, that people can't help loving each other any more than Madeline and I could have helped ourselves. And I saw how fair you both were to Dad—what a good wife you were, Mother—what a true friend you were, Darrell—and how damn much he loved you both! So all I wanted to say is, now he's dead, I hope you'll get married and I hope you'll be as happy as you both deserve— (*Here he breaks down, kissing her and then breaking away*) I've got to say good-bye—got to fly back before dark—Madeline's waiting. (*He takes* DARRELL'S *hand and shakes it again. They have both been staring at him stupidly*) Good-bye Darrell! Good luck!

DARRELL (*thinking sufferingly*)

> Why does he keep on calling me Darrell . . . he's my boy . . . I'm his father . . . I've got to make him realize I'm his father! . . .

(*Holding* GORDON'S *hand*) Listen, son. It's my turn. I've got to tell you something—

NINA (*thinking torturedly*)

> Oh, he mustn't! . . . I feel he mustn't! . . .

(*Sharply*) Ned! First, let me ask Gordon a question. (*Then looking her son in the eyes, slowly and impressively*) Do you think I was ever unfaithful to your father, Gordon?

GORDON (*startled, stares at her—shocked and horrified—then suddenly he blurts out indignantly*) Mother, what do you think I am—as rotten-minded as that! (*Pleadingly*) Please, Mother, I'm not as bad as that! I know you're the best woman that ever lived—the best of all! I don't even except Madeline!

NINA (*with a sobbing triumphant cry*) My dear Gordon! You do love me, don't you?

GORDON (*kneeling beside her and kissing her*) Of course!

NINA (*pushing him away—tenderly*) And now go! Hurry! Madeline is waiting! Give her my love! Come to see me once in a while in the years to come! Good-bye, dear! (*Turning to* DARRELL, *who is standing with a sad resigned expression—imploringly*) Did you still want to tell Gordon something, Ned?

DARRELL (*forcing a tortured smile*) Not for anything in the world! Good-bye, son.

GORDON Good-bye, sir. (*He hurries off around the corner of the house at left, rear, thinking troubledly*)

> What does she think I am? . . . I've never thought that! . . . I couldn't! . . . my own mother! I'd kill myself if I ever even caught myself thinking . . . !

(*He is gone*).

NINA (*turns to* NED, *gratefully taking his hand and pressing it*) Poor dear Ned, you've always had to give! How can I ever thank you?

DARRELL (*with an ironical smile—forcing a joking tone*) By refusing me when I ask you to marry me! For I've got to ask you! Gordon expects it! And he'll be so pleased when he knows you turned me down. (MARSDEN *comes out of the house*) Hello, here comes Charlie. I must hurry. Will you marry me, Nina?

NINA (*with a sad smile*) No. Certainly not. Our ghosts would torture us to death! (*Then forlornly*) But I wish I did love you, Ned! Those were wonderful afternoons long ago! The Nina of those afternoons will always live in me, will always love her lover, Ned, the father of her baby!

DARRELL (*lifting her hands to his lips—tenderly*) Thank you for that! And that Ned will always adore his beautiful Nina! Remember him! Forget me! I'm going back to work. (*He laughs softly and sadly*) I leave you to Charlie. You'd better marry him, Nina—if you want peace. And after all, I think you owe it to him for his life-long devotion.

MARSDEN (*thinking uneasily*)

They're talking about me . . . why doesn't he go? . . . she doesn't love him any more . . . even now he's all heat and energy and the tormenting drive of noon . . . can't he see she is in love with evening? . . .

(*Clearing his throat uneasily*) Do I hear my name taken in vain?

NINA (*looking at* MARSDEN *with a strange yearning*)

Peace! . . . yes . . . that is all I desire . . . I can no longer imagine happiness . . . Charlie has found peace . . . he will be tender . . . as my father was when I was a girl . . . when I could imagine happiness . . .

(*With a girlish coquettishness and embarrassment—making way for him on the bench beside her—strangely*) Ned's just proposed to me. I refused him, Charlie. I don't love him any more.

MARSDEN (*sitting down beside her*) I suspected as much. Then whom do you love, Nina Cara Nina?

NINA (*sadly smiling*) You, Charlie, I suppose. I have always loved your love for me. (*She kisses him—wistfully*) Will you let me rot away in peace?

MARSDEN (*strongly*) All my life I've waited to bring you peace.

NINA (*sadly teasing*) If you've waited that long, Charlie, we'd better get married tomorrow. But I forgot. You haven't asked me yet, have you? Do you want me to marry you, Charlie?

MARSDEN (*humbly*) Yes, Nina. (*Thinking with a strange ecstasy*)

I knew the time would come at last when I would hear her ask that! . . . I could never have said it, never! . . . oh, russet-golden afternoon, you are a mellow fruit of happiness ripely falling! . . .

DARRELL (*amused—with a sad smile*) Bless you, my children! (*He turns to go*).

NINA I don't suppose we'll ever see you again, Ned.

DARRELL I hope not, Nina. A scientist shouldn't believe in ghosts. (*With a mocking smile*) But perhaps we'll become part of cosmic positive and negative electric charges and meet again.

NINA In our afternoons—again?

DARRELL (*smiling sadly*) Again. In our afternoons.

MARSDEN (*coming out of his day dream*) We'll be married in the afternoon, decidedly. I've already picked out the church, Nina—a gray ivied chapel, full of restful shadow, symbolical of the peace we have found. The crimsons and purples in the windows will stain our faces with faded passion. It must be in the hour before sunset when the earth dreams in afterthoughts and mystic premonitions of life's beauty. And then we'll go up to your old home to live. Mine wouldn't be suitable for us. Mother and Jane live there in memory. And I'll work in your father's old study. He won't mind me. (*From the bay below comes the roaring hum of an airplane motor.* NINA *and* DARRELL *jump startledly and go to the rear of the terrace to watch the plane ascend from the water, standing side by side.* MARSDEN *remains oblivious*).

NINA (*with anguish*) Gordon! Good-bye, dear! (*Pointing as the plane climbs higher moving away off to the left—bitterly*) See, Ned! He's leaving me without a backward look!

DARRELL (*joyfully*) No! He's circling. He's coming back! (*The roar of the engine grows steadily nearer now*) He's going to pass directly over us! (*Their eyes follow the plane as it comes swiftly nearer and passes directly over them*) See! He's waving to us!

NINA Oh, Gordon! My dear son! (*She waves frantically*).

DARRELL (*with a last tortured protest*) Nina! Are you forgetting? He's my son, too! (*He shouts up at the sky*) You're my son, Gordon! You're my— (*He controls himself abruptly—with a smile of cynical self-pity*) He can't hear! Well, at least I've done my duty! (*Then with a grim fatalism—with a final wave of his hand at the sky*) Good-bye, Gordon's son!

NINA (*with tortured exultance*) Fly up to heaven, Gordon! Fly with your love to heaven! Fly always! Never crash to earth like my old Gordon! Be happy, dear! You've got to be happy!

DARRELL (*sardonically*) I've heard that cry for happiness before, Nina! I remember hearing myself cry it—once—it must have been long ago! I'll get back to my cells—sensible unicellular life that floats in the sea and has never learned the cry for happiness! I'm going, Nina. (*As she remains oblivious, staring after the plane—thinking fatalistically*)

She doesn't hear, either. . . .

(*He laughs up at the sky*)

Oh, God, so deaf and dumb and blind! . . . teach me to be resigned to be an atom! . . .

(*He walks off, right, and enters the house*).

NINA (*finally lowering her eyes—confusedly*) Gone. My eyes are growing dim. Where is Ned? Gone, too. And Sam is gone. They're all dead. Where are Father and Charlie? (*With a shiver of fear she hurries over and sits on the bench beside* MARSDEN, *huddling against him*) Gordon is dead, Father. I've just had a cable. What I mean is, he flew away to another life—my son, Gordon, Charlie. So we're alone again—just as we used to be.

MARSDEN (*putting his arm around her—affectionately*) Just as we used to be, dear Nina Cara Nina, before Gordon came.

NINA (*looking up at the sky—strangely*) My having a son was a failure, wasn't it? He couldn't give me happiness. Sons are always their fathers. They pass through the mother to become their father again. The Sons of the Father have all been failures! Failing they died for us, they flew away to other lives, they could not stay with us, they could not give us happiness!

MARSDEN (*paternally—in her father's tone*) You had best forget the whole affair of your association with the Gordons. After all, dear Nina, there was something unreal in all that has happened since you first met Gordon Shaw, something extravagant and fantastic, the sort of thing that isn't done, really, in our afternoons. So let's you and me forget the whole distressing episode, regard it as an interlude, of trial and preparation, say, in which our souls have been scraped clean of impure flesh and made worthy to bleach in peace.

NINA (*with a strange smile*) Strange interlude! Yes, our lives are merely strange dark interludes in the electrical display of God the Father! (*Resting her head on his shoulder*) You're so restful, Charlie. I feel as if I were a girl again and you were my father and the Charlie of those days made into one. I wonder is our old garden the same? We'll pick flowers together in the aging afternoons of spring and summer, won't we? It will be a comfort to get home—to be old and to be home again at last—to be in love with peace together—to love each other's peace—to sleep with peace together!— (*She kisses him—then shuts her eyes with a deep sigh of requited weariness*) —to die in peace! I'm so contentedly weary with life!

MARSDEN (*with a serene peace*) Rest, dear Nina. (*Then tenderly*) It has been a long day. Why don't you sleep now—as you used to, remember?—for a little while?

NINA (*murmurs with drowsy gratitude*) Thank you, Father—have I been wicked?—you're so good—dear old Charlie!

MARSDEN (*reacting automatically and wincing with pain—thinking mechanically*)

God damn dear old . . . !

(*Then with a glance down at* NINA'S *face, with a happy smile*)

No, God bless dear old Charlie . . . who, passed beyond desire, has all the luck at last! . . .

(NINA *has fallen asleep. He watches with contented eyes the evening shadows closing in around them*).

CURTAIN

Mourning Becomes Electra

A TRILOGY

To Carlotta, my wife

Part One

HOMECOMING

A Play in Four Acts

Part Two

THE HUNTED

A Play in Five Acts

Part Three

THE HAUNTED

A Play in Four Acts

GENERAL SCENE OF THE TRILOGY

The action of the trilogy, with the exception of an act of the second play, takes place in or immediately outside the Mannon residence, on the outskirts of one of the small New England seaport towns.

A special curtain shows the house as seen from the street. From this, in each play, one comes to the exterior of the house in the opening act and enters it in the following act.

This curtain reveals the extensive grounds—about thirty acres—which surround the house, a heavily wooded ridge in the background, orchards at the right and in the immediate rear, a large flower garden and a greenhouse to the left.

In the foreground, along the street, is a line of locust and elm trees. The property is enclosed by a white picket fence and a tall hedge. A driveway curves up to the house from two entrances with white gates. Between the house and the street is a lawn. By the right corner of the house is a grove of pine trees. Farther forward, along the driveway, maples and locusts. By the left corner of the house is a big clump of lilacs and syringas.

The house is placed back on a slight rise of ground about three hundred feet from the street. It is a large building of the Greek temple type that was the vogue in the first half of the nineteenth century. A white wooden portico with six tall columns contrasts with the wall of the house proper which is of gray cut stone. There are five windows on the upper floor and four on the ground floor, with the main entrance in the middle, a doorway with squared transom and sidelights flanked by intermediate columns. The window shutters are painted a dark green. Before the doorway a flight of four steps leads from the ground to the portico.

The three plays take place in either spring or summer of the years 1865-1866.

Homecoming

CHARACTERS

BRIGADIER-GENERAL EZRA MANNON

CHRISTINE, *his wife*

LAVINIA, *their daughter*

CAPTAIN ADAM BRANT, *of the clipper "Flying Trades"*

CAPTAIN PETER NILES, *U. S. Artillery*

HAZEL NILES, *his sister*

SETH BECKWITH

AMOS AMES

LOUISA, *his wife*

MINNIE, *her cousin*

SCENES

ACT ONE: Exterior of the Mannon house in New England—April, 1865.

ACT TWO: Ezra Mannon's study in the house—no time has elapsed.

ACT THREE: The same as Act One—exterior of the house—a night a week later.

ACT FOUR: A bedroom in the house—later the same night.

Homecoming

ACT ONE

SCENE—*Exterior of the Mannon house on a late afternoon in April, 1865. At front is the driveway which leads up to the house from the two entrances on the street. Behind the driveway the white Grecian temple portico with its six tall columns extends across the stage. A big pine tree is on the lawn at the edge of the drive before the right corner of the house. Its trunk is a black column in striking contrast to the white columns of the portico. By the edge of the drive, left front, is a thick clump of lilacs and syringas. A bench is placed on the lawn at front of this shrubbery which partly screens anyone sitting on it from the front of the house.*

It is shortly before sunset and the soft light of the declining sun shines directly on the front of the house, shimmering in a luminous mist on the white portico and the gray stone wall behind, intensifying the whiteness of the columns, the somber grayness of the wall the green of the open shutters, the green of the lawn and shrubbery, the black and green of the pine tree. The white columns cast black bars of shadow on the gray wall behind them. The windows of the lower floor reflect the sun's rays in a resentful glare. The temple portico is like an incongruous white mask fixed on the house to hide its somber gray ugliness.

In the distance, from the town, a band is heard playing "John Brown's Body." Borne on the light puffs of wind this music is at times quite loud, then sinks into faintness as the wind dies.

From the left rear, a man's voice is heard singing the chanty "Shenandoah"—a song that more than any other holds in it the brooding rhythm of the sea. The voice grows quickly nearer. It is thin and aged, the wraith of what must once have been a good baritone.

"Oh, Shenandoah, I long to hear you
A-way, my rolling river
Oh, Shenandoah, I can't get near you
Way-ay, I'm bound away
Across the wide Missouri."

The singer, SETH BECKWITH, *finishes the last line as he enters from around the corner of the house. Closely following him are* AMOS AMES, *his wife* LOUISA, *and her cousin* MINNIE.

SETH BECKWITH, *the Mannons' gardener and man of all work, is an old man of seventy-five with white hair and beard, tall, raw-boned and stoop-shouldered, his joints stiffened by rheumatism, but still sound and hale. He has a gaunt face that in repose gives one the strange impression of a life-like mask. It is set in a grim expression, but his small, sharp eyes still peer at life with a shrewd prying avidity and his loose mouth has a strong suggestion of ribald humor. He wears his earth-stained working clothes.*

AMOS AMES, *carpenter by trade but now taking a holiday and dressed in his Sunday best, as are his wife and her cousin, is a fat man in his fifties. In character he is the townsfolk type of garrulous gossip-monger who is at the same time devoid of evil intent, scandal being for him merely the subject most popular with his audience.*

His wife, LOUISA, *is taller and stouter than he and about the same age. Of a similar scandal-bearing type, her tongue is sharpened by malice.*

Her cousin, MINNIE, *is a plump little woman of forty, of the meek, eager-listener type, with a small round face, round stupid eyes, and a round mouth pursed out to drink in gossip.*

These last three are types of townsfolk rather than individuals, a chorus representing the town come to look and listen and spy on the rich and exclusive Mannons.

Led by SETH, *they come forward as far as the lilac clump and stand staring at the house.* SETH, *in a mood of aged playfulness, is trying to make an impression on* MINNIE. *His singing has been for her benefit. He nudges her with his elbow, grinning.*

SETH How's that fur singin' fur an old feller? I used to be noted fur my chanties. (*Seeing she is paying no attention to him but is staring with open-mouthed awe at the house, he turns to* AMES—*jubilantly*) By jingo, Amos, if that news is true, there won't be a sober man in town tonight! It's our patriotic duty to celebrate!

AMES (*with a grin*) We'd ought to, that's sartin!

LOUISA You ain't goin' to git Amos drunk tonight, surrender or no surrender! An old reprobate, that's what you be!

SETH (*pleased*) Old nothin'! On'y seventy-five! My old man lived to be ninety! Licker can't kill the Beckwiths! (*He and* AMES *laugh.* LOUISA *smiles in spite of herself.* MINNIE *is oblivious, still staring at the house*).

MINNIE My sakes! What a purty house!

SETH Wal, I promised Amos I'd help show ye the sights when you came to visit him. 'Taint everyone can git to see the Mannon place close to. They're strict about trespassin'.

MINNIE My! They must be rich! How'd they make their money?

SETH Ezra's made a pile, and before him, his father, Abe Mannon, he inherited some and made a pile more in shippin'. Started one of the fust Western Ocean packet lines.

MINNIE Ezra's the General, ain't he?

SETH (*proudly*) Ayeh. The best fighter in the hull of Grant's army!

MINNIE What kind is he?

SETH (*boastfully expanding*) He's able, Ezra is! Folks think he's cold-blooded and uppish, 'cause he's never got much to say to 'em. But that's only the Mannons' way. They've been top dog around here for near on two hundred years and don't let folks fergit it.

MINNIE How'd he come to jine the army if he's so rich?

SETH Oh, he'd been a soldier afore this war. His paw made him go to West P'int. He went to the Mexican war and come out a major. Abe died that same year and Ezra give up the army and took holt of the shippin' business here. But he didn't stop there. He learned law on the side and got made a judge. Went in fur politics and got 'lected mayor. He was mayor when this war broke out but he resigned to once and jined the army again. And now he's riz to be General. Oh, he's able, Ezra is!

AMES Ayeh. This town's real proud of Ezra.

LOUISA Which is more'n you kin say fur his wife. Folks all hates her! She ain't the Mannon kind. French and Dutch descended, she is. Furrin lookin' and queer. Her father's a doctor in New York, but he can't be much of a one 'cause she didn't bring no money when Ezra married her.

SETH (*his face growing grim—sharply*) Never mind her. We ain't talkin' 'bout her. (*Then abruptly changing the subject*) Wal, I've got to see Vinnie. I'm goin' round by the kitchen. You wait here. And if Ezra's wife starts to run you off fur trespassin', you tell her I got permission from Vinnie to show you round. (*He goes off around the corner of the house, left. The three stare about them gawkily, awed and uncomfortable. They talk in low voices*).

LOUISA Seth is so proud of his durned old Mannons! I couldn't help givin' him a dig about Ezra's wife.

AMES Wal, don't matter much. He's allus hated her.

LOUISA Ssshh! Someone's comin' out. Let's get back here! (*They crowd to the rear of the bench by the lilac clump and peer through the leaves as the front door is opened and* CHRISTINE MANNON *comes out to the edge of the portico at the top of the steps.* LOUISA *prods her cousin and whispers excitedly*) That's her! (CHRISTINE MANNON *is a tall striking-looking woman of forty but she appears younger. She has a fine, voluptuous figure and she moves with a flowing animal grace. She wears a green satin dress, smartly cut and expensive, which brings out the peculiar color of her thick curly hair, partly a copper brown, partly a bronze gold, each shade distinct and yet blending with the other. Her face is unusual, handsome rather than beautiful. One is struck at once by the strange impression it gives in repose of being not living flesh but a wonderfully life-like pale mask, in which only the deep-set eyes, of a dark violet-blue, are alive. Her black eyebrows meet in a pronounced straight line above her strong nose. Her chin is heavy, her mouth large and sensual, the lower lip full, the upper a thin bow, shadowed by a line of hair. She stands and listens defensively, as if the music held some meaning that threatened her. But at once she shrugs her shoulders with disdain and comes down the steps and walks off toward the flower garden, passing behind the lilac clump without having noticed* AMES *and the women*).

MINNIE (*in an awed whisper*) My! She's awful handsome, ain't she?

LOUISA Too furrin lookin' fur my taste.

MINNIE Ayeh. There's somethin' queer lookin' about her face.

AMES Secret lookin'—'s if it was a mask she'd put on. That's the Mannon look. They all has it. They grow it on their wives. Seth's growed it on too, didn't you notice—from bein' with 'em all his life. They don't want folks to guess their secrets.

MINNIE (*breathlessly eager*) Secrets?

LOUISA The Mannons got skeletons in their closets same as

others! Worse ones. (*Lowering her voice almost to a whisper—to her husband*) Tell Minnie about old Abe Mannon's brother David marryin' that French Canuck nurse girl he'd got into trouble.

AMES Ssshh! Shet up, can't you? Here's Seth comin'. (*But he whispers quickly to* MINNIE) That happened way back when I was a youngster. I'll tell you later. (SETH *has appeared from around the left corner of the house and now joins them*).

SETH That durned nigger cook is allus askin' me to fetch wood fur her! You'd think I was her slave! That's what we get fur freein' 'em! (*Then briskly*) Wal, come along, folks. I'll show you the peach orchard and then we'll go to my greenhouse. I couldn't find Vinnie. (*They are about to start when the front door of the house is opened and* LAVINIA *comes out to the top of the steps where her mother had stood. She is twenty-three but looks considerably older. Tall like her mother, her body is thin, flat-breasted and angular, and its unattractiveness is accentuated by her plain black dress. Her movements are stiff and she carries herself with a wooden, square-shouldered, military bearing. She has a flat dry voice and a habit of snapping out her words like an officer giving orders. But in spite of these dissimilarities, one is immediately struck by her facial resemblance to her mother. She has the same peculiar shade of copper-gold hair, the same pallor and dark violet-blue eyes, the black eyebrows meeting in a straight line above her nose, the same sensual mouth, the same heavy jaw. Above all, one is struck by the same strange, life-like mask impression her face gives in repose. But it is evident* LAVINIA *does all in her power to emphasize the dissimilarity rather than the resemblance to her parent. She wears her hair pulled tightly back, as if to conceal its natural curliness, and there is not a touch of feminine allurement to her severely plain get-up. Her head is the same size as her mother's, but on her thin body it looks too large and heavy*).

SETH (*seeing her*) There she be now. (*He starts for the steps—then sees she has not noticed their presence, and stops and stands waiting, struck by something in her manner. She is looking off right, watching her mother as she strolls through the garden to the green house. Her eyes are bleak and hard with an intense, bitter enmity. Then her mother evidently disappears in the greenhouse, for* LAVINIA *turns her head, still oblivious to* SETH *and his friends, and looks off left, her attention caught by the band, the music of which, borne on a fresh-*

ening breeze, has suddenly become louder. It is still playing "John Brown's Body." LAVINIA *listens, as her mother had a moment before, but her reaction is the direct opposite to what her mother's had been. Her eyes light up with a grim satisfaction, and an expression of strange vindictive triumph comes into her face*).

LOUISA (*in a quick whisper to* MINNIE) That's Lavinia!

MINNIE She looks like her mother in face—queer lookin'—but she ain't purty like her.

SETH You git along to the orchard, folks. I'll jine you there. (*They walk back around the left of the house and disappear. He goes to* LAVINIA *eagerly*) Say, I got fine news fur you, Vinnie. The telegraph feller says Lee is a goner sure this time! They're only waitin' now fur the news to be made official. You can count on your paw comin' home!

LAVINIA (*grimly*) I hope so. It's time.

SETH (*with a keen glance at her—slowly*) Ayeh.

LAVINIA (*turning on him sharply*) What do you mean, Seth?

SETH (*avoiding her eyes—evasively*) Nothin'—'cept what you mean. (LAVINIA *stares at him. He avoids her eyes—then heavily casual*) Where was you gallivantin' night afore last and all yesterday?

LAVINIA (*starts*) Over to Hazel and Peter's house.

SETH Ayeh. There's where Hannah said you'd told her you was goin'. That's funny now—'cause I seen Peter upstreet yesterday and he asked me where you was keepin' yourself.

LAVINIA (*again starts—then slowly as if admitting a secret understanding between them*) I went to New York, Seth.

SETH Ayeh. That's where I thought you'd gone, mebbe. (*Then with deep sympathy*) It's durned hard on you, Vinnie. It's a durned shame.

LAVINIA (*stiffening—curtly*) I don't know what you're talking about.

SETH (*nods comprehendingly*) All right, Vinnie. Just as you say. (*He pauses—then after hesitating frowningly for a moment, blurts out*) There's somethin' been on my mind lately I want to warn you about. It's got to do with what's worryin' you—that is, if there's anythin' in it.

LAVINIA (*stiffly*) There's nothing worrying me. (*Then sharply*) Warn me? About what?

SETH Mebbe it's nothin'—and then again mebbe I'm right,

and if I'm right, then you'd ought t'be warned. It's to do with that Captain Brant.

LAVINIA (*starts again but keeps her tone cold and collected*) What about him?

SETH Somethin' I calc'late no one'd notice 'specially 'ceptin' me, because— (*Then hastily as he sees someone coming up the drive*) Here's Peter and Hazel comin'. I'll tell you later, Vinnie. I ain't got time now anyways. Those folks are waitin' for me.

LAVINIA I'll be sitting here. You come back afterwards. (*Then her cold disciplined mask breaking for a moment—tensely*) Oh, why do Peter and Hazel have to come now? I don't want to see anyone! (*She starts as if to go into the house*).

SETH You run in. I'll get rid of 'em fur you.

LAVINIA (*recovering herself—curtly*) No. I'll see them. (SETH *goes back around the corner of the house, left. A moment later* HAZEL *and* PETER NILES *enter along the drive from left, front.* HAZEL *is a pretty, healthy girl of nineteen, with dark hair and eyes. Her features are small but clearly modelled. She has a strong chin and a capable, smiling mouth. One gets a sure impression of her character at a glance—frank, innocent, amiable and good—not in a negative but in a positive, self-possessed way. Her brother,* PETER, *is very like her in character—straightforward, guileless and good-natured. He is a heavily built young fellow of twenty-two, awkward in movement and hesitating in speech. His face is broad, plain, with a snubby nose, curly brown hair, fine gray eyes and a big mouth. He wears the uniform of an artillery captain in the Union Army*).

LAVINIA (*with forced cordiality*) Good afternoon. How are you? (*She and* HAZEL *kiss and she shakes hands with* PETER).

HAZEL Oh, we're all right. But how are you, Vinnie, that's the question? Seems as if we hadn't seen you in ages! You haven't been sick, I hope!

LAVINIA Well—if you call a pesky cold sick.

PETER Gosh, that's too bad! All over it now?

LAVINIA Yes—almost. Do sit down, won't you? (HAZEL *sits at left of bench,* LAVINIA *beside her in the middle.* PETER *sits gingerly on the right edge so that there is an open space between him and* LAVINIA).

HAZEL Peter can stay a while if you want him to, but I

just dropped in for a second to find out if you'd had any more news from Orin.

LAVINIA Not since the letter I showed you.

HAZEL But that was ages ago! And I haven't had a letter in months. I guess he must have met another girl some place and given me the go by. (*She forces a smile but her tone is really hurt*).

PETER Orin not writing doesn't mean anything. He never was much of a hand for letters.

HAZEL I know that, but—you don't think he's been wounded, do you, Vinnie?

LAVINIA Of course not. Father would have let us know.

PETER Sure he would. Don't be foolish, Hazel! (*Then after a little pause*) Orin ought to be home before long now. You've heard the good news, of course, Vinnie?

HAZEL Peter won't have to go back. Isn't that fine?

PETER My wound is healed and I've got orders to leave tomorrow, but they'll be cancelled, I guess. (*Grinning*) I won't pretend I'm the sort of hero that wants to go back, either! I've had enough!

HAZEL (*impulsively*) Oh, it will be so good to see Orin again. (*Then embarrassed, forces a self-conscious laugh and gets up and kisses* LAVINIA) Well, I must run. I've got to meet Emily. Good-bye, Vinnie. Do take care of yourself and come to see us soon. (*With a teasing glance at her brother*) And be kind to Peter. He's nice—when he's asleep. And he has something he's just dying to ask you!

PETER (*horribly embarrassed*) Darn you! (HAZEL *laughs and goes off down the drive, left front.* PETER *fidgets, his eyes on the ground.* LAVINIA *watches him. Since* HAZEL'S *teasing statement, she has visibly withdrawn into herself and is on the defensive. Finally* PETER *looks up and blurts out awkwardly*) Hazel feels bad about Orin not writing. Do you think he really —loves her?

LAVINIA (*stiffening—brusquely*) I don't know anything about love! I don't want to know anything! (*Intensely*) I hate love!

PETER (*crushed by this but trying bravely to joke*) Gosh, then, if that's the mood you're in, I guess I better not ask—something I'd made up my mind to ask you today.

LAVINIA It's what you asked me a year ago when you were home on leave, isn't it?

PETER And you said wait till the war was over. Well, it's over now.

LAVINIA (*slowly*) I can't marry anyone, Peter. I've got to stay home. Father needs me.

PETER He's got your mother.

LAVINIA (*sharply*) He needs me more! (*A pause. Then she turns pityingly and puts her hand on his shoulder*) I'm sorry, Peter.

PETER (*gruffly*) Oh, that's all right.

LAVINIA I know it's what girls always say in books, but I do love you as a brother, Peter. I wouldn't lose you as a brother for anything. We've been like that ever since we were little and started playing together—you and Orin and Hazel and I. So please don't let this come between us.

PETER 'Course it won't. What do you think I am? (*Doggedly*) Besides, I'm not giving up hope but what you'll change your mind in time. That is, unless it's because you love someone else—

LAVINIA (*snatching her hand back*) Don't be stupid, Peter!

PETER But how about this mysterious clipper captain that's been calling?

LAVINIA (*angrily*) Do you think I care anything about that —that—!

PETER Don't get mad. I only meant, folks say he's courting you.

LAVINIA Folks say more than their prayers!

PETER Then you don't—care for him?

LAVINIA (*intensely*) I hate the sight of him!

PETER Gosh! I'm glad to hear you say that, Vinnie. I was afraid—I imagined girls all liked him. He's such a darned romantic-looking cuss. Looks more like a gambler or a poet than a ship captain. I got a look as he was coming out of your gate—I guess it was the last time he was here. Funny, too. He reminded me of someone. But I couldn't place who it was.

LAVINIA (*startled, glances at him uneasily*) No one around here, that's sure. He comes from out West. Grandfather Hamel happened to meet him in New York and took a fancy to him, and Mother met him at Grandfather's house.

PETER Who is he, anyway, Vinnie?

LAVINIA I don't know much about him in spite of what you think. Oh, he did tell me the story of his life to make himself out romantic, but I didn't pay much attention. He went to sea when he was young and was in California for the Gold Rush. He's sailed all over the world—he lived on a South Sea island once, so he says.

PETER (*grumpily*) He seems to have had plenty of romantic experience, if you can believe him!

LAVINIA (*bitterly*) That's his trade—being romantic! (*Then agitatedly*) But I don't want to talk any more about him. (*She gets up and walks toward right to conceal her agitation, keeping her back turned to* PETER).

PETER (*with a grin*) Well, I don't either. I can think of more interesting subjects. (CHRISTINE MANNON *appears from left, between the clump of lilacs and the house. She is carrying a big bunch of flowers.* LAVINIA *senses her presence and whirls around. For a moment, mother and daughter stare into each other's eyes. In their whole tense attitudes is clearly revealed the bitter antagonism between them. But* CHRISTINE *quickly recovers herself and her air resumes its disdainful aloofness*).

CHRISTINE Ah, here you are at last! (*Then she sees* PETER, *who is visibly embarrassed by her presence*) Why, good afternoon, Peter, I didn't see you at first.

PETER Good afternoon, Mrs. Mannon. I was just passing and dropped in for a second. I guess I better run along now, Vinnie.

LAVINIA (*with an obvious eagerness to get him off—quickly*) All right. Good-bye, Peter.

PETER Good-bye. Good-bye, Mrs. Mannon.

CHRISTINE Good-bye, Peter. (*He disappears from the drive, left.* CHRISTINE *comes forward*) I must say you treat your one devoted swain pretty rudely. (LAVINIA *doesn't reply.* CHRISTINE *goes on coolly*) I was wondering when I was going to see you. When I returned from New York last night you seemed to have gone to bed.

LAVINIA I had gone to bed.

CHRISTINE You usually read long after that. I tried your door—but you had locked yourself in. When you kept yourself locked in all day I was sure you were intentionally avoiding me. But Annie said you had a headache. (*While she has been speaking she has come toward* LAVINIA *until she is now within arm's reach of her. The facial resemblance, as they stand there, is extraordinary.* CHRISTINE *stares at her coolly, but one senses an uneasy wariness beneath her pose*) Did you have a headache?

LAVINIA No. I wanted to be alone—to think over things.

CHRISTINE What things, if I may ask? (*Then, as if she were afraid of an answer to this question, she abruptly changes the subject*) Who are those people I saw wandering about the grounds?

LAVINIA Some friends of Seth's.

CHRISTINE Because they know that lazy old sot, does it give them the privilege of trespassing?

LAVINIA I gave Seth permission to show them around.

CHRISTINE And since when have you the right without consulting me?

LAVINIA I couldn't very well consult you when Seth asked me. You had gone to New York— (*She pauses a second—then adds slowly, staring fixedly at her mother*) to see Grandfather. Is he feeling any better? He seems to have been sick so much this past year.

CHRISTINE (*casually, avoiding her eyes*) Yes. He's much better now. He'll soon be going the rounds to his patients again, he hopes. (*As if anxious to change the subject, looking at the flowers she carries*) I've been to the greenhouse to pick these. I felt our tomb needed a little brightening. (*She nods scornfully toward the house*) Each time I come back after being away it appears more like a sepulchre! The "whited" one of the Bible—pagan temple front stuck like a mask on Puritan gray ugliness! It was just like old Abe Mannon to build such a monstrosity—as a temple for his hatred. (*Then with a little mocking laugh*) Forgive me, Vinnie. I forgot you liked it. And you ought to. It suits your temperament. (LAVINIA *stares at her but remains silent.* CHRISTINE *glances at her flowers again and turns toward the house*) I must put these in water. (*She moves a few steps toward the house—then turns again—with a studied casualness*) By the way, before I forget, I happened to run into Captain Brant on the street in New York. He said he was coming up here today to take over his ship and asked me if he might drop in to see you. I told him he could—and stay to supper with us. (*Without looking at* LAVINIA, *who is staring at her with a face grown grim and hard*) Doesn't that please you, Vinnie? Or do you remain true to your one and only beau, Peter?

LAVINIA Is that why you picked the flowers—because he is coming? (*Her mother does not answer. She goes on with a threatening undercurrent in her voice*) You have heard the news, I suppose? It means Father will be home soon!

CHRISTINE (*without looking at her—coolly*) We've had so

many rumors lately. This report hasn't been confirmed yet, has it? I haven't heard the fort firing a salute.

LAVINIA You will before long!

CHRISTINE I'm sure I hope so as much as you.

LAVINIA You can say that!

CHRISTINE (*concealing her alarm—coldly*) What do you mean? You will kindly not take that tone with me, please! (*Cuttingly*) If you are determined to quarrel, let us go into the house. We might be overheard out here. (*She turns and sees* SETH *who has just come to the corner of the house, left, and is standing there watching them*) See. There is your old crony doing his best to listen now! (*Moving to the steps*) I am going in and rest a while. (*She walks up the steps*).

LAVINIA (*harshly*) I've got to have a talk with you, Mother —before long!

CHRISTINE (*turning defiantly*) Whenever you wish. To-night after the Captain leaves you, if you like. But what is it you want to talk about?

LAVINIA You'll know soon enough!

CHRISTINE (*staring at her with a questioning dread—forcing a scornful smile*) You always make such a mystery of things, Vinnie. (*She goes into the house and closes the door behind her.* SETH *comes forward from where he had withdrawn around the corner of the house.* LAVINIA *makes a motion for him to follow her, and goes and sits on the bench at left. A pause. She stares straight ahead, her face frozen, her eyes hard. He regards her understandingly*).

LAVINIA (*abruptly*) Well? What is it about Captain Brant you want to warn me against? (*Then as if she felt she must defend her question from some suspicion that she knows is in his mind*) I want to know all I can about him because—he seems to be calling to court me.

SETH (*managing to convey his entire disbelief of this statement in onc word*) Ayeh.

LAVINIA (*sharply*) You say that as if you didn't believe me.

SETH I believe anything you tell me to believe. I ain't been with the Mannons for sixty years without learning that. (*A pause. Then he asks slowly*) Ain't you noticed this Brant reminds you of someone in looks?

LAVINIA (*struck by this*) Yes. I have—ever since I first saw him—but I've never been able to place who— Who do you mean?

SETH Your Paw, ain't it, Vinnie?

LAVINIA (*startled—agitatedly*) Father? No! It can't be! (*Then as if the conviction were forcing itself on her in spite of herself*) Yes! He does—something about his face—that must be why I've had the strange feeling I've known him before—why I've felt— (*Then tensely as if she were about to break down*) Oh! I won't believe it! You must be mistaken, Seth! That would be too—!

SETH He ain't only like your Paw. He's like Orin, too—and all the Mannons I've known.

LAVINIA (*frightenedly*) But why—why should he—?

SETH More speshully he calls to my mind your Grandpaw's brother, David. How much do you know about David Mannon, Vinnie? I know his name's never been allowed to be spoke among Mannons since the day he left—but you've likely heard gossip, ain't you—even if it all happened before you was born.

LAVINIA I've heard that he loved the Canuck nurse girl who was taking care of Father's little sister who died, and had to marry her because she was going to have a baby; and that Grandfather put them both out of the house and then afterwards tore it down and built this one because he wouldn't live where his brother had disgraced the family. But what has that old scandal got to do with—

SETH Wait. Right after they was throwed out they married and went away. There was talk they'd gone out West, but no one knew nothin' about 'em afterwards—'ceptin' your Grandpaw let out to me one time she'd had the baby—a boy. He was cussin' it. (*Then impressively*) It's about her baby I've been thinkin', Vinnie.

LAVINIA (*a look of appalled comprehension growing on her face*) Oh!

SETH How old is that Brant, Vinnie?

LAVINIA Thirty-six, I think.

SETH Ayeh! That'd make it right. And here's another funny thing—his name. Brant's sort of queer fur a name. I ain't never heard tell of it before. Sounds made up to me—like short fur somethin' else. Remember what that Canuck girl's name was, do you, Vinnie? Marie Brantôme! See what I'm drivin' at?

LAVINIA (*agitatedly, fighting against a growing conviction*) But—don't be stupid, Seth—his name would be Mannon and he'd be only too proud of it.

SETH He'd have good reason not to use the name of Mannon when he came callin' here, wouldn't he? If your Paw ever guessed—!

LAVINIA (*breaking out violently*) No! It can't be! God wouldn't let it! It would be too horrible—on top of—! I won't even think of it, do you hear? Why did you have to tell me?

SETH (*calmingly*) There now! Don't take on, Vinnie. No need gettin' riled at me. (*He waits—then goes on insistently*) All I'm drivin' at is that it's durned funny—his looks and the name—and you'd ought fur your Paw's sake to make sartin.

LAVINIA How can I make certain?

SETH Catch him off guard sometime and put it up to him strong—as if you knowed it—and see if mebbe he don't give himself away. (*He starts to go—looks down the drive at left*) Looks like him comin' up the drive now, Vinnie. There's somethin' about his walk calls back David Mannon, too. If I didn't know it was him I'd think it was David's ghost comin' home. (*He turns away abruptly*) Wal, calc'late I better git back to work. (*He walks around the left corner of the house. A pause. Then* CAPTAIN ADAM BRANT *enters from the drive, left, front. He starts on seeing* LAVINIA *but immediately puts on his most polite, winning air. One is struck at a glance by the peculiar quality his face in repose has of being a life-like mask rather than living flesh. He has a broad, low forehead, framed by coal-black straight hair which he wears noticeably long, pushed back carelessly from his forehead as a poet's might be. He has a big aquiline nose, bushy eyebrows, swarthy complexion, hazel eyes. His wide mouth is sensual and moody—a mouth that can be strong and weak by turns. He wears a mustache, but his heavy cleft chin is clean-shaven. In figure he is tall, broad-shouldered and powerful. He gives the impression of being always on the offensive or defensive, always fighting life. He is dressed with an almost foppish extravagance, with touches of studied carelessness, as if a romantic Byronic appearance were the ideal in mind. There is little of the obvious ship captain about him, except his big, strong hands and his deep voice*).

BRANT (*bowing with an exaggerated politeness*) Good afternoon. (*Coming and taking her hand which she forces herself to hold out to him*) Hope you don't mind my walking in on you without ceremony. Your mother told me—

LAVINIA I know. She had to go out for a while and she said I was to keep you company until she returned.

BRANT (*gallantly*) Well, I'm in good luck, then. I hope she doesn't hurry back to stand watch over us. I haven't had a chance to be alone with you since—that night we went walking in the moonlight, do you remember? (*He has kept her hand

and he drops his voice to a low, lover-like tone. LAVINIA *cannot repress a start, agitatedly snatching her hand from his and turning away from him*).

LAVINIA (*regaining command of herself—slowly*) What do you think of the news of Lee surrendering, Captain? We expect my father home very soon now. (*At something in her tone he stares at her suspiciously, but she is looking straight before her*) Why don't you sit down?

BRANT Thank you. (*He sits on the bench at her right. He has become wary now, feeling something strange in her attitude but not able to make her out—casually*) Yes, you must be very happy at the prospect of seeing your father again. Your mother has told me how close you've always been to him.

LAVINIA Did she? (*Then with intensity*) I love Father better than anyone in the world. There is nothing I wouldn't do—to protect him from hurt!

BRANT (*watching her carefully—keeping his casual tone*) You care more for him than for your mother?

LAVINIA Yes.

BRANT Well, I suppose that's the usual way of it. A daughter feels closer to her father and a son to his mother. But I should think you ought to be a born exception to that rule.

LAVINIA Why?

BRANT You're so like your mother in some ways. Your face is the dead image of hers. And look at your hair. You won't meet hair like yours and hers again in a month of Sundays. I only know of one other woman who had it. You'll think it strange when I tell you. It was my mother.

LAVINIA (*with a start*) Ah!

BRANT (*dropping his voice to a reverent, hushed tone*) Yes, she had beautiful hair like your mother's, that hung down to her knees, and big, deep, sad eyes that were blue as the Caribbean Sea!

LAVINIA (*harshly*) What do looks amount to? I'm not a bit like her! Everybody knows I take after Father!

BRANT (*brought back with a shock, astonished at her tone*) But—you're not angry at me for saying that, are you? (*Then filled with uneasiness and resolving he must establish himself on an intimate footing with her again—with engaging bluntness*) You're puzzling today, Miss Lavinia. You'll excuse me if I come out with it bluntly. I've lived most of my life at sea and in camps and I'm used to straight speaking. What are you holding against me? If I've done anything to offend you, I swear it wasn't meant. (*She is silent, staring before her with hard eyes, rigidly upright. He appraises her with a calculating look, then goes on*) I wouldn't have bad feeling come between us for the world. I may only be flattering myself, but I thought you liked me. Have you forgotten that night walking along the shore?

LAVINIA (*in a cold, hard voice*) I haven't forgotten. Did Mother tell you you could kiss me?

BRANT What—what do you mean? (*But he at once attributes the question to her naïveté—laughingly*) Oh! I see! But, come now, Lavinia, you can't mean, can you, I should have asked her permission?

LAVINIA Shouldn't you?

BRANT (*again uneasy—trying to joke it off*) Well, I wasn't brought up that strictly and, should or shouldn't, at any rate, I didn't—and it wasn't the less sweet for that! (*Then at something in her face he hurriedly goes off on another tack*) I'm afraid I gabbed too much that night. Maybe I bored you with my talk of clipper ships and my love for them?

LAVINIA (*dryly*) "Tall, white clippers," you called them. You said they were like beautiful, pale women to you. You said you loved them more than you'd ever loved a woman. Is that true, Captain?

BRANT (*with forced gallantry*) Aye. But I meant, before I met you. (*Then thinking he has at last hit on the cause of her changed attitude toward him—with a laugh*) So that's what you're holding against me, is it? Well, I might have guessed. Women are jealous of ships. They always suspect the sea. They know they're three of a kind when it comes to a man! (*He laughs again but less certainly this time, as he regards her grim, set expression*) Yes, I might have seen you didn't appear much taken by my sea gamming that night. I suppose clippers are too old a story to the daughter of a shipbuilder. But unless I'm much mistaken, you were interested when I told you of the islands in the South Seas where I was shipwrecked my first voyage at sea.

LAVINIA (*in a dry, brittle tone*) I remember your admiration for the naked native women. You said they had found the secret of happiness because they had never heard that love can be a sin.

BRANT (*surprised—sizing her up puzzledly*) So you remember that, do you? (*Then romantically*) Aye! And they live in as near the Garden of Paradise before sin was discovered as you'll find on this earth! Unless you've seen it, you can't picture the green beauty of their land set in the blue of the sea! The clouds like down on the mountain tops, the sun drowsing in your blood, and always the surf on the barrier reef singing a croon in your ears like a lullaby! The Blessed Isles, I'd call them! You can forget there all men's dirty dreams of greed and power!

LAVINIA And their dirty dreams—of love?

BRANT (*startled again—staring at her uneasily*) Why do you say that? What do you mean, Lavinia?

LAVINIA Nothing. I was only thinking—of your Blessed Isles.

BRANT (*uncertainly*) Oh! But you said— (*Then with a confused, stupid persistence he comes closer to her, dropping his voice again to his love-making tone*) Whenever I remember those islands now, I will always think of you, as you walked beside me that night with your hair blowing in the sea wind and the moonlight in your eyes! (*He tries to take her hand, but at his touch she pulls away and springs to her feet*).

LAVINIA (*with cold fury*) Don't you touch me! Don't you dare—! You liar! You—! (*Then as he starts back in confusion, she seizes this opportunity to follow* SETH'S *advice—staring at him with deliberately insulting scorn*) But I suppose it would be foolish to expect anything but cheap romantic lies from the son of a low Canuck nurse girl!

BRANT (*stunned*) What's that? (*Then rage at the insult to his mother overcoming all prudence—springs to his feet threateningly*) Belay, damn you!—or I'll forget you're a woman—no Mannon can insult her while I—

LAVINIA (*appalled now she knows the truth*) So—it is true— You are her son! Oh!

BRANT (*fighting to control himself—with harsh defiance*) And what if I am? I'm proud to be! My only shame is my dirty Mannon blood! So that's why you couldn't stand my touching you just now, is it? You're too good for the son of a servant, eh? By God, you were glad enough before—!

LAVINIA (*fiercely*) It's not true! I was only leading you on to find out things!

BRANT Oh, no! It's only since you suspected who I was! I suppose your father has stuffed you with his lies about my mother! But, by God, you'll hear the truth of it, now you know who I am— And you'll see if you or any Mannon has the right to look down on her!

LAVINIA I don't want to hear— (*She starts to go toward the house*).

BRANT (*grabbing her by the arm—tauntingly*) You're a coward, are you, like all Mannons, when it comes to facing the truth about themselves? (*She turns on him defiantly. He drops her arm and goes on harshly*) I'll bet he never told you your grandfather, Abe Mannon, as well as his brother, loved my mother!

LAVINIA It's a lie!

BRANT It's the truth. It was his jealous revenge made him disown my father and cheat him out of his share of the business they'd inherited!

LAVINIA He didn't cheat him! He bought him out!

BRANT Forced him to sell for one-tenth its worth, you mean! He knew my father and mother were starving! But the money didn't last my father long! He'd taken to drink. He was a coward—like all Mannons—once he felt the world looked down on him. He skulked and avoided people. He grew ashamed of my mother—and me. He sank down and down and my mother worked and supported him. I can remember when men from the corner saloon would drag him home and he'd fall in the door, a sodden carcass. One night when I was seven he came home crazy drunk and hit my mother in the face. It was the first time he'd ever struck her. It made me blind mad. I hit at him with the poker and cut his head. My mother pulled me back and gave me a hiding. Then she cried over him. She'd never stopped loving him.

LAVINIA Why do you tell me this? I told you once I don't want to hear—

BRANT (*grimly*) You'll see the point of it damned soon! (*Unheeding—as if the scene were still before his eyes*) For days after, he sat and stared at nothing. One time when we were alone he asked me to forgive him hitting her. But I hated him and I wouldn't forgive him. Then one night he went out and he didn't come back. The next morning they found him hanging in a barn!

LAVINIA (*with a shudder*) Oh!

BRANT (*savagely*) The only decent thing he ever did!

LAVINIA You're lying! No Mannon would ever—

BRANT Oh, wouldn't they? They are all fine, honorable gentlemen, you think! Then listen a bit and you'll hear something about another of them! (*Then going on bitterly with his story*) My mother sewed for a living and sent me to school.

She was very strict with me. She blamed me for his killing himself. But she was bound she'd make a gentleman of me—like he was!—if it took her last cent and her last strap! (*With a grim smile*) She didn't succeed, as you notice! At seventeen I ran away to sea—and forgot I had a mother, except I took part of her name—Brant was short and easy on ships—and I wouldn't wear the name of Mannon. I forgot her until two years ago when I came back from the East. Oh, I'd written to her now and then and sent her money when I happened to have any. But I'd forgotten her just the same—and when I got to New York I found her dying—of sickness and starvation! And I found out that when she'd been laid up, not able to work, not knowing where to reach me, she'd sunk her last shred of pride and written to your father asking for a loan. He never answered her. And I came too late. She died in my arms. (*With vindictive passion*) He could have saved her—and he deliberately let her die! He's as guilty of murder as anyone he ever sent to the rope when he was a judge!

LAVINIA (*springing to her feet—furiously*) You dare say that about Father! If he were here—

BRANT I wish to God he was! I'd tell him what I tell you now—that I swore on my mother's body I'd revenge her death on him.

LAVINIA (*with cold deadly intensity*) And I suppose you boast that now you've done so, don't you?—in the vilest, most cowardly way—like the son of a servant you are!

BRANT (*again thrown off guard—furiously*) Belay, I told you, with that kind of talk!

LAVINIA She is only your means of revenge on Father, is that it?

BRANT (*stunned—stammers in guilty confusion*) What?—She?—Who?—I don't know what you're talking about!

LAVINIA Then you soon will know! And so will she! I've found out all I wanted to from you. I'm going in to talk to her now. You wait here until I call you!

BRANT (*furious at her tone*) No! Be damned if you can order me about as if I was your servant!

LAVINIA (*icily*) If you have any consideration for her, you'll do as I say and not force me to write my father. (*She turns her back on him and walks to the steps woodenly erect and square-shouldered*).

BRANT (*desperately now—with a grotesque catching at his lover's manner*) I don't know what you mean, Lavinia. I swear before God it is only you I— (*She turns at the top of the steps at this and stares at him with such a passion of hatred that he is silenced. Her lips move as if she were going to speak, but she fights back the words, turns stiffly and goes into the house and closes the door behind her*).

CURTAIN

ACT TWO

SCENE—*In the house*—EZRA MANNON'S *study. No time has elapsed. The study is a large room with a stiff, austere atmosphere. The furniture is old colonial. The walls are plain plastered surfaces tinted a dull gray with a flat white trim. At rear, right, is a door leading to the hall. On the right wall is a painting of George Washington in a gilt frame, flanked by smaller portraits of Alexander Hamilton and John Marshall. At rear, center, is an open fireplace. At left of fireplace, a bookcase filled with law books. Above the fireplace, in a plain frame, is a large portrait of* EZRA MANNON *himself, painted ten years previously. One is at once struck by the startling likeness between him and* ADAM BRANT. *He is a tall man in his early forties, with a spare, wiry frame, seated stiffly in an armchair, his hands on the arms, wearing his black judge's robe. His face is handsome in a stern, aloof fashion. It is cold and emotionless and has the same strange semblance of a life-like mask that we have already seen in the faces of his wife and daughter and* BRANT.

On the left are two windows. Between them a desk. A large table with an armchair on either side, right and left, stands at left center, front. At right center is another chair. There are hooked rugs on the floor.

Outside the sun is beginning to set and its glow fills the room with a golden mist. As the action progresses this becomes brighter, then turns to crimson, which darkens to somberness at the end.

LAVINIA *is discovered standing by the table. She is fighting to control herself, but her face is torn by a look of stricken anguish. She turns slowly to her father's portrait and for a moment stares at it fixedly. Then she goes to it and puts her hand over one of his hands with a loving, protecting gesture.*

LAVINIA Poor Father! (*She hears a noise in the hall and moves hastily away. The door from the hall is opened and* CHRISTINE *enters. She is uneasy underneath, but affects a scornful indignation*).

CHRISTINE Really, this unconfirmed report must have turned your head—otherwise I'd find it difficult to understand your sending Annie to disturb me when you knew I was resting.

LAVINIA I told you I had to talk to you.

CHRISTINE (*looking around the room with aversion*) But why in this musty room, of all places?

LAVINIA (*indicating the portrait—quietly*) Because it's Father's room.

CHRISTINE (*starts, looks at the portrait and quickly drops her eyes.* LAVINIA *goes to the door and closes it.* CHRISTINE *says with forced scorn*) More mystery?

LAVINIA You better sit down. (CHRISTINE *sits in the chair at rear center.* LAVINIA *goes back to her father's chair at left of table*).

CHRISTINE Well—if you're quite ready, perhaps you will explain.

LAVINIA I suppose Annie told you I'd been to visit Hazel and Peter while you were away.

CHRISTINE Yes. I thought it peculiar. You never visit anyone overnight. Why did you suddenly take that notion?

LAVINIA I didn't.

CHRISTINE You didn't visit them?

LAVINIA No.

CHRISTINE Then where did you go?

LAVINIA (*accusingly*) To New York! (CHRISTINE *starts.* LAVINIA *hurries on a bit incoherently*) I've suspected something—lately—the excuse you've made for all your trips there the past year, that Grandfather was sick— (*As* CHRISTINE *is about to protest indignantly*) Oh! I know he has been—and you've stayed at his house—but I've suspected lately that wasn't the real reason—and now I can prove it isn't! Because I waited outside Grandfather's house and followed you. I saw you meet Brant!

CHRISTINE (*alarmed but concealing it—coolly*) Well, what if you did? I told you myself I ran into him by accident—

LAVINIA You went to his room!

CHRISTINE (*shaken*) He asked me to meet a friend of his—a lady. It was her house we went to.

LAVINIA I asked the woman in the basement. He had hired the room under another name, but she recognized his description. And yours too. She said you had come there often in the past year.

CHRISTINE (*desperately*) It was the first time I had ever been there. He insisted on my going. He said he had to talk to me about you. He wanted my help to approach your father—

LAVINIA (*furiously*) How can you lie like that? How can you be so vile as to try to use me to hide your adultery?

CHRISTINE (*springing up—with weak indignation*) Vinnie!

LAVINIA Your adultery, I said!

CHRISTINE No!

LAVINIA Stop lying, I tell you! I went upstairs! I heard you telling him—"I love you, Adam"—and kissing him! (*with a cold bitter fury*) You vile—! You're shameless and evil! Even if you are my mother, I say it! (CHRISTINE *stares at her, overwhelmed by this onslaught, her poise shattered for the moment. She tries to keep her voice indifferent but it trembles a little*).

CHRISTINE I—I knew you hated me, Vinnie—but not as bitterly as that! (*Then with a return of her defiant coolness*) Very well! I love Adam Brant. What are you going to do?

LAVINIA How you say that—without any shame! You don't give one thought to Father—who is so good—who trusts you! Oh, how could you do this to Father? How could you?

CHRISTINE (*with strident intensity*) You would understand if you were the wife of a man you hated!

LAVINIA (*horrified—with a glance at the portrait*) Don't! Don't say that—before him! I won't listen!

CHRISTINE (*grabbing her by the arm*) You will listen! I'm talking to you as a woman now, not as mother to daughter! That relationship has no meaning between us! You've called me vile and shameless! Well, I want you to know that's what I've felt about myself for over twenty years, giving my body to a man I—

LAVINIA (*trying to break away from her, half putting her hands up to her ears*) Stop telling me such things! Let me go! (*She breaks away, shrinking from her mother with a look of sick repulsion. A pause. She stammers*) You—then you've always hated Father?

CHRISTINE (*bitterly*) No. I loved him once—before I married him—incredible as that seems now! He was handsome in his lieutenant's uniform! He was silent and mysterious and romantic! But marriage soon turned his romance into—disgust!

LAVINIA (*wincing again—stammers harshly*) So I was born of your disgust! I've always guessed that, Mother—ever since I was little—when I used to come to you—with love—but you would always push me away! I've felt it ever since I can remember—your disgust! (*Then with a flare-up of bitter hatred*) Oh, I hate you! It's only right I should hate you!

CHRISTINE (*shaken—defensively*) I tried to love you. I told myself it wasn't human not to love my own child, born of my body. But I never could make myself feel you were born of any body but his! You were always my wedding night to me—and my honeymoon!

LAVINIA Stop saying that! How can you be so—! (*Then suddenly—with a strange jealous bitterness*) You've loved Orin! Why didn't you hate him, too?

CHRISTINE Because by then I had forced myself to become resigned in order to live! And most of the time I was carrying him, your father was with the army in Mexico. I had forgotten him. And when Orin was born he seemed my child, only mine, and I loved him for that! (*Bitterly*) I loved him until he let you and your father nag him into the war, in spite of my begging him not leave me alone. (*Staring at* LAVINIA *with hatred*) I know his leaving me was your doing principally, Vinnie!

LAVINIA (*sternly*) It was his duty as a Mannon to go! He'd have been sorry the rest of his life if he hadn't! I love him better than you! I was thinking of him!

CHRISTINE Well, I hope you realize I never would have fallen in love with Adam if I'd had Orin with me. When he had gone there was nothing left—but hate and a desire to be revenged—and a longing for love! And it was then I met Adam. I saw he loved me—

LAVINIA (*with taunting scorn*) He doesn't love you! You're only his revenge on Father! Do you know who he really is? He's the son of that low nurse girl Grandfather put out of our house!

CHRISTINE (*concealing a start—coolly*) So you've found that out? Were you hoping it would be a crushing surprise to me? I've known it all along. He told me when he said he loved me.

LAVINIA Oh! And I suppose knowing who he was gave you all the more satisfaction—to add that disgrace!

CHRISTINE (*cuttingly*) Will you kindly come to the point and tell me what you intend doing? I suppose you'll hardly let your father get in the door before you tell him!

LAVINIA (*suddenly becoming rigid and cold again—slowly*) No. Not unless you force me to. (*Then as she sees her mother's astonishment—grimly*) I don't wonder you're surprised! You know you deserve the worst punishment you could get. And Father would disown you publicly, no matter how much the scandal cost him!

CHRISTINE I realize that. I know him even better than you do!

LAVINIA And I'd like to see you punished for your wickedness! So please understand this isn't for your sake. It's for Father's. He hasn't been well lately. I'm not going to have him hurt! It's my first duty to protect him from you!

CHRISTINE I know better than to expect any generosity on my account.

LAVINIA I won't tell him, provided you give up Brant and never see him again—and promise to be a dutiful wife to Father and make up for the wrong you've done him!

CHRISTINE (*stares at her daughter—a pause—then she laughs dryly*) What a fraud you are, with your talk of your father and your duty! Oh, I'm not denying you want to save his pride—and I know how anxious you are to keep the family from more scandal! But all the same, that's not your real reason for sparing me!

LAVINIA (*confused—guiltily*) It is!

CHRISTINE You wanted Adam Brant yourself!

LAVINIA That's a lie!

CHRISTINE And now you know you can't have him, you're determined that at least you'll take him from me!

LAVINIA No!

CHRISTINE But if you told your father, I'd have to go away with Adam. He'd be mine still. You can't bear that thought, even at the price of my disgrace, can you?

LAVINIA It's your evil mind!

CHRISTINE I know you, Vinnie! I've watched you ever since you were little, trying to do exactly what you're doing now! You've tried to become the wife of your father and the mother of Orin! You've always schemed to steal my place!

LAVINIA (*wildly*) No! It's you who have stolen all love from me since the time I was born! (*Then her manner becoming threatening*) But I don't want to listen to any more of your lies and excuses! I want to know right now whether you're going to do what I told you or not!

CHRISTINE Suppose I refuse! Suppose I go off openly with Adam! Where will you and your father and the family name be after that scandal? And what if I were disgraced myself? I'd have the man I love, at least!

LAVINIA (*grimly*) Not for long! Father would use all his influence and get Brant blacklisted so he'd lose his command and never get another! You know how much the "Flying

Trades" means to him. And Father would never divorce you. You could never marry. You'd be an anchor around his neck. Don't forget you're five years older than he is! He'll still be in his prime when you're an old woman with all your looks gone! He'd grow to hate the sight of you!

CHRISTINE (*stung beyond bearing—makes a threatening move as if to strike her daughter's face*) You devil! You mean little—! (*But* LAVINIA *stares back coldly into her eyes and she controls herself and drops her hand*).

LAVINIA I wouldn't call names if I were you! There is one you deserve!

CHRISTINE (*turning away—her voice still trembling*) I'm a fool to let you make me lose my temper—over your jealous spite! (*A pause.* LAVINIA *stares at her.* CHRISTINE *seems considering something. A sinister expression comes to her face. Then she turns back to* LAVINIA*—coldly*) But you wanted my answer, didn't you? Well, I agree to do as you said. I promise you I'll never see Adam again after he calls this evening. Are you satisfied?

LAVINIA (*stares at her with cold suspicion*) You seem to take giving him up pretty easily!

CHRISTINE (*hastily*) Do you think I'll ever give you the satisfaction of seeing me grieve? Oh, no, Vinnie! You'll never have a chance to gloat!

LAVINIA (*still suspiciously—with a touch of scorn*) If I loved anyone—!

CHRISTINE (*tauntingly*) If? I think you do love him—as much as you can love! (*With a sudden flurry of jealousy*) You little fool! Don't you know I made him flirt with you, so you wouldn't be suspicious?

LAVINIA (*gives a little shudder—then fiercely*) He didn't fool me! I saw what a liar he was! I just led him on—to find out things! I always hated him! (CHRISTINE *smiles mockingly and turns away, as if to go out of the room.* LAVINIA'S *manner becomes threatening again*) Wait! I don't trust you! I know you're thinking already how you can fool me and break the promise you've just made! But you better not try it! I'll be watching you every minute! And I won't be the only one! I wrote to Father and Orin as soon as I got back from New York!

CHRISTINE (*startled*) About Adam?

LAVINIA Only enough so they'd be suspicious and watch

you too. I said a Captain Brant had been calling and folks had begun to gossip.

CHRISTINE Ah! I see what it's going to mean—that you'll always have this to hold over me and I'll be under your thumb for the rest of my life! (*She cannot restrain her rage—threateningly*) Take care, Vinnie! You'll be responsible if—! (*She checks herself abruptly*).

LAVINIA (*suspiciously*) If what?

CHRISTINE (*quickly*) Nothing. I only meant if I went off with Adam. But of course you know I won't do that. You know there's nothing I can do now—but obey your orders!

LAVINIA (*continues to stare at her suspiciously—grimly*) You ought to see it's your duty to Father, not my orders—if you had any honor or decency! (*Then brusquely*) Brant is waiting outside. You can tell him what you've got to do— and tell him if he ever dares come here again—! (*Forcing back her anger*) And see that you get rid of him right now! I'm going upstreet to get the latest news. I won't be gone more than a half-hour and I want him out of the house by the time I get back, do you hear? If he isn't, I'll write Father again. I won't even wait for him to come home! (*She turns her back on her mother and marches out the door, square-shouldered and stiff, without a backward glance.* CHRISTINE *looks after her, waiting until she hears the side door of the house close after her. Then she turns and stands in tense calculating thought. Her face has become like a sinister evil mask. Finally, as if making up her mind irrevocably, she comes to the table, tears off a slip of paper and writes two words on it. She tucks this paper in the sleeve of her dress and goes to the open window and calls*).

CHRISTINE Adam! (*She moves toward the door to wait for him. Her eyes are caught by the eyes of her husband in the portrait over the fireplace. She stares at him with hatred and addresses him vindictively, half under her breath*) You can thank Vinnie, Ezra! (*She goes to the door and reaches it just as* BRANT *appears from the hall. She takes his hand and draws him into the room, closing the door behind him. One is immediately struck by the resemblance between his face and that of the portrait of* EZRA MANNON).

BRANT (*glancing uneasily at her, as they come to the center of the room*) She knows—?

CHRISTINE Yes. She followed me to New York. And she's found out who you are too, Adam.

BRANT (*with a grim smile*) I know. She got that out of me—the proof of it, at any rate. Before I knew what was up I'd given myself away.

CHRISTINE She must have noticed your resemblance to Orin. I was afraid that might start her thinking.

BRANT (*sees the portrait for the first time. Instantly his body shifts to a fighting tenseness. It is as if he were going to spring at the figure in the painting. He says slowly*) That, I take it, is General Mannon?

CHRISTINE Judge Mannon then. Don't forget he used to be a judge. He won't forget it.

BRANT (*his eyes still fixed on the portrait—comes and sits in* MANNON'S *chair on the left of table. Unconsciously he takes the same attitude as* MANNON, *sitting erect, his hands on the arms of the chair—slowly*) Does Orin by any chance resemble his father?

CHRISTINE (*stares at him—agitatedly*) No! Of course not! What put such a stupid idea in your head?

BRANT It would be damned queer if you fell in love with me because I recalled Ezra Mannon to you!

CHRISTINE (*going to him and putting an arm around his shoulder*) No, no, I tell you! It was Orin you made me think of! It was Orin!

BRANT I remember that night we were introduced and I heard the name Mrs. Ezra Mannon! By God, how I hated you then for being his! I thought, by God, I'll take her from him and that'll be part of my revenge! And out of that hatred my love came! It's damned queer, isn't it?

CHRISTINE (*hugging him to her*) Are you going to let him take me from you now, Adam?

BRANT (*passionately*) You ask that!

CHRISTINE You swear you won't—no matter what you must do?

BRANT By God, I swear it!

CHRISTINE (*kisses him*) Remember that oath! (*She glances at the portrait—then turns back to* BRANT *with a little shiver—nervously*) What made you sit there? It's his chair. I've so often seen him sitting there— (*Forcing a little laugh*) Your silly talk about resemblances— Don't sit there. Come. Bring that chair over here. (*She moves to the chair at right center. He brings the chair at right of table close to hers*).

BRANT We've got to decide what we must do. The time for skulking and lying is over—and by God I'm glad of it! It's a coward's game I have no stomach for! (*He has placed the chair beside hers. She is staring at the portrait*) Why don't you sit down, Christine?

CHRISTINE (*slowly*) I was thinking—perhaps we had better go to the sitting-room. (*Then defiantly*) No! I've been afraid of you long enough, Ezra! (*She sits down*).

BRANT I felt there was something wrong the moment I saw her. I tried my damnedest to put her off the course by giving her some softsoap—as you'd told me to do to blind her. (*Frowning*) That was a mistake, Christine. It made her pay too much attention to me—and opened her eyes!

CHRISTINE Oh, I know I've made one blunder after another. It's as if love drove me on to do everything I shouldn't. I never should have brought you to this house. Seeing you in New York should have been enough for me. But I loved you too much. I wanted you every possible moment we could steal! And I simply couldn't believe that he ever would come home. I prayed that he should be killed in the war so intensely that I finally believed it would surely happen! (*With savage intensity*) Oh, if he were only dead!

BRANT That chance is finished now.

CHRISTINE (*slowly—without looking at him*) Yes—in that way.

BRANT (*stares at her*) What do you mean? (*She remains silent. He changes the subject uneasily*) There's only one thing to do! When he comes home I'll wait for him and not give Vinnie the satisfaction of telling him. I'll tell him myself. (*Vindictively*) By God! I'd give my soul to see his face when he knows you love Marie Brantôme's son! And then I'll take you away openly and laugh at him! And if he tries to stop me—! (*He stops and glances with savage hatred at the portrait*).

CHRISTINE What would you do then?

BRANT If ever I laid hands on him, I'd kill him!

CHRISTINE And then? You would be hanged for murder! And where would I be? There would be nothing left for me but to kill myself!

BRANT If I could catch him alone, where no one would interfere, and let the best man come out alive—as I've often seen it done in the West!

CHRISTINE This isn't the West.

BRANT I could insult him on the street before everyone and make him fight me! I could let him shoot first and then kill him in self-defense.

CHRISTINE (*scornfully*) Do you imagine you could force him to fight a duel with you? Don't you know duelling is illegal? Oh, no! He'd simply feel bound to do his duty as a former judge and have you arrested! (*She adds calculatingly, seeing he is boiling inside*) It would be a poor revenge for your mother's death to let him make you a laughing stock!

BRANT But when I take you off, the laugh will be on him! You can come on the "Flying Trades."

CHRISTINE (*calculatingly reproachful*) I don't think you'd propose that, Adam, if you stopped thinking of your revenge for a moment and thought of me! Don't you realize he would never divorce me, out of spite? What would I be in the world's eyes? My life would be ruined and I would ruin yours! You'd grow to hate me!

BRANT (*passionately*) Don't talk like that! It's a lie and you know it!

CHRISTINE (*with bitter yearning*) If I could only believe that, Adam! But I'll grow old so soon! And I'm afraid of time! (*Then abruptly changing tone*) As for my sailing on your ship, you'll find you won't have a ship! He'll see to it you lose this command and get you blacklisted so you'll have no chance of getting another.

BRANT (*angrily*) Aye! He can do that if he sets about it. There are twice as many skippers as ships these days.

CHRISTINE (*calculatingly—without looking at him*) If he had only been killed, we could be married now and I would bring you my share of the Mannon estate. That would only be justice. It's yours by right. It's what his father stole from yours.

BRANT That's true enough, damn him!

CHRISTINE You wouldn't have to worry about commands or owners' favors then. You could buy your own ship and be your own master!

BRANT (*yearningly*) That's always been my dream—some day to own my own clipper! And Clark and Dawson would be willing to sell the "Flying Trades." (*Then forgetting everything in his enthusiasm*) You've seen her, Christine. She's as beautiful a ship as you're a woman. Aye, the two of you are like sisters. If she was mine, I'd take you on a honeymoon then! To China—and on the voyage back, we'd stop at the South Pacific Islands I've told you about. By God, there's the right place for love and a honeymoon!

CHRISTINE (*slowly*) Yes—but Ezra is alive!

BRANT (*brought back to earth—gloomily*) I know it's only a dream.

CHRISTINE (*turning to stare at him—slowly*) You can have your dream—and I can have mine. There is a way. (*Then turning away again*) You remember my telling you he had written complaining of pains about his heart?

BRANT You're surely not hoping—

CHRISTINE No. He said it was nothing serious. But I've let it be known that he has heart trouble. I went to see our old family doctor and told him about Ezra's letter. I pretended to be dreadfully worried, until I got him worried too. He's the town's worst old gossip. I'm sure everyone knows about Ezra's weak heart by this time.

BRANT What are you driving at, Christine?

CHRISTINE Something I've been thinking of ever since I realized he might soon come home. And now that Vinnie—but even if we didn't have to consider her, it'd be the only way! I couldn't fool him long. He's a strange, hidden man. His silence always creeps into my thoughts. Even if he never spoke, I would feel what was in his mind and some night, lying beside him, it would drive me mad and I'd have to kill his silence by screaming out the truth! (*She has been staring before her—now she suddenly turns on* BRANT*—slowly*) If he died suddenly now, no one would think it was anything but heart failure. I've been reading a book in Father's medical library. I saw it there one day a few weeks ago—it was as if some fate in me forced me to see it! (*She reaches in the sleeve of her dress and takes out the slip of paper she had written on*) I've written something here. I want you to get it for me. (*His fingers close on it mechanically. He stares at it with a strange stupid dread. She hurries on so as not to give him time for reflection*) The work on the "Flying Trades" is all finished, isn't it? You sail to Boston tomorrow, to wait for cargo?

BRANT (*dully*) Aye.

CHRISTINE Get this at some druggist's down by the waterfront the minute you reach there. You can make up some story about a sick dog on your ship. As soon as you get it, mail it to me here. I'll be on the look out, so Vinnie will never know it came. Then you must wait on the "Flying Trades" until you hear from me or I come to you—afterward!

BRANT (*dully*) But how can you do it—so no one will suspect?

CHRISTINE He's taking medicine. I'll give him his medicine. Oh, I've planned it carefully.

BRANT But—if he dies suddenly, won't Vinnie—

CHRISTINE There'll be no reason for her to suspect. She's worried already about his heart. Besides, she may hate me, but she would never think—

BRANT Orin will be coming home, too.

CHRISTINE Orin will believe anything I want him to. As for the people here, they'd never dream of such a thing in the Mannon house! And the sooner I do it, the less suspicion there'll be! They will think the excitement of coming home and the reaction were too much for his weak heart! Doctor Blake will think so. I'll see that's what he thinks.

BRANT (*harshly*) Poison! It's a coward's trick!

CHRISTINE (*with fierce scorn now, seeing the necessity of goading him*) Do you think you would be braver to give me up to him and let him take away your ship?

BRANT No!

CHRISTINE Didn't you say you wanted to kill him?

BRANT Aye! But I'd give him his chance!

CHRISTINE Did he give your mother her chance?

BRANT (*aroused*) No, damn him!

CHRISTINE Then what makes you suddenly so scrupulous about his death? (*With a sneer*) It must be the Mannon in you coming out! Are you going to prove, the first time your love is put to a real test, that you're a weak coward like your father?

BRANT Christine! If it was any man said that to me—!

CHRISTINE (*passionately*) Have you thought of this side of his homecoming—that he's coming back to my bed? If you love me as much as you claim, I should think that would rid you of any scruples! If it was a question of some woman taking you from me, I wouldn't have qualms about which was or wasn't the way to kill her! (*More tauntingly*) But perhaps your love has been only a lie you told me—to take the sneaking revenge on him of being a backstairs lover! Perhaps—

BRANT (*stung, grabbing her by the shoulders—fiercely*) Stop it! I'll do anything you want! You know it! (*Then with a change to somber grimness—putting the paper in his pocket*) And you're right. I'm a damn fool to have any feeling about how Ezra Mannon dies!

CHRISTINE (*a look of exultant satisfaction comes to her face as she sees he is definitely won over now. She throws her arms around him and kisses him passionately*) Ah! Now you're the man I love again, not a hypocritical Mannon! Promise me, no more cowardly romantic scruples! Promise me!

BRANT I promise. (*The boom of a cannon sounds from the fort that guards the harbor. He and* CHRISTINE *start frightenedly and stand staring at each other. Another boom comes, reverberating, rattling the windows.* CHRISTINE *recovers herself*).

CHRISTINE You hear? That's the salute to his homecoming! (*She kisses him—with fierce insistence*) Remember your mother's death! Remember your dream of your own ship! Above all, remember you'll have me!—all your own—your wife! (*Then urgently*) And now you must go! She'll be coming back—and you're not good at hiding your thoughts. (*Urging him toward the door*) Hurry! I don't want you to meet her! (*The cannon at the fort keep booming at regular intervals until the end of the scene.* BRANT *goes out in the hall and a moment later the front door is heard closing after him.* CHRISTINE *hurries from the door to the window and watches him from behind the curtains as he goes down the drive. She is in a state of tense, exultant excitement. Then, as if an idea had suddenly come to her, she speaks to his retreating figure with a strange sinister air of elation*) You'll never dare leave me now, Adam—for your ships or your sea or your naked Island girls—when I grow old and ugly! (*She turns back from the window. Her eyes are caught by the eyes of her husband in the portrait and for a moment she stares back into them, as if fascinated. Then she jerks her glance away and, with a little shudder she cannot repress, turns and walks quickly from the room and closes the door behind her*).

CURTAIN

ACT THREE

SCENE—*The same as Act One, Scene One—exterior of the Mannon house. It is around nine o'clock of a night a week later. The light of a half moon falls on the house, giving it an unreal, detached, eerie quality. The pure white temple front seems more than ever like an incongruous mask fixed on the somber, stone house. All the shutters are closed. The white columns of the portico cast black bars of shadow on the gray wall behind them. The trunk of the pine at right is an ebony pillar, its branches a mass of shade.*

LAVINIA *is sitting on the top of the steps to the portico. She is dressed, as before, severely in black. Her thin figure, seated stiffly upright, arms against her sides, the legs close together, the shoulders square, the head upright, is like that of an Egyptian statue. She is staring straight before her. The sound of* SETH'S *thin, aged baritone mournfully singing the chanty "Shenandoah" is heard from down the drive, off right front. He is approaching the house and the song draws quickly nearer:*

"Oh, Shenandoah, I long to hear you
A-way, my rolling river.
Oh, Shenandoah, I can't get near you
Way-ay, I'm bound away
Across the wide Missouri.

"Oh, Shenandoah, I love your daughter
A-way, my rolling river."

He enters right front. He is a bit drunk but holding his liquor well. He walks up by the lilacs starting the next line "Oh, Shenandoah"—then suddenly sees LAVINIA *on the steps and stops abruptly, a bit sheepish.*

LAVINIA (*disapprovingly*) This is the second time this week I've caught you coming home like this.

SETH (*unabashed, approaches the steps—with a grin*) I'm aimin' to do my patriotic duty, Vinnie. The first time was celebratin' Lee's surrender and this time is drownin' my sorrow for the President gittin' shot! And the third'll be when your Paw gits home!

LAVINIA Father might arrive tonight.

SETH Gosh, Vinnie, I never calc'lated he could git here so soon!

LAVINIA Evidently you didn't. He'd give you fits if he caught you drunk. Oh, I don't believe he'll come, but it's possible he might.

SETH (*is evidently trying to pull himself together. He suddenly leans over toward her and, lowering his voice, asks soberly*) Did you find out anything about that Brant?

LAVINIA (*sharply*) Yes. There's no connection. It was just a silly idea of yours.

SETH (*stares at her—then understandingly*) Wal, if you want it left that way, I'll leave it that way. (*A pause. He continues to stand looking at her, while she stares in front of her*).

LAVINIA (*in a low voice*) What was that Marie Brantôme like, Seth?

SETH Marie? She was always laughin' and singin'—frisky and full of life—with something free and wild about her like an animile. Purty she was, too! (*Then he adds*) Hair just the color of your Maw's and yourn she had.

LAVINIA I know.

SETH Oh, everyone took to Marie—couldn't help it. Even your Paw. He was only a boy then, but he was crazy about her, too, like a youngster would be. His mother was stern with him, while Marie, she made a fuss over him and petted him.

LAVINIA Father, too!

SETH Ayeh—but he hated her worse than anyone when it got found out she was his Uncle David's fancy woman.

LAVINIA (*in a low voice, as if to herself, staring at the house*) It's all so strange! It frightens me! (*She checks herself abruptly—turns to* SETH, *curtly*) I don't believe that about Father. You've had too much whiskey. Go to bed and sleep it off. (*She walks up the steps again*).

SETH (*gazes at her with understanding*) Ayeh. (*Then warningly, making a surreptitious signal as he sees the front door opening behind her*) Ssstt! (CHRISTINE *appears outlined in the light from the hall. She is dressed in a gown of green velvet that sets off her hair. The light behind her glows along the edges of the dress and in the color of her hair. She closes the door and comes into the moonlight at the edge of the steps, standing above and a little to the right of* LAVINIA. *The moonlight, falling full on them, accentuates strangely the resemblance between their faces and at the same time the hostile dissimi-*

larity in body and dress. LAVINIA *does not turn or give any sign of knowing her mother is behind her. There is a second's uncomfortable silence.* SETH *moves off left*) Wal, I'll trot along! (*He disappears around the corner of the house. There is a pause. Then* CHRISTINE *speaks in a dry mocking tone*)

CHRISTINE What are you moongazing at? Puritan maidens shouldn't peer too inquisitively into Spring! Isn't beauty an abomination and love a vile thing? (*She laughs with bitter mockery—then tauntingly*) Why don't you marry Peter? You don't want to be left an old maid, do you?

LAVINIA (*quietly*) You needn't hope to get rid of me that way. I'm not marrying anyone. I've got my duty to Father.

CHRISTINE Duty! How often I've heard that word in this house! Well, you can't say I didn't do mine all these years. But there comes an end.

LAVINIA (*grimly*) And there comes another end—and you must do your duty again!

CHRISTINE (*starts as if to retort defiantly—then says calmly*) Yes, I realize that.

LAVINIA (*after a pause—suspiciously*) What's going on at the bottom of your mind? I know you're plotting something!

CHRISTINE (*controlling a start*) Don't be stupid, please!

LAVINIA Are you planning how you can see Adam again? You better not!

CHRISTINE (*calmly*) I'm not so foolish. I said good-bye once. Do you think I want to make it harder for myself?

LAVINIA Has it been hard for you? I'd never guess it—and I've been watching you.

CHRISTINE I warned you you would have no chance to gloat! (*After a pause*) When do you expect your father home? You want me to play my part well when he comes, don't you?—for his sake. I'd like to be forewarned.

LAVINIA His letter said he wouldn't wait until his brigade was disbanded but would try to get leave at once. He might arrive tonight—or tomorrow—or the next day. I don't know.

CHRISTINE You think he might come tonight? (*Then with a mocking smile*) So he's the beau you're waiting for in the spring moonlight! (*Then after a pause*) But the night train got in long ago.

LAVINIA (*glances down the drive, left front—then starts to her feet excitedly*) Here's someone! (CHRISTINE *slowly rises. There is the sound of footsteps. A moment later* EZRA MANNON *enters from left, front. He stops short in the shadow for a sec-*

ond and stands, erect and stiff, as if at attention, staring at his house, his wife and daughter. He is a tall, spare, big-boned man of fifty, dressed in the uniform of a brigadier-general. One is immediately struck by the mask-like look of his face in repose, more pronounced in him than in the others. He is exactly like the portrait in his study, which we have seen in Act Two, except that his face is more lined and lean and the hair and beard are grizzled. His movements are exact and wooden and he has a mannerism of standing and sitting in stiff, posed attitudes that suggest the statues of military heroes. When he speaks, his deep voice has a hollow repressed quality, as if he were continually withholding emotion from it. His air is brusque and authoritative).

LAVINIA (*seeing the man' figure top in the shadow—calls excitedly*) Who's that?

MANNON (*stepping forward into the moonlight*) It's I.

LAVINIA (*with a cry of joy*) Father! (*She runs to him and throws her arms around him and kisses him*) Oh, Father! (*She bursts into tears and hides her face against his shoulder*).

MANNON (*embarrassed—patting her head—gruffly*) Come! I thought I'd taught you never to cry.

LAVINIA (*obediently forcing back her tears*) I'm sorry, Father—but I'm so happy!

MANNON (*awkwardly moved*) Tears are queer tokens of happiness! But I appreciate your—your feeling.

CHRISTINE (*has slowly descended the steps, her eyes fixed on him—tensely*) Is it really you, Ezra? We had just given up hope of your coming tonight.

MANNON (*going stiffly to meet her*) Train was late. The railroad is jammed up. Everybody has got leave. (*He meets her at the foot of the steps and kisses her with a chill dignity—formally*) I am glad to see you, Christine. You are looking well. (*He steps back and stares at her—then in a voice that betrays a deep undercurrent of suppressed feeling*) You have changed, somehow. You are prettier than ever— But you always were pretty.

CHRISTINE (*forcing a light tone*) Compliments from one's husband! How gallant you've become, Ezra! (*Then solicitously*) You must be terribly tired. Wouldn't you like to sit here on the steps for a while? The moonlight is so beautiful.

LAVINIA (*who has been hovering about jealously, now manages to worm herself between them—sharply*) No. It's too damp out here. And Father must be hungry. (*Taking his arm*)

Come inside with me and I'll get you something to eat. You poor dear! You must be starved.

MANNON (*really revelling in his daughter's coddling but embarrassed before his wife—pulling his arm back—brusquely*) No, thanks! I would rather rest here for a spell. Sit down, Vinnie. (CHRISTINE *sits on the top step at center; he sits on the middle step at right;* LAVINIA *on the lowest step at left. While they are doing this he keeps on talking in his abrupt sentences, as if he were trying to cover up some hidden uneasiness*) I've got leave for a few days. Then I must go back and disband my brigade. Peace ought to be signed soon. The President's assassination is a frightful calamity. But it can't change the course of events.

LAVINIA Poor man! It's dreadful he should die just at his moment of victory.

MANNON Yes! (*Then after a pause—somberly*) All victory ends in the defeat of death. That's sure. But does defeat end in the victory of death? That's what I wonder! (*They both stare at him,* LAVINIA *in surprise,* CHRISTINE *in uneasy wonder. A pause*).

CHRISTINE Where is Orin? Couldn't you get leave for him too?

MANNON (*hesitates—then brusquely*) I've been keeping it from you. Orin was wounded.

LAVINIA Wounded! You don't mean—badly hurt?

CHRISTINE (*half starting to her feet impulsively—with more of angry bitterness than grief*) I knew it! I knew when you forced him into your horrible war—! (*Then sinking back —tensely*) You needn't trouble to break the news gradually, Ezra. Orin is dead, isn't he?

LAVINIA Don't say that! It isn't true, is it, Father?

MANNON (*curtly—a trace of jealousy in his tone*) Of course it isn't! If your mother would permit me to finish instead of jumping at conclusions about her baby—! (*With a grim, proud satisfaction*) He's no baby now. I've made a man of him. He did one of the bravest things I've seen in the war. He was wounded in the head—a close shave but it turned out only a scratch. But he got brain fever from the shock. He's all right now. He was in a rundown condition, they say at the hospital. I never guessed it. Nerves. I wouldn't notice nerves. He's always been restless. (*Half turning to* CHRISTINE) He gets that from you.

CHRISTINE When will he be well enough to come home?

MANNON Soon. The doctor advised a few more days' rest. He's still weak. He was out of his head for a long time. Acted as if he were a little boy again. Seemed to think you were with him. That is, he kept talking to "Mother."

CHRISTINE (*with a tense intake of breath*) Ah!

LAVINIA (*pityingly—with a tinge of scorn in her voice*) Poor Orin!

MANNON I don't want you to baby him when he comes home, Christine. It would be bad for him to get tied to your apron strings again.

CHRISTINE You needn't worry. That passed—when he left me. (*Another pause. Then* LAVINIA *speaks*).

LAVINIA How is the trouble with your heart, Father? I've been so afraid you might be making it out less serious than it really was to keep us from worrying.

MANNON (*gruffly*) If it was serious, I'd tell you, so you'd be prepared. If you'd seen as much of death as I have in the past four years, you wouldn't be afraid of it. (*Suddenly jumping to his feet—brusquely*) Let's change the subject! I've had my fill of death. What I want now is to forget it. (*He turns and paces up and down to the right of steps.* LAVINIA *watches him worriedly*) All I know is the pain is like a knife. It puts me out of commission while it lasts. The doctor gave me orders to avoid worry or any over-exertion or excitement.

CHRISTINE (*staring at him*) You don't look well. But probably that's because you're so tired. You must go to bed soon, Ezra.

MANNON (*comes to a stop in his pacing directly before her and looks into her eyes—a pause—then he says in a voice that he tries to make ordinary*) Yes, I want to—soon.

LAVINIA (*who has been watching him jealously—suddenly pulling him by the arm—with a childish volubility*) No! Not yet! Please, Father! You've only just come! We've hardly talked at all! (*Defiantly to her mother*) How can you tell him he looks tired? He looks as well as I've ever seen him. (*Then to her father with a vindictive look at Christine*) We've so much to tell you. All about Captain Brant. (*If she had expected her mother to flinch at this, she is disappointed.* CHRISTINE *is prepared and remains unmoved beneath the searching, suspicious glance Mannon now directs at her*).

MANNON Vinnie wrote me you'd had company. I never heard of him. What business had he here?

CHRISTINE (*with an easy smile*) You had better ask Vinnie!

He's her latest beau! She even went walking in the moonlight with him!

LAVINIA (*with a gasp at being defied so brazenly*) Oh!

MANNON (*now jealous and suspicious of his daughter*) I notice you didn't mention that in your letter, young lady!

LAVINIA I only went walking once with him—and that was before— (*She checks herself abruptly*).

MANNON Before what?

LAVINIA Before I knew he's the kind who chases after every woman he sees.

MANNON (*angrily to* CHRISTINE) A fine guest to receive in my absence!

LAVINIA I believe he even thought Mother was flirting with him. That's why I felt it my duty to write you. You know how folks in town gossip, Father. I thought you ought to warn Mother she was foolish to allow him to come here.

MANNON Foolish! It was downright—!

CHRISTINE (*coldly*) I would prefer not to discuss this until we are alone, Ezra—if you don't mind! And I think Vinnie is extremely inconsiderate the moment you're home—to annoy you with such ridiculous nonsense! (*She turns to* LAVINIA) I think you've done enough mischief. Will you kindly leave us?

LAVINIA No.

MANNON (*sharply*) Stop your squabbling, both of you! I hoped you had grown out of that nonsense! I won't have it in my house!

LAVINIA (*obediently*) Yes, Father.

MANNON It must be your bedtime, Vinnie.

LAVINIA Yes, Father. (*She comes and kisses him—excitedly*) Oh, I'm so happy you're here! Don't let Mother make you believe I— You're the only man I'll ever love! I'm going to stay with you!

MANNON (*patting her hair—with gruff tenderness*) I hope so. I want you to remain my little girl—for a while longer, at least. (*Then suddenly catching* CHRISTINE'S *scornful glance—pushes* LAVINIA *away—brusquely*) March now!

LAVINIA Yes, Father. (*She goes up the steps past her mother without a look. Behind her mother, in the portico, she stops and turns*) Don't let anything worry you, Father. I'll always take care of you. (*She goes in.* MANNON *looks at his wife who stares before her. He clears his throat as if about to say something—then starts pacing self-consciously up and down at the right of steps*).

CHRISTINE (*forcing a gentle tone*) Sit down, Ezra. You will only make yourself more tired, keeping on your feet. (*He sits awkwardly two steps below her, on her left, turned sideways to face her. She asks with disarming simplicity*) Now please tell me just what it is you suspect me of?

MANNON (*taken aback*) What makes you think I suspect you?

CHRISTINE Everything! I've felt your distrust from the moment you came. Your eyes have been probing me, as if you were a judge again and I were the prisoner.

MANNON (*guiltily*) I—?

CHRISTINE And all on account of a stupid letter Vinnie had no business to write. It seems to me a late day, when I am an old woman with grown-up children, to accuse me of flirting with a stupid ship captain!

MANNON (*impressed and relieved—placatingly*) There's no question of accusing you of that. I only think you've been foolish to give the gossips a chance to be malicious.

CHRISTINE Are you sure that's all you have in your heart against me?

MANNON Yes! Of course! What else? (*Patting her hand embarrassedly*) We'll say no more about it. (*Then he adds gruffly*) But I'd like you to explain how this Brant happened—

CHRISTINE I'm only too glad to! I met him at Father's. Father has taken a fancy to him for some reason. So when he called here I couldn't be rude, could I? I hinted that his visits weren't welcome, but men of his type don't understand hints. But he's only been here four times in all, I think. And as for there having been gossip, that's nonsense! The only talk has been that he came to court Vinnie! You can ask anyone in town.

MANNON Damn his impudence! It was your duty to tell him flatly he wasn't wanted!

CHRISTINE (*forcing a contrite air*) Well, I must confess I didn't mind his coming as much as I might have—for one reason. He always brought me news of Father. Father's been sick for the past year, as I wrote you. (*Then with a twitch of the lips, as if she were restraining a derisive smile*) You can't realize what a strain I've been under—worrying about Father and Orin and—you.

MANNON (*deeply moved, turns to her and takes her hand in both of his—awkwardly*) Christine—I deeply regret—having been unjust. (*He kisses her hand impulsively—then em-*

barrassed by this show of emotion, adds in a gruff, joking tone) Afraid old Johnny Reb would pick me off, were you?

CHRISTINE (*controlling a wild impulse to burst into derisive laughter*) Do you need to ask that? (*A pause. He stares at her, fascinated and stirred*).

MANNON (*finally blurts out*) I've dreamed of coming home to you, Christine! (*Leans toward her, his voice trembling with desire and a feeling of strangeness and awe—touching her hair with an awkward caress*) You're beautiful! You look more beautiful than ever—and strange to me. I don't know you. You're younger. I feel like an old man beside you. Only your hair is the same—your strange beautiful hair I always—

CHRISTINE (*with a start of repulsion, shrinking from his hand*) Don't! (*Then as he turns away, hurt and resentful at this rebuff—hastily*) I'm sorry, Ezra. I didn't mean—I—I'm nervous tonight. (MANNON *paces to the right and stands looking at the trees.* CHRISTINE *stares at his back with hatred. She sighs with affected weariness and leans back and closes her eyes*).

CHRISTINE I'm tired, Ezra.

MANNON (*blurts out*) I shouldn't have bothered you with that foolishness about Brant tonight. (*He forces a strained smile*) But I was jealous a mite, to tell you the truth. (*He forces himself to turn and, seeing her eyes are shut, suddenly comes and leans over her awkwardly, as if to kiss her, then is stopped by some strangeness he feels about her still face*).

CHRISTINE (*feeling his desire and instinctively shrinking —without opening her eyes*) Why do you look at me like that?

MANNON (*turns away guiltily*) Like what? (*Uneasily*) How do you know? Your eyes are shut. (*Then, as if some burden of depression were on him that he had to throw off, he blurts out heavily*) I can't get used to home yet. It's so lonely. I've got used to the feel of camps with thousands of men around me at night—a sense of protection, maybe! (*Suddenly uneasy again*) Don't keep your eyes shut like that! Don't be so still! (*Then, as she opens her eyes—with an explosive appeal*) God, I want to talk to you, Christine! I've got to explain some things—inside me—to my wife—try to, anyway! (*He sits down beside her*) Shut your eyes again! I can talk better. It has always been hard for me to talk—about feelings. I never could when you looked at me. Your eyes were always so—so full of silence! That is, since we've been married. Not before, when I was courting you.

They used to speak then. They made me talk—because they answered.

CHRISTINE (*her eyes closed—tensely*) Don't talk, Ezra.

MANNON (*as if he had determined, once started, to go on doggedly without heeding any interruption*) It was seeing death all the time in this war got me to thinking these things. Death was so common, it didn't mean anything. That freed me to think of life. Queer, isn't it? Death made me think of life. Before that life had only made me think of death!

CHRISTINE (*without opening her eyes*) Why are you talking of death?

MANNON That's always been the Mannons' way of thinking. They went to the white meeting-house on Sabbaths and meditated on death. Life was a dying. Being born was starting to die. Death was being born. (*Shaking his head with a dogged bewilderment*) How in hell people ever got such notions! That white meeting-house. It stuck in my mind—clean-scrubbed and whitewashed—a temple of death! But in this war I've seen too many white walls splattered with blood that counted no more than dirty water. I've seen dead men scattered about, no more important than rubbish to be got rid of. That made the white meeting-house seem meaningless—making so much solemn fuss over death!

CHRISTINE (*opens her eyes and stares at him with a strange terror*) What has this talk of death to do with me?

MANNON (*avoiding her glance—insistently*) Shut your eyes again. Listen and you'll know. (*She shuts her eyes. He plods on with a note of desperation in his voice*) I thought about my life—lying awake nights—and about your life. In the middle of battle I'd think maybe in a minute I'll be dead. But my life as just me ending, that didn't appear worth a thought one way or another. But listen, me as your husband being killed that seemed queer and wrong—like something dying that had never lived. Then all the years we've been man and wife would rise up in my mind and I would try to look at them. But nothing was clear except that there'd always been some barrier between us—a wall hiding us from each other! I would try to make up my mind exactly what that wall was but I never could discover. (*With a clumsy appealing gesture*) Do you know?

CHRISTINE (*tensely*) I don't know what you're talking about.

MANNON But you've known it was there! Don't lie, Christine! (*He looks at her still face and closed eyes, imploring her to reassure him—then blunders on doggedly*) Maybe you've always known you didn't love me. I call to mind the Mexican War. I could see you wanted me to go. I had a feeling you'd grown to hate me. Did you? (*She doesn't answer*) That was why I went. I was hoping I might get killed. Maybe you were hoping that too. Were you?

CHRISTINE (*stammers*) No, no, I— What makes you say such things?

MANNON When I came back you had turned to your new baby, Orin. I was hardly alive for you any more. I saw that. I tried not to hate Orin. I turned to Vinnie, but a daughter's not a wife. Then I made up my mind I'd do my work in the world and leave you alone in your life and not care. That's why the shipping wasn't enough—why I became a judge and a mayor and such vain truck, and why folks in town look on me as so able! Ha! Able for what? Not for what I wanted most in life! Not for your love! No! Able only to keep my mind from thinking of what I'd lost! (*He stares at her—then asks pleadingly*) For you did love me before we were married. You won't deny that, will you?

CHRISTINE (*desperately*) I don't deny anything!

MANNON (*drawing himself up with a stern pride and dignity and surrendering himself like a commander against hopeless odds*) All right, then. I came home to surrender to you—what's inside me. I love you. I loved you then, and all the years between, and I love you now.

CHRISTINE (*distractedly*) Ezra! Please!

MANNON I want that said! Maybe you have forgotten it. I wouldn't blame you. I guess I haven't said it or showed it much—ever. Something queer in me keeps me mum about the things I'd like most to say—keeps me hiding the things I'd like to show. Something keeps me sitting numb in my own heart—like a statue of a dead man in a town square. (*Suddenly he reaches over and takes her hand*) I want to find what that wall is marriage put between us! You've got to help me smash it down! We have twenty good years still before us! I've been thinking of what we could do to get back to each other. I've a notion if we'd leave the children and go off on a voyage together—to the other side of the world—find some island where we could be alone a while. You'll find I have changed, Christine. I'm sick of death! I want life! Maybe you could love me now! (*In a note of final desperate pleading*) I've got to make you love me!

CHRISTINE (*pulls her hand away from him and springs to her feet wildly*) For God's sake, stop talking. I don't know what you're saying. Leave me alone! What must be, must be! You make me weak! (*Then abruptly*) It's getting late.

MANNON (*terribly wounded, withdrawn into his stiff soldier armor—takes out his watch mechanically*) Yes—six past eleven. Time to turn in. (*He ascends two steps, his face toward the door. He says bitterly*) You tell me to stop talking! By God, that's funny!

CHRISTINE (*collected now and calculating—takes hold of his arm, seductively*) I meant—what is the good of words? There is no wall between us. I love you.

MANNON (*grabs her by the shoulders and stares into her face*) Christine! I'd give my soul to believe that—but—I'm afraid! (*She kisses him. He presses her fiercely in his arms—passionately*) Christine! (*The door behind him is opened and* LAVINIA *appears at the edge of the portico behind and above him. She wears slippers over her bare feet and has a dark dressing-gown over her night dress. She shrinks back from their embrace with aversion. They separate, startled*).

MANNON (*embarrassed—irritably*) Thought you'd gone to bed, young lady!

LAVINIA (*woodenly*) I didn't feel sleepy. I thought I'd walk a little. It's such a fine night.

CHRISTINE We are just going to bed. Your father is tired. (*She moves up, past her daughter, taking* MANNON'S *hand, leading him after her to the door*).

MANNON No time for a walk, if you ask me. See you turn in soon.

LAVINIA Yes, Father.

MANNON Good night. (*The door closes behind them.* LAVINIA *stands staring before her—then walks stiffly down the steps and stands again. Light appears between the chinks of the shutters in the bedroom on the second floor to the left. She looks up*).

LAVINIA (*in an anguish of jealous hatred*) I hate you! You steal even Father's love from me again! You stole all love from me when I was born! (*Then almost with a sob, hiding her face in her hands*) Oh, Mother! Why have you done this to me? What harm had I done you? (*Then looking up at the window again—with passionate disgust*) Father, how can you love that shameless harlot? (*Then frenziedly*) I can't bear it! I won't! It's my duty to tell him about her! I will! (*She calls desperately*)

Father! Father! (*The shutter of the bedroom is pushed open and* MANNON *leans out*).

MANNON (*sharply*) What is it? Don't shout like that!

LAVINIA (*stammers lamely*) I—I remembered I forgot to say good night, Father.

MANNON (*exasperated*) Good heavens! What— (*Then gently*) Oh—all right—good night, Vinnie. Get to bed soon, like a good girl.

LAVINIA Yes, Father. Good night. (*He goes back in the bedroom and pulls the shutter closed. She stands staring fascinatedly up at the window, wringing her hands in a pitiful desperation*).

CURTAIN

ACT FOUR

SCENE—EZRA MANNON'S *bedroom. A big four-poster bed is at rear, center, the foot front, the head against the rear wall. A small stand, with a candle on it, is by the head of the bed on the left. To the left of the stand is a door leading into* CHRISTINE'S *room. The door is open. In the left wall are two windows. At left, front, is a table with a lamp on it and a chair beside it. In the right wall, front, is a door leading to the hall. Further back, against the wall, is a bureau.*

None of these details can be discerned at first because the room is in darkness, except for what moonlight filters feebly through the shutters. It is around dawn of the following morning.

CHRISTINE'S *form can be made out, a pale ghost in the darkness, as she slips slowly and stealthily from the bed. She tiptoes to the table, left front, and picks up a light-colored dressing-gown that is flung over the chair and puts it on. She stands listening for some sound from the bed. A pause. Then* MANNON'S *voice comes suddenly from the bed, dull and lifeless.*

MANNON Christine.

CHRISTINE (*starts violently—in a strained voice*) Yes.

MANNON Must be near daybreak, isn't it?

CHRISTINE Yes. It is beginning to get gray.

MANNON What made you jump when I spoke? Is my voice so strange to you?

CHRISTINE I thought you were asleep.

MANNON I haven't been able to sleep. I've been lying here thinking. What makes you so uneasy?

CHRISTINE I haven't been able to sleep either.

MANNON You slunk out of bed so quietly.

CHRISTINE I didn't want to wake you.

MANNON (*bitterly*) Couldn't you bear it—lying close to me?

CHRISTINE I didn't want to disturb you by tossing around.

MANNON We'd better light the light and talk a while.

CHRISTINE (*with dread*) I don't want to talk! I prefer the dark.

MANNON I want to see you. (*He takes matches from the*

stand by the bed and lights the candle on it. CHRISTINE *hastily sits down in the chair by the table, pushing it so she sits facing left, front, with her face turned three-quarters away from him. He pushes his back up against the head of the bed in a half-sitting position. His face, with the flickering candle light on its side, has a grim, bitter expression*) You like the dark where you can't see your old man of a husband, is that it?

CHRISTINE I wish you wouldn't talk like that, Ezra. If you are going to say stupid things, I'll go in my own room. (*She gets to her feet but keeps her face turned away from him*).

MANNON Wait! (*Then a note of pleading in his voice*) Don't go. I don't want to be alone. (*She sits again in the same position as before. He goes on humbly*) I didn't mean to say those things. I guess there's bitterness inside me—my own cussedness, maybe—and sometimes it gets out before I can stop it.

CHRISTINE You have always been bitter.

MANNON Before we married?

CHRISTINE I don't remember.

MANNON You don't want to remember you ever loved me!

CHRISTINE (*tensely*) I don't want to talk of the past! (*Abruptly changing the subject*) Did you hear Vinnie the first part of the night? She was pacing up and down before the house like a sentry guarding you. She didn't go to bed until two. I heard the clock strike.

MANNON There is one who loves me, at least! (*Then after a pause*) I feel strange, Christine.

CHRISTINE You mean—your heart? You don't think you are going to be—taken ill, do you?

MANNON (*harshly*) No! (*A pause—then accusingly*) Is that what you're waiting for? Is that why you were so willing to give yourself tonight? Were you hoping—?

CHRISTINE (*springing up*) Ezra! Stop talking like that! I can't stand it! (*She moves as if to go into her own room*).

MANNON Wait! I'm sorry I said that. (*Then, as she sits down again, he goes on gloomily*) It isn't my heart. It's something uneasy troubling my mind—as if something in me was listening, watching, waiting for something to happen.

CHRISTINE Waiting for what to happen?

MANNON I don't know. (*A pause—then he goes on somberly*) This house is not my house. This is not my room nor my bed. They are empty—waiting for someone to move in! And you are not my wife! You are waiting for something!

CHRISTINE (*beginning to snap under the strain—jumps to her feet again*) What would I be waiting for?

MANNON For death—to set you free!

CHRISTINE Leave me alone! Stop nagging at me with your crazy suspicions! (*Then anger and hatred come into her voice*) Not your wife! You acted as if I were your wife—your property—not so long ago!

MANNON (*with bitter scorn*) Your body? What are bodies to me? I've seen too many rotting in the sun to make grass greener! Ashes to ashes, dirt to dirt! Is that your notion of love? Do you think I married a body? (*Then, as if all the bitterness and hurt in him had suddenly burst its dam*) You were lying to me tonight as you've always lied! You were only pretending love! You let me take you as if you were a nigger slave I'd bought at auction! You made me appear a lustful beast in my own eyes!—as you've always done since our first marriage night! I would feel cleaner now if I had gone to a brothel! I would feel more honor between myself and life!

CHRISTINE (*in a stifled voice*) Look out, Ezra! I won't stand—

MANNON (*with a harsh laugh*) And I had hoped my homecoming would mark a new beginning—new love between us! I told you my secret feelings. I tore my insides out for you—thinking you'd understand! By God, I'm an old fool!

CHRISTINE (*her voice grown strident*) Did you think you could make me weak—make me forget all the years? Oh, no, Ezra! It's too late! (*Then her voice changes, as if she had suddenly resolved on a course of action, and becomes deliberately taunting*) You want the truth? You've guessed it! You've used me, you've given me children, but I've never once been yours! I never could be! And whose fault is it? I loved you when I married you! I wanted to give myself! But you made me so I couldn't give! You filled me with disgust!

MANNON (*furiously*) You say that to me! (*Then trying to calm himself—stammers*) No! Be quiet! We mustn't fight! I mustn't lose my temper! It will bring on—!

CHRISTINE (*goading him with calculating cruelty*) Oh, no! You needn't adopt that pitiful tone! You wanted the truth and you're going to hear it now!

MANNON (*frightened—almost pleading*) Be quiet, Christine!

CHRISTINE I've lied about everything! I lied about Captain

Brant! He is Marie Brantôme's son! And it was I he came to see, not Vinnie! I made him come!

MANNON (*seized with fury*) You dared—! You—! The son of that—!

CHRISTINE Yes, I dared! And all my trips to New York weren't to visit Father but to be with Adam! He's gentle and tender, he's everything you've never been. He's what I've longed for all these years with you—a lover! I love him! So now you know the truth!

MANNON (*in a frenzy—struggling to get out of bed*) You—you whore—I'll kill you! (*Suddenly he falls back, groaning, doubled up on his left side, with intense pain*).

CHRISTINE (*with savage satisfaction*) Ah! (*She hurries through the doorway into her room and immediately returns with a small box in her hand. He is facing away from her door, and, even if the intense pain left him any perception, he could not notice her departure and return, she moves so silently*).

MANNON (*gaspingly*) Quick—medicine!

CHRISTINE (*turned away from him, takes a pellet from the box, asking tensely as she does so*) Where is your medicine?

MANNON On the stand! Hurry!

CHRISTINE Wait. I have it now. (*She pretends to take something from the stand by the head of the bed—then holds out the pellet and a glass of water which is on the stand*) Here. (*He turns to her groaning and opens his mouth. She puts the pellet on his tongue and presses the glass of water to his lips*) Now drink.

MANNON (*takes a swallow of water—then suddenly a wild look of terror comes over his face. He gasps*) That's not—my medicine! (*She shrinks back to the table, the hand with the box held out behind her, as if seeking a hiding place. Her fingers release the box on the table top and she brings her hand in front of her as if instinctively impelled to prove to him she has nothing. His eyes are fixed on her in a terrible accusing glare. He tries to call for help but his voice fades to a wheezy whisper*) Help! Vinnie! (*He falls back in a coma, breathing stertorously.* CHRISTINE *stares at him fascinatedly—then starts with terror as she hears a noise from the hall and frantically snatches up the box from the table and holds it behind her back, turning to face the door as it opens and* LAVINIA *appears in the doorway. She is dressed as at the end of Act Three, in nightgown, wrapper and slippers. She stands, dazed and frightened and hesitating, as if she had just awakened*).

LAVINIA I had a horrible dream—I thought I heard Father calling me—it woke me up—

CHRISTINE (*trembling with guilty terror—stammers*) He just had—an attack.

LAVINIA (*hurries to the bed*) Father! (*She puts her arms around him*) He's fainted!

CHRISTINE No. He's all right now. Let him sleep. (*At this moment* MANNON, *with a last dying effort, straightens up in a sitting position in* LAVINIA'S *arms, his eyes glaring at his wife, and manages to raise his arm and point an accusing finger at her*).

MANNON (*gasps*) She's guilty—not medicine! (*He falls back limply*).

LAVINIA Father!(*Frightenedly she feels for his pulse, puts her ear against his chest to listen for a heartbeat*).

CHRISTINE Let him alone. He's asleep.

LAVINIA He's dead!

CHRISTINE (*repeats mechanically*) Dead? (*Then in a strange flat tone*) I hope—he rests in peace.

LAVINIA (*turning on her with hatred*) Don't you dare pretend—! You wanted him to die! You— (*She stops and stares at her mother with a horrified suspicion—then harshly accusing*) Why did he point at you like that? Why did he say you were guilty? Answer me!

CHRISTINE (*stammers*) I told him—Adam was my lover.

LAVINIA (*aghast*) You told him that—when you knew his heart—! Oh! You did it on purpose! You murdered him!

CHRISTINE No—it was your fault—you made him suspicious—he kept talking of love and death—he forced me to tell him! (*Her voice becomes thick, as if she were drowsy and fighting off sleep. Her eyes half close*).

LAVINIA (*grabbing her by the shoulders—fiercely*) Listen! Look at me! He said "not medicine"! What did he mean?

CHRISTINE (*keeping the hand with the poison pressed against her back*) I—I don't know.

LAVINIA You do know! What was it? Tell me!

CHRISTINE (*with a last effort of will manages to draw her herself up and speak with a simulation of outraged feeling*) Are you accusing your mother of—

LAVINIA Yes! I—! (*Then distractedly*) No—you can't be that evil!

CHRISTINE (*her strength gone—swaying weakly*) I don't know what—you're talking about. (*She edges away from* LA-

VINIA *toward her bedroom door, the hand with the poison stretched out behind her—weakly*) I—feel faint. I must go—and lie down. I— (*She turns as if to run into the room, takes a tottering step—then her knees suddenly buckle under her and she falls in a dead faint at the foot of the bed. As her hand strikes the floor the fingers relax and the box slips out onto one of the hooked rugs*).

LAVINIA (*does not notice this. Startled by* CHRISTINE'S *collapse, she automatically bends on one knee beside her and hastily feels for her pulse. Then satisfied she has only fainted, her anguished hatred immediately returns and she speaks with strident denunciation*) You murdered him just the same—by telling him! I suppose you think you'll be free to marry Adam now! But you won't! Not while I'm alive! I'll make you pay for your crime! I'll find a way to punish you! (*She is starting to her feet when her eyes fall on the little box on the rug. Immediately she snatches it up and stares at it, the look of suspicion changing to a dreadful, horrified certainty. Then with a shuddering cry she shrinks back along the side of the bed, the box clutched in her hand, and sinks on her knees by the head of the bed, and flings her arms around the dead man. With anguished beseeching*) Father! Don't leave me alone! Come back to me! Tell me what to do!

CURTAIN

The Hunted

CHARACTERS

CHRISTINE, *Ezra Mannon's widow*

LAVINIA (VINNIE), *her daughter*

ORIN, *her son, First Lieutenant of Infantry*

CAPTAIN ADAM BRANT

HAZEL NILES

PETER, *her brother, Captain of Artillery*

JOSIAH BORDEN, *manager of the shipping company*

EMMA, *his wife*

EVERETT HILLS, D.D., *of the First Congregational Church*

HIS WIFE

DOCTOR JOSEPH BLAKE

THE CHANTYMAN

SCENES

ACT ONE: Exterior of the Mannon house—a moonlight night two days after the murder of EZRA MANNON.

ACT TWO: Sitting-room in the house—immediately follows Act One.

ACT THREE: EZRA MANNON'S study—immediately follows Act Two.

ACT FOUR: The stern of the clipper ship "Flying Trades," at a wharf in East Boston—a night two days later.

ACT FIVE: Same as Act One—Exterior of the Mannon house the night of the following day.

The Hunted

ACT ONE

SCENE—*The same as Acts One and Three of "Homecoming"—Exterior of the Mannon House.*

It is a moonlight night two days after the murder of EZRA MANNON. *The house has the same strange eerie appearance, its white portico like a mask in the moonlight, as it had on that night. All the shutters are closed. A funeral wreath is fixed to the column at the right of steps. Another wreath is on the door.*

There is a sound of voices from inside the house, the front door is opened and JOSIAH BORDEN *and his wife,* EVERETT HILLS, *the Congregational minister, and his wife, and* DOCTOR JOSEPH BLAKE, *the Mannons' family physician, come out.* CHRISTINE *can be seen in the hall just inside the door. There is a chorus of "Good night, Mrs. Mannon," and then turn to the steps and the door is closed.*

These people—the BORDENS, HILLS *and his wife and* DOCTOR BLAKE—*are, as were the Ames of Act one of "Homecoming," types of townsfolk, a chorus representing as those others had, but in a different stratum of society, the town as a human background for the drama of the Mannons.*

JOSIAH BORDEN, *the manager of the Mannon shipping company, is shrewd and competent. He is around sixty, small and wizened, white hair and beard, rasping nasal voice, and little sharp eyes. His wife, about ten years his junior, is a typical New England woman of pure English ancestry, with a horse face, buck teeth and big feet, her manner defensively sharp and assertive.* HILLS *is the type of well-fed minister of a prosperous small-town congregation—stout and unctuous, snobbish and ingratiating, conscious of godliness, but timid and always feeling his way. He is in the fifties, as is his wife, a sallow, flabby, self-effacing minister's wife.* DOCTOR BLAKE *is the old kindly best-family physician—a stout, self-important old man with a stubborn opinionated expression.*

They come down the steps to the drive. MRS. BORDEN *and* MRS. HILLS *walk together toward left front until they are by the bench. There they stop to wait for the men who stand at the foot of the steps while* BORDEN *and* BLAKE *light cigars.*

MRS. BORDEN (*tartly*) I can't abide that woman!

MRS. HILLS No. There's something queer about her.

MRS. BORDEN (*grudgingly honest*) Still and all, I come nearer to liking her now than I ever did before when I see how broken down she is over her husband's death.

MRS. HILLS Yes. She looks terrible, doesn't she? Doctor Blake says she will have herself in bed sick if she doesn't look out.

MRS. BORDEN I'd never have suspected she had that much feeling in her. Not but what she hasn't always been a dutiful wife, as far as anyone knows.

MRS. HILLS Yes. She's seemed to be.

MRS. BORDEN Well, it only goes to show how you can misjudge a person without meaning to—especially when that person is a Mannon. They're not easy to make head or tail of. Queer, the difference in her and Lavinia—the way they take his death. Lavinia is cold and calm as an icicle.

MRS. HILLS Yes. She doesn't seem to feel as much sorrow as she ought.

MRS. BORDEN That's where you're wrong. She feels it as much as her mother. Only she's too Mannon to let anyone see what she feels. But did you notice the look in her eyes?

MRS. HILLS I noticed she never said a word to anyone. Where did she disappear to all of a sudden?

MRS. BORDEN Went to the train with Peter Niles to meet Orin, I overheard her mother talking to Lavinia in the hall. She was insisting Peter should escort her to meet the train. Lavinia must have been starting to go alone. Her mother seemed real angry about it. (*Then glancing toward the men who have moved a little away from the steps and are standing talking in low tones*) Whatever are those men gossiping about? (*She calls*) Josiah! It's time we were getting home.

BORDEN I'm coming, Emma. (*The three men join the women by the bench,* BORDEN *talking as they come*) It isn't for me to question the arrangements she's made, Joe, but it does seem as if Ezra should have been laid out in the town hall where the whole town could have paid their respects to him, and had a big public funeral tomorrow.

HILLS That's my opinion. He was mayor of the town and a national war hero—

BLAKE She says it was Ezra's wish he'd often expressed that everything should be private and quiet. That's just like Ezra. He never was one for show. He did the work and let others do the showing off.

HILLS (*unctuously*) He was a great man. His death is a real loss to everyone in this community. He was a power for good.

BORDEN Yes. He got things done.

HILLS What a tragedy to be taken his first night home after passing unharmed through the whole war!

BORDEN I couldn't believe the news. Who'd ever suspect— It's queer. It's like fate.

MRS. HILLS (*breaks in tactlessly*) Maybe it is fate. You remember, Everett, you've always said about the Mannons that pride goeth before a fall and that some day God would humble them in their sinful pride. (*Everyone stares at her, shocked and irritated*).

HILLS (*flusteredly*) I don't remember ever saying—

BLAKE (*huffily*) If you'll excuse me, that's darn nonsense! I've known Ezra Mannon all my life, and to those he wanted to know he was as plain and simple—

HILLS (*hastily*) Of course, Doctor. My wife entirely misunderstood me. I was, perhaps wrongly, referring to Mrs. Mannon.

BLAKE She's all right too—when you get to know her.

HILLS (*dryly*) I have no doubt.

BLAKE And it's a poor time, when this household is afflicted by sudden death, to be—

HILLS You are quite right, Doctor. My wife should have remembered—

MRS. HILLS (*crushed*) I didn't mean anything wrong, Doctor.

BLAKE (*mollifiedly*) Let's forget it then. (*Turning to* BORDEN—*with a self-satisfied, knowing air*) As for your saying who'd ever expect it—well, you and Emma know I expected Ezra wouldn't last long.

BORDEN Yes. I remember you said you were afraid his heart was bad.

MRS. BORDEN I remember you did too.

BLAKE From the symptoms Mrs. Mannon described from his letter to her, I was as certain as if I'd examined him he had angina. And I wasn't surprised neither. I'd often told Ezra he was attempting more than one man could handle and if he didn't rest he'd break down. The minute they sent for me I knew what'd happened. And what she told me about waking up to find him groaning and doubled with pain confirmed it. She'd given him his medicine—it was what I would have prescribed myself—but it was too late. And as for dying, his first night home—well, the war was over, he was worn out, he'd had a long, hard trip home—and angina is no respecter of time and place. It strikes when it has a mind to.

BORDEN (*shaking his head*) Too bad. Too durned bad. The town won't find another as able as Ezra in a hurry. (*They all shake their heads and look sad. A pause*).

MRS. BORDEN Well, we aren't doing anyone any good standing here. We ought to get home, Josiah.

MRS. HILLS Yes. We must, too, Everett. (*They begin moving slowly off left,* HILLS *going with the two women.* DOCTOR BLAKE *nudges* BORDEN *and motions him to stay behind. After the others disappear, he whispers with a meaning grin*).

BLAKE I'll tell you a secret, Josiah—strictly between you and me.

BORDEN (*sensing something from his manner—eagerly*) Of course. What is it, Joe?

BLAKE I haven't asked Christine Mannon any embarrassing questions, but I have a strong suspicion it was love killed Ezra!

BORDEN Love?

BLAKE That's what! Leastways, love made angina kill him, if you take my meaning. She's a damned handsome woman and he'd been away a long time. Only natural between man and wife—but not the treatment I'd recommend for angina. He should have known better, but—well—he was human.

BORDEN (*with a salacious smirk*) Can't say as I blame him! She's a looker! I don't like her and never did but I can imagine worse ways of dying! (*They both chuckle*) Well, let's catch up with the folks. (*They go off, left. They have hardly disappeared before the door of the house is opened and* CHRISTINE MANNON *comes out and stands at the head of the steps a moment, then descends to the drive. She is obviously in a terrible state of strained nerves. Beneath the mask-like veneer of her face there are deep lines about her mouth, and her eyes burn with a feverish light. Feeling herself free from observation for a moment she lets go, her mouth twitches, her eyes look desperately on all sides, as if she longed to fly from something.* HAZEL NILES *comes out of the house to the head of the steps. She is the same as in "Homecoming."* CHRISTINE *at once senses her presence behind her and regains her tense control of herself).*

HAZEL (*with a cheering, sympathetic air*) So here you are. I looked everywhere around the house and couldn't find you.

CHRISTINE (*tensely*) I couldn't stay in. I'm so nervous. It's been a little harrowing—all these people coming to stand around and stare at the dead—and at me.

HAZEL I know. But there won't be any more now. (*Then a tone of eagerness breaking through in spite of herself*) Peter and Vinnie ought to be back soon, if the train isn't late. Oh, I hope Orin will surely come!

CHRISTINE (*strangely*) The same train! It was late that night he came! Only two days ago! It seems a lifetime! I've grown old.

HAZEL (*gently*) Try not to think of it.

CHRISTINE (*tensely*) As if I hadn't tried! But my brain keeps on—over and over and over!

HAZEL I'm so afraid you will make yourself sick.

CHRISTINE (*rallying herself and forcing a smile*) There, I'm all right. I mustn't appear too old and haggard when Orin comes, must I? He always liked me to be pretty.

HAZEL It will be so good to see him again! (*Then quickly*) He ought to be such a comfort to you in your grief.

CHRISTINE Yes. (*Then strangely*) He used to be my baby, you know—before he left me. (*Suddenly staring at* HAZEL, *as if struck by an idea*) You love Orin, don't you?

HAZEL (*embarrassed—stammers shyly*) I—I—

CHRISTINE I am glad. I want you to. I want him to marry you. (*Putting an arm around her—in a strained tone*) We'll be secret conspirators, shall we, and I'll help you and you'll help me?

HAZEL I don't understand.

CHRISTINE You know how possessive Vinnie is with Orin. She's always been jealous of you. I warn you she'll do everything she can to keep him from marrying you.

HAZEL (*shocked*) Oh, Mrs. Mannon, I can't believe Vinnie—!

CHRISTINE (*unheeding*) So you must help me. We mustn't let Orin come under her influence again. Especially now in the morbid, crazy state of grief she's in! Haven't you noticed how queer she's become? She hasn't spoken a single word since her father's death! When I talk to her she won't answer me. And yet she follows me around everywhere—she hardly leaves me alone a minute. (*Forcing a nervous laugh*) It gets on my nerves until I could scream!

HAZEL Poor Vinnie! She was so fond of her father. I don't wonder she—

CHRISTINE (*staring at her—strangely*) You are genuinely good and pure of heart, aren't you?

HAZEL (*embarrassed*) Oh, no! I'm not at all—

CHRISTINE I was like you once—long ago—before— (*Then with bitter longing*) If I could only have stayed as I was then! Why can't all of us remain innocent and loving and trusting? But God won't leave us alone. He twists and wrings and tortures our lives with others' lives until—we poison each other to death! (*Seeing* HAZEL'S *look, catches herself—quickly*) Don't mind what I said! Let's go in, shall we? I would rather wait for Orin inside. I couldn't bear to wait and watch him coming up the drive—just like—he looks so much like his father at times—and like—but what nonsense I'm talking! Let's go in. I hate moonlight. It makes everything so haunted. (*She turns abruptly and goes into the house.* HAZEL *follows her and shuts the door. There is a pause. Then footsteps and voices are heard from off right front and a moment later* ORIN MANNON *enters with* PETER *and* LAVINIA. *One is at once struck by his startling family resemblance to* EZRA MANNON *and* ADAM BRANT (*whose likeness to each other we have seen in "Homecoming"*). *There is the same lifelike mask quality of his face in repose, the same aquiline nose, heavy eyebrows, swarthy complexion, thick straight black hair, light hazel eyes. His mouth and chin have the same general characteristics as his father's had, but the expression of his mouth gives an impression of tense oversensitiveness quite foreign to the General's, and his chin is a refined, weakened version of the dead man's. He is about the same height as* MANNON *and* BRANT, *but his body is thin and his swarthy complexion sallow. He wears a bandage around his head high up on his forehead. He carries himself by turns with a marked slouchiness or with a self-conscious square-shouldered stiffness that indicates a soldierly bearing is unnatural to him. When he speaks it is jerkily, with a strange vague, preoccupied air. But when he smiles naturally his face has a gentle boyish charm which makes women immediately want to mother him. He wears a mustache similar to* BRANT'S *which serves to increase their resemblance to each other. Although he is only twenty, he looks thirty. He is dressed in a baggy, ill-fitting uniform—that of a first lieutenant of infantry in the Union Army*).

ORIN (*as they enter looks eagerly toward the house—then with bitter, hurt disappointment in his tone*) Where's Mother? I thought she'd surely be waiting for me. (*He stands staring at the house*) God, how I've dreamed of coming home! I thought it would never end, that we'd go on murdering and being murdered until no one was left alive! Home at last! No, by God, I must be dreaming again! (*Then in an awed tone*) But the house looks strange. Or is it something in me? I was out of my head so long, everything has seemed queer since I came back to earth. Did the house always look so ghostly and dead?

PETER That's only the moonlight, you chump.

ORIN Like a tomb. That's what mother used to say it reminded her of, I remember.

LAVINIA (*reproachfully*) It is a tomb—just now, Orin.

ORIN (*hurriedly—shamefacedly*) I—I'd forgotten. I simply can't realize he's dead yet. I suppose I'd come to expect he would live forever. (*A trace of resentment has crept into his tone*) Or, at least outlive me. I never thought his heart was weak. He told me the trouble he had wasn't serious.

LAVINIA (*quickly*) Father told you that, too? I was hoping he had. (*Then turning to* PETER) You go ahead in, Peter. Say we're coming a little behind. I want to speak to Orin a moment.

PETER Sure thing, Vinnie. (*He goes in the front door, closing it behind him*).

ORIN I'm glad you got rid of him. Peter is all right but—I want to talk to you alone. (*With a boyish brotherly air—putting an arm around her*) You certainly are a sight for sore eyes, Vinnie! How are you, anyway, you old bossy fuss-buzzer! Gosh, it seems natural to hear myself calling you that old nickname again. Aren't you glad to see me?

LAVINIA (*affectionately*) Of course I am!

ORIN I'd never guess it! You've hardly spoken a word since you met me. What's happened to you? (*Then, as she looks at him reproachfully, he takes away his arm—a bit impatiently*) I told you I can't get used to the idea of his being dead. Forgive me, Vinnie. I know what a shock it must be to you.

LAVINIA Isn't it a shock to you, Orin?

ORIN Certainly! What do you think I am? But—oh, I can't explain! You wouldn't understand, unless you'd been at the front. I hardened myself to expect my own death and everyone else's, and think nothing of it. I had to—to keep alive! It was part of my training as a soldier under him. He taught it to me, you might say! So when it's his turn he can hardly expect— (*He has talked with increasing bitterness.* LAVINIA *interrupts him sharply*).

LAVINIA Orin! How can you be so unfeeling?

ORIN (*again shamefaced*) I didn't mean that. My mind is still full of ghosts. I can't grasp anything but war, in which he was so alive. He was the war to me—the war that would never end until I died. I can't understand peace—his end! (*Then with exasperation*) God damn it, Vinnie, give me a chance to get used to things!

LAVINIA Orin!

ORIN (*resentfully*) I'm sorry! Oh, I know what you're thinking! I used to be such a nice gentlemanly cuss, didn't I?— and now—Well, you wanted me to be a hero in blue, so you better be resigned! Murdering doesn't improve one's manners! (*Abruptly changing the subject*) But what the devil are we talking about me for? Listen, Vinnie. There's something I want to ask you before I see Mother.

LAVINIA Hurry, then! She'll be coming right out! I've got to tell you something too!

ORIN What was that stuff you wrote about some Captain Brant coming to see Mother? Do you mean to tell me there's actually been gossip started about her? (*Then without waiting for a reply, bursting into jealous rage*) By God, if he dares come here again, I'll make him damned sorry he did!

LAVINIA (*grimly*) I'm glad you feel that way about him. But there's no time to talk now. All I want to do is warn you to be on your guard. Don't let her baby you the way she used to and get you under her thumb again. Don't believe the lies she'll tell you! Wait until you've talked to me! Will you promise me?

ORIN (*staring at her bewilderedly*) You mean—Mother? (*Then angrily*) What the hell are you talking about, anyway? Are you loony? Honestly, Vinnie, I call that carrying your everlasting squabble with Mother a bit too far! You ought to be ashamed of yourself! (*Then suspiciously*) What are you being so mysterious about? Is it Brant—?

LAVINIA (*at a sound from inside the house*) Ssshh! (*The front door of the house is opened and* CHRISTINE *hurries out*).

CHRISTINE (*angrily to* PETER *who is in the hall*) Why

didn't you call me, Peter? You shouldn't have left him alone! (*She calls uncertainly*) Orin.

ORIN Mother! (*She runs down the steps and flings her arms around him*).

CHRISTINE My boy! My baby! (*She kisses him*).

ORIN (*melting, all his suspicion forgotten*) Mother! God, it's good to see you! (*Then almost roughly, pushing her back and staring at her*) But you're different! What's happened to you?

CHRISTINE (*forcing a smile*) I? Different? I don't think so, dear. Certainly I hope not—to you! (*Touching the bandage on his head—tenderly*) Your head! Does it pain dreadfully? You poor darling, how you must have suffered! (*She kisses him*) But it's all over now, thank God. I've got you back again! (*Keeping her arm around him, she leads him up the steps*) Let's go in. There's someone else waiting who will be glad to see you.

LAVINIA (*who has come to the foot of the steps—harshly*) Remember, Orin! (CHRISTINE *turns around to look down at her. A look of hate flashes between mother and daughter.* ORIN *glances at his mother suspiciously and draws away from her*).

CHRISTINE (*immediately recovers her poise—to* ORIN, *as if* LAVINIA *hadn't spoken*) Come on in, dear. It's chilly. Your poor head— (*She takes his hand and leads him through the door and closes it behind them.* LAVINIA *remains by the foot of the steps, staring after them. Then the door is suddenly opened again and* CHRISTINE *comes out, closing it behind her, and walks to the head of the steps. For a moment mother and daughter stare into each other's eyes. Then* CHRISTINE *begins haltingly in a tone she vainly tries to make kindly and persuasive*) Vinnie, I—I must speak with you a moment—now Orin is here. I appreciate your grief has made you—not quite normal—and I make allowances. But I cannot understand your attitude toward me. Why do you keep following me everywhere—and stare at me like that? I had been a good wife to him for twenty-three years—until I met Adam. I was guilty then, I admit. But I repented and put him out of my life. I would have been a good wife again as long as your father had lived. After all, Vinnie, I am your mother. I brought you into the world. You ought to have some feeling for me. (*She pauses, waiting for some response but* LAVINIA *simply stares at her, frozen and silent. Fear creeps into* CHRISTINE'S *tone*) Don't stare like that! What are you thinking? Surely you can't still have that insane suspicion—that I— (*Then guiltily*) What did you do that night after I fainted? I—I've missed something—some medicine I take to put me to sleep— (*Something like a grim smile of satisfaction forms on* LAVINIA'S *lips.* CHRISTINE *exclaims frightenendly*) Oh, you did—you found—and I suppose you connect that—but don't you see how insane—to suspect—when Doctor Blake knows he died of—! (*Then angrily*) I know what you've been waiting for—to tell Orin your lies and get him to go to the police! You don't dare do that on your own responsibility—but if you can make Orin— Isn't that it? Isn't that what you've been planning the last two days? Tell me! (*Then, as* LAVINIA *remains silent,* CHRISTINE *gives way to fury and rushes down the steps and grabs her by the arm and shakes her*) Answer me when I speak to you! What are you plotting? What are you going to do? Tell me! (LAVINIA *keeps her body rigid, her eyes staring into her mother's.* CHRISTINE *lets go and steps away from her. Then* LAVINIA, *turning her back, walks slowly and woodenly off left between the lilac clump and the house.* CHRISTINE *stares after her, her strength seems to leave her, she trembles with dread. From inside the house comes the sound of* ORIN'S *voice calling sharply "Mother! Where are you?"* CHRISTINE *starts and immediately by an effort of will regains control over herself. She hurries up the steps and opens the door. She speaks to* ORIN *and her voice is tensely quiet and normal*) Here I am, dear! (*She shuts the door behind her*).

CURTAIN

ACT TWO

SCENE—*The sitting-room of the Mannon house. Like the study, but much larger, it is an interior composed of straight severe lines with heavy detail. The walls are plain plastered surfaces, light gray with a white trim. It is a bleak room without intimacy, with an atmosphere of uncomfortable, stilted stateliness. The furniture is stationed about with exact precision. On the left, front, is a doorway leading to the dining-room. Further back, on the left, are a wall table and chair and a writing desk and chair. In the rear wall, center, is the doorway giving on the main hall and the stairs. At right is a fireplace with a chimney-piece of black marble, flanked by two windows. Portraits of ancestors hangs on the walls. At the rear of the fireplace, on the right, is one of a grim-visaged minister of the witch-burning era. Between fireplace and front is another of* EZRA MANNON'S *grandfather, in the uniform of an officer in Washington's army. Directly over the fireplace is the portrait of* EZRA'S *father,* ABE MANNON, *done when he was sixty. Except for the difference in ages, his face looks exactly like* EZRA'S *in the painting in the study.*

Of the three portraits on the other walls, two are of women— ABE MANNON'S *wife and the wife of Washington's officer. The third has the appearance of a prosperous shipowner of Colonial days. All the faces in the portraits have the same mask quality of those of the living characters in the play.*

At the left center of the room, front, is a table with two chairs. There is another chair at center, front, and a sofa at right, front, facing left.

The opening of this scene follows immediately the close of the preceding one. HAZEL *is discovered sitting on the chair at center, front.* PETER *is sitting on the sofa at right. From the hall* ORIN *is heard calling "Mother! Where are you?" as at the close of the preceding act.*

HAZEL Where can she have gone? She's worked herself into such a state of grief I don't think she knows what she's doing.

PETER Vinnie's completely knocked out, too.

HAZEL And poor Orin! What a terrible homecoming this is for him! How sick and changed he looks, doesn't he, Peter?

PETER Head wounds are no joke. He's darned lucky to have come out alive. (*They stop talking self-consciously as* ORIN *and* CHRISTINE *enter from the rear.* ORIN *is questioning her suspiciously*).

ORIN Why did you sneak away like that? What were you doing?

CHRISTINE (*forcing a wan smile*) The happiness of seeing you again was a little too much for me, I'm afraid, dear. I suddenly felt as if I were going to faint, so I rushed out in the fresh air.

ORIN (*immediately ashamed of himself—tenderly, putting his arm around her*) Poor Mother! I'm sorry— Look here, then. You sit down and rest. Or maybe you better go right to bed.

HAZEL That's right, Orin, you make her. I've been trying to get her to but she won't listen to me.

CHRISTINE Go to bed the minute he comes home! I should say not!

ORIN (*worried and pleased at the same time*) But you mustn't do anything to—

CHRISTINE (*patting his cheek*) Fiddlesticks! Having you again is just the medicine I need to give me strength—to bear things. (*She turns to* HAZEL) Listen to him, Hazel! You'd think I was the invalid and not he.

HAZEL Yes. You've got to take care of yourself, too, Orin.

ORIN Oh, forget me. I'm all right.

CHRISTINE We'll play nurses, Hazel and I, and have you your old self again before you know it. Won't we, Hazel?

HAZEL (*smiling happily*) Of course we will.

CHRISTINE Don't stand, dear. You must be worn out. Wait. We'll make you comfortable. Hazel, will you bring me a cushion? (HAZEL *gets a cushion and helps to place it behind his back in the chair at right of table.* ORIN'S *eyes light up and he grins boyishly, obviously revelling in being coddled*).

ORIN How's this for the comforts of home, Peter? The front was never like this, eh?

PETER Not so you'd notice it!

ORIN (*with a wink at* HAZEL) Peter will be getting jealous! You better call Vinnie in to put a pillow behind him!

HAZEL (*with a smile*) I can't picture Vinnie being that soft.

ORIN (*a jealous resentment creeping into his voice*) She can be soft—on occasion. She's always coddling Father and he likes it, although he pretends—

CHRISTINE (*turning away and restraining a shudder*) Orin! You're talking as if he were—alive! (*There is an uncomfortable silence.* HAZEL *goes quietly back to her chair at center.* CHRISTINE *goes around the table to the chair opposite* ORIN *and sits down*).

ORIN (*with a wry smile*) We'd all forgotten he's dead, hadn't we? Well, I can't believe it even yet. I feel him in this house—alive!

CHRISTINE Orin!

ORIN (*strangely*) Everything is changed—in some queer way—this house, Vinnie, you, I—everything but Father. He's the same and always will be—here—the same! Don't you feel that, Mother? (*She shivers, looking before her but doesn't answer*).

HAZEL (*gently*) You mustn't make your mother think of it, Orin.

ORIN (*staring at her—in a queer tone of gratitude*) You're the same, Hazel—sweet and good. (*He turns to his mother accusingly*) At least Hazel hasn't changed, thank God!

CHRISTINE (*rousing herself—turns to force a smile at him*) Hazel will never change, I hope. I am glad you appreciate her. (HAZEL *looks embarrassed.* CHRISTINE *goes on—with motherly solicitude*) Wasn't the long train trip terribly hard on you, dear?

ORIN Well, it wasn't a pleasure trip exactly. My head got aching till I thought it would explode.

CHRISTINE (*leans over and puts her hand on his forehead*) Poor boy! Does it pain now?

ORIN Not much. Not at all when your hand is there. (*Impulsively he takes her hand and kisses it—boyishly*) Gosh, Mother, it feels so darned good to be home with you! (*Then staring at her suspiciously again*) Let me have a good look at you. You're so different. I noticed it even outside. What is it?

CHRISTINE (*avoiding his eyes—forcing a smile*) It's just that I'm getting old, I'm afraid, dear.

ORIN No. You're more beautiful than ever! You're younger, too, somehow. But it isn't that. (*Almost pushing her hand away—bitterly*) Maybe I can guess!

CHRISTINE (*forces a laugh*) Younger and more beautiful! Do you hear him going on, Hazel? He has learned to be very gallant, I must say! (LAVINIA *appears in the doorway at rear. She enters but remains standing just inside the doorway and keeps her eyes fixed on her mother and* ORIN).

ORIN (*who is again looking at* HAZEL, *breaks out harshly*)

Do you remember how you waved your handkerchief, Hazel, the day I set off to become a hero? I thought you would sprain your wrist! And all the mothers and wives and sisters and girls did the same! Sometime in some war they ought to make the women take the men's place for a month or so. Give them a taste of murder!

CHRISTINE Orin!

ORIN Let them batter each other's brains out with rifle butts and rip each other's guts with bayonets! After that, maybe they'd stop waving handkerchiefs and gabbing about heroes! (HAZEL *gives a shocked exclamation*).

CHRISTINE Please!

PETER (*gruffly*) Give it a rest, Orin! It's over. Give yourself a chance to forget it. None of us liked it any more than you did.

ORIN (*immediately shamefaced*) You're right, Peter. I'm a damned whining fool! I'm sorry, Hazel. That was rotten of me.

HAZEL It was nothing, Orin. I understand how you feel. Really I do.

ORIN I—I let off steam when I shouldn't. (*Then suddenly*) Do you still sing, Hazel? I used to hear you singing—down there. It made me feel life might still be alive somewhere—that, and my dreams of Mother, and the memory of Vinnie bossing me around like a drill sergeant. I used to hear you singing at the queerest times—so sweet and clear and pure! It would rise above the screams of the dying—

CHRISTINE (*tensely*) I wish you wouldn't talk of death!

LAVINIA (*from the doorway—in a brusque commanding tone like her father's*) Orin! Come and see Father.

ORIN (*starts up from his chair and makes an automatic motion as if to salute—mechanically*) Yes, sir. (*Then confusedly*) What the devil—? You sounded just like him. Don't do that again, for heaven's sake! (*He tries to force a laugh—then shamefacedly*) I meant to look at him the first thing—but I got talking—I'll go in right now.

CHRISTINE (*her voice tense and strained*) No! Wait! (*Angrily to* LAVINIA) Can't you let your brother have a minute to rest? You can see how worn out he is! (*Then to* ORIN) I've hardly had a chance to say a word to you yet—and it has been so long! Stay with me a little while, won't you?

ORIN (*touched, coming back to her*) Of course, Mother! You come before everything!

LAVINIA (*starts to make a bitter retort, glances at* PETER *and* HAZEL, *then remarks evenly*) Very well. Only remember what I said, Orin. (*She turns her back and starts to go into the hall*).

CHRISTINE (*frightenedly*) Vinnie! Where are you going?

LAVINIA (*does not answer her but calls back to her brother over her shoulder*) You'll come in a little while, won't you? (*She disappears across the hall.* ORIN *gives his mother a sidelong glance of uneasy suspicion.* CHRISTINE *is desperately trying to appear calm.* PETER *and* HAZEL *stand up, feeling uncomfortable*).

HAZEL Peter, we really must be getting home.

PETER Yes.

CHRISTINE It was so kind of you to come.

HAZEL (*giving her hand to* ORIN) You must rest all you can now, Orin—and try not to think about things.

ORIN You're darned kind, Hazel. It's fine to see you again—the same as ever!

HAZEL (*delighted but pulling her hand away shyly*) I'm glad, too. Good night, Orin.

PETER (*shakes his hand*) Good night. Rest up and take it easy.

ORIN Good night, Peter. Thanks for meeting me.

CHRISTINE (*goes with them to the hall*) I'm afraid this isn't a very cheerful house to visit just now—but please come soon again. You will do Orin more good than anyone, Hazel. (*The look of suspicion again comes to* ORIN'S *eyes. He sits down in the chair at left of table and stares before him bitterly.* CHRISTINE *returns from the hall, closing the sliding doors behind her silently. She stands for a moment looking at* ORIN, *visibly bracing herself for the ordeal of the coming interview, her eyes full of tense calculating fear*).

ORIN (*without looking at her*) What's made you take such a fancy to Hazel all of a sudden? You never used to think much of her. You didn't want me going around with her.

CHRISTINE (*coming forward and sitting across the table from him—in her gentle motherly tone*) I was selfish then. I was jealous, too, I'll confess. But all I want now is your happiness, dear. I know how much you used to like Hazel—

ORIN (*blurts out*) That was only to make you jealous! (*Then bitterly*) But now you're a widow, I'm not home an hour before you're trying to marry me off! You must be damned anxious to get rid of me again! Why?

CHRISTINE You mustn't say that! If you knew how horribly lonely I've been without you—

ORIN So lonely you've written me exactly two letters in the last six months!

CHRISTINE But I wrote you much more! They must have been lost—

ORIN I received all of Hazel's letters—and Vinnie's. It's darned funny yours should be the only ones to get lost! (*Unable to hold back any longer, he bursts forth*) Who is this Captain Brant who's been calling on you?

CHRISTINE (*prepared for this—with well-feigned astonishment*) On me? You mean on Vinnie, don't you? (*Then as* ORIN *looks taken aback*) Wherever did you get that silly idea? Oh, of course, I know! Vinnie must have written you the same nonsense she did your father.

ORIN She wrote him? What did he do?

CHRISTINE Why, he laughed at it, naturally! Your father was very fond of Vinnie but he knew how jealous she's always been of me and he realized she'd tell any lie she could to—

ORIN Oh, come on now, Mother! Just because you're always getting on each other's nerves it doesn't mean Vinnie would ever deliberately—

CHRISTINE Oh, doesn't it, though? I think you'll discover before you're much older that there isn't anything your sister will stop at—that she will even accuse me of the vilest, most horrible things!

ORIN Mother! Honestly now! You oughtn't to say that!

CHRISTINE (*reaching out and taking his hand*) I mean it, Orin. I wouldn't say it to anyone but you. You know that. But we've always been so close, you and I. I feel you are really—my flesh and blood! She isn't! She is your father's! You're a part of me!

ORIN (*with strange eagerness*) Yes! I feel that, too, Mother!

CHRISTINE I know I can trust you to understand now as you always used to. (*With a tender smile*) We had a secret little world of our own in the old days, didn't we?—which no one but us knew about.

ORIN (*happily*) You bet we did! No Mannons allowed was our password, remember!

CHRISTINE And that's what your father and Vinnie could never forgive us! But we'll make that little world of our own again, won't we?

ORIN Yes.

CHRISTINE I want to make up to you for all the injustice you suffered at your father's hands. It may seem a hard thing to say about the dead, but he was jealous of you. He hated you because he knew I loved you better than anything in the world!

ORIN (*pressing her hand in both of his—intensely*) Do you, Mother? Do you honestly? (*Then he is struck by what she said about his father—woundedly*) I knew he had it in for me. But I never thought he went as far as to—hate me.

CHRISTINE He did, just the same!

ORIN (*with resentful bitterness*) All right, then! I'll tell you the truth, Mother! I won't pretend to you I'm sorry he's dead!

CHRISTINE (*lowering her voice to a whisper*) Yes. I am glad, too!—that he has left us alone! Oh, how happy we'll be together, you and I, if you only won't let Vinnie poison your mind against me with her disgusting lies!

ORIN (*immediately uneasy again*) What lies? (*He releases her hand and stares at her, morbidly suspicious*) You haven't told me about that Brant yet.

CHRISTINE There's nothing to tell—except in Vinnie's morbid revengeful mind! I tell you, Orin, you can't realize how she's changed while you've been away! She's always been a moody and strange girl, you know that, but since you've gone she has worried and brooded until I really believe she went a little out of her head. She got so she'd say the most terrible things about everyone. You simply wouldn't believe it, if I told you some of the things. And now, with the shock of your father's death on top of everything, I'm convinced she's actually insane. Haven't you noticed how queerly she acts? You must have!

ORIN I saw she'd changed a lot. She seemed strange. But—

CHRISTINE And her craziness all works out in hatred for me! Take this Captain Brant affair, for example—

ORIN Ah!

CHRISTINE A stupid ship captain I happened to meet at your grandfather's who took it into his silly head to call here a few times without being asked. Vinnie thought he was coming to court her. I honestly believe she fell in love with him, Orin. But she soon discovered that he wasn't after her at all!

ORIN Who was he after—you?

CHRISTINE (*sharply*) Orin! I'd be very angry with you if it weren't so ridiculous! (*She forces a laugh*) You don't seem to realize I'm an old married woman with two grown-up children! No, all he was after was to insinuate himself as a family friend and use your father when he came home to get him a better ship! I soon saw through his little scheme and he'll never call here again, I promise you that! (*She laughs—then with a teasing air*) And that's the whole of the great Captain Brant scandal! Are you satisfied now, you jealous goose, you?

ORIN (*penitent and happy*) I'm a fool! The war has got me silly, I guess! If you knew all the hell I've been through!

CHRISTINE It was Vinnie's fault you ever went to war! I'll never forgive her for that! It broke my heart, Orin! (*Then quickly*) But I was going to give you an example of her insane suspicions from the Captain Brant incident. Would you believe it that she has worked it all out that because his name is Brant, he must be the son of that nurse girl Marie Brantôme? Isn't that crazy? And to imagine for a moment, if he were, he'd ever come here to visit!

ORIN (*his face hardening*) By God, I'd like to see him! His mother brought disgrace enough on our family without—

CHRISTINE (*frightened, shrinking from him*) Orin! Don't look like that! You're so like your father! (*Then hurrying on*) But I haven't told you the worst yet. Vinnie actually accuses me—your mother—of being in love with that fool and of having met him in New York and gone to his room! I am no better than a prostitute in your sister's eyes!

ORIN (*stunned*) I don't believe it! Vinnie couldn't!

CHRISTINE I told you she'd gone crazy! She even followed me to New York, when I went to see your sick grandfather, to spy on me. She saw me meet a man—and immediately to her crazy brain the man was Brant. Oh, it's too revolting, Orin! You don't know what I've had to put up with from Vinnie, or you'd pity me!

ORIN Good God! Did she tell Father that? No wonder he's dead! (*Then harshly*) Who was this man you met in New York?

CHRISTINE It was Mr. Lamar, your grandfather's old friend who has known me ever since I was a baby! I happened to meet him and he asked me to go with him to call on his daughter. (*Then, seeing* ORIN *wavering, pitifully*) Oh, Orin! You pretend to love me! And yet you question me as if you suspected me, too! And you haven't Vinnie's excuse! You aren't out of your mind! (*She weeps hysterically*).

ORIN (*overcome at once by remorse and love*) No! I swear to you! (*He throws himself on his knees beside her and puts *his arm around her*) Mother! Please! Don't cry! I do love you! I do!

CHRISTINE I haven't told you the most horrible thing of all! Vinnie suspects me of having poisoned your father!

ORIN (*horrified*) What! No, by God, that's too much! If that's true, she ought to be put in an asylum!

CHRISTINE She found some medicine I take to make me sleep, but she is so crazy I know she thinks— (*Then, with real terror, clinging to him*) Oh, Orin, I'm so afraid of her! God knows what she might do, in her state! She might even go to the police and— Don't let her turn you against me! Remember you're all I have to protect me! You are all I have in the world, dear!

ORIN (*tenderly soothing her*) Turn me against you? She can't be so crazy as to try that! But listen. I honestly think you— You're a little hysterical, you know. That—about Father —is all such damned nonsense! And as for her going to the police—do you suppose I wouldn't prevent that—for a hundred reasons—the family's sake—my own sake and Vinnie's, too, as well as yours—even if I knew—

CHRISTINE (*staring at him—in a whisper*) Knew? Orin, you don't believe—?

ORIN No! For God's sake! I only meant that no matter what you ever did, I love you better than anything in the world and—

CHRISTINE (*in an outburst of grateful joy—pressing him to her and kissing him*) Oh, Orin, you are my boy, my baby! I love you!

ORIN Mother! (*Then seizing her by the shoulders and staring into her eyes—with somber intensity*) I could forgive anything—anything!—in my mother—except that other—that about Brant!

CHRISTINE I swear to you—!

ORIN If I thought that damned—! (*With savage vengefulness*) By God, I'd show you then I hadn't been taught to kill for nothing!

CHRISTINE (*full of new terror now—for* BRANT'S *life—distractedly*) For God's sake, don't talk like that! You're not like my Orin! You're cruel and horrible! You frighten me!

ORIN (*immediately contrite and soothing, petting her*) There, there, Mother! We won't ever think about it again! We'll talk of something else. I want to tell you something. (*He *sits on the floor at her feet and looks up into her face. A pause. Then he asks tenderly, taking her hand*) Did you really want me to come back, Mother?

CHRISTINE (*has calmed herself, but her eyes are still terrified and her voice trembles*) What a foolish question, dear.

ORIN But your letters got farther and farther between—and they seemed so cold! It drove me crazy! I wanted to desert and run home—or else get killed! If you only knew how I longed to be here with you—like this! (*He leans his head against her knee. His voice becomes dreamy and low and caressing*) I used to have the most wonderful dreams about you. Have you ever read a book called "Typee"—about the South Sea Islands?

CHRISTINE (*with a start—strangely*) Islands! Where there is peace?

ORIN Then you did read it?

CHRISTINE No.

ORIN Someone loaned me the book. I read it and reread it until finally those Islands came to mean everything that wasn't war, everything that was peace and warmth and security. I used to dream I was there. And later on all the time I was out of my head I seemed really to be there. There was no one there but you and me. And yet I never saw you, that's the funny part. I only felt you all around me. The breaking of the waves was your voice. The sky was the same color as your eyes. The warm sand was like your skin. The whole island was you. (*He smiles with a dreamy tenderness*) A strange notion, wasn't it? But you needn't be provoked at being an island because this was the most beautiful island in the world—as beautiful as you, Mother!

CHRISTINE (*has been staring over his head, listening fascinatedly, more and more deeply moved. As he stops, an agonizing tenderness for him wells up in her—with tortured longing*) Oh, if only you had never gone away! If you only hadn't let them take you from me!

ORIN (*uneasily*) But I've come back. Everything is all right now, isn't it?

CHRISTINE (*hastily*) Yes! I didn't mean that. It had to be.

ORIN (*With a tender grin*) You're my only girl!

CHRISTINE (*again with tenderness, stroking his hair—smiling*) You're a big man now, aren't you? I can't believe it. It seems only yesterday when I used to find you in your nightshirt hiding in the hall upstairs on the chance that I'd come up and you'd get one more good-night kiss! Do you remember?

ORIN (*with a boyish grin*) You bet I remember! And what a row there was when Father caught me! And do you remember how you used to let me brush your hair and how I loved to? He hated me doing that, too. You've still got the same beautiful hair, Mother. That hasn't changed. (*He reaches up and touches her hair caressingly. She gives a little shudder of repulsion and draws away from him but he is too happy to notice*) Oh, Mother, it's going to be wonderful from now on! We'll get Vinnie to marry Peter and there will be just you and I! (*The sliding doors in rear are opened a little and* LAVINIA *slips silently in and stands looking at them*)

CHRISTINE (*immediately senses her presence—controlling a start, harshly*) What do you want? (ORIN *turns to look at his sister resentfully*).

LAVINIA (*in a flat, emotionless voice*) Aren't you coming in to see Father, Orin?

ORIN (*scrambling to his feet—irritably*) Oh, all right, I'll come now. (*He hurries out past* LAVINIA *with the air of one with a disagreeable duty he wants to get over quickly and closes the door with a bang behind him.* LAVINIA *stares at her mother a moment—then about-faces stiffly to follow him*).

CHRISTINE (*springs to her feet*) Vinnie! (*As* LAVINIA *turns to face her—sharply*) Come here—please. I don't want to shout across the room. (LAVINIA *comes slowly forward until she is at arm's length. Her eyes grow bleak and her mouth tightens to a thin line. The resemblance between mother and daughter as they stand confronting each other is strikingly brought out.* CHRISTINE *begins to speak in a low voice, coolly defiant, almost triumphant*) Well, you can go ahead now and tell Orin anything you wish! I've already told him—so you might as well save yourself the trouble. He said you must be insane! I told him how you lied about my trips to New York—for revenge!—because you loved Adam yourself! (LAVINIA *makes a movement like a faint shudder but is immediately stiff and frozen again.* CHRISTINE *smiles tauntingly*) So hadn't you better leave Orin out of it? You can't get him to go to the police for you. Even if you convinced him I poisoned your father, you couldn't! He doesn't want—any more than you do, or your father, or any of the Mannon dead—such a public disgrace as a murder trial would be! For it would all come out! Everything! Who Adam is and my adultery and your knowledge of it—and your love for Adam! Oh, believe me, I'll see to it that comes out if anything ever gets to a trial! I'll show you to the world as a daughter who desired her mother's lover and then tried to get her mother hanged out of hatred and jealousy! (*She laughs tauntingly.* LAVINIA *is trembling but her face remains hard and emotionless. Her lips open as if to speak but she closes them again.* CHRISTINE *seems drunk with her own defiant recklessness*) Go on! Try and convince Orin of my wickedness! He loves me! He hated his father! He's glad he's dead! Even if he knew I had killed him, he'd protect me! (*Then all her defiant attitude collapses and she pleads, seized by an hysterical terror, by some fear she has kept hidden*) For God's sake, keep Orin out of this! He's still sick! He's changed! He's grown hard and cruel! All he thinks of is death! Don't tell him about Adam! He would kill him! I couldn't live then! I would kill myself! (LAVINIA *starts and her eyes light up with a cruel hatred. Again her pale lips parts as if she were about to say something but she controls the impulse and about-faces abruptly and walks with jerky steps from the room like some tragic mechanical doll.* CHRISTINE *stares after her—then as she disappears, collapses, catching at the table for support—terrifiedly*) I've got to see Adam! I've got to warn him! (*She sinks in the chair at right of table*).

CURTAIN

ACT THREE

SCENE—*The same as Act Two of "Homecoming"*—EZRA MANNON'S *study. His body, dressed in full uniform, is laid out on a bier draped in black which is placed lengthwise directly before the portrait of him over the fireplace. His head is at right. His mask-like face is a startling reproduction of the face in the portrait above him, but grimly remote and austere in death, like the carven face of a statue.*

The table and chairs which had been at center have been moved to the left. There is a lamp on this table. Two stands of three lighted candles are at each end of the black marble chimneypiece, throwing their light above on the portrait and below on the dead man. There is a chair by the dead man's head, at front of bier.

ORIN *is standing by the head of the bier, at the rear of it, stiffly-erect like a sentinel at attention. He is not looking down at his father but is staring straight before him, deep in suspicious brooding. His face in the candlelight bears a striking resemblance to that of the portrait above him and the dead man's.*

The time of the opening of this act precedes by a few moments that of the end of the previous act.

ORIN (*ashamed and guilty—bursts out angrily at himself*) Christ, I won't have such thoughts! I am a rotten swine to—Damn Vinnie! She must be crazy! (*Then, as if to distract his mind from these reflections, he turns to gaze down at his father. At the same moment* LAVINIA *appears silently in the doorway from the hall and stands looking at him. He does not notice her entrance. He stares at his father's mask-like face and addresses it with a strange friendly mockery*) Who are you? Another corpse! You and I have seen fields and hillsides sown with them—and they meant nothing!—nothing but a dirty joke life plays on life! (*Then with a dry smile*) Death sits so naturally on you! Death becomes the Mannons! You were always like a statue of an eminent dead man—sitting on a chair in a park or straddling a horse in a town square—looking over the head of life without a sign of recognition—cutting it dead for the impropriety of living! (*He chuckles to himself with a queer affectionate amusement*) You never cared to know me in life—but I really think we might be friends now you are dead!

LAVINIA (*sternly*) Orin!

ORIN (*turns to her startledly*) Damn it, don't sneak around like that! What are you trying to do, anyway? I'm jumpy enough without— (*Then as she turns and locks the door behind her—suspiciously*) What are you locking the door for?

LAVINIA I've got to talk to you—and I don't want to be interrupted. (*Then sternly*) What made you say such things just then? I wouldn't believe you could have grown so callous to all feeling of respect—

ORIN (*guilty and resentful*) You folks at home take death so solemnly! You would have soon learned at the front that it's only a joke! You don't understand, Vinnie. You have to learn to mock or go crazy, can't you see? I didn't mean it in an unkind way. It simply struck me he looks so strangely familiar —the same familiar stranger I've never known. (*Then glancing at the dead man with a kindly amused smile*) Do you know his nickname in the army? Old Stick—short for Stick-in-the-Mud. Grant himself started it—said Father was no good on an offensive but he'd trust him to stick in the mud and hold a position until hell froze over!

LAVINIA Orin! Don't you realize he was your father and he is dead?

ORIN (*irritably*) What Grant said was a big compliment in a way.

LAVINIA When I think of how proud of you he was when he came home! He boasted that you had done one of the bravest things he'd seen in the war!

ORIN (*astonished—then grins with bitter mockery*) One of the bravest things he'd seen! Oh, that's too rich! I'll tell you the joke about that heroic deed. It really began the night before when I sneaked through their lines. I was always volunteering for extra danger. I was so scared anyone would guess I was afraid! There was a thick mist and it was so still you could hear the fog seeping into the ground. I met a Reb crawling toward our lines. His face drifted out of the mist toward mine. I shortened my sword and let him have the point under the ear. He stared at me with an idiotic look as if he'd sat on a tack—and his eyes dimmed and went out— (*His voice has sunk lower and lower, as if he were talking to himself. He pauses and stares over his father's body fascinatedly at nothing*).

LAVINIA (*with a shudder*) Don't think of that now!

ORIN (*goes on with the same air*) Before I'd gotten back I had to kill another in the same way. It was like murdering the same man twice. I had a queer feeling that war meant murdering the same man over and over, and that in the end I would discover the man was myself! Their faces keep coming back in dreams—and they change to Father's face—or to mine— What does that mean, Vinnie?

LAVINIA I don't know! I've got to talk to you! For heaven's sake, forget the war! It's over now!

ORIN Not inside us who killed! (*Then quickly—with a bitter, joking tone*) The rest is all a joke! The next morning I was in the trenches. This was at Petersburg. I hadn't slept. My head was queer. I thought what a joke it would be on the stupid generals like Father if everyone on both sides suddenly saw the joke war was on them and laughed and shook hands! So I began to laugh and walked toward their lines with my hand out. Of course, the joke was on me and I got this wound in the head for my pains. I went mad, wanted to kill, and ran on, yelling. Then a lot of our fools went crazy, too, and followed me and we captured a part of their line we hadn't dared tackle before. I had acted without orders, of course—but Father decided it was better policy to overlook that and let me be a hero! So do you wonder I laugh!

LAVINIA (*soothingly, coming to him and taking his arm*) You were brave and you know it. I'm proud of you, too.

ORIN (*helplessly*) Oh, all right! Be proud, then! (*He leaves her and sprawls in the chair at left of table. She stands by the head of the bier and faces him. He says resentfully*) Well? Fire away and let's get this over! But you're wasting your breath. I know what you're going to say. Mother warned me. (*The whole memory of what his mother had said rushes over him*) My God, how can you think such thinks of Mother? What the hell's got into you? (*Then humoringly*) But I realize you're not yourself. I know how hard his death has hit you. Don't you think it would be better to postpone our talk until—

LAVINIA No! (*Bitterly*) Has she succeeded in convincing you I'm out of my mind? Oh, Orin, how can you be so stupid? (*She goes to him and, grasping him by his shoulders, brings her face close to him—compellingly*) Look at me! You know in your heart I'm the same as I always was—your sister—who loves you, Orin!

ORIN (*moved*) I didn't mean—I only think the shock of his death—

LAVINIA I've never lied to you, have I? Even when we were little you always knew I told you the truth, didn't you?

ORIN Yes—but—

LAVINIA Then you must believe I wouldn't lie to you now!

ORIN No one is saying you'd deliberately lie. It's a question of—

LAVINIA And even if she's got you so under her thumb again that you doubt my word, you can't doubt the absolute proof!

ORIN (*roughly*) Never mind what you call proofs! I know all about them already! (*Then excitedly*) Now, listen here, if you think you're going to tell me a lot of crazy stuff about Mother, I warn you I won't listen! So shut up before you start!

LAVINIA (*threateningly now*) If you don't, I'll go to the police!

ORIN Don't be a damn fool!

LAVINIA As a last resort I will—if you force me to!

ORIN By God, you must be crazy even to talk of—!

LAVINIA They won't think so!

ORIN Vinnie! Do you realize what it would mean—?

LAVINIA I realize only too well! You and I, who are innocent, would suffer a worse punishment than the guilty—for we'd have to live on! It would mean that Father's memory and that of all the honorable Mannon dead would be dragged through the horror of a murder trial! But I'd rather suffer that than let the murder of our father go unpunished!

ORIN Good God, do you actually believe—?

LAVINIA Yes! I accuse her of murder! (*She takes the little box she has found in* CHRISTINE'S *room right after the murder* [*Act Four "Homecoming"*] *from the bosom of her dress and holds it out to him*) You see this? I found it right after Father died!

ORIN Don't be a damned lunatic! She told me all about that! It's only some stuff she takes to make her sleep!

LAVINIA (*goes on implacably, ignoring his interruptions*) And Father knew she'd poisoned him! He said to me, "She's guilty!"

ORIN That's all your crazy imagination! God, how can you think—? Do you realize you're deliberately accusing your own mother— It's too horrible and mad! I'll have you declared insane by Doctor Blake and put away in an asylum!

LAVINIA I swear by our dead father I am telling you the truth! (*She puts her hand on the dead man and addresses him*) Make Orin believe me, Father!

ORIN (*harshly*) Don't drag him in! He always sided with

you against Mother and me! (*He grabs her arm and forces the box from her hand*) Here! Give me that! (*He slips it into his coat pocket*).

LAVINIA Ah! So you are afraid it's true!

ORIN No! But I'm going to stop your damned— But I'm a fool to pay any attention to you! The whole thing is too insane! I won't talk to a crazy woman! But, by God, you look out, Vinnie! You leave Mother alone or—!

LAVINIA (*regarding him bitterly*) Poor Father! He thought the war had made a man of you! But you're not! You're still the spoiled crybaby that she can make a fool of whenever she pleases!

ORIN (*stung*) That's enough from you!

LAVINIA Oh, she warned me just now what to expect! She boasted that you wouldn't believe me, and that even if you knew she'd murdered Father you would be glad because you hated him! (*Then a note of entreaty in her voice*) Orin! For God's sake—here, before him!—tell me that isn't true, at least!

ORIN (*overcome by a sense of guilt—violently defensive*) Of course, I never said that—and I don't believe she did. But Mother means a thousand times more to me than he ever did! I say that before him now as I would if he could hear me!

LAVINIA (*with a calculated scornful contempt now*) Then if I can't make you see your duty one way, I will another! If you won't help me punish her, I hope you're not such a coward that you're willing to let her lover escape!

ORIN (*in a tone of awakening suspicion*) Lover? Who do you mean?

LAVINIA I mean the man who plotted Father's murder with her, who must have got the poison for her! I mean the Captain Brant I wrote you about!

ORIN (*thickly, trying to fight back his jealous suspicion*) You lie! She told me your rotten lies—about him—about following her to New York. That was Mr. Lamar she met.

LAVINIA So that's what she told you! As if I could mistake Lamar for Adam Brant! What a fool you are, Orin! She kisses you and pretends she loves you—when she'd forgotten you were ever alive, when all she's thought of is this low lover of hers—!

ORIN (*wildly*) Stop! I won't stand—!

LAVINIA When all she is thinking of right now is how she can use you to keep me from doing anything, so she'll get a chance to run off and marry him!

ORIN You lie!

LAVINIA She pets you and plays the loving mother and you're so blind you can't see through her! I tell you she went to his room! I followed them upstairs. I heard her telling him, "I love you, Adam." She was kissing him!

ORIN (*grabs her by the shoulder and shakes her, forcing her to her knees—frenziedly*) Damn you! Tell me you're lying or—!

LAVINIA (*unafraid—looking up into his eyes—coldly*) You know I'm not lying! She's been going to New York on the excuse of visiting Grandfather Hamel, but really to give herself to—!

ORIN (*in anguish*) You lie, damn you! (*Threateningly*) You dare say that about Mother! Now you've got to prove it or else—! You're not insane! You know what you're saying! So you prove it—or by God, I'll—!

LAVINIA (*taking his hands off her shoulders and rising*) All I ask is a chance to prove it! (*Then intensely*) But when I do, will you help me punish Father's murderers?

ORIN (*in a burst of murderous rage*) I'll kill that bastard! (*In anguished uncertainty again*) But you haven't proved anything yet! It's only your word against hers! I don't believe you! You say Brant is her lover! If that's true, I'll hate her! I'll know she murdered Father then! I'll help you punish her! But you've got to prove it!

LAVINIA (*coldly*) I can do that very soon. She's frightened out of her wits! She'll go to see Brant the first chance she gets. We must give her that chance. Will you believe me when you find them together?

ORIN (*torturedly*) Yes. (*Then in a burst of rage*) God damn him, I'll—!

LAVINIA (*sharply*) Ssshh! Be quiet. There's someone in the hall! (*They wait, staring at the door. Then someone knocks loudly*).

CHRISTINE (*her voice comes through the door, frightened and strained*) Orin!

ORIN (*stammers*) God! I can't face her now!

LAVINIA (*in a quick whisper*) Don't let her know you suspect her. Pretend you think I'm out of my mind, as she wanted you to.

CHRISTINE Orin! Why don't you answer me? (*She tries the doorknob, and finding the door locked, her voice becomes terri-*

fied) Why have you locked me out? Let me in! (*She pounds on the door violently*).

LAVINIA (*in a whisper*) Answer her. Let her in.

ORIN (*obeying mechanically—calls in a choked voice*) All right. I'm coming. (*He moves reluctantly toward the door*).

LAVINIA (*struck by a sudden idea—grasps his arm*) Wait! (*Before he can prevent it, she reaches in his pocket and gets possession of the box and puts it conspicuously on the body over the dead man's heart*) Watch her when she sees that—if you want proof!

CHRISTINE Open the door! (*He forces himself to open the door and steps aside.* CHRISTINE *almost falls in. She is in a state bordering on collapse. She throws her arms around* ORIN *as if seeking protection from him*) Orin! I got so afraid—when I found the door locked!

ORIN (*controls a furious jealous impulse to push her violently away from him—harshly*) What made you afraid, Mother?

CHRISTINE (*stammers*) Why do you look at me—like that? You look—so like—your father!

ORIN I am his son, too, remember that!

LAVINIA (*warningly*) Orin!

CHRISTINE (*turning on* LAVINIA *who stands by the head of the bier*) I suppose you've been telling him your vile lies, you—

ORIN (*remembering his instructions, forces himself to blurt out*) She—she's out of her head, Mother.

CHRISTINE Didn't I tell you! I knew you'd see that! (*Then anxiously, keeping her eyes on* LAVINIA) Did she tell you what she's going to do, Orin? I know she's plotting something—crazy! Did she threaten to go to the police? They might not believe she's crazy— (*Pleading desperately, her eyes still on* LAVINIA) You won't let her do anything dreadful like that, will you?

ORIN (*feeling her guilt, stammers*) No, Mother.

CHRISTINE (*her eyes, which have been avoiding the corpse, now fasten on the dead man's face with fascinated horror*) No—remember your father wouldn't want—any scandal—he mustn't be worried, he said—he needs rest and peace— (*She addresses the dead man directly in a strange tone of defiant scorn*) You seem the same to me in death, Ezra! You were always dead to me! I hate the sight of death! I hate the thought of it! (*Her eyes shift from his face and she sees the box of poison. She starts back with a stifled scream and stares at it with guilty fear).*

ORIN Mother! For God's sake, be quiet! (*The strain snaps for him and he laughs with savage irony*) God! To think I hoped home would be an escape from death! I should never have come back to life—from my island of peace! (*Then staring at his mother strangely*) But that's lost now! You're my lost island, aren't you, Mother? (*He turns and stumbles blindly from the room.* LAVINIA *reaches out stealthily and snatches up the box. This breaks the spell for* CHRISTINE *whose eyes have been fixed on it hypnotically. She looks wildly at* LAVINIA'S *frozen accusing face*).

LAVINIA (*in a cold, grim voice*) It was Brant who got you this—medicine to make you sleep—wasn't it?

CHRISTINE (*distractedly*) No! No! No!

LAVINIA You're telling me it was. I knew it—but I wanted to make sure. (*She puts the box back in the bosom of her dress —turns, rigid and square-shouldered, and walks woodenly from the room*).

CHRISTINE (*stares after her wildly, then her eyes fasten again on the dead man's face. Suddenly she appeals to him distractedly*) Ezra! Don't let her harm Adam! I am the only guilty one! Don't let Orin—! (*Then, as if she read some answer in the dead man's face, she stops in terror and, her eyes still fixed on his face, backs to the door and rushes out*).

CURTAIN

ACT FOUR

The stern section of a clipper ship moored alongside a wharf in East Boston, with the floor of the wharf in the foreground. The vessel lies with her bow and amidships off left and only the part aft of the mizzenmast is visible with the curve of the stern at right. The ship is unloaded and her black side rises nine or ten feet above the level of the wharf. On the poop deck above, at right, is the wheel. At left is the chart room and the entrance to the companionway stairs leading below to the cabin. At extreme left is the mizzenmast, the lowest yard just visible above, the boom of the spanker extending out above the deck to the right. Below the deck the portholes show a faint light from the interior of the cabin. On the wharf the end of a warehouse is at left front.

It is a night two days after Act Two—the day following EZRA MANNON'S *funeral. The moon is rising above the horizon off left rear, its light accentuating the black outlines of the ship.*

Borne on the wind the melancholy refrain of the capstan chanty "Shenandoah," sung by a chantyman with the crew coming in on the chorus, drifts over the water from a ship that is weighing anchor in the harbor. Half in and half out of the shadow of the warehouse, the CHANTYMAN *lies sprawled on his back, snoring in a drunken slumber. The sound of the singing seems to strike a responsive chord in his brain, for he stirs, grunts, and with difficulty raises himself to a sitting position in the moonlight beyond the shadow.*

He is a thin, wiry man of sixty-five or so, with a tousled mop of black hair, unkempt black beard and mustache. His weather-beaten face is dissipated, he has a weak mouth, his big round blue eyes are bloodshot, dreamy and drunken. But there is something romantic, a queer troubadour-of-the-sea quality about him.

CHANTYMAN (*listens to the singing with critical disapproval*) A hell of a chantyman that feller be! Screech owls is op'ry singers compared to him! I'll give him a taste of how "Shenandoah" ought t' be sung! (*He begins to sing in a surprisingly good tenor voice, a bit blurry with booze now and sentimentally mournful to a degree, but still managing to get full value out of the chanty*)

> *"Oh, Shenandoah, I long to hear you—*
> *A-way, my rolling river!*
> *Oh, Shenandoah, I can't get near you—*
> *Way—ay, I'm bound away*
> *Across the wide Missouri!*
>
> *"Oh, Shenandoah, I love your daughter*
> *A-way, my rolling river!"*

(*He stops abruptly, shaking his head—mournfully*) No good! Too drunk to do myself jestice! Pipe down, my John! Sleep it off! (*He sprawls back on his elbows—confusedly*) Where am I? What the hell difference is it? There's plenty o' fresh air and the moon fur a glim. Don't be so damn pertic'lar! What ye want anyways? Featherbed an' a grand piany? (*He sings with a maudlin zest*).

> *"A bottle o' wine and a bottle o' beer*
> *And a bottle of Irish whiskey oh!*
> *So early in the morning*
> *The sailor likes his bottle oh!"*

(*He stops and mutters*) Who'll buy a drink fur the slickest chantyman on the Western or any other damn ocean? Go to hell then! I kin buy it myself! (*He fumbles in his pants pocket*) I had it in this pocket—I remember I put it there pertic'lar—ten dollars in this pocket— (*He pulls the pocket inside out—with bewildered drunken anger*) By Christ, it's gone! I'm plucked clean! (*He struggles to a sitting position*) Where was I last? Aye, I remember! That yaller-haired pig with the pink dress on! Put her arm around me so lovin'! Told me how fine I could sing! (*He scrambles unsteadily to his feet*) By Christ, I'll go back an' give her a seaboot in her fat tail that'll learn her—! (*He takes a step but lurches into the shadow and leans against the warehouse*) Hard down! Heavy gales around Cape Stiff! All is sunk but honor, as the feller says, an' there's damn little o' that afloat! (*He stands against the warehouse, waiting for the swaying world to subside. The companionway door on the poop deck of the vessel is opened and* ADAM BRANT *comes cautiously out. He looks around him quickly with an uneasy suspicious air. He is dressed in a merchant captain's blue uniform. Satisfied that there is no one on the deck, he comes to the rail and stares expectantly up the wharf, off left. His attitude is tense and nervous and he keeps one hand in his coat pocket. The* CHANTYMAN *loses his balance, lurches forward, then back against the warehouse with a thump.* BRANT *leaps back from the rail startledly, jerking a revolver from his coat pocket—then leans over the rail again and calls threateningly*).

BRANT Who's there? Come out and let me have a look at you or by God I'll shoot!

CHANTYMAN (*stares up, startled in his turn and momentarily sobered—hastily*) Easy goes, shipmate! Stow that pistol! I'm doin' you no harm. (*He lurches out into the moonlight—suddenly pugnacious*) Not that I'm skeered o' you or your shooter! Who the hell are you to be threatenin' the life of an honest chantyman? Tryin' to hold me up, air ye? I been robbed once tonight! I'll go to the police station and tell 'em there's a robber here—

BRANT (*hastily, with a placating air*) No harm meant. I'm skipper of this vessel and there have been a lot of waterfront thieves around here lately. I'm lacking a watchman and I've got to keep my weather eye open.

CHANTYMAN (*again momentarily sobered—touching his forehead*) Aye—aye, sir. Mind your eye. I heer'd tell robbers broke in the "Annie Lodge's" cabin two nights back. Smashed everything and stole two hundred dollars off her skipper. Murderous, too, they be! Near beat the watchman's brains out! (*Then drunken pugnaciousness comes over him again*) Think I'm one o' that gang, do ye? Come down out o' that and I'll show ye who's a thief! I don't give a damn if ye air a skipper! Ye could be Bully Watermann himself an' I'd not let you insult me! I ain't signed on your old hooker! You've got no rights over me! I'm on dry land, by Christ, and this is a free country and— (*His voice has risen to a shout.* BRANT *is alarmed that this uproar will attract someone. He puts the pistol back in his pocket hastily and peers anxiously down the wharf. Then he interrupts the* CHANTYMAN'S *tirade by a sharp command*).

BRANT Stow your damned jaw! Or, by the Eternal, I'll come down and pound some sense in your head!

CHANTYMAN (*automatically reacts to the voice of authority—quietly*) Aye—aye, sir. (*Then inconsequentially*) You ain't needin' a chantyman fur your next vi'ge, are ye, sir?

BRANT I'm not sailing for a month yet. If you're still out of a job then—

CHANTYMAN (*proudly*) You don't know me, that's plain!

I'm the finest damn chantyman that ever put a tune to his lip! I ain't lookin' fur berths—they're lookin' fur me! Aye! Skippers are on'y too glad to git me! Many's a time I've seed a skipper an' mates sweatin' blood to beat work out of a crew but nary a lick could they git into 'em till I raised a tune—and then there'd be full sail on her afore ye knowed it!

BRANT (*impatiently*) I'm not doubting your ability. But I'd advise you to turn in and sleep it off.

CHANTYMAN (*not heeding this—sadly*) Aye, but it ain't fur long, steam is comin' in, the sea is full o' smoky tea-kettles, the old days is dyin', an' where'll you an' me be then? (*Lugubriously drunken again*) Everything is dyin'! Abe Lincoln is dead. I used to ship on the Mannon packets an' I seed in the paper where Ezra Mannon was dead! (BRANT *starts guiltily. The* CHANTYMAN *goes on maudlinly*) Heart failure killed him, it said, but I know better! I've sailed on Mannon hookers an' been worked t' death and gotten swill fur grub, an' I know he didn't have not heart in him! Open him up an' you'd find a dried turnip! The old skinflint must have left a pile o' money. Who gits it, I wonder? Leave a widder, did he?

BRANT (*harshly*) How would I know? (*Changing the subject calculatingly*) What are you doing here, Chantyman? I'd expect a man with your voice would be in a saloon, singing and making merry!

CHANTYMAN So I would! So I would! But I was robbed, sir—aye—an' I know who done it—a yaller-haired wench had her arm around me. Steer clear o' gals or they'll skin your hide off an' use it fur a carpet! I warn ye, skipper! They're not fur sailormen like you an' me, 'less we're lookin' fur sorrow! (*Then insinuatingly*) I ain't got the price of a drink, that's why I'm here, sir.

BRANT (*reaches in his pocket and tosses him down a silver dollar*) Here!

CHANTYMAN (*fumbles around and finds the dollar*) Thank ye sir. (*Then flatteringly*) It's a fine ship you've got there, sir. Crack sail on her and she'll beat most of 'em—an' you're the kind to crack sail on, I kin tell by your cut.

BRANT (*pleased, glancing up at his ship's lofty rig*) Aye! I'll make her go right enough!

CHANTYMAN All you need is a good chantyman to help ye. Here's "Hanging Johnny" fur ye! (BRANT *starts at this. The* CHANTYMAN *suddenly begins to sing the chanty "Hanging Johnny" with sentimental mournfulness*)

"Oh, they call me Hanging Johnny
Away—ay—i—oh!
They says I hangs for money
Oh, hang, boys, hang!"

BRANT (*harshly*) Stop that damned dirge! And get out of here! Look lively now!

CHANTYMAN (*starting to go*) Aye—aye, sir. (*Then resentfully*) I see ye ain't got much ear fur music. Good night.

BRANT (*with exasperated relief*) Good night. (*The* CHANTYMAN *goes unsteadily off left, between the warehouse and the ship. He bursts again into his mournful dirge, his voice receding*)

"They say I hanged my mother
Away—ay—i—oh!
They say I hanged my mother
Oh, hang, boys, hang!"

Coward

(BRANT, *standing by the rail looking after him, mutters a curse and starts pacing up and down the deck*) Damn that chanty! It's sad as death! I've a foreboding I'll never take this ship to sea. She doesn't want me now—a coward hiding behind a woman's skirts! The sea hates a coward! (*A woman's figure dressed in black, heavily veiled, moves stealthily out from the darkness between the ship and the warehouse, left. She sees the figure on the deck above her and shrinks back with a stifled gasp of fear.* BRANT *hears the noise. Immediately his revolver is in his hand and he peers down into the shadows of the warehouse*) Who's there?

CHRISTINE (*with a cry of relief*) Adam!

BRANT Christine! (*Then quickly*) Go back to the gangplank. I'll meet you there. (*She goes back. He hurries along the deck and dissappears off left to meet her. Their voices are heard and a moment later they enter on the poop deck, from left. She leans against him weakly and he supports her with his arm around her*) I have to bring you this way. I bolted the door to the main deck.

CHRISTINE I was so frightened! I wasn't sure which ship! Some drunken man came along singing—

BRANT Aye. I just got rid of him. I fired the watchman this morning so I'd be alone at night. I was hoping you'd come soon. Did that drunk see you?

CHRISTINE No. I hid behind some boxes. (*Then frightenedly*) Why have you got that pistol?

BRANT (*grimly*) I was going to give them a fight for it—if things went wrong.

CHRISTINE Adam!

BRANT By God, you don't think I'll ever let them take me alive, do you?

CHRISTINE Please, please! Don't talk of that for a moment! Only hold me close to you! Tell me you love me!

BRANT (*harshly*) It's no time! I want to know what's happened! (*Then immediately repentant he kisses her—with rough tenderness*) Don't mind me! My nerves are gone from waiting alone here not knowing anything but what I read in the papers—that he was dead. These last days have been hell!

CHRISTINE If you knew what they have been for me!

BRANT There's something gone wrong! I can read that in your face! What is it, Christine?

CHRISTINE (*falteringly*) Vinnie knows—! She came into the room when he was dying! He told her—

BRANT (*harshly*) God! What is she going to do? (*Then, without giving her time to answer his question, he suddenly looks around uneasily*) Christine! How did you get away? She'd suspect you weren't going to your father's now. She followed you once before—

CHRISTINE No. It's all right. This morning Orin said his cousins, the Bradfords, had invited him and Vinnie to visit them overnight at Blackridge and he was taking Vinnie with him because he thought a change would bring her back to her senses. I've made him think she's out of her head with grief—so he wouldn't listen to her—

BRANT (*eagerly*) And he believes that?

CHRISTINE (*weakly*) Yes—he does—now—but I don't know how long—

BRANT Ah!

CHRISTINE So I told him by all means to go. It gave me the chance I wanted to come to you. They went this morning. They don't know I've gone and even after they've found out they can't prove where I went. I can only stay a little while, Adam—we've got to plan—so many things have happened I couldn't foresee—I came to warn you—

BRANT Ssshh! Come below in the cabin! We're fools to be talking out here. (*He guides her with his arm around her through the door to the companionway stairs and closes it quietly behind them. A pause in which the singing of the crew on the ship in the harbor comes mournfully over the water. Then* ORIN *and* LAVINIA *come in stealthily along the deck from the left. She is dressed in black as before. He wears a long cloak over his uniform and has a slouch hat pulled down over his eyes. Her manner is cold and grim.* ORIN *is holding in a savage, revengeful rage. They approach the cabin skylight silently.* ORIN *bends down by it to listen. His face, in the light from the skylight, becomes distorted with jealous fury.* LAVINIA *puts a restraining hand on his arm.*

The scene fades out into darkness. Several minutes are supposed to elapse. When the light comes on again, a section of the ship has been removed to reveal the interior of the cabin, a small compartment, the walls newly painted a light brown. The skylight giving in the deck above is in the middle of the ceiling. Suspended in the skylight is a ship's compass. Beneath it is a pine table with three chairs, one at rear, the other two at the table ends, left and right. On the table is a bottle of whiskey, half full, with a glass and a pitcher of water.

Built against the right wall of the cabin is a long narrow couch, like a bunk, with leather cushions. In the rear wall, at right, is a door leading into the captain's stateroom. A big sideboard stands against the left wall, center. Above it, a ship's clock. Farther back is a door opening on the alleyway leading to the main deck. The companionway stairs lead down to this alleyway.

There is a lighted lamp on the sideboard and a ship's lantern, also lighted, at the right end of the table.

In the cabin, BRANT *is seated at the right of table,* CHRISTINE *to the rear of it. Her face looks haggard and ageing, the mouth pinched and drawn down at the corners, and her general appearance, the arrangement of her hair and clothes, has the dishevelled touch of the fugitive. She is just finishing her story of the murder and the events following it. He is listening tensely.*

On the deck above, ORIN *and* LAVINIA *are discovered as before, with* ORIN *bending down by the transom, listening*).

CHRISTINE When he was dying he pointed at me and told her I was guilty! And afterwards she found the poison—

BRANT (*springing to his feet*) For God's sake, why didn't you—

CHRISTINE (*pitifully*) I fainted before I could hide it! And I had planned it all so carefully. But how could I foresee that she would come in just at that moment? And how could I know he would talk to me the way he did? He drove me crazy! He kept talking of death! He was torturing me! I only wanted him to die and leave me alone!

BRANT (*his eyes lighting up with savage satisfaction*) He knew before he died whose son I was, you said? By God, I'll bet that maddened him!

CHRISTINE (*repeats pitifully*) I'd planned it so carefully—but something made things happen!

BRANT (*overcome by gloomy dejection, sinks down on his chair again*) I knew it! I've had a feeling in my bones! It serves me right, what has happened and is to happen! It wasn't that kind of revenge I had sworn on my mother's body! I should have done as I wanted—fought with Ezra Mannon as two men fight for love of a woman! (*With bitter self-contempt*) I have my father's rotten coward blood in me, I think! Aye!

CHRISTINE Adam! You make me feel so guilty!

BRANT (*rousing himself—shamefacedly*) I didn't mean to blame you, Christine. (*Then harshly*) It's too late for regrets now, anyway. We've got to think what to do.

CHRISTINE Yes! I'm so terrified of Vinnie! Oh, Adam, you must promise me to be on your guard every minute! If she convinces Orin you are my lover— Oh, why can't we go away, Adam? Once we're out of her reach, she can't do anything.

BRANT The "Flying Trades" won't be sailing for a month or more. We can't get cargo as soon as the owners thought.

CHRISTINE Can't we go on another ship—as passengers—to the East—we could be married out there—

BRANT (*gloomily*) But everyone in the town would know you were gone. It would start suspicion—

CHRISTINE No. Orin and Vinnie would lie to people. They'd have to for their own sakes. They'd say I was in New York with my father. Oh, Adam, it's the only thing we can do! If we don't get out of Vinnie's reach right away I know something horrible will happen!

BRANT (*dejectedly*) Aye. I suppose it's the only way out for us now. The "Atlantis" is sailing on Friday for China. I'll arrange with her skipper to give us passage—and keep his mouth shut. She sails at daybreak Friday. You'd better meet me here Thursday night. (*Then with an effort*) I'll write Clark and Dawson tonight they'll have to find another skipper for the "Flying Trades."

CHRISTINE (*noticing the hurt in his tone—miserably*) Poor Adam! I know how it hurts you to give up your ship.

BRANT (*rousing himself guiltily—pats her hand—with gruff tenderness*) There are plenty of ships—but there is only one you, Christine!

CHRISTINE I feel so guilty! I've brought you nothing but misfortune!

BRANT You've brought love—and the rest is only the price. It's worth it a million times! You're all mine now, anyway! (*He hugs her to him, staring over her head with sad blank eyes*).

CHRISTINE (*her voice trembling*) But I'm afraid I'm not much to boast about having—now. I've grown old in the past few days. I'm ugly. But I'll make myself beautiful again—for you—! I'll make up to you for everything! Try not to regret your ship too much, Adam!

BRANT (*gruffly*) Let's not talk of her any more. (*Then forcing a wry smile*) I'll give up the sea. I think it's through with me now, anyway! The sea hates a coward.

CHRISTINE (*trying pitifully to cheer him*) Don't talk like that! You have me, Adam! You have me! And we will be happy—once we're safe on your Blessed Islands! (*Then suddenly, with a little shudder*) It's strange. Orin was telling me of an island— (*On the deck above,* ORIN, *who has bent closer to the transom, straightens up with a threatening movement.* LAVINIA *grips his arm, restraining him*).

BRANT (*with a bitter, hopeless yearning*) Aye—the Blessed Isles—Maybe we can still find happiness and forget! (*Then strangely, as if to himself*) I can see them now—so close—and a million miles away! The warm earth in the moonlight, the trade winds rustling the coco palms, the surf on the barrier reef singing a croon in your ears like a lullaby! Aye! There's peace, and forgetfulness for us there—if we can ever find those islands now!

CHRISTINE (*desperately*) We will find them! We will! (*She kisses him. A pause. Suddenly she glances frightenedly at the clock*) Look at the time! I've got to go, Adam!

BRANT For the love of God, watch out for Vinnie. If anything happened to you now—!

CHRISTINE Nothing will happen to me. But you must be on your guard in case Orin— Good-bye, my lover! I must go! I must! (*She tears herself from his arms but immediately throws herself in them again—terrifiedly*) Oh! I feel so strange—so sad—as if I'd never see you again! (*She begins to sob hysteri-*

cally) Oh, Adam, tell me you don't regret! Tell me we're going to be happy! I can't bear this horrible feeling of despair!

BRANT Of course we'll be happy! Come now! It's only a couple of days. (*They start for the door*) We'll go by the main deck. It's shorter. I'll walk to the end of the wharf with you. I won't go further. We might be seen.

CHRISTINE Then we don't have to say good-bye for a few minutes yet! Oh, thank God! (*They go out to the alleyway,* BRANT *closing the door behind him. A pause. On the deck above* ORIN *pulls a revolver from under his cloak and makes a move, as if to rush off left down to the main deck after them.* LAVINIA *has been dreading this and throws herself in his way, grasping his arm*).

ORIN (*in a furious whisper*) Let me go!

LAVINIA (*struggling with him*) No! Be quiet! Ssshh! I hear them on the main deck! Quick! Come to his cabin! (*She urges him to the companionway door, gets him inside and shuts the door behind them. A moment later the door on the left of the cabin below is opened and they enter*).

LAVINIA He's going to the end of the wharf. That gives us a few minutes. (*Grimly*) You wanted proof! Well, are you satisfied now?

ORIN Yes! God damn him! Death is too good for him! He ought to be—

LAVINIA (*sharply commanding*) Orin! Remember you promised not to lose your head. You've got to do everything exactly as we planned it, so there'll be no suspicion about us. There would be no justice if we let ourselves—

ORIN (*impatiently*) You've said all that before! Do you think I'm a fool? I'm not anxious to be hanged—for that skunk! (*Then with bitter anguish*) I heard her asking him to kiss her! I heard her warn him against me! (*He gives a horrible chuckle*) And my island I told her about—which was she and I—she wants to go there—with him! (*Then furiously*) Damn you! Why did you stop me? I'd have shot his guts out in front of her!

LAVINIA (*scornfully*) Outside on deck where the shot would be sure to be heard? We'd have been arrested—and then I'd have to tell the truth to save us. She'd be hanged, and even if we managed to get off, our lives would be ruined! The only person to come off lucky would be Brant! He could die happy, knowing he'd revenged himself on us more than he ever dared hope! Is that what you want?

ORIN (*sullenly*) No.

LAVINIA Then don't act like a fool again. (*Looks around the cabin calculatingly—then in a tone of command*) Go and hide outside. He won't see you when he passes along the alleyway in the dark. He'll come straight in here. That's the time for you—

ORIN (*grimly*) You needn't tell me what to do. I've had a thorough training at this game—thanks to you and Father.

LAVINIA Quick! Go out now! He won't be long!

ORIN (*goes to the door—then quickly*) I hear him coming. (*He slips out silently. She hurriedly hides herself by the sideboard at left, front. A moment later* BRANT *appears in the doorway and stands just inside it blinking in the light. He looks around the cabin sadly*)

BRANT (*huskily*) So it's good-bye to you, "Flying Trades"! And you're right! I wasn't man enough for you! (ORIN *steps through the door and with the pistol almost against* BRANT'S *body fires twice.* BRANT *pitches forward to the floor by the table, rolls over, twitches a moment on his back and lies still.* ORIN *springs forward and stands over the body, his pistol aimed down at it, ready to fire again*).

LAVINIA (*stares fascinatedly at* BRANT'S *still face*) Is he—dead?

ORIN Yes.

LAVINIA (*sharply*) Don't stand there! Where's the chisel you brought? Smash open everything in his stateroom. We must make it look as if thieves killed him, remember! Take anything valuable! We can sink it overboard afterwards! Hurry! (ORIN *puts his revolver on the table and takes a chisel that is stuck in his belt under his cloak and goes into the stateroom. A moment later there is the sound of splintering wood as he pries open a drawer*).

LAVINIA (*goes slowly to the body and stands looking down into* BRANT'S *face. Her own is frozen and expressionless. A pause.* ORIN *can be heard in the stateroom prying open* BRANT'S *desk and scattering the contents of drawers around. Finally* LAVINIA *speaks to the corpse in a grim bitter tone*) How could you love that vile old woman so? (*She throws off this thought—harshly*) But you're dead! It's ended! (*She turns away from him resolutely—then suddenly turns back and stands stiffly upright and grim beside the body and prays coldly, as if carrying out a duty*) May God find forgiveness for your sins! May the soul of our cousin, Adam Mannon, rest in peace! (ORIN *comes in from the stateroom and overhears the last of her prayer).*

ORIN (*harshly*) Rest in hell, you mean! (*He comes to her*) I've pried open everything I could find.

LAVINIA Then come along. Quick. There's your pistol. Don't forget that. (*She goes to the door*).

ORIN (*putting it in his pocket*) We've got to go through his pockets to make everything look like a burglary. (*He quickly turns* BRANT'S *pockets inside out and puts the revolver he finds, along with bills and coins, watch and chain, knife, etc., into his own*) I'll sink these overboard from the dock, along with what was in his stateroom. (*Having finished this, he still remains stooping over the body and stares into* BRANT'S *face, a queer fascinated expression in his eyes*).

LAVINIA (*uneasily*) Orin!

ORIN By God, he does look like Father!

LAVINIA No! Come along!

ORIN (*as if talking to himself*) This is like my dream. I've killed him before—over and over.

LAVINIA Orin!

ORIN Do you remember me telling you how the faces of the men I killed came back and changed to Father's face and finally became my own? (*He smiles grimly*) He looks like me, too! Maybe I've committed suicide!

LAVINIA (*frightenedly—grabbing his arm*) Hurry! Someone may come!

ORIN (*not heeding her, still staring at* BRANT—*strangely*) If I had been he I would have done what he did! I would have loved her as he loved her—and killed Father too—for her sake!

LAVINIA (*tensely—shaking him by the arm*) Orin, for God's sake, will you stop talking crazy and come along? Do you want us to be found here? (*She pulls him away forcibly*).

ORIN (*with a last look at the dead man*) It's queer! It's a rotten dirty joke on someone! (*He lets her hustle him out to the alleyway*).

CURTAIN

ACT FIVE

SCENE—*The same as Act Three of "Homecoming"—exterior of the Mannon house. It is the following night. The moon has just risen. The right half of the house is in the black shadow cast by the pine trees but the moonlight falls full on the part to the left of the doorway. The door at center is open and there is a light in the hall behind. All the shutters of the windows are closed.*

CHRISTINE *is discovered walking back and forth on the drive before the portico, passing from moonlight into the shadow of the pines and back again. She is in a frightful state of tension, unable to keep still.*

She sees someone she is evidently expecting approaching the house from up the drive, off left, and she hurries down as far as the bench to meet her.

HAZEL (*enters from left—with a kindly smile*) Here I am! Seth brought your note and I hurried right over.

CHRISTINE (*kissing her—with unnatural effusiveness*) I'm so glad you've come! I know I shouldn't have bothered you.

HAZEL It's no bother at all, Mrs. Mannon. I'm only too happy to keep you company.

CHRISTINE I was feeling so terribly sad—and nervous here. I had let Hannah and Annie have the night off. I'm all alone. (*She sits on the bench*) Let's sit out here. I can't bear it in the house. (HAZEL *sits beside her*).

HAZEL (*pityingly*) I know. It must be terribly lonely for you. You must miss him so much.

CHRISTINE (*with a shudder*) Please don't talk about— He is buried! He is gone!

HAZEL (*gently*) He is at peace, Mrs. Mannon.

CHRISTINE (*with bitter mockery*) I was like you once! I believed in heaven! Now I know there is only hell!

HAZEL Ssshh! You mustn't say that.

CHRISTINE (*rousing herself—forcing a smile*) I'm not fit company for a young girl, I'm afraid. You should have youth and beauty and freedom around you. I'm old and ugly and haunted by death! (*Then, as if to herself—in a low desperate tone*) I can't let myself get ugly! I can't!

HAZEL You're only terribly worn out. You ought to try and sleep.

CHRISTINE I don't believe there's such a thing on this earth as sleep! It's only in the earth one sleeps! One must feel so at peace—at last—with all one's fears ended! (*Then forcing a laugh*) Good heavens, what a bore it must be for you, listening to my gloomy thoughts! I honestly didn't send for you to— I wanted to ask if you or Peter had heard anything from Orin and Vinnie.

HAZEL (*surprised*) Why, no. We haven't seen them since the funeral.

CHRISTINE (*forcing a smile*) They seem to have deserted me. (*Then quickly*) I mean they should have been home before this. I can't imagine what's keeping them. They went to Blackridge to stay overnight at the Bradfords'.

HAZEL Then there's nothing to worry about. But I don't see how they could leave you alone—just now.

CHRISTINE Oh, that part is all right. I urged them to go. They left soon after the funeral, and afterwards I thought it would be a good opportunity for me to go to New York and see my father. He's sick, you know, but I found him so much better I decided to come home again last night. I expected Vinnie and Orin back this noon, but here it's night and no sign of them. I—I must confess I'm worried—and frightened. You can't know the horror of being all night—alone in that house! (*She glances at the house behind her with a shudder*).

HAZEL Would it help you if I stayed with you tonight—I mean if they don't come?

CHRISTINE (*eagerly*) Oh, would you? (*Hysterical tears come to her eyes. She kisses* HAZEL *with impulsive gratitude*) I can't tell you how grateful I'd be! You're so good! (*Then forcing a laugh*) But it's an imposition to ask you to face such an ordeal. I can't stay still. I'm terrified at every sound. You would have to sit up.

HAZEL Losing a little sleep won't hurt me any.

CHRISTINE I mustn't sleep! If you see me falling asleep you must promise to wake me!

HAZEL But it's just what you need.

CHRISTINE Yes—afterwards—but not now. I must keep awake. (*In tense desperation*) I wish Orin and Vinnie would come!

HAZEL (*worriedly*) Perhaps Orin got so sick he wasn't able to. Oh, I hope that isn't it! (*Then getting up*) If I'm going to stay all night I'll have to run home and tell Mother, so she won't worry.

CHRISTINE Yes—do. (*Then frightenedly*) You won't be long, will you? I'm afraid—to be alone.

HAZEL (*kisses her—pityingly*) I'll be as quick as I possibly can. (*She walks down the drive, off left, waving her hand as she disappears.* CHRISTINE *stands by the bench—then begins to pace back and forth again*).

CHRISTINE (*her eyes caught by something down the drive—in a tense whisper*) She's met someone by the gate! Oh, why am I so afraid! (*She turns, seized by panic, and runs to the house—then stops at the top of the steps and faces around, leaning against a column for support*) Oh, God, I'm afraid to know! (*A moment later* ORIN *and* LAVINIA *come up the drive from the left.* LAVINIA *is stiffly square-shouldered, her eyes hard, her mouth grim and set.* ORIN *is in a state of morbid excitement. He carries a newspaper in his hand*).

ORIN (*speaking to* VINNIE *as they enter—harshly*) You let me do the talking! I want to be the one— (*He sees his mother—startledly*) Mother! (*Then with vindictive mockery*) Ah! So this time at least you are waiting to meet me when I come home!

CHRISTINE (*stammers*) Orin! What kept you—?

ORIN We just met Hazel. She said you were terribly frightened at being alone here. That is strange—when you have the memory of Father for company!

CHRISTINE You—you stayed all this time—at the Bradfords'?

ORIN We didn't go to the Bradfords'!

CHRISTINE (*stupidly*) You didn't go—to Blackridge?

ORIN We took the train there but we decided to stay right on and go to Boston instead.

CHRISTINE (*terrifiedly*) To—Boston—?

ORIN And in Boston we waited until the evening train got in. We met that train.

CHRISTINE Ah!

ORIN We had an idea you would take advantage of our being in Blackridge to be on it—and you were! And we followed you when you called on your lover in his cabin!

CHRISTINE (*with a pitiful effort at indignation*) Orin! How dare you talk—! (*Then brokenly*) Orin! Don't look at me like that! Tell me—

ORIN Your lover! Don't lie! You've lied enough, Mother!

I was on deck, listening! What would you have done if you had discovered me? Would you have gotten your lover to murder me, Mother? I heard you warning him against me! But your warning was no use!

CHRISTINE (*chokingly*) What—? Tell me—!

ORIN I killed him!

CHRISTINE (*with a cry of terror*) Oh—oh! I knew! (*Then clutching at* ORIN) No—Orin! You—you're just telling me that—to punish me, aren't you? You said you loved me—you'd protect me—protect your mother—you couldn't murder—!

ORIN (*harshly, pushing her away*) You could murder Father, couldn't you? (*He thrusts the newspaper into her hands, pointing to the story*) Here! Read that, if you don't believe me! We got it in Boston to see whom the police would suspect. It's only a few lines. Brant wasn't important—except to you! (*She looks at the paper with fascinated horror. Then she lets it slip through her fingers, sinks down on the lowest step and begins to moan to herself, wringing her hands together in stricken anguish.* ORIN *turns from her and starts to pace up and down by the steps.* LAVINIA *stands at the left of the steps, rigid and erect, her face mask-like*).

ORIN (*harshly*) They think exactly what we planned they should think—that he was killed by waterfront thieves. There's nothing to connect us with his death! (*He stops by her. She stares before her, wringing her hands and moaning. He blurts out*) Mother! Don't moan like that! (*She gives no sign of having heard him. He starts to pace up and down again—with savage resentment*) Why do you grieve for that servant's bastard? I know he was the one who planned Father's murder! You couldn't have done that! He got you under his influence to revenge himself! He hypnotized you! I saw you weren't yourself the minute I got home, remember? How else could you ever have imagined you loved that low swine! How else could you ever have said the things— (*He stops before her*) I heard you planning to go with him to the island I had told you about—our island—that was you and I! (*He starts to pace up and down again distractedly. She remains as before except that her moaning has begun to exhaust itself.* ORIN *stops before her again and grasps her by the shoulders, kneeling on the steps beside her—desperately pleading now*) Mother! Don't moan like that! You're still under his influence! But you'll forget him! I'll make you forget him! I'll make you happy! We'll leave

Vinnie here and go away on a long voyage—to the South Seas—

LAVINIA (*sharply*) Orin!

ORIN (*not heeding her, stares into his mother's face. She has stopped moaning, the horror in her eyes is dying into blankness, the expression of her mouth congealing to one of numbed grief. She gives no sign of having heard him.* ORIN *shakes her—desperately*) Mother! Don't you hear me? Why won't you speak to me? Will you always love him? Do you hate me now? (*He sinks on his knees before her*) Mother! Answer me! Say you forgive me!

LAVINIA (*with bitter scorn*) Orin! After all that's happened, are you becoming her crybaby again? (ORIN *starts and gets to his feet, staring at her confusedly, as if he had forgotten her existence.* LAVINIA *speaks again in curt commanding tone that recalls her father*) Leave her alone! Go in the house! (*As he hesitates—more sharply*) Do you hear me? March!

ORIN (*automatically makes a confused motion of military salute—vaguely*) Yes, sir. (*He walks mechanically up the steps—gazing up at the house—strangely*) Why are the shutters still closed? Father has gone. We ought to let in the moonlight. (*He goes into the house.* LAVINIA *comes and stands beside her mother.* CHRISTINE *continues to stare blankly in front of her. Her face has become a tragic death mask. She gives no sign of being aware of her daughter's presence.* LAVINIA *regards her with bleak, condemning eyes*).

LAVINIA (*finally speaks sternly*) He paid the just penalty for his crime. You know it was justice. It was the only way true justice could be done. (*Her mother starts. The words shatter her merciful numbness and awaken her to agony again. She springs to her feet and stands glaring at her daughter with a terrible look in which a savage hatred fights with horror and fear. In spite of her frozen self-control,* LAVINIA *recoils before this. Keeping her eyes on her,* CHRISTINE *shrinks backward up the steps until she stands at the top between the two columns of the portico before the front door.* LAVINIA *suddenly makes a motion, as if to hold her back. She calls shakenly as if the words were wrung out of her against her will*) Mother! What are you going to do? You can live!

CHRISTINE (*glares at her as if this were the last insult—with strident mockery*) Live! (*She bursts into shrill laughter, stops it abruptly, raises her hands between her face and her *daughter and pushes them out in a gesture of blotting* LAVINIA *forever from her sight. Then she turns and rushes into the house.* LAVINIA *again makes a movement to follow her. But she immediately fights down this impulse and turns her back on the house determinedly, standing square-shouldered and stiff like a grim sentinel in black*).

LAVINIA (*implacably to herself*) It is justice! (*From the street, away off right front,* SETH'S *thin wraith of a baritone is raised in his favorite mournful "Shenandoah," as he nears the gateway to the drive, returning from his nightly visit to the saloon*).

> *"Oh, Shenandoah, I long to hear you*
> *A-way, my rolling river!*
> *Oh, Shenandoah, I can't get near you*
> *Way—ay, I'm bound away*
> *Across the wide—"*

(*There is the sharp report of a pistol from the left ground floor of the house where* EZRA MANNON'S *study is.* LAVINIA *gives a shuddering gasp, turns back to the steps, starts to go up them, stops again and stammers shakenly*) It is justice! It is your justice, Father! (ORIN'S *voice is heard calling from the sitting-room at right "What's that"! A door slams. Then* ORIN'S *horrified cry comes from the study as he finds his mother's body, and a moment later he rushes out frantically to* LAVINIA).

ORIN Vinnie! (*He grabs her arm and stammers distractedly*) Mother—shot herself—Father's pistol—get a doctor—(*Then with hopeless anguish*) No—it's too late—she's dead! (*Then wildly*) Why—why did she, Vinnie? (*With tortured self-accusation*) I drove her to it! I wanted to torture her! She couldn't forgive me! Why did I have to boast about killing him? Why—?

LAVINIA (*frightenedly, puts her hand over his mouth*) Be quiet!

ORIN (*tears her hand away—violently*) Why didn't I let her believe burglars killed him? She wouldn't have hated me then! She would have forgotten him! She would have turned to me! (*In a final frenzy of self-denunciation*) I murdered her!

LAVINIA (*grabbing him by the shoulders*) For God's sake, will you be quiet?

ORIN (*frantically—trying to break away from her*) Let me go! I've got to find her! I've got to make her forgive me! I—! (*He suddenly breaks down and weeps in hysterical anguish.*

LAVINIA *puts her arm around him soothingly. He sobs despairingly*) But she's dead— She's gone—how can I ever get her to forgive me now?

LAVINIA (*soothingly*) Ssshh! Ssshh! You have me, haven't you? I love you. I'll help you to forget. (*He turns to go back into the house, still sobbing helplessly.* SETH'S *voice comes from the drive, right, close at hand:*

"She's far across the stormy water
Way-ay, I'm bound away—"

(*He enters right, front.* LAVINIA *turns to face him*).

SETH (*approaching*) Say, Vinnie, did you hear a shot—?

LAVINIA (*sharply*) I want you to go for Doctor Blake. Tell him Mother has killed herself in a fit of insane grief over Father's death. (*Then as he stares, dumbfounded and wondering, but keeping his face expressionless—more sharply*) Will *you remember to tell him that?*

SETH (*slowly*) Ayeh. I'll tell him, Vinnie—anything you say. (*His face set grimly, he goes off, right front.* LAVINIA *turns and, stiffly erect, her face stern and mask-like, follows* ORIN *into the house*).

CURTAIN

The Haunted

CHARACTERS

LAVINIA MANNON

ORIN, *her brother*

PETER NILES

HAZEL, *his sister*

SETH

AMOS AMES

IRA MACKEL

JOE SILVA

ABNER SMALL

SCENES

ACT ONE—*Scene* I: Exterior of the Mannon house—an evening in the summer of 1866.

ACT ONE—*Scene* II: Sitting-room in the house (immediately follows Scene One).

ACT TWO: The study—an evening a month later.

ACT THREE: The sitting-room (immediately follows Act Two).

ACT FOUR: Same as Act One, Scene One—Exterior of the Mannon house—a late afternoon three days later.

The Haunted

ACT ONE · SCENE ONE

Exterior of the Mannon house (as in the two preceding plays) on an evening of a clear day in summer a year later. It is shortly after sunset but the afterglow in the sky still bathes the white temple portico in a crimson light. The columns cast black bars of shadow on the wall behind them. All the shutters are closed and the front door is boarded up, showing that the house is unoccupied.

A group of five men is standing on the drive by the bench at left, front. SETH BECKWITH *is there and* AMOS AMES, *who appeared in the first Act of "Homecoming." The others are* ABNER SMALL, JOE SILVA *and* IRA MACKEL.

*These four—*AMES, SMALL, SILVA *and* MACKEL*—are, as were the townsfolk of the first acts of "Homecoming" and "The Hunted," a chorus of types representing the town as a human background for the drama of the Mannons.*

SMALL *is a wiry little old man of sixty five, a clerk in a hardware store. He has white hair and a wispy goat's beard, bright inquisitive eyes, ruddy complexion, and a shrill rasping voice.* SILVA *is a Portuguese fishing captain—a fat, boisterous man, with a hoarse bass voice. He has matted gray hair and a big grizzled mustache. He is sixty.* MACKEL, *who is a farmer, hobbles along with the aid of a cane. His shiny wrinkled face is oblong with a square white chin whisker. He is bald. His yellowish brown eyes are sly. He talks in a drawling wheezy cackle.*

All five are drunk. SETH *has a stone jug in his hand. There is a grotesque atmosphere of boys out on a forbidden lark about these old men.*

SMALL God A'mighty, Seth, be you glued to that jug?
MACKEL Gol durn him, he's gittin' stingy in his old age!
SILVA (*bursts into song*)

"A bottle of beer and a bottle of gin
And a bottle of Irish whiskey oh!
So early in the morning
A sailor likes his bottle oh!"

AMES (*derisively*) You like your bottle 'ceptin' when your old woman's got her eye on ye!

SILVA She's visitin' her folks to New Bedford. What the hell I care! (*Bursts into song again*)

"Hurrah! Hurrah! I sing the jubilee
Hurrah! Hurrah! Her folks has set me free!"

AMES (*slapping him on the back*) God damn you, Joe, you're gittin' to be a poet! (*They all laugh*).

SMALL God A'mighty, Seth, ain't ye got no heart in ye? Watch me perishin' fur lack o' whiskey and ye keep froze to that jug! (*He reaches out for it*).

SETH No, ye don't! I'm onto your game! (*With a wink at the others*) He's aimin' to git so full of Injun courage he wouldn't mind if a ghost sot on his lap! Purty slick you be, Abner! Swill my licker so's you kin skin me out o' my bet!

MACKEL That's it, Seth! Don't let him play no skin games!

JOE By God, if ghosts look like the livin', I'd let Ezra's woman's ghost set on my lap! M'm! (*He smacks his lips lasciviously*).

AMES Me, too! She was a looker!

SMALL (*with an uneasy glance at the house*) It's her ghost folks is sayin' haunts the place, ain't it?

SETH (*with a wink at the others*) Oh, hers and a hull passel of others. The graveyard's full of Mannons and they all spend their nights to hum here. You needn't worry but you'll have plenty o' company, Abner! (*The others laugh, their mirth a bit forced, but* SMALL *looks rather sick*).

SMALL It ain't in our bet for you to put sech notions in my head afore I go in, be it? (*Then forcing a perky bravado*) Think you kin scare me? There ain't no sech thing as ghosts!

SETH An' I'm sayin' you're scared to prove there ain't! Let's git our bet set out plain afore witnesses. I'm lettin' you in the Mannon house and I'm bettin' you ten dollars and a gallon of licker you dasn't stay there till moonrise at ten o'clock. If you come out afore then, you lose. An' you're to stay in the dark and not even strike a match! Is that agreed?

SMALL (*trying to put a brave face on it*) That's agreed—an' it's like stealin' ten dollars off you!

SETH We'll see! (*Then with a grin*) An' you're supposed to go in sober! But I won't make it too dead sober! I ain't that hardhearted. I wouldn't face what you'll face with a gallon under my belt! (*Handing him the jug*) Here! Take a good swig! You're lookin' a mite pale about the gills a'ready!

SMALL No sech thing! (*But he puts the jug to his lips and takes an enormous swallow*).

MACKEL Whoa thar! Ye ain't drinkin' fur all on us! (SMALL *hands the jug to him and he drinks and passes it around until it finally reaches* SETH *again. In the meantime* SMALL *talks to* SETH).

SMALL Be it all right fur me to go in afore dark? I'd like to know where I'm at while I kin see.

SETH Wal, I calc'late you kin. Don't want you runnin' into furniture an' breakin' things when them ghosts git chasin' you! Vinnie an' Orin's liable to be back from Chiny afore long an' she'd give me hell if anythin' was broke. (*The jug reaches him. He takes a drink—then sets it down on the drive*) Come along! I've took the screws out o' that door. I kin let you right in. (*He goes toward the portico,* SMALL *following him, whistling with elaborate nonchalance*).

SMALL (*to the others who remain where they are*) So long, fellers. We'll have a good spree on that ten dollars.

MACKEL (*with a malicious cackle*) Mebbe! Would you like me fur one o' your pallbearers, Abner?

AMES I'll comfort your old woman—providin' she'll want comfortin', which ain't likely!

SILVA And I'll water your grave every Sunday after church! That's the kind of man I be, by God. I don't forget my friends when they're gone!

SETH (*from the portico*) We'll all jine in, Joe! If he ain't dead, by God, we'll drown him! (*They all roar with laughter.* SMALL *looks bitter. The jest strikes him as being unfeeling—All glow has faded from the sky and it is getting dark*).

SMALL To hell with ye! (SETH *pries off the board door and unlocks the inner door*).

SETH Come on. I'll show you the handiest place to say your prayers. (*They go in. The group outside becomes serious*).

AMES (*voicing the opinion of all of them*) Wal, all the same, I wouldn't be in Abner's boots. It don't do to monkey with them thin's.

MACKEL You believe in ghosts, Amos?

AMES Mebbe. Who knows there ain't?

MACKEL Wal, I believe in 'em. Take the Nims' place out my way. Asa Nims killed his wife with a hatchet—she'd nagged him—then hung himself in the attic. I knew Ben Willett that bought the place. He couldn't live thar—had to move away. It's fallen to runs now. Ben used to hear things clawin' at the walls an' winders and see the chairs move about. He wasn't a liar nor chicken-hearted neither.

SILVA There is ghosts, by God! My cousin, Manuel, he seen one! Off on a whaler in the Injun Ocean, that was. A man got knifed and pushed overboard. After that, on moonlight nights, they'd see him a-settin' on the yards and hear him moanin' to himself. Yes, sir, my cousin Manuel, he ain't no liar neither—'ceptin' when he's drunk—and he seen him with his own eyes!

AMES (*with an uneasy glance around, reaching for the jug*) Wal, let's have a drink. (*He takes a swig just as* SETH *comes out of the house, shutting the door behind him*).

MACKEL That's Seth. He ain't anxious to stay in thar long, I notice! (SETH *hurries down to them, trying to appear to saunter*).

SETH (*with a forced note to his joking*) God A'mighty, ye'd ought to see Abner! He's shyin' at the furniture covers an' his teeth are clickin' a'ready. He'll come runnin' out hell fur leather afore long. All I'm wonderin' is, has he got ten dollars.

MACKEL (*slyly*) You seem a mite shaky.

SETH (*with a scowl*) You're a liar. What're ye all lookin' glum as owls about?

MACKEL Been talkin' of ghosts. Do you really believe that there house is haunted, Seth, or are ye only jokin' Abner?

SETH (*sharply*) Don't be a durned fool! I'm on'y jokin' him, of course!

MACKEL (*insistently*) Still, it'd be only natural if it was haunted. She shot herself there. Do you think she done it fur grief over Ezra's death, like the daughter let on to folks?

SETH 'Course she did!

MACKEL Ezra dyin' sudden his first night to hum—that was durned queer!

SETH (*angrily*) It's durned queer old fools like you with one foot in the grave can't mind their own business in the little time left to 'em. That's what's queer!

MACKEL (*angry in his turn*) Wal, all I say is if they hadn't been Mannons with the town lickin' their boots, there'd have been queer doin's come out! And as fur me bein' an old fool, you're older an' a worse fool! An' your foot's deeper in the grave than mine be!

SETH (*shaking his fist in* MACKEL'S *face*) It ain't so deep but what I kin whale the stuffin' out o' you any day in the week!

SILVA (*comes between them*) Here, you old roosters! No fightin' allowed!

MACKEL (*subsiding grumpily*) This is a free country, ain't it? I got a right to my opinions!

AMES (*suddenly looking off down left*) Ssshh! Look, Seth! There's someone comin' up the drive.

SETH (*peering*) Ayeh! Who the hell—? It's Peter'n Hazel. Hide that jug, durn ye! (*The jug is hidden under the lilacs. A moment later,* HAZEL *and* PETER *enter. They stop in surprise on seeing* SETH *and his friends.* SETH *greets them self-consciously*) Good evenin'. I was just showin' some friends around—

PETER Hello, Seth. Just the man we're looking for. We've just had a telegram. Vinnie and Orin have landed in New York and— (*He is interrupted by a muffled yell of terror from the house. As they all turn to look, the front door is flung open and* SMALL *comes tearing out and down the portico steps, his face chalky white and his eyes popping*).

SMALL (*as he reaches them—terrifiedly*) God A'mighty! I heard 'em comin' after me, and I run in the room opposite, an' I seed Ezra's ghost dressed like a judge comin' through the wall—and, by God, I run! (*He jerks a bill out of his pocket and thrusts it on* SETH) Here's your money, durn ye! I wouldn't stay in there fur a million! (*This breaks the tension, and the old men give way to an hysterical, boisterous, drunken mirth, roaring with laughter, pounding each other on the back*).

PETER (*sharply*) What's this all about? What was he doing in there?

SETH (*controlling his laughter—embarrassedly*) Only a joke, Peter. (*Then turning on* SMALL—*scornfully*) That was Ezra's picture hangin' on the wall, not a ghost, ye durned idjut!

SMALL (*indignantly*) I know pictures when I see 'em an' I knowed him. This was him! Let's get out o' here. I've had enough of this durned place!

SETH You fellers trot along. I'll jine you later. (*They all mutter good evenings to* PETER *and* HAZEL *and go off, left front.* SMALL'S *excited voice can be heard receding as he begins to embroider on the horrors of his adventure.* SETH *turns to*

PETER *apologetically*) Abner Small's always braggin' how brave he is—so I bet him he dasn't stay in there—

HAZEL (*indignantly*) Seth! What would Vinnie say if she knew you did such things?

SETH There ain't no harm done. I calc'late Abner didn't break nothin'. And Vinnie wouldn't mind when she knew why I done it. I was aimin' to stop the durned gabbin' that's been goin' round town about this house bein' haunted. You've heard it, ain't ye?

PETER I heard some silly talk but didn't pay any attention—

SETH That durned idjut female I got in to clean a month after Vinnie and Orin sailed started it. Said she'd felt ghosts around. You know how them things grow. Seemed to me Abner's braggin' gave me a good chance to stop it by turnin' it all into a joke on him folks'd laugh at. An' when I git through tellin' my story of it round town tomorrow you'll find folks'll shet up and not take it serious no more.

PETER (*appreciatively*) You're right, Seth. That was a darned slick notion! Nothing like a joke to lay a ghost!

SETH Ayeh. But— (*He hesitates—then decides to say it*) Between you 'n' me 'n' the lamp-post, it ain't all sech a joke as it sounds—that about the hauntin', I mean.

PETER (*incredulously*) You aren't going to tell me you think the house is haunted too!

SETH (*grimly*) Mebbe, and mebbe not. All I know is I wouldn't stay in there all night if you was to give me the town!

HAZEL (*impressed but forcing a teasing tone*) Seth! I'm ashamed of you!

PETER First time I ever heard you say you were afraid of anything!

SETH There's times when a man's a darn fool not to be scared! Oh, don't git it in your heads I take stock in spirits trespassin' round in windin' sheets or no sech lunatic doin's. But there is sech a thing as evil spirit. An' I've felt it, goin' in there daytimes to see to things—like somethin' rottin' in the walls!

PETER Bosh!

SETH (*quietly*) 'Tain't bosh, Peter. There's been evil in that house since it was first built in hate—and it's kept growin' there ever since, as what's happened there has proved. You understand I ain't sayin' this to no one but you two. An' I'm only tellin' you fur one reason—because you're closer to Vinnie and Orin than anyone and you'd ought to persuade them, now they're back, not to live in it. (*He adds impressively*) Fur their own good! (*Then with a change of tone*) An' now I've got that off my chest, tell me about 'em. When are they comin'?

PETER Tomorrow. Vinnie asked us to open the house. So let's start right in.

SETH (*with evident reluctance*) You want to do it tonight?

HAZEL We must, Seth. We've got so little time. We can at least tidy up the rooms a little and get the furniture covers off.

SETH Wal, I'll go to the barn and git lanterns. There's candles in the house. (*He turns abruptly and goes off left between the lilacs and the house*).

HAZEL (*looking after him—uneasily*) I can't get over Seth acting so strangely.

PETER Don't mind him. It's rum and old age.

HAZEL (*shaking her head—slowly*) No. There is something queer about this house. I've always felt it, even before the General's death and her suicide. (*She shudders*) I can still see her sitting on that bench as she was that last night. She was so frightened of being alone. But I thought when Vinnie and Orin came back she would be all right. (*Then sadly*) Poor Orin! I'll never forget to my dying day the way he looked when we saw him at the funeral. I hardly recognized him, did you?

PETER No. He certainly was broken up.

HAZEL And the way he acted—like someone in a trance! I don't believe when Vinnie rushed him off on this trip to the East he knew what he was doing or where he was going or anything.

PETER A long voyage like that was the best thing to help them both forget.

HAZEL (*without conviction*) Yes. I suppose it was—but—(*She stops and sighs—then worriedly*) I wonder how Orin is. Vinnie's letters haven't said much about him, or herself, for that matter—only about the trip. (*She sees* SETH *approaching, whistling loudly, from left, rear, with two lighted lanterns*) Here's Seth. (*She walks up the steps to the portico.* PETER *follows her. She hesitates and stands looking at the house—in a low tone, almost of dread*) Seth was right. You feel something cold grip you the moment you set foot—

PETER Oh, nonsense! He's got you going, too! (*Then with a chuckle*) Listen to him whistling to keep his courage up! (SETH *comes in from the left. He hands one of the lanterns to* PETER).

SETH Here you be, Peter.

HAZEL Well, let's go in. You better come out to the kitchen and help me first, Peter. We ought to start a fire. (*They go in. There is a pause in which* PETER *can be heard opening windows behind the shutters in the downstairs rooms. Then silence. Then* LAVINIA *enters, coming up the drive from left, front, and stands regarding the house. One is at once aware of an extraordinary change in her. Her body, formerly so thin and undeveloped, has filled out. Her movements have lost their square-shouldered stiffness. She now bears a striking resemblance to her mother in every respect, even to being dressed in the green her mother had affected. She walks to the clump of lilacs and stands there staring at the house*).

LAVINIA (*turns back and calls coaxingly in the tone one would use to a child*) Don't stop there, Orin! What are you afraid of? Come on! (*He comes slowly and hesitatingly in from left, front. He carries himself woodenly erect now like a soldier. His movements and attitudes have the statue-like quality that was so marked in his father. He now wears a close-cropped beard in addition to his mustache, and this accentuates his resemblance to his father. The Mannon semblance of his face in repose to a mask is more pronounced than ever. He has grown dreadfully thin and his black suit hangs loosely on his body. His haggard swarthy face is set in a blank lifeless expression*).

LAVINIA (*glances at him uneasily—concealing her apprehension under a coaxing motherly tone*) You must be brave! This is the test! You have got to face it! (*Then anxiously as he makes no reply*) Do you feel you can—now we're here?

ORIN (*dully*) I'll be all right—with you.

LAVINIA (*takes his hand and pats it encouragingly*) That's all I wanted—to hear you say that. (*Turning to the house*) Look, I see a light through the shutters of the sitting-room. That must be Peter and Hazel. (*Then as she sees he still keeps his eyes averted from the house*) Why don't you look at the house? Are you afraid? (*Then sharply commanding*) Orin! I want you to look now! Do you hear me?

ORIN (*dully obedient*) Yes, Vinnie. (*He jerks his head around and stares at the house and draws a deep shuddering breath*).

LAVINIA (*her eyes on his face—as if she were willing her strength into him*) Well? You don't see any ghosts, do you? Tell me!

ORIN (*obediently*) No.

LAVINIA Because there are none! Tell me you know there are none, Orin!

ORIN (*as before*) Yes.

LAVINIA (*searches his face uneasily—then is apparently satisfied*) Come. Let's go in. We'll find Hazel and Peter and surprise them— (*She takes his arm and leads him to the steps. He walks like an automaton. When they reach the spot where his mother had sat moaning, the last time he had seen her alive* [*Act Five of "The Hunted"*] *he stops with a shudder*).

ORIN (*stammers—pointing*) It was here—she—the last time I saw her alive—

LAVINIA (*quickly, urging him on commandingly*) That is all past and finished! The dead have forgotten us! We've forgotten them! Come! (*He obeys woodenly. She gets him up the steps and they pass into the house*).

CURTAIN

SCENE TWO

Same as Act Two of "The Hunted"—The sitting-room in the Mannon house. PETER *has lighted two candles on the mantel and put the lantern on the table at front. In this dim, spotty light the room is full of shadows. It has the dead appearance of a room long shut up, and the covered furniture has a ghostly look. In the flickering candlelight the eyes of the Mannon portraits stare with a grim forbiddingness.*

LAVINIA *appears in the doorway at rear. In the lighted room, the change in her is strikingly apparent. At a first glance, one would mistake her for her mother as she appeared in the First Act of "Homecoming." She seems a mature woman, sure of her feminine attractiveness. Her brown-gold hair is arranged as her mother's had been. Her green dress is like a copy of her mother's in Act One of "Homecoming." She comes forward slowly. The movements of her body now have the feminine grace her mother's had possessed. Her eyes are caught by the eyes of the Mannons in the portraits and she approaches as if compelled in spite of herself until she stands directly under them in front of the fireplace. She suddenly addresses them in a harsh resentful voice*).

LAVINIA Why do you look at me like that? I've done my duty by you! That's finished and forgotten! (*She tears her eyes from theirs and, turning away, becomes aware that* ORIN *has not followed her into the room, and is immediately frightened and uneasy and hurries toward the door, calling*) Orin!

ORIN (*his voice comes from the dark hall*) I'm here.

LAVINIA What are you doing out there? Come here! (ORIN *appears in the doorway. His face wears a dazed expression and his eyes have a wild, stricken look. He hurries to her as if seeking protection. She exclaims frightenedly*) Orin! What is it?

ORIN (*strangely*) I've just been in the study. I was sure she'd be waiting for me in there, where— (*Torturedly*) But she wasn't! She isn't anywhere. It's only they— (*He points to the portraits*) They're everywhere! But she's gone forever. She'll never forgive me now!

LAVINIA (*harshly*) Orin! Will you be quiet!

ORIN (*unheeding—with a sudden turn to bitter resentful defiance*) Well, let her go! What is she to me? I'm not her son any more! I'm Father's! I'm a Mannon! And they'll welcome me home!

LAVINIA (*angrily commanding*) Stop it, do you hear me!

ORIN (*shocked back to awareness by her tone—pitifully confused*) I—I didn't—don't be angry, Vinnie!

LAVINIA (*soothing him now*) I'm not angry, dear—only do get hold of yourself and be brave. (*Leading him to the sofa*) Here. Come. Let's sit down for a moment, shall we, and get used to being home? (*They sit down. She puts an arm around him reproachfully*) Don't you know how terribly you frighten me when you act so strangely? You don't mean to hurt me, do you?

ORIN (*deeply moved*) God knows I don't, Vinnie! You're all I have in the world! (*He takes her hand and kisses it humbly*).

LAVINIA (*soothingly*) That's a good boy. (*Then with a cheerful matter-of-fact note*) Hazel and Peter must be back in the kitchen. Won't you be glad to see Hazel again?

ORIN (*dully now*) You've kept talking about them all the voyage home. Why? What can they have to do with us—now?

LAVINIA A lot. What we need most is to get back to simple normal things and begin a new life. And their friendship and love will help us more than anything to forget.

ORIN (*with sudden harshness*) Forget? I thought you'd forgotten long ago—if you ever remembered, which you never seemed to! (*Then with somber bitterness*) Love! What right have I—or you—to love?

LAVINIA (*defiantly*) Every right!

ORIN (*grimly*) Mother felt the same about— (*Then with a strange, searching glance at her*) You don't know how like Mother you've become, Vinnie. I don't mean only how pretty you've gotten—

LAVINIA (*with a strange shy eagerness*) Do you really think I'm as pretty now as she was, Orin?

ORIN (*as if she hadn't interrupted*) I mean the change in your soul, too. I've watched it ever since we sailed for the East. Little by little it grew like Mother's soul—as if you were stealing hers—as if her death had set you free—to become her!

LAVINIA (*uneasily*) Now don't begin talking nonsense again, please!

ORIN (*grimly*) Don't you believe in souls any more? I think you will after we've lived in this house awhile! The Mannon dead will convert you. (*He turns to the portraits mockingly*) Ask them if I'm not right!

LAVINIA (*sharply*) Orin! What's come over you? You haven't had one of these morbid spells since we left the Islands. You swore to me you were all over them, or I'd never have agreed to come home.

ORIN (*with a strange malicious air*) I had to get you away from the Islands. My brotherly duty! If you'd stayed there much longer. (*He chuckles disagreeably*).

LAVINIA (*with a trace of confusion*) I don't know what you're talking about. I only went there for your sake.

ORIN (*with another chuckle*) Yes—but afterwards—

LAVINIA (*sharply*) You promised you weren't going to talk any more morbid nonsense. (*He subsides meekly. She goes on reproachfully*) Remember all I've gone through on your account. For months after we sailed you didn't know what you were doing. I had to live in constant fear of what you might say. I wouldn't live through those horrible days again for anything on earth. And remember this homecoming is what you wanted. You told me that if you could come home and face your ghosts, you knew you could rid yourself forever of your silly guilt about the past.

ORIN (*dully*) I know, Vinnie.

LAVINIA And I believed you, you seemed so certain of yourself. But now you've suddenly become strange again. You frighten me. So much depends on how you start in, now we're home. (*Then sharply commanding*) Listen, Orin! I want you to start again—by facing all your ghosts right now! (*He turns and his eyes remain fixed on hers from now on. She asks sternly*) Who murdered Father?

ORIN (*falteringly*) Brant did—for revenge because—

LAVINIA (*more sternly*) Who murdered Father? Answer me!

ORIN (*with a shudder*) Mother was under his influence—

LAVINIA That's a lie! It was he who was under hers. You know the truth!

ORIN Yes.

LAVINIA She was an adulteress and a murderess, wasn't she?

ORIN Yes.

LAVINIA If we'd done our duty under the law, she would have been hanged, wouldn't she?

ORIN Yes.

LAVINIA But we protected her. She could have lived, couldn't she? But she chose to kill herself as a punishment for her crime—of her own free will! It was an act of justice! You had nothing to do with it! You see that now, don't you? (*As he hesitates, trembling violently, she grabs his arm fiercely*) Tell me!

ORIN (*hardly above a whisper*) Yes.

LAVINIA And your feeling of being responsible for her death was only your morbid imagination! You don't feel it now! You'll never feel it again!

ORIN No.

LAVINIA (*gratefully—and weakly because the strength she has willed into him has left her exhausted*) There! You see! You can do it when you will to! (*She kisses him. He breaks down, sobbing weakly against her breast. She soothes him*) There! Don't cry! You ought to feel proud. You've proven you can laugh at your ghosts from now on. (*Then briskly, to distract his mind*) Come now. Help me to take off these furniture covers. We might as well start making ourselves useful. (*She starts to work. For a moment he helps. Then he goes to one of the windows and pushes back a shutter and stands staring out.* PETER *comes in the door from rear. At the sight of* LAVINIA *he stops startledly, thinks for a second it is her mother's ghost and gives an exclamation of dread. At the same moment she sees him. She stares at him with a strange eager possessiveness. She calls softly*).

LAVINIA Peter! (*She goes toward him, smiling as her mother might have smiled*) Don't you know me any more, Peter?

PETER (*stammers*) Vinnie! I—I thought you were—! I can't realize it's you! You've grown so like your— (*Checking himself awkwardly*) I mean you've changed so—and we weren't looking for you until— (*He takes her hand automatically, staring at her stupidly*).

LAVINIA I know. We had intended to stay in New York tonight but we decided later we'd better come right home. (*Then taking him in with a smiling appreciative possessiveness*) Let me look at you, Peter. You haven't gone and changed, have you? No, you're the same, thank goodness! I've been thinking of you all the way home and wondering—I was so afraid you might have.

PETER (*plucking up his courage—blurts out*) You—you ought to know I'd never change—with you! (*Then, alarmed by his own boldness, he hastily looks away from her*).

LAVINIA (*teasingly*) But you haven't said yet you're glad to see me!

PETER (*has turned back and is staring fascinatedly at her. A surge of love and desire overcomes his timidity and he bursts out*) I—you know how much I—! (*Then he turns away again in confusion and takes refuge in a burst of talk*) Gosh, Vinnie, you ought to have given us more warning. We've only just started to open the place up. I was with Hazel, in the kitchen, starting a fire—

LAVINIA (*laughing softly*) Yes. You're the same old Peter! You're still afraid of me. But you mustn't be now. I know I used to be an awful old stick, but—

PETER Who said so? You were not! (*Then with enthusiasm*) Gosh, you look so darned pretty—and healthy. Your trip certainly did you good! (*Staring at her again, drinking her in*) I can't get over seeing you dressed in color. You always used to wear black.

LAVINIA (*with a strange smile*) I was dead then.

PETER You ought always to wear color.

LAVINIA (*immensely pleased*) Do you think so?

PETER Yes. It certainly is becoming. I— (*Then embarrassedly changing the subject*) But where's Orin?

LAVINIA (*turning to look around*) Why, he was right here. (*She sees him at the window*) Orin, what are you doing there? Here's Peter. (ORIN *closes the shutter he has pushed open and turns back from the window. He comes forward, his eyes fixed in a strange preoccupation, as if he were unaware of their presence.* LAVINIA *watches him uneasily and speaks sharply*) Don't you see Peter? Why don't you speak to him? You mustn't be so rude.

PETER (*good-naturedly*) Give him a chance. Hello, Orin. Darned glad to see you back. (*They shake hands.* PETER *has difficulty in hiding his pained surprise at* ORIN'S *sickly appearance*).

ORIN (*rousing himself, forces a smile and makes an effort at his old friendly manner with* PETER) Hello, Peter. You know I'm glad to see you without any polite palaver. Vinnie is the same old bossy fuss-buzzer—you remember—always trying to teach me manners!

PETER You bet I remember! But say, hasn't she changed, though? I didn't know her, she's grown so fat! And I was just telling her how well she looked in color. Don't you agree?

ORIN (*in a sudden strange tone of jeering malice*) Did you ask her why she stole Mother's colors? I can't see why—yet—and I don't think she knows herself. But it will prove a strange reason, I'm certain of that, when I do discover it!

LAVINIA (*making a warning sign to* PETER *not to take this seriously—forcing a smile*) Don't mind him, Peter.

ORIN (*his tone becoming sly, insinuating and mocking*) And she's become romantic! Imagine that! Influence of the "dark and deep blue ocean"—and of the Islands, eh, Vinnie?

PETER (*surprised*) You stopped at the Islands?

ORIN Yes. We took advantage of our being on a Mannon ship to make the captain touch there on the way back. We stopped a month. (*With resentful bitterness*) But they turned out to be Vinnie's islands, not mine. They only made me sick—and the naked women disgusted me. I guess I'm too much of a Mannon, after all, to turn into a pagan. But you should have seen Vinnie with the men—!

LAVINIA (*indignantly but with a certain guiltiness*) How can you—!

ORIN (*jeeringly*) Handsome and romantic-looking, weren't they, Vinnie?—with colored rags around their middles and flowers stuck over their ears! Oh, she was a bit shocked at first by their dances, but afterwards she fell in love with the Islanders. If we'd stayed another month, I know I'd have found her some moonlight night dancing under the palm trees—as naked as the rest!

LAVINIA Orin! Don't be disgusting!

ORIN (*points to the portraits mockingly*) Picture, if you can, the feelings of the God-fearing Mannon dead at that spectacle!

LAVINIA (*with an anxious glance at* PETER) How can you make up such disgusting fibs?

ORIN (*with a malicious chuckle*) Oh, I wasn't as blind as I pretended to be! Do you remember Avahanni?

LAVINIA (*angrily*) Stop talking like a fool! (*He subsides meekly again. She forces a smile and a motherly tone*) You're a naughty boy, do you know it? What will Peter think? Of course, he knows you're only teasing me—but you shouldn't go on like that. It isn't nice. (*Then changing the subject abruptly*) Why don't you go and find Hazel? Here. Let me look at you. I want you to look your best when she sees you. (*She arranges him as a mother would a boy, pulling down his coat, giving a touch to his shirt and tie.* ORIN *straightens woodenly to a soldierly attention. She is vexed by this*) Don't stand like a ramrod! You'd be so handsome if you'd only shave off that silly beard and not carry yourself like a tin soldier!

ORIN (*with a sly cunning air*) Not look so much like Father, eh? More like a romantic clipper captain, is that it? (*As she starts and stares at him frightenedly, he smiles an ugly taunting smile*) Don't look so frightened, Vinnie!

LAVINIA (*with an apprehensive glance at* PETER—*pleading and at the same time warning*) Ssshh! You weren't to talk nonsense, remember! (*Giving him a final pat*) There! Now run along to Hazel.

ORIN (*looks from her to* PETER *suspiciously*) You seem damned anxious to get rid of me. (*He turns and stalks stiffly with hurt dignity from the room.* LAVINIA *turns to* PETER. *The strain of* ORIN'S *conduct has told on her. She seems suddenly weak and frightened*)

PETER (*in shocked amazement*) What's come over him?

LAVINIA (*in a strained voice*) It's the same thing—what the war did to him—and on top of that Father's death—and the shock of Mother's suicide.

PETER (*puts his arm around her impulsively—comfortingly*) It'll be all right! Don't worry, Vinnie!

LAVINIA (*nestling against him gratefully*) Thank you, Peter. You're so good. (*Then looking into his eyes*) Do you still love me, Peter?

PETER Don't have to ask that, do you? (*He squeezes her*

awkwardly—then stammers) But do you—think now—you maybe—can love me?

LAVINIA Yes!

PETER You really mean that!

LAVINIA Yes! I do! I've thought of you so much! Things were always reminding me of you—the ship and the sea—everything that was honest and clean! And the natives on the Islands reminded me of you too. They were so simple and fine— (*Then hastily*) You mustn't mind what Orin was saying about the Islands. He's become a regular bigoted Mannon.

PETER (*amazed*) But, Vinnie—!

LAVINIA Oh, I know it must sound funny hearing me talk like that. But remember I'm only half Mannon. (*She looks at the portraits defiantly*) And I've done my duty by them! They can't say I haven't!

PETER (*mystified but happy*) Gosh, you certainly have changed! But I'm darned glad!

LAVINIA Orin keeps teasing that I was flirting with that native he spoke about, simply because he used to smile at me and I smiled back.

PETER (*teasingly*) Now, I'm beginning to get jealous, too.

LAVINIA You mustn't. He made me think of you. He made me dream of marrying you—and everything.

PETER Oh, well then, I take it all back! I owe him a vote of thanks! (*He hugs her*).

LAVINIA (*dreamily*) I loved those Islands. They finished setting me free. There was something there mysterious and beautiful—a good spirit—of love—coming out of the land and sea. It made me forget death. There was no hereafter. There was only this world—the warm earth in the moonlight—the trade wind in the coco palms—the surf on the reef—the fires at night and the drum throbbing in my heart—the natives dancing naked and innocent—without knowledge of sin! (*She checks herself abruptly and frightenedly*) But what in the world! I'm gabbing on like a regular chatterbox. You must think I've become awfully scatter-brained!

PETER (*with a chuckle*) Gosh no! I'm glad you've grown that way! You never used to say a word unless you had to!

LAVINIA (*suddenly filled with grateful love for him, lets herself go and throws her arms around him*) Oh, Peter, hold me close to you! I want to feel love! Love is all beautiful! I never used to know that! I was a fool! (*She kisses him pas-*

sionately. He returns it, aroused and at the same time a little shocked by her boldness. She goes on longingly) We'll be married soon, won't we, and settle out in the country away from folks and their evil talk. We'll make an island for ourselves on land, and we'll have children and love them and teach them to love life so that they can never be possessed by hate and death! (*She gives a start—in a whisper as if to herself*) But I'm forgetting Orin!

PETER What's Orin got to do with us marrying?

LAVINIA I can't leave him—until he's all well again. I'd be afraid—

PETER Let him live with us.

LAVINIA (*with sudden intensity*) No! I want to be rid of the past. (*Then after a quick look at him—in a confiding tone*) I want to tell you what's wrong with Orin—so you and Hazel can help me. He feels guilty about Mother killing herself. You see, he'd had a quarrel with her that last night. He was jealous and mad and said things he was sorry for after and it preyed on his mind until he blames himself for her death.

PETER But that's crazy!

LAVINIA I know it is, Peter, but you can't do anything with him when he gets his morbid spells. Oh, I don't mean he's the way he is tonight most of the time. Usually he's like himself, only quiet and sad—so sad it breaks my heart to see him—like a little boy who's been punished for something he didn't do. Please tell Hazel what I've told you, so she'll make allowances for any crazy thing he might say.

PETER I'll warn her. And now don't you worry any more about him. We'll get him all right again one way or another.

LAVINIA (*again grateful for his simple goodness—lovingly*) Bless you, Peter! (*She kisses him. As she does so,* HAZEL *and* ORIN *appear in the doorway at rear.* HAZEL *is a bit shocked, then smiles happily.* ORIN *starts as if he'd been struck. He glares at them with jealous rage and clenches his fists as if he were going to attack them*).

HAZEL (*with a teasing laugh*) I'm afraid we're interrupting, Orin. (PETER *and* VINNIE *jump apart in confusion*).

ORIN (*threateningly*) So that's it! By God—!

LAVINIA (*frightened but managing to be stern*) Orin!

ORIN (*pulls himself up sharply—confusedly, forcing a sickly smile*) Don't be so solemn—Fuss Buzzer! I was only trying to scare you—for a joke! (*Turning to* PETER *and holding out his hand, his smile becoming ghastly*) I suppose congratulations are in order. I—I'm glad. (PETER *takes his hand awkwardly.* HAZEL *moves toward* LAVINIA *to greet her, her face full of an uneasy bewilderment.* LAVINIA *stares at* ORIN *with eyes full of dread*).

CURTAIN

ACT TWO

SCENE—*Same as Act Three of "The Hunted"*—EZRA MANNON'S *study—on an evening a month later. The shutters of the windows are closed. Candles on the mantel above the fireplace light up the portrait of* EZRA MANNON *in his judge's robes.* ORIN *is sitting in his father's chair at left of table, writing by the light of a lamp. A small pile of manuscript is stacked by his right hand. He is intent on his work. He has aged in the intervening month. He looks almost as old now as his father in the portrait. He is dressed in black and the resemblance between the two is uncanny. A grim smile of satisfaction twitches his lips as he stops writing and reads over the paragraph he has just finished. Then he puts the sheet down and stares up at the portrait, sitting back in his chair.*

ORIN (*sardonically, addressing the portrait*) The truth, the whole truth and nothing but the truth! Is that what you're demanding, Father? Are you sure you want the whole truth? What will the neighbors say if this whole truth is ever known? (*He chuckles grimly*) A ticklish decision for you, Your Honor! (*There is a knock on the door. He hastily grabs the script and puts it in the drawer of the desk*) Who's there?

LAVINIA It's I.

ORIN (*hastily locking the drawer and putting the key in his pocket*) What do you want?

LAVINIA (*sharply*) Please open the door!

ORIN All right. In a minute. (*He hurriedly straightens up the table and grabs a book at random from the bookcase and lays it open on the table as if he had been reading. Then he unlocks the door and comes back to his chair as* LAVINIA *enters. She wears a green velvet gown similar to that worn by* CHRISTINE *in Act Three of "Homecoming." It sets off her hair and eyes. She is obviously concealing beneath a surface calm a sense of dread and desperation*).

LAVINIA (*glances at him suspiciously, but forces a casual air*) Why did you lock yourself in? (*She comes over to the table*) What are you doing?

ORIN Reading.

LAVINIA (*picks up the book*) Father's law books?

ORIN (*mockingly*) Why not? I'm considering studying law. He wanted me to, if you remember.

LAVINIA Do you expect me to believe that, Orin? What is it you're really doing?

ORIN Curious, aren't you?

LAVINIA (*forcing a smile*) Good gracious, why wouldn't I be? You've acted so funny lately, locking yourself in here with the blinds closed and the lamp burning even in the daytime. It isn't good for you staying in this stuffy room in this weather. You ought to get out in the fresh air.

ORIN (*harshly*) I hate the daylight. It's like an accusing eye! No, we've renounced the day, in which normal people live —or rather it has renounced us. Perpetual night—darkness of death in life—that's the fitting habitat for guilt! You believe you can escape that, but I'm not so foolish!

LAVINIA Now you're being stupid again!

ORIN And I find artificial light more appropriate for my work—man's light, not God's—man's feeble striving to understand himself, to exist for himself in the darkness! It's a symbol of his life—a lamp burning out in a room of waiting shadows!

LAVINIA (*sharply*) Your work? What work?

ORIN (*mockingly*) Studying the law of crime and punishment, as you saw.

LAVINIA (*forcing a smile again and turning away from him*) All right, if you won't tell me. Go on being mysterious, if you like. (*In a tense voice*) It's so close in here! It's suffocating! It's bad for you! (*She goes to the window and throws the shutters open and looks out*) It's black as pitch tonight. There isn't a star.

ORIN (*somberly*) Darkness without a star to guide us! Where are we going, Vinnie? (*Then with a mocking chuckle*) Oh, I know you think you know where you're going, but there's many a slip, remember!

LAVINIA (*her voice strident, as if her will were snapping*) Be quiet! Can't you think of anything but —(*Then controlling herself, comes to him—gently*) I'm sorry. I'm terribly nervous tonight. It's the heat, I guess. And you get me so worried with your incessant brooding over the past. It's the worst thing for your health. (*She pats him on the arm—soothingly*) That's all I'm thinking about, dear.

ORIN Thank you for your anxiety about my health! But I'm afraid there isn't much hope for you there! I happen to feel quite well!

LAVINIA (*whirling on him—distractedly*) How can you insinuate such horrible—! (*Again controlling herself with a great effort, forcing a smile*) But you're only trying to rile me—and I'm not going to let you. I'm so glad you're feeling better. You ate a good supper tonight—for you. The long walk we took with Hazel did you good.

ORIN (*dully*) Yes. (*He slumps down in his chair at left of table*) Why is it you never leave me alone with her more than a minute? You approved of my asking her to marry me—and now we're engaged you never leave us alone! (*Then with a bitter smile*) But I know the reason well enough. You're afraid I'll let something slip.

LAVINIA (*sits in the chair opposite him—wearily*) Can you blame me, the way you've been acting?

ORIN (*somberly*) No. I'm afraid myself of being too long alone with her—afraid of myself. I have no right in the same world with her. And yet I feel so drawn to her purity! Her love for me makes me appear less vile to myself! (*Then with a harsh laugh*) And, at the same time, a million times more vile, that's the hell of it! So I'm afraid you can't hope to get rid of me through Hazel. She's another lost island! It's wiser for you to keep Hazel away from me, I warn you. Because when I see love for a murderer in her eyes my guilt crowds up in my throat like poisonous vomit and I long to spit it out—and confess!

LAVINIA (*in a low voice*) Yes, that is what I live in terror of—that in one of your fits you'll say something before someone—now after it's all past and forgotten—when there isn't the slightest suspicion—

ORIN (*harshly*) Were you hoping you could escape retribution? You can't! Confess and atone to the full extent of the law! That's the only way to wash the guilt of our mother's blood from our souls!

LAVINIA (*distractedly*) Ssshh! Will you stop!

ORIN Ask our father, the Judge, if it isn't! He knows! He keeps telling me!

LAVINIA Oh, God! Over and over and over! Will you never lose your stupid guilty conscience! Don't you see how you torture me? You're becoming my guilty conscience, too! (*With an instinctive flare-up of her old jealousy*) How can you still love that vile woman so—when you know all she wanted was to leave you without a thought and marry that—

ORIN (*with fierce accusation*) Yes! Exactly as you're scheming now to leave me and marry Peter! But, by God, you won't!

You'll damn soon stop your tricks when you know what I've been writing!

LAVINIA (*tensely*) What have you written?

ORIN (*his anger turned to gloating satisfaction*) Ah! That frightens you, does it? Well, you better be frightened!

LAVINIA Tell me what you've written!

ORIN None of your damned business.

LAVINIA I've got to know!

ORIN Well, as I've practically finished it—I suppose I might as well tell you. At his earnest solicitation— (*He waves a hand to the portrait mockingly*) as the last male Mannon—thank God for that, eh!—I've been writing the history of our family! (*He adds with a glance at the portrait and a malicious chuckle*) But I don't wish to convey that he approves of all I've set down—not by a damned sight!

LAVINIA (*trying to keep calm—tensely*) What kind of history do you mean?

ORIN A true history of all the family crimes, beginning with Grandfather Abe's—all of the crimes, including ours, do you understand?

LAVINIA (*aghast*) Do you mean to tell me you've actually written—

ORIN Yes! I've tried to trace to its secret hiding place in the Mannon past the evil destiny behind our lives! I thought if I could see it clearly in the past I might be able to foretell what fate is in store for us, Vinnie—but I haven't dared predict that—not yet—although I can guess— (*He gives a sinister chuckle*).

LAVINIA Orin!

ORIN Most of what I've written is about you! I found you the most interesting criminal of us all!

LAVINIA (*breaking*) How can you say such dreadful things to me, after all I—

ORIN (*as if he hadn't heard—inexorably*) So many strange hidden things out of the Mannon past combine in you! For one example, do you remember the first mate, Wilkins, on the voyage to Frisco? Oh, I know you thought I was in a stupor of grief—but I wasn't blind! I saw how you wanted him!

LAVINIA (*angrily, but with a trace of guilty confusion*) I never gave him a thought! He was an officer of the ship to me, and nothing more!

ORIN (*mockingly*) Adam Brant was a ship's officer, too, wasn't he? Wilkins reminded you of Brant—

LAVINIA No!

ORIN And that's why you suddenly discarded mourning in Frisco and bought new clothes—in Mother's colors!

LAVINIA (*furiously*) Stop talking about her! You'd think, to hear you, I had no life of my own!

ORIN You wanted Wilkins just as you'd wanted Brant!

LAVINIA That's a lie!

ORIN You're doing the lying! You know damned well that behind all your pretense about Mother's murder being an act of justice was your jealous hatred! She warned me of that and I see it clearly now! You wanted Brant for yourself!

LAVINIA (*fiercely*) It's a lie! I hated him!

ORIN Yes, after you knew he was her lover! (*He chuckles with a sinister mockery*) But we'll let that pass for the present—I know it's the last thing you could ever admit to yourself!—and come to what I've written about your adventures on my lost islands. Or should I say, Adam Brant's islands! He had been there too, if you'll remember! Probably he'd lived with one of the native women! He was that kind! Were you thinking of that when we were there?

LAVINIA (*chokingly*) Stop it! I—I warn you—I won't bear it much longer!

ORIN (*as if he hadn't heard—in the same sinister mocking tone*) What a paradise the Islands were for you, eh? All those handsome men staring at you and your strange beautiful hair! It was then you finally became pretty—like Mother! You knew they all desired you, didn't you? It filled you with pride! Especially Avahanni! You watched him stare at your body through your clothes, stripping you naked! And you wanted him!

LAVINIA No!

ORIN Don't lie! (*He accuses her with fierce jealousy*) What did you do with him the night I was sick and you went to watch their shameless dance? Something happened between you! I saw your face when you came back and stood with him in front of our hut!

LAVINIA (*quietly—with simple dignity now*) I had kissed him good night, that was all—in gratitude! He was innocent and good. He had made me feel for the first time in my life that everything about love could be sweet and natural.

ORIN So you kissed him, did you? And that was all?

LAVINIA (*with a sudden flare of deliberately evil taunting that recalls her mother in the last act of "Homecoming," when she was goading Ezra Mannon to fury just before his murder*)

And what if it wasn't? I'm not your property! I have a right to love!

ORIN (*reacting as his father had—his face grown livid—with a hoarse cry of fury grabs her by the throat*) You—you whore! I'll kill you! (*Then suddenly he breaks down and becomes weak and pitiful*) No! You're lying about him, aren't you? For God's sake, tell me you're lying, Vinnie!

LAVINIA (*strangely shaken and trembling—stammers*) Yes —it was a lie—how could you believe I—Oh, Orin, something made me say that to you—against my will—something rose up in me—like an evil spirit!

ORIN (*laughs wildly*) Ghosts! You never seemed so much like Mother as you did just then!

LAVINIA (*pleading distractedly*) Don't talk about it! Let's forget it ever happened! Forgive me! Please forget it!

ORIN All right—if the ghosts will let us forget! (*He stares at her fixedly for a moment—then satisfied*) I believe you about Avahanni. I never really suspected, or I'd have killed him—and you, too! I hope you know that! (*Then with his old obsessed insistence*) But you were guilty in your mind just the same!

LAVINIA (*in a flash of distracted anger*) Stop harping on that! Stop torturing me or I—! I've warned you! I warn you again! I can't bear any more! I won't!

ORIN (*with a mocking diabolical sneer—quietly*) Then why don't you murder me? I'll help you plan it, as we planned Brant's, so there will be no suspicion on you! And I'll be grateful! I loathe my life!

LAVINIA (*speechless with horror—can only gasp*) Oh!

ORIN (*with a quiet mad insistence*) Can't you see I'm now in Father's place and you're Mother? That's the evil destiny out of the past I haven't dared predict! I'm the Mannon you're chained to! So isn't it plain—

LAVINIA (*putting her hands over her ears*) For God's sake, won't you be quiet! (*Then suddenly her horror turning into a violent rage—unconsciously repeating the exact threat she had goaded her mother to make to her in Act Two of "Homecoming"*) Take care, Orin! You'll be responsible if—! (*She stops abruptly, terrified by her own words*).

ORIN (*with a diabolical mockery*) If what? If I should die mysteriously of heart failure?

LAVINIA Leave me alone! Leave me alone! Don't keep saying that! How can you be so terrible? Don't you know I'm your sister, who loves you, who would give her life to bring you peace?

ORIN (*with a change to a harsh threatening tone*) I don't believe you! I know you're plotting something! But you look out! I'll be watching you! And I warn you I won't stand your leaving me for Peter! I'm going to put this confession I've written in safe hands—to be read in case you try to marry him—or if I should die—

LAVINIA (*frantically grabbing his arm and shaking him fiercely*) Stop having such thoughts! Stop making me have them! You're like a devil torturing me! I won't listen! (*She breaks down and sobs brokenly.* ORIN *stares at her dazedly—seems half to come back to his natural self and the wild look fades from his eyes leaving them glazed and lifeless*).

ORIN (*strangely*) Don't cry. The damned don't cry. (*He slumps down heavily in his father's chair and stares at the floor. Suddenly he says harshly again*) Go away, will you? I want to be alone—to finish my work. (*Still sobbing, her hand over her eyes,* LAVINIA *feels blindly for the door and goes out closing it after her.* ORIN *unlocks the table drawer, pulls out his manuscript, and takes up his pen*).

CURTAIN

ACT THREE

SCENE—*Same as Act One, Scene Two—the sitting-room. The lamp on the table is lighted but turned low. Two candles are burning on the mantel over the fireplace at right, shedding their flickering light on the portrait of* ABE MANNON *above, and of the other Mannons on the walls on each side of him. The eyes of the portraits seem to possess an intense bitter life, with their frozen stare "looking over the head of life, cutting it dead for the impropriety of living," as* ORIN *had said of his father in Act Two of "The Hunted."*

No time has elapsed since the preceding act. LAVINIA *enters from the hall in the rear, having just come from the study. She comes to the table and turns up the lamp. She is in a terrific state of tension. The corners of her mouth twitch, she twines and untwines the fingers of her clasped hands with a slow wringing movement which recalls her mother in the last Act of "The Hunted."*

LAVINIA (*torturedly—begins to pace up and down, muttering her thoughts aloud*) I can't bear it! Why does he keep putting his death in my head? He would be better off if— Why hasn't he the courage—? (*Then in a frenzy of remorseful anguish, her eyes unconsciously seeking the Mannon portraits on the right wall, as if they were the visible symbol of her God*) Oh, God, don't let me have such thoughts! You know I love Orin! Show me the way to save him! Don't let me think of death! I couldn't bear another death! Please! Please (*At a noise from the hall she controls herself and pretends to be glancing through a book on the table.* SETH *appears in the doorway*).

SETH Vinnie!

LAVINIA What is it, Seth?

SETH That durned idjut, Hannah, is throwin' fits agin. Went down cellar and says she felt ha'nts crawlin' behind her. You'd better come and git her calmed down—or she'll be leavin'. (*Then he adds disgustedly*) That's what we git fur freein' 'em!

LAVINIA (*wearily*) All right. I'll talk to her. (*She goes out with* SETH. *A pause. Then a ring from the front door bell. A moment later* SETH *can be seen coming back along the hall. He opens the front door and is heard greeting* HAZEL *and* PETER *and follows them in as they enter the room*).

SETH Vinnie's back seein' to somethin'. You set down and she'll be here soon as she kin.

PETER All right, Seth. (SETH *goes out again. They come forward and sit down.* PETER *looks hearty and good-natured, the same as ever, but* HAZEL'S *face wears a nervous, uneasy look although her air is determined*).

PETER I'll have to run along soon and drop in at the Council meeting. I can't get out of it. I'll be back in half an hour—maybe sooner.

HAZEL (*suddenly with a little shiver*) I hate this house now. I hate coming here. If it wasn't for Orin—He's getting worse. Keeping him shut up here is the worst thing Vinnie could do.

PETER He won't go out. You know very well she has to force him to walk with you.

HAZEL And comes along herself! Never leaves him alone hardly a second!

PETER (*with a grin*) Oh, that's what you've got against her, eh?

HAZEL (*sharply*) Don't be silly, Peter! I simply think, and I'd say it to her face, that she's a bad influence for Orin! I feel there's something awfully wrong—somehow. He scares me at times—and Vinnie—I've watched her looking at you. She's changed so. There's something bold about her.

PETER (*getting up*) If you're going to talk like that—! You ought to be ashamed, Hazel!

HAZEL Well, I'm not! I've got some right to say something about how he's cared for! And I'm going to from now on! I'm going to make her let him visit us for a spell. I've asked Mother and she'll be glad to have him.

PETER Say, I think that's a darned good notion for both of them. She needs a rest from him, too.

HAZEL Vinnie doesn't think it's a good notion! I mentioned it yesterday and she gave me such a look! (*Determinedly*) But I'm going to make him promise to come over tomorrow, no matter what she says!

PETER (*soothingly, patting her shoulder*) Don't get angry now—about nothing. I'll help you persuade her to let him come. (*Then with a grin*) I'll help you do anything to help Orin get well—if only for selfish reasons. As long as Vinnie's tied down to him we can't get married.

HAZEL (*stares at him—slowly*) Do you really want to marry her—now?

PETER Why do you ask such a fool question? What do you mean, do I want to now?

HAZEL (*her voice trembles and she seems about to burst into tears*) Oh, I don't know, Peter! I don't know!

PETER (*sympathetic and at the same time exasperated*) What in the dickens is the matter with you?

HAZEL (*hears a noise from the hall and collects herself—warningly*) Ssshh! (ORIN *appears in the doorway at rear. He glances at them, then quickly around the room to see if* LAVINIA *is there. They both greet him with "Hello, Orin"*).

ORIN Hello! (*Then in an excited whisper, coming to them*) Where's Vinnie?

HAZEL She's gone to see to something, Seth said.

PETER (*glancing at his watch*) Gosh, I've got to hurry to that darned Council meeting.

ORIN (*eagerly*) You're going?

PETER (*jokingly*) You needn't look so darned tickled about it! It isn't polite!

ORIN I've got to see Hazel alone!

PETER All right! You don't have to put me out! (*He grins, slapping* ORIN *on the back and goes out.* ORIN *follows him with his eyes until he hears the front door close behind him*).

ORIN (*turning to* HAZEL*—with queer furtive excitement*) Listen, Hazel! I want you to do something! But wait! I've got to get— (*He rushes out and can be heard going across the hall to the study.* HAZEL *looks after him worriedly. A moment later he hurries back with a big sealed envelope in his hand which he gives to* HAZEL, *talking breathlessly, with nervous jerks of his head, as he glances apprehensively at the door*) Here! Take this! Quick! Don't let her see it! I want you to keep it in a safe place and never let anyone know you have it! It will be stolen if I keep it here! I know her! Will you promise?

HAZEL But—what is it, Orin?

ORIN I can't tell you. You mustn't ask me. And you must promise never to open it—unless something happens to me.

HAZEL (*frightened by his tone*) What do you mean?

ORIN I mean if I should die—or—but this is the most important, if she tries to marry Peter—the day before the wedding—I want you to make Peter read what's inside.

HAZEL You don't want her to marry Peter?

ORIN No! She can't have happiness! She's got to be punished! (*Suddenly taking her hand—excitedly*) And listen, Hazel! You mustn't love me any more. The only love I can know now is the love of guilt for guilt which breeds more guilt—until you get so deep at the bottom of hell there is no lower you can sink and you rest there in peace! (*He laughs harshly and turns away from her*).

HAZEL Orin! Don't talk like that! (*Then conquering her horror—resolutely tender and soothing*) Ssshh! Poor boy! Come here to me. (*He comes to her. She puts an arm around him*) Listen. I know something is worrying you—and I don't want to seem prying—but I've had such a strong feeling at times that it would relieve your mind if you could tell me what it is. Haven't you thought that, Orin?

ORIN (*longingly*) Yes! Yes! I want to confess to your purity! I want to be forgiven! (*Then checking himself abruptly as he is about to speak—dully*) No. I can't. Don't ask me. I love her.

HAZEL But, you silly boy, Vinnie told Peter herself what it is and told him to tell me.

ORIN (*staring at her wildly*) What did she tell?

HAZEL About your having a quarrel with your poor mother that night before she—and how you've brooded over it until you blame yourself for her death.

ORIN (*harshly*) I see! So in case I did tell you—oh, she's cunning! But not cunning enough this time! (*Vindictively*) You remember what I've given you, Hazel, and you do exactly what I said with it. (*Then with desperate pleading*) For God's sake, Hazel, if you love me help me to get away from here—or something terrible will happen!

HAZEL That's just what I want to do! You come over tomorrow and stay with us.

ORIN (*bitterly*) Do you suppose for a moment she'll ever let me go?

HAZEL But haven't you a right to do as you want to?

ORIN (*furtively*) I could sneak out when she wasn't looking—and then you could hide me and when she came for me tell her I wasn't there.

HAZEL (*indignantly*) I won't do any such thing! I don't tell lies, Orin! (*Then scornfully*) How can you be so scared of Vinnie?

ORIN (*hearing a noise from the hall—hastily*) Ssshh! She's coming! Don't let her see what I gave you. And go home right away and lock it up! (*He tiptoes away as if he were afraid of being found close to her and sits on the sofa at right, adopting a suspiciously careless attitude.* HAZEL *looks self-conscious and stiff.* LAVINIA *appears in the doorway and gives a start as she sees* HAZEL *and* ORIN *are alone. She quickly senses something in the atmosphere and glances sharply from one to the other as she comes into the room*).

LAVINIA (*to* HAZEL, *forcing a casual air*) I'm sorry being so long.

HAZEL I didn't mind waiting.

LAVINIA (*sitting down on the chair at center*) Where's Peter?

HAZEL He had to go to a Council meeting. He's coming back.

LAVINIA (*uneasiness creeping into her tone*) Has he been gone long?

HAZEL Not very long.

LAVINIA (*turning to* ORIN—*sharply*) I thought you were in the study.

ORIN (*sensing her uneasiness—mockingly*) I finished what I was working on.

LAVINIA You finished—? (*She glances sharply at* HAZEL—*forcing a joking tone*) My, but you two look mysterious! What have you been up to?

HAZEL (*trying to force a laugh*) Why, Vinnie? What makes you think—?

LAVINIA You're hiding something. (HAZEL *gives a start and instinctively moves the hand with the envelope farther behind her back.* LAVINIA *notices this. So does* ORIN *who uneasily comes to* HAZEL'S *rescue*).

ORIN We're not hiding anything. Hazel has invited me over to their house to stay for a while—and I'm going.

HAZEL (*backing him up resolutely*) Yes. Orin is coming tomorrow.

LAVINIA (*alarmed and resentful—coldly*) It's kind of you. I know you mean it for the best. But he can't go.

HAZEL (*sharply*) Why not?

LAVINIA I don't care to discuss it, Hazel. You ought to know—

HAZEL (*angrily*) I don't know! Orin is of age and can go where he pleases!

ORIN Let her talk all she likes, Hazel. I'll have the upper hand for a change, from now on! (LAVINIA *looks at him, frightened by the triumphant satisfaction in his voice*).

HAZEL (*anxious to score her point anad keep* ORIN'S *mind on it*) I should think you'd be glad. It will be the best thing in the world for him.

LAVINIA (*turns on her—angrily*) I'll ask you to please mind your own business, Hazel!

HAZEL (*springs to her feet, in her anger forgetting to hide the envelope which she now holds openly in her hand*) It is my business! I love Orin better than you! I don't think you love him at all, the way you've been acting!

ORIN (*sees the envelope in plain sight and calls to her warningly*) Hazel! (*She catches his eye and hastily puts her hand behind her.* LAVINIA *sees the movement but doesn't for a moment realize the meaning of it.* ORIN *goes on warningly*) You said you had to go home early. I don't want to remind you but—

HAZEL (*hastily*) Yes, I really must. (*Starting to go, trying to keep the envelope hidden, aware that* LAVINIA *is watching her suspiciously—defiantly to* ORIN) We'll expect you tomorrow, and have your room ready. (*Then to* LAVINIA*—coldly*) After the way you've insulted me, Vinnie, I hope you realize there's no more question of any friendship between us. (*She tries awkwardly to sidle toward the door*).

LAVINIA (*suddenly gets between her and the door—with angry accusation*) What are you hiding behind your back? (HAZEL *flushes guiltily, but refusing to lie, says nothing.* LAVINIA *turns on* ORIN) Have you given her what you've written? (*As he hesitates—violently*) Answer me!

ORIN That's my business! What if I have?

LAVINIA You—you traitor! You coward! (*Fiercely to* HAZEL) Give it to me! Do you hear?

HAZEL Vinnie! How dare you talk that way to me! (*She tries to go but* LAVINIA *keeps directly between her and the door*).

LAVINIA You shan't leave here until—! (*Then breaking down and pleading*) Orin! Think what you're doing! Tell her to give it to me!

ORIN No!

LAVINIA (*goes and puts her arms around him—beseechingly as he avoids her eyes*) Think sanely for a moment! You can't do this! You're a Mannon!

ORIN (*harshly*) It's because I'm one!

LAVINIA For Mother's sake, you can't! You loved her!

ORIN A lot she cared! Don't call on her!

LAVINIA (*desperately*) For my sake, then! You know I love you! Make Hazel give that up and I'll do anything—anything you want me to!

ORIN (*stares into her eyes, bending his head until his face is close to hers—with morbid intensity*) You mean that?

LAVINIA (*shrinking back from him—falteringly*) Yes.

ORIN (*laughs with a crazy triumph—checks this abruptly—and goes to* HAZEL *who has been standing bewilderedly, not understanding what is behind their talk but sensing something sinister, and terribly frightened.* ORIN *speaks curtly, his eyes fixed on* LAVINIA) Let me have it, Hazel.

HAZEL (*hands him the envelope—in a trembling voice*) I'll go home. I suppose—we can't expect you tomorrow—now.

ORIN No. Forget me. The Orin you loved was killed in the war. (*With a twisted smile*) Remember only that dead hero and not his rotting ghost! Good-bye! (*Then harshly*) Please go! (HAZEL *begins to sob and hurries blindly from the room.* ORIN *comes back to* LAVINIA *who remains kneeling by the chair. He puts the envelope in her hand—harshly*) Here! You realize the promise you made means giving up Peter? And never seeing him again?

LAVINIA (*tensely*) Yes.

ORIN And I suppose you think that's all it means, that I'll be content with a promise I've forced out of you, which you'll always be plotting to break? Oh, no! I'm not such a fool! I've got to be sure— (*She doesn't reply or look at him. He stares at her and slowly a distorted look of desire comes over his face*) You said you would do anything for me. That's a large promise, Vinnie—anything!

LAVINIA (*shrinking from him*) What do you mean? What terrible thing have you been thinking lately—behind all your crazy talk? No, I don't want to know! Orin! Why do you look at me like that?

ORIN You don't seem to feel all you mean to me now—all you have made yourself mean—since we murdered Mother!

LAVINIA Orin!

ORIN I love you now with all the guilt in me—the guilt we share! Perhaps I love you too much, Vinnie!

LAVINIA You don't know what you're saying!

ORIN There are times now when you don't seem to be my sister, nor Mother, but some stranger with the same beautiful hair— (*He touches her hair caressingly. She pulls violently *away. He laughs wildly*) Perhaps you're Marie Brantôme, eh? And you say there are no ghosts in this house?

LAVINIA (*staring at him with fascinated horror*) For God's sake—! No! You're insane! You can't mean—!

ORIN How else can I be sure you won't leave me? You would never dare leave me—then! You would feel as guilty then as I do! You would be as damned as I am! (*Then with sudden anger as he sees the growing horrified repulsion on her face*) Damn you, don't you see I must find some certainty some way or go mad? You don't want me to go mad, do you? I would talk too much! I would confess! (*Then as if the word stirred something within him his tone instantly changes to one of passionate pleading*) Vinnie! For the love of God, let's go now and confess and pay the penalty for Mother's murder, and find peace together!

LAVINIA (*tempted and tortured, in a longing whisper*) Peace! (*Then summoning her will, springs to her feet wildly*) No! You coward! There is nothing to confess! There was only justice!

ORIN (*turns and addresses the portraits on the wall with a crazy mockery*) You hear her? You'll find Lavinia Mannon harder to break than me! You'll have to haunt and hound her for a lifetime!

LAVINIA (*her control snapping—turning on him now in a burst of frantic hatred and rage*) I hate you! I wish you were dead! You're too vile to live! You'd kill yourself if you weren't a coward!

ORIN (*starts back as if he'd been struck, the tortured mad look on his face changing to a stricken terrified expression*) Vinnie!

LAVINIA I mean it! I mean it! (*She breaks down and sobs hysterically*).

ORIN (*in a pitiful pleading whisper*) Vinnie! (*He stares at her with the lost stricken expression for a moment more—then the obsessed wild look returns to his eyes—with harsh mockery*) Another act of justice, eh? You want to drive me to suicide as I drove Mother! An eye for an eye, is that it? But—(*He stops abruptly and stares before him, as if this idea were suddenly taking hold of his tortured imagination and speaks fascinatedly to himself*) Yes! That would be justice—now you are Mother! She is speaking now through you! (*More and more hypnotized by this train of thought*) Yes! It's the way to peace—to find her again—my lost island—Death is an island of peace, too—Mother will be waiting for me there— (*With excited eagerness now, speaking to the dead*) Mother! Do you know what I'll do then? I'll get on my knees and ask your forgiveness—and say— (*His mouth grows convulsed, as if he were retching up poison*) I'll say, I'm glad you found love, Mother! I'll wish you happiness—you and Adam! (*He laughs exultantly*) You've heard me! You're here in the house now! You're calling me! You're waiting to take me home! (*He turns and strides toward the door*).

LAVINIA (*who has raised her head and has been staring at him with dread during the latter part of his talk—torn by remorse, runs after him and throws her arms around him*) No, Orin! No!

ORIN (*pushes her away—with a rough brotherly irritation*) Get out of my way, can't you? Mother's waiting! (*He gets to the door. Then he turns back and says sharply*) Ssshh! Here's Peter! Shut up, now! (*He steps back in the room as* PETER *appears in the doorway*).

PETER Excuse my coming right in. The door was open. Where's Hazel?

ORIN (*with unnatural casualness*) Gone home. (*Then with a quick, meaning, mocking glance at* LAVINIA) I'm just going in the study to clean my pistol. Darn thing's gotten so rusty. Glad you came now, Peter. You can keep Vinnie company. (*He turns and goes out the door.* PETER *stares after him puzzledly*).

LAVINIA (*with a stifled cry*) Orin! (*There is no answer but the sound of the study door being shut. She starts to run after him, stops herself, then throws herself into* PETER'S *arms, as if for protection against herself and begins to talk volubly to drown out thought*) Hold me close, Peter! Nothing matters but love, does it? That must come first! No price is too great, is it? Or for peace! One must have peace—one is too weak to forget—no one has the right to keep anyone from peace! (*She makes a motion to cover her ears with her hands*).

PETER (*alarmed by her hectic excitement*) He's a darned fool to monkey with a pistol—in his state. Shall I get it away from him?

LAVINIA (*holding him tighter—volubly*) Oh, won't it be wonderful, Peter—once we're married and have a home with a garden and trees! We'll be so happy! I love everything that grows simply—up toward the sun—everything that's straight and strong! I hate what's warped and twists and eats into itself and dies for a lifetime in shadow. (*Then her voice rising as if it were about to break hysterically—again with the instinctive movement to cover her ears*) I can't bear waiting—waiting and waiting and waiting—! (*There is a muffled shot from the study across the hall*).

PETER (*breaking from her and running for the door*) Good God! What's that? (*He rushes into the hall*).

LAVINIA (*sags weakly and supports herself against the table —in a faint, trembling voice*) Orin! Forgive me! (*She controls herself with a terrible effort of will. Her mouth congeals into a frozen line. Mechanically she hides the sealed envelope in a drawer of the table and locks the drawer*) I've got to go in— (*She turns to go and her eyes catch the eyes of the* MANNONS *in the portraits fixed accusingly on her—defiantly*) Why do you look at me like that? Wasn't it the only way to keep your secret, too? But I'm through with you forever now, do you hear? I'm Mother's daughter—not one of you! I'll live in spite of you! (*She squares her shoulders, with a return of the abrupt military movement copied from her father which she had of old—as if by the very act of disowining the* MANNONS *she had returned to the fold—and marches stiffly from the room*).

CURTAIN

ACT FOUR

SCENE—*Same as Act One, Scene One—exterior of the house. It is in the late afternoon of a day three days later. The Mannon house has much the same appearance as it had in the first act of "Homecoming." Soft golden sunlight shimmers in a luminous mist on the Greek temple portico, intensifying the whiteness of the columns, the deep green of the shutters, the green of the shrubbery, the black and green of the pines. The columns cast black bars of shadow on the gray stone wall behind them. The shutters are all fastened back, the windows open. On the ground floor, the upper part of the windows, raised from the bottom, reflect the sun in a smouldering stare, as of brooding revengeful eyes.*

SETH *appears walking slowly up the drive from right, front. He has a pair of grass clippers and potters along pretending to trim the edge of the lawn along the drive. But in reality he is merely killing time, chewing tobacco, and singing mournfully to himself, in his aged, plaintive wraith of a once good baritone, the chanty "Shenandoah":*

SETH *"Oh, Shenandoah, I long to hear you*
A-way, my rolling river,
Oh, Shenandoah, I can't get near you
Way-ay, I'm bound away
Across the wide Missouri.

"Oh, Shenandoah, I love your daughter
A-way, you rolling river."

SETH (*stops singing and stands peering off left toward the flower garden—shakes his head and mutters to himself*) There she be pickin' my flowers agin. Like her Maw used to—on'y wuss. She's got every room in the house full of 'em a'ready. Durn it, I hoped she'd stop that once the funeral was over. There won't be a one left in my garden! (*He looks away and begins pottering about again, and mutters grimly*) A durn queer thin' fur a sodger to kill himself cleanin' his gun, folks is sayin'. They'll fight purty shy of her now. A Mannon has come to mean sudden death to 'em. (*Then with a grim pride*)

But Vinnie's able fur 'em. They'll never git her to show nothin'. Clean Mannon strain!

(LAVINIA *enters from the left. The three days that have intervened have effected a remarkable change in her. Her body, dressed in deep mourning, again appears flat-chested and thin. The* MANNON *mask-semblance of her face appears intensified now. It is deeply lined, haggard with sleeplessness and strain, congealed into a stony emotionless expression. Her lips are bloodless, drawn taut in a grim line. She is carrying a large bunch of flowers. She holds them out to* SETH *and speaks in a strange, empty voice*).

LAVINIA Take these, Seth, and give them to Hannah. Tell her to set them around inside. I want the house to be full of flowers. Peter is coming, and I want everything to be pretty and cheerful. (*She goes and sits at the top of the steps, bolt upright, her arms held stiffly to her sides, her legs and feet pressed together, and stares back into the sun-glare with unblinking, frozen, defiant eyes*).

SETH (*stands holding the flowers and regarding her worriedly*). I seed you settin' out here on the steps when I got up at five this mornin'—and every mornin' since Orin— Ain't you been gittin' no sleep? (*She stares before her as if she had not heard him. He goes on coaxingly*) How'd you like if I hauled one of them sofas out fur you to lie on, Vinnie? Mebbe you could take a couple o' winks an' it'd do you good.

LAVINIA No, thank you, Seth. I'm waiting for Peter. (*Then after a pause, curiously*) Why didn't you tell me to go in the house and lie down? (SETH *pretends not to hear the question, avoiding her eyes*) You understand, don't you? You've been with us Mannons so long! You know there's no rest in this house which Grandfather built as a temple of Hate and Death!

SETH (*blurts out*) Don't you try to live here, Vinnie! You marry Peter and git clear!

LAVINIA I'm going to marry him! And I'm going away with him and forget this house and all that ever happened in it!

SETH That's talkin', Vinnie!

LAVINIA I'll close it up and leave it in the sun and rain to die. The portraits of the Mannons will rot on the walls and the ghosts will fade back into death. And the Mannons will be forgotten. I'm the last and I won't be one long. I'll be Mrs. Peter Niles. Then they're finished! Thank God! (*She leans back in the sunlight and closes her eyes.* SETH *stares at her worriedly, shakes his head and spits. Then he hears something and peers down the drive, off left)*

SETH Vinnie. Here's Hazel comin'.

LAVINIA (*jerks up stiffly with a look of alarm*) Hazel? What does she want? (*She springs up as if she were going to run in the house, then stands her ground on the top of the steps, her voice hardening*) Seth, you go work in back, please!

SETH Ayeh. (*He moves slowly off behind the lilacs as* HAZEL *enters from left, front—calling back*) Evenin', Hazel.

HAZEL Good evening, Seth. (*She stops short and stares at* LAVINIA. LAVINIA'S *eyes are hard and defiant as she stares back.* HAZEL *is dressed in mourning. Her face is sad and pale, her eyes show evidence of much weeping, but there is an air of stubborn resolution about her as she makes up her mind and walks to the foot of the steps*).

LAVINIA What do you want? I've got a lot to attend to.

HAZEL (*quietly*) It won't take me long to say what I've come to say, Vinnie. (*Suddenly she bursts out*) It's a lie about Orin killing himself by accident! I know it is! He meant to!

LAVINIA You better be careful what you say. I can prove what happened. Peter was here—

HAZEL I don't care what anyone says!

LAVINIA I should think you'd be the last one to accuse Orin—

HAZEL I'm not accusing him! Don't you dare say that! I'm accusing you! You drove him to it! Oh, I know I can't prove it—any more than I can prove a lot of things Orin hinted at! But I know terrible things must have happened—and that you're to blame for them, somehow!

LAVINIA (*concealing a start of fear—changing to a forced reproachful tone*) What would Orin think of you coming here the day of his funeral to accuse me of the sorrow that's afflicted our family?

HAZEL (*feeling guilty and at the same time defiant and sure she is right*) All right, Vinnie. I won't say anything more. But I know there's something—and so do you—something that was driving Orin crazy— (*She breaks down and sobs*) Poor Orin!

LAVINIA (*stares straight before her. Her lips twitch. In a stifled voice between her clenched teeth*) Don't—do that!

HAZEL (*controlling herself—after a pause*) I'm sorry. I didn't come to talk about Orin.

LAVINIA (*uneasily*) What did you come for?

HAZEL About Peter.

LAVINIA (*as if this were something she had been dreading—harshly*) You leave Peter and me alone!

HAZEL I won't! You're not going to marry Peter and ruin his life! (*Pleading now*) You can't! Don't you see he could never be happy with you, that you'll only drag him into this terrible thing—whatever it is—and make him share it?

LAVINIA There is no terrible thing!

HAZEL I know Peter can't believe evil of anyone, but living alone with you, married, you couldn't hide it, he'd get to feel what I feel. You could never be happy because it would come between you! (*Pleading again*) Oh, Vinnie, you've got to be fair to Peter! You've got to consider his happiness—if you really love him!

LAVINIA (*hoarsely*) I do love him!

HAZEL It has started already—his being made unhappy through you!

LAVINIA You're lying!

HAZEL He fought with Mother last night when she tried to talk to him—the first time he ever did such a thing! It isn't like Peter. You've changed him. He left home and went to the hotel to stay. He said he'd never speak to Mother or me again. He's always been such a wonderful son before—and brother. We three have been so happy. It's broken Mother's heart. All she does is sit and cry. (*Desperately*) Oh, Vinnie, you can't do it! You will be punished if you do! Peter would get to hate you in the end!

LAVINIA No!

HAZEL Do you want to take the risk of driving Peter to do what Orin did? He might—if he ever discovered the truth!

LAVINIA (*violently*) What truth, you little fool! Discover what?

HAZEL (*accusingly*) I don't know—but you know! Look in your heart and ask your conscience before God if you ought to marry Peter!

LAVINIA (*desperately—at the end of her tether*) Yes! Before God! Before anything! (*Then glaring at her—with a burst of rage*) You leave me alone—go away—or I'll get Orin's pistol and kill you! (*Her rage passes, leaving her weak and shaken. She goes to her chair and sinks on it*).

HAZEL (*recoiling*) Oh! You are wicked! I believe you would—! Vinnie! What's made you like this?

LAVINIA Go away!

HAZEL Vinnie! (LAVINIA *closes her eyes.* HAZEL *stands staring at her. After a pause—in a trembling voice*) All right. I'll go. All I can do is trust you. I know in your heart you can't be dead to all honor and justice—you, a Mannon! (LAVINIA *gives a little bitter laugh without opening her eyes*) At least you owe it to Peter to let him read what Orin had in that envelope. Orin asked me to make him read it before he married you. I've told Peter about that, Vinnie.

LAVINIA (*without opening her eyes—strangely, as if to herself*) The dead! Why can't the dead die!

HAZEL (*stares at her frightenedly, not knowing what to do—looks around her uncertainly and sees someone coming from off left, front—quickly*) Here he comes now. I'll go by the back. I don't want him to meet me. (*She starts to go but stops by the clump of lilacs—pityingly*) I know you're suffering, Vinnie—and I know your conscience will make you do what's right—and God will forgive you. (*She goes quickly behind the lilacs and around the house to the rear*).

LAVINIA (*looks after her and calls defiantly*) I'm not asking God or anybody for forgiveness. I forgive myself! (*She leans back and closes her eyes again—bitterly*) I hope there is a hell for the good somewhere! (PETER *enters from the left, front. He looks haggard and tormented. He walks slowly, his eyes on the ground—then sees* LAVINIA *and immediately makes an effort to pull himself together and appear cheerful*).

PETER Hello, Vinnie. (*He sits on the edge of the portico beside her. She still keeps her eyes closed, as if afraid to open them. He looks at her worriedly*) You look terribly worn out. Haven't you slept? (*He pats her hand with awkward tenderness. Her mouth twitches and draws down at the corners as she stifles a sob. He goes on comfortingly*) You've had an awfully hard time of it, but never mind, we'll be married soon.

LAVINIA (*without opening her eyes—longingly*) You'll love me and keep me from remembering?

PETER You bet I will! And the first thing is to get you away from this darned house! I may be a fool but I'm beginning to feel superstitious about it myself.

LAVINIA (*without opening her eyes—strangely*) Yes. Love can't live in it. We'll go away and leave it alone to die—and we'll forget the dead.

PETER (*a bitter resentful note coming into his voice*) We can't move too far away to suit me! I hate this damned town now and everyone in it!

LAVINIA (*opens her eyes and looks at him startledly*) I never heard you talk that way before, Peter—bitter!

PETER (*avoiding her eyes*) Some things would make anyone bitter!

LAVINIA You've quarreled with your mother and Hazel—on account of me—is that it?

PETER How did you know?

LAVINIA Hazel was just here.

PETER She told you? The darned fool! What did she do that for?

LAVINIA She doesn't want me to marry you.

PETER (*angrily*) The little sneak! What right has she—? (*Then a bit uneasily—forcing a smile*) Well, you won't pay any attention to her, I hope.

LAVINIA (*more as if she were answering some voice in herself than him—stiffening in her chair—defiantly*) No!

PETER She and Mother suddenly got a lot of crazy notions in their heads. But they'll get over them.

LAVINIA (*staring at him searchingly—uneasily*) Supposing they don't?

PETER They will after we are married—or I'm through with them!

LAVINIA (*a pause. Then she takes his face in her hands and turns it to hers*) Peter! Let me look at you! You're suffering! Your eyes have a hurt look! They've always been so trustful! They look suspicious and afraid of life now! Have I done this to you already, Peter? Are you beginning to suspect me? Are you wondering what it was Orin wrote?

PETER (*protesting violently*) No! Of course I'm not! Don't I know Orin was out of his mind? Why would I pay any attention—?

LAVINIA You swear you'll never suspect me—of anything?

PETER What do you think I am?

LAVINIA And you'll never let anyone come between us? Nothing can keep us from being happy, can it? You won't let anything, will you?

PETER Of course I won't!

LAVINIA (*more and more desperately*) I want to get married right away, Peter! I'm afraid! Would you marry me now—this evening? We can find a minister to do it. I can change my clothes in a second and put on the color you like! Marry me today, Peter! I'm afraid to wait!

PETER (*bewildered and a bit shocked*) But—you don't

mean that, do you? We couldn't. It wouldn't look right the day Orin—out of respect for him. (*Then suspicious in spite of himself*) I can't see why you're so afraid of waiting. Nothing can happen, can it? Was there anything in what Orin wrote that would stop us from—?

LAVINIA (*with a wild beaten laugh*) The dead coming between! They always would, Peter! You trust me with your happiness! But that means trusting the Mannon dead—and they're not to be trusted with love! I know them too well! And I couldn't bear to watch your eyes grow bitter and hidden from me and wounded in their trust of life! I love you too much!

PETER (*made more uneasy and suspicious by this*) What are you talking about, Vinnie? You make me think there was something—

LAVINIA (*desperately*) No—nothing! (*Then suddenly throwing her arms around him*) No! Don't think of that—not yet! I want a little while of happiness—in spite of all the dead! I've earned it! I've done enough—! (*Growing more desperate—pleading wildly*) Listen, Peter! Why must we wait for marriage? I want a moment of joy—of love—to make up for what's coming! I want it now! Can't you be strong, Peter? Can't you be simple and pure? Can't you forget sin and see that all love is beautiful? (*She kisses him with desperate passion*) Kiss me! Hold me close! Want me! Want me so much you'd murder anyone to have me! I did that—for you! Take me in this house of the dead and love me! Our love will drive the dead away! It will shame them back into death! (*At the topmost pitch of desperate, frantic abandonment*) Want me! Take me, Adam! (*She is brought back to herself with a start by this name escaping her—bewilderedly, laughing idiotically*) Adam? Why did I call you Adam? I never even heard that name before—outside of the Bible! (*Then suddenly with a hopeless, dead finality*) Always the dead between! It's no good trying any more!

PETER (*convinced she is hysterical and yet shocked and repelled by her display of passion*) Vinnie! You're talking crazy! You don't know what you're saying! You're not—like that!

LAVINIA (*in a dead voice*) I can't marry you, Peter. You mustn't ever see me again. (*He stares at her, stunned and stupid*) Go home. Make it up with your mother and Hazel. Marry someone else. Love isn't permitted to me. The dead are too strong!

PETER (*his mind in a turmoil*) Vinnie! You can't—! You've gone crazy—! What's changed you like this? (*Then suspiciously*) Is it—what Orin wrote? What was it? I've got a right to know, haven't I? (*Then as she doesn't answer—more suspiciously*) He acted so queer about—what happened to you on the Islands. Was it something there—something to do with that native—?

LAVINIA (*her first instinctive reaction one of hurt insult*) Peter! Don't you dare—! (*Then suddenly seizing on this as a way out—with calculated coarseness*) All right! Yes, if you must know! I won't lie any more! Orin suspected I'd lusted with him! And I had!

PETER (*shrinking from her aghast—brokenly*) Vinnie! You've gone crazy! I don't believe— You—you couldn't!

LAVINIA (*stridently*) Why shouldn't I? I wanted him! I wanted to learn love from him—love that wasn't a sin! And I did, I tell you! He had me! I was his fancy woman!

PETER (*wincing as if she had struck him in the face, stares at her with a stricken look of horrified repulsion—with bitter, broken anger*) Then—Mother and Hazel were right about you—you are bad at heart—no wonder Orin killed himself—God, I—I hope you'll be punished—I—! (*He hurries blindly off down the drive to the left*).

LAVINIA (*watches him go—then with a little desperate cry starts after him*) Peter! It's a lie! I didn't—! (*She stops abruptly and stiffens into her old, square-shouldered attitude. She looks down the drive after him—then turns away, saying in a lost, empty tone*) Good-bye, Peter. (SETH *enters from the left rear, coming around the corner of the house. He stands for a moment watching her, grimly wondering. Then to call her attention to his presence, he begins singing half under his breath his melancholy "Shenandoah" chanty, at the same time looking at the ground around him as if searching for something*).

SETH *"Oh, Shenandoah, I can't get near you*
Way-ay, I'm bound away—"

LAVINIA (*without looking at him, picking up the words of the chanty—with a grim writhen smile*) I'm not bound away—not now, Seth. I'm bound here—to the Mannon dead! (*She gives a dry little cackle of laughter and turns as if to enter the house*).

SETH (*frightened by the look on her face, grabs her by the arm*) Don't go in there, Vinnie!

LAVINIA (*grimly*) Don't be afraid. I'm not going the way Mother and Orin went. That's escaping punishment. And there's no one left to punish me. I'm the last Mannon. I've got to punish myself! Living alone here with the dead is a worse act of justice than death or prison! I'll never go out or see anyone! I'll have the shutters nailed closed so no sunlight can ever get in. I'll live alone with the dead, and keep their secrets, and let them hound me, until the curse is paid out and the last Mannon is let die! (*With a strange cruel smile of gloating over the years of self-torture*) I know they will see to it I live for a long time! It takes the Mannons to punish themselves for being born!

SETH (*with grim understanding*) Ayeh. And I ain't heard a word you've been sayin', Vinnie. (*Pretending to search the ground again*) Left my clippers around somewheres.

LAVINIA (*turns to him sharply*) You go now and close the shutters and nail them tight.

SETH Ayeh.

LAVINIA And tell Hannah to throw out all the flowers.

SETH Ayeh. (*He goes past her up the steps and into the house. She ascends to the portico—and then turns and stands for a while, stiff and square-shouldered, staring into the sunlight with frozen eyes.* SETH *leans out of the window at the right of the door and pulls the shutters closed with a decisive bang. As if this were a word of command,* LAVINIA *pivots sharply on her heel and marches woodenly into the house, closing the door behind her*).

CURTAIN

EUGENE O'NEILL was born on October 16, 1888, in New York City. His father was James O'Neill, the famous dramatic actor; and during his early years O'Neill traveled much with his parents. In 1909 he went on a gold-prospecting expedition to South America; he later shipped as a seaman to Buenos Aires, worked at various occupations in the Argentine and tended mules on a cattle steamer to South Africa. He returned to New York destitute, then worked briefly as a reporter on a newspaper in New London, Connecticut, at which point an attack of tuberculosis sent him for six months to a sanitarium. This event marked the turning point in his career, and shortly after, at the age of twenty-four, he began his first play. His major works include *The Emperor Jones*, 1920; *The Hairy Ape*, 1921; *Desire Under the Elms*, 1924; *The Great God Brown*, 1925; *Strange Interlude*, 1926, 1927; *Mourning Becomes Electra*, 1929, 1931; *Ah, Wilderness*, 1933; *Days Without End*, 1934; *A Moon for the Misbegotten*, 1945; *The Iceman Cometh*, 1946; and several plays produced posthumously, including *Long Day's Journey into Night*, *A Touch of the Poet* and *Hughie*.

Many of his plays are available in Vintage Books and in the Modern Library. Eugene O'Neill died in 1953.

VINTAGE BIOGRAPHY AND AUTOBIOGRAPHY

V-658	ALINSKY, SAUL D. *John L. Lewis: An Unauthorized Biography*
V-250	BURCKHARDT, C. J. *Richelieu: His Rise to Power*
V-725	CARR, E. H. *Michael Bakunin*
V-746	DEUTSCHER, ISAAC *The Prophet Armed*
V-747	DEUTSCHER, ISAAC *The Prophet Unarmed*
V-748	DEUTSCHER, ISAAC *The Prophet Outcast*
V-617	DEVLIN, BERNADETTE *The Price of My Soul*
V-225	FISCHER, LOUIS (ed.) *The Essential Gandhi*
V-132	FREUD, SIGMUND *Leonardo Da Vinci*
V-147	GIDE, ANDRE *If It Die*
V-499	GOODMAN, PAUL *Five Years*
V-449	GRAY, FRANCINE DU PLESSIX *Divine Disobedience*
V-268	JUNG, C. G. *Memories, Dreams, Reflections*
V-50	KELLY, AMY *Eleanor of Aquitaine and the Four Kings*
V-728	KLYUCHEVSKY, V. *Peter the Great*
V-581	KRAMER, JANE *Allen Ginsberg in America*
V-215	LACOUTURE, JEAN *Ho Chi Minh*
V-677	LESTER, JULIUS *The Seventh Son,* Volume I
V-678	LESTER, JULIUS *The Seventh Son,* Volume II
V-280	LEWIS, OSCAR *Children of Sánchez*
V-634	LEWIS, OSCAR *A Death in the Sánchez Family*
V-92	MATTINGLY, GARRETT *Catherine of Aragon*
V-490	MYRDAL, JAN *Confessions of a Disloyal European*
V-624	PARKINSON, G. H. R. *Georg Lukacs: The Man, His Work, and His Ideas*
V-373	PAUSTOVSKY, KONSTANTIN *The Story of a Life*
V-133	STEIN, GERTRUDE *The Autobiography of Alice B. Toklas*
V-100	SULLIVAN, J. W. N. *Beethoven: His Spiritual Development*
V-287	TAYLOR, A. J. P. *Bismarck: The Man and the Statesman*
V-256	WILDE, OSCAR *De Profundis*
V-106	WINSTON, RICHARD *Charlemagne: From the Hammer to the Cross*